Palgrave Studies in Classical Liberalism

Series Editors
David F. Hardwick
Department of Pathology and Laboratory Medicine
The University of British Columbia
Vancouver, BC, Canada

Leslie Marsh
Department of Pathology and Laboratory Medicine
The University of British Columbia
Vancouver, BC, Canada

This series offers a forum to writers concerned that the central presuppositions of the liberal tradition have been severely corroded, neglected, or misappropriated by overly rationalistic and constructivist approaches.

The hardest-won achievement of the liberal tradition has been the wrestling of epistemic independence from overwhelming concentrations of power, monopolies and capricious zealotries. The very precondition of knowledge is the exploitation of the epistemic virtues accorded by society's situated and distributed manifold of spontaneous orders, the DNA of the modern civil condition.

With the confluence of interest in situated and distributed liberalism emanating from the Scottish tradition, Austrian and behavioral economics, non-Cartesian philosophy and moral psychology, the editors are soliciting proposals that speak to this multidisciplinary constituency. Sole or joint authorship submissions are welcome as are edited collections, broadly theoretical or topical in nature.

Ferenc Hörcher

Art and Politics in Roger Scruton's Conservative Philosophy

palgrave
macmillan

Ferenc Hörcher
Institute of Philosophy
Hungarian Academy of Sciences
Budapest, Hungary

ISSN 2662-6470   ISSN 2662-6489   (electronic)
Palgrave Studies in Classical Liberalism
ISBN 978-3-031-13590-3   ISBN 978-3-031-13591-0   (eBook)
https://doi.org/10.1007/978-3-031-13591-0

This Palgrave Macmillan imprint is published by the registered company Springer Nature Switzerland AG.
The registered company address is: Gewerbestrasse 11, 6330 Cham, Switzerland

Preface

This book has its root in my decades-long acquaintance with the late Sir Roger Scruton. We kept meeting at academic events, and I also interviewed him regularly, when I had been working as a journalist for ten years after the millennium. Without the first-hand impressions I gained during those years of him as a character, this book would have been a different one. For philosophy is not simply about epistemic claims—for example, of certain truths concerning the natural world and the human realm. It is also about character formation, and the efforts to live a meaningful and whole life. Although Scruton was not exactly an extrovert, when getting into human relationships, he was able to open up and show something of his own internal mental landscape. Yet he died painfully early, and I had to realise that I missed the opportunity to get to know him in a deep enough manner. What remained, instead, was to get a more intimate knowledge of his thoughts, as presented in his philosophical and autobiographical texts. I made the decision in the year of his death to write this book, and Palgrave Macmillan was ready to embark with me on this project—I am grateful to them for this trust and confidence. Its main idea is to shed a new light on Scruton's achievements, by connecting the two fields of philosophy he was engaged in most: Scruton, the political philosopher and Scruton, the aesthete and art critic.

During the one and the half years of intensive work on this book after his death I ran into great debts. First of all, it was Sophie Scruton who encouraged me to take the path I intended. Sir Roger's one time personal assistant, Izzy Larthe, also offered her help when I needed. As for the academic support, the list is too long. Yet the most important was the help I received from Bob Grant and Anthony O'Hear, from among the closest friends of Sir Roger, who both saw the first version of the text of the whole book, and tried to help me polishing it. John O'Sullivan, president of the Danube Institute, and his wife, Melissa, also believed in my project. Of the younger generation I had the chance to meet and work together to cultivate the memory of Sir Roger, with Alicja Gescinska, and Samuel Hughes. I earned a friend in the person of Marek Matraszek, another close ally and disciple of Sir Roger. Two organisers of the Humane Philosophy Project and the Vanenburg Society, Mikolaj Slawkowski-Rode and Jonathan Price were also very helpful. I thank the invitation of Fisher Derderian, founder and executive director of the Roger Scruton Legacy Foundation to join the scientific committee of the Foundation. I also owe a lot to the Common Sense Society, and especially to Anna (Stumpf) Smith Lacey and Marion Smith, two of its founding pillars. I found the non-partisan, civil and educative aims of Liberty Fund also extremely fruitful, and I appreciate the activity of a number of its board members and fellows, including Emilio J. Pacheco, Douglas J. Den Uyl, Christine Henderson and Peter C. Mentzel. Since I began working on this project, a great number of senior, as well as junior academics contacted me on Twitter, academia.edu and ResearchGate, giving me advice and encouragement. Especially promising is the recent establishment of an online friendly circle, the Conservative Philosophy Club, inspired by the Conservative Philosophy Group, established, among others, by Sir Roger.

The two institutions where I am affiliated, The Research Institute of Politics and Government of the University of Public Service and the Institute of Philosophy of the Research Centre for the Humanities, both in Budapest, provided for me excellent working conditions for the project. I am especially grateful to Bernát Török, earlier student of mine at the Catholic University, present-day director of the Research Centre of the University of Public Service, for his great support, as well as to András Koltay, who invited me to the university. I am also grateful to the present rector of the University, Prof. Gergely Deli, as well as to Dániel Schmal, diector of the Institute of Philosophy. I also benefited from the kind support of the network of Scruton Cafés in Budapest, in these friendly loci some of my ideas could be tried with a benevolent audience.

As usual, Steve Patrick edited the English of my book, and Andrea Robotka took care of the copy editing of the text. I am grateful to both, as to Palgrave Macmillan's reviewers and editors who also did their best to raise its quality. All the remaining spots are my own responsibility.

I dedicate this book to my grandson, Sámuel Hörcher, who was born only a week ago (June, 2022).

Budapest, Hungary   Ferenc Hörcher
June 2022

Contents

1 **Introduction: Politics, Art and Philosophy**   1
   Fields of Human Activity   1
      Oakeshott's Modes of Experience   1
      Aristotle's Forms of Knowledge and Activity   5
      Plato on Beauty, Poetry and the Divine   9
      Practical Life and Contemplation   12
   Art and Politics   14
   Politics and Philosophy   16
   Art and Philosophy   20
   Scruton's Triangle: Philosophy, Art and Politics   24

2 **The Emergence of a Philosophy of Art and Politics**   33
   Paris 1968   35
   Casey and The Peterhouse Right   37
      John Casey   37
      Maurice Cowling   40
      David Watkin   43
   Cultural Criticism   46
      F.R. Leavis   46
   Studying the Law   47

3   The Political Philosophy of Conservatism (*Vita Activa*)   55
The Salisbury Group and the Salisbury Review   55
Underground Teaching in Communist Central Europe   58
Conservatism: Doctrine or Philosophy   60
    The Meaning of Conservatism (1980)   61
    A Political Philosophy: Arguments for Conservatism (2006)   67
    How to Be a Conservative (2014)   76
    Conservatism: An Invitation to the Great Tradition (2017)   86
National Attachment   97
    England. An Elegy (2000)   98
    The Need for Nations (2004)   104
The Concept of *Oikophilia*   112

4   The Theory of Art and Culture   135
The Theory of Culture   136
    Modern Culture (1998)   137
    Culture Counts (2007)   142
The Theory of Beauty   149
    Beauty (2009)   149
In Praise of the Vernacular: Aesthetics, Politics and
Architecture   157
    The Example of Watkin   159
    The Aesthetics of Architecture (1979)   168
    The Classical Vernacular: Architectural Principles in an Age
    of Nihilism (1994)   185
    New Urbanism, Poundbury and the Building Better
    Commission   200
In Praise of Wagner: Metaphysics, Politics and Music   213
    The Politics and Metapolitics of Wagner   215
    Music as a Communal Experience   228

**5   From the Philosophy of Art to Metaphysics (Vita
Contemplativa)**   255
Metaphysics I. The Face of God   257
    Painting the Fall of Man   257
    The Gifford Lectures and Natural Theology   259

Community and Communion   260
Interpersonal Dialogue   262
Aesthetic and Moral Judgement   264
The Human Face   266
The Face of Nature   270
The Face of God   274
Wagner and Redemption Through Suffering   280
Metaphysics II. The Soul of the World   281
Poussin's Landscape   282
The Religious Urge   287
Human Nature   289
From I to We   294
The Transcendental Ties of a Covenant   296
The World in Which We Feel at Home   298
The Gift of Music   303
"Seeking God"   309

6   Conclusion. The Duality of Scruton's Philosophy of
    Politics and Art   323
    Vita Activa: The British Idea of the Rule of Law 326
    Vita Contemplativa: Philosophy of Art   332
    The Philosophy of Politics, Art—and Religion   334

Sir Roger Scruton's Own Works   343

Author Index   359

Subject Index   371

1

Introduction: Politics, Art and Philosophy

The late Sir Roger Scruton was a Cambridge-educated philosopher, who had two major fields of interests: the philosophy of art and political philosophy. Both of these philosophies address a form of human activity: political philosophy focuses on the *zoon politikon*, the political being, while the philosophy of art describes the human being engaged in artistic activity, fascinated by beauty. This book tries to make sense of these two major themes of the philosopher. Politics and art can be viewed both as separate forms and as overlapping spheres of human activity. This first chapter is an introduction, about the relationship of philosophy, politics and art.

Fields of Human Activity

Oakeshott's Modes of Experience

Let us start our story with the name of the British philosopher, Michael Oakeshott. Although Oakeshott and Scruton were both representatives of twentieth-century British conservatism, their particular ways of philosophical thinking were remarkably different.[1] While they both represent

© The Author(s), under exclusive license to Springer Nature Switzerland AG 2023
F. Hörcher, *Art and Politics in Roger Scruton's Conservative Philosophy*, Palgrave Studies in Classical Liberalism, https://doi.org/10.1007/978-3-031-13591-0_1

perhaps the best of twentieth-century British conservative thought, it does not follow from this that they were similar, either in their careers or as regards their philosophical positions. Anthony O'Hear even suggested, in a personal note to me, that there was something almost "flippant" about Oakeshott's philosophical attitude, particularly in his aestheticism, which can be contrasted with Scruton's "seriousness."[2]

The reason to start with him is Oakeshott's theory of human activities, which I will apply here.

It was in his early book of philosophy, *Experience and Its Modes* (1933), that Oakeshott embarked on a distinction between the major forms of human activity or what he called "modes of experience." Humans relate to the world, he thought, either theoretically or practically. I assume that one can comfortably apply Oakeshott's analysis to discussing the relationship between politics, art and philosophy, which he regarded as distinct *modes of experience*, or *forms of discourse*, or, finally, *voices*.[3]

To my knowledge Scruton never embarked on a theoretical reflection on the relationship between his own interests in politics and art. The Oakeshottian classification is a convenient way, however, to give a general account of the interactions of philosophy with art and politics. This general account was first articulated by the philosophers of ancient Greece. Socrates, Plato and Aristotle are of particular interest for us here. Both Oakeshott and Scruton made an effort to relate to the great tradition of European philosophy.[4]

Oakeshott's major interest was in the *differentia specifica* of engagement with the field traditionally called philosophy. He often returned to a philosophy of philosophy, or metaphilosophy. To do so he needed to distinguish philosophy from other forms of perception and other modes of experience.[5] We can confront the world, he thought, only through particular experiences. This is expressed in Kantian epistemology, according to which there is no way to look at the world beyond our experiential horizon. The substance of experience is thought. It is this element that makes Oakeshott's philosophical account of experience an idealist one: even in our relationships to the material world we cannot escape our ideas of it. Ideas are arranged in an orderly fashion in the human consciousness. When a critical mass of corresponding ideas is collected, they begin to work as a body of ideas, a mode of experience. They become "autonomous," in the sense of "specifiable in terms of exact conditions." Modes of experience are separate items, because they are "logically incapable of denying or confirming the conclusions of any other mode."[6] This sort of internal cohesion, and the external differences between the ideas of a mode of experience result in a "whole of interlocking meanings."[7]

In *Experience and Its Modes* Oakeshott identifies history, science and practice as distinct modes, to which he later adds poetry and arguably, politics, which he regarded as a special branch of practice.[8] Practice is separable from the rest due to the fact that it is directly involved in acting, while history, science and poetry are all special, reflective, indirect kinds of action. Even poetry involves activity. In fact, I shall view both poetry and politics as parts of a bridge between the realm of practical concerns (i.e. practice) and ideas for their own sake (i.e. theory). This distinction is parallel with Dilthey's conceptual pair of *Erklären* (explanation) in the *Naturwissenschaften* and *Verstehen* (understanding) in the *Geisteswissenschaften*.[9]

Modes of experience are distinguished by Oakeshott by what he calls modal distinctions. Nardin argues that in this claim Oakeshott is closer to Hegel, who first made use of the Kantian claim that there are no "things in themselves" except for the transcendental ego which experiences when defending the view that experience is both a form of knowing and explains a form of being. Nardin tends to identify particular experiences with their specific "universe of discourse," supposing that each of them has "its own arguments and ways of assessing and grounding them."[10] This supposition is strict: modes hardly ever overlap.[11] However, Oakeshott does not exclude the possibility of a specific form of communication—a conversation between them. Indeed, in his later works he goes so far as to claim that modes of experiences are, in fact, voices in an intermodal conversation.[12] In a conversation, the functional approach of communication is relaxed, the intercourse is not strictly argumentative, but rather dialogical. There is no definite conclusion to such a conversation, and there is no metanarrative. Neither does it allow a hierarchy of modes of experience, or of voices: each of them has its own undisputable merits, or, one might also argue, all of them are for their own sake. Importantly, Oakeshott also argues that, as soon as philosophy takes charge of it, the conversation between or among coequal discourses is by definition civilised, as it expects voices to accept and respect the differences between or among them.

Besides Dilthey and the German classical idealist tradition, Nardin also cites certain works by Benedetto Croce and Collingwood, as representing efforts comparable to Oakeshott's theory of different modes. Unlike the other two, however, Oakeshott claims that there is no hierarchy between the modes, and he seems to imply that both art and religion are, in fact, parts of practice. For him, philosophy itself constituted more than just one of the modes. It is a metadiscourse, which enables its subject, the philosopher, to reflect upon the nature of other modes in a critical manner. Yet unlike major theories of idealism, in which philosophy enables its subject to gain an insight into the workings of the Absolute, it is not clear that this is possible in Oakeshott's own account of philosophy. The philosopher is just as much on a perpetual "voyage" as the political agent is, because she cannot find the harbour of absolute knowledge. Even so, the sum total of the forms of knowledge, as overviewed by philosophy, is not much less than the absolute.

As Oakeshott, Scruton was also brought up in the analytical tradition, which—under the impact of logical positivism and ordinary language philosophy—pushed metaphysics into the background.[13] For him, politics and art are forms of knowledge (i.e. consisting of ideas or thought), yet he also recognised that they both had their practical aspects.

Due to Scruton's appreciation of Kant's metaphysical system, he was always rather careful not to touch upon supra-philosophical problems, like that of the existence of God. However, the late Scruton took advantage of the metaphysically more robust enquiries into metaphysics from the last third of the twentieth century, and in his parallel books, *The Face of God* and *The Soul of the World* he embarked on enquiries which implied an approach towards a transcendental realm of being. Although, as we shall see, religious thought remained an enigma for him, this book will argue that Scruton's late thought was directly involved in an effort to show how art can be interpreted as one of the most promising way to evoke, show or simply intimate the metaphysical realm of the sacred.[14] While expanding his attitude towards the absolute did not leave his political philosophy untouched, I will argue that his premises of what constitutes a sound political regime remained largely unchanged. He remained more or less Burkean until the very end of his life, defending the virtues of the British political tradition, with its cherished ideas of the King-in-Parliament, the unwritten constitution, habeas corpus and Bill of Rights. What did change perhaps, over the years, is that he discovered in that very tradition ideas which had religious roots, like the relevance of authority, pietas and human friendship. All of these concepts, however, had ancient Greek philosophical backgrounds as well.

Aristotle's Forms of Knowledge and Activity

In his late book on Conservatism, Scruton claimed that "most of the ideas purveyed by modern conservatives are foreshadowed in Aristotle's great work."[15] It seems appropriate, therefore, to have a look at Aristotle's own concept of the forms of knowledge, a topic he developed in the sixth book of *Nicomachean Ethics* (*NE*). Oakeshott's modes of experience and Aristotle's forms of knowledge are not the same, yet the Aristotelian distinctions between the forms of knowledge have had a long career, and they remain relevant even in a modern context. In the sixth book of *NE* the Greek philosopher distinguishes between "craft knowledge (*techné*), scientific knowledge (*epistémé*), practical wisdom (*phronesis*), theoretical wisdom (*sophia*), and understanding (*nous*)."[16] Scientific knowledge involves grasping what cannot be otherwise, that is, what is eternal, and what can therefore be taught. It also allows for demonstration. "What admits of being otherwise includes both what is producible and what is doable in action."[17] The example Aristotle gives for production is building. It is a sort of action, which has an end product, which is different from the action. The activity of building a house has a conclusion, a house which is out there, in the world. To produce properly requires a form of knowledge, which might also be called competence. What we consider art belongs to this form of knowledge, to *techné*. This is underlined by Aristotle when he mentions two famous sculptors, Phidias and Polyclitus, both practitioners of the craft of sculpture. One special type of craft is poetry (*poiesis*), where what are created are poems, which Aristotle deals with in a specific treatise, *Poetics*. While *techné* is concerned with how to create something, *phronesis* is concerned with how to behave.

Phronesis is practical wisdom, the sort of wisdom which concerns praxis—practical activity. A man of practical wisdom is "able to deliberate correctly about what is good and advantageous for himself, not partially... but about what sorts of things further living well as a whole."[18] In other words, this is knowledge about practical activity, but it also concerns human life as a whole—which would be an important issue for Scruton, too, when he discussed what lies beyond the momentary in our action. Practical wisdom is clearly distinguished from scientific knowledge and craft knowledge: it is "not scientific knowledge because what is doable in action admits of being otherwise, not craft knowledge because action and production differ in kind."[19] Aristotle also claims that household managers (*oikonomos*) and politicians are men of practical wisdom, and he gives Pericles as his prime example of the latter. Within politics, which comprises practical wisdom about the political community, Aristotle distinguishes between legislative science and politics, as it is properly called, of which one part is deliberative, the other judicial. He thus defines the three branches of political action: legislation, execution and judicial activity.

Both people of *techné* (creative persons) and people of *phronesis* (practically wise people) are practically wise in a particular way. But there are also those who are "wise about things as a whole."[20] This consists of grasping the truth of starting points, and knowing "what follows from the starting-points." Thus, "theoretical wisdom must be understanding plus scientific knowledge."[21] Importantly, theoretical wisdom or *sophia* "produces happiness." [22] The love of theoretical wisdom, or *sophia*, is philosophy. Importantly, both practical wisdom and theoretical wisdom require experience, becoming acquainted with things. This is why a young man cannot be called either practically wise or theoretically wise, even though he may possess both craft knowledge and *epistémé*.

The above categorical scheme shows that Aristotle distinguished between different types of knowledge. Oakeshott's analysis of modes of experience was inspired by this classification. He, too, differentiated between practice, science and philosophy. Aristotle also defined history in the ninth part of *Poetics*, where he distinguished between history, poetry and philosophy. "Poetry, therefore, is a more philosophical and a higher thing than history: for poetry tends to express the universal, history the particular."[23] Both of them have the function of reconstructing (or as he puts it, imitating) human action. But while history presents a particular person (Aristotle illustrates this point with the name of Alcibiades), poetry represents how "a person of a certain type will on occasion speak or act, according to the law of probability or necessity."[24] In other words: while history presents the particular and the accidental, poetry is interested in that human speech and action which has a kind of general validity, that is, which expresses a kind or type, and not simply an individual case.[25] What Aristotle does here is to juxtapose history, as the imitation of the accidental and particular, and philosophy, as that of the necessary and universal, of human action. He claims that poetry is somewhere in between the two, confronting its audience with what could be called the concrete universal.[26] Poetry, then, is able to show the universal in the particular, the philosophy that can be found in history and to reveal what is necessary in the accidental.

Aristotle's categories of knowledge explain both Oakeshott's and Scruton's terminology. We are interested here in the latter, but Oakeshott's modes of experience also seem to come from this ancient Greek source, while certainly not directly, but most probably through the mediation of German classical idealism. To take the key terms of this book: poetry turns out to be a form of craft knowledge, politics a form of practical wisdom, and philosophy is theoretical wisdom. Obviously theoretical wisdom stands on higher ground, as it is concerned with universals, while both *techné* and *phronesis* are concerned with particulars. *Theoria* is "the most exact of the sciences."[27] Presumably it is this exactness of theoretical wisdom which explains why it produces happiness. Thales, through his knowledge of astronomy, for example, was able to make a fortune predicting when there would be a large harvest of olives, and buying up of all the olive presses which people could only hire from him for large amounts of money.[28] Moreover, Aristotle demonstrates through the example of Anaxagoras that theorising "about the heavens and the whole order of the universe," as Reeve puts it, "constitutes the most blessedly happy life and thus is the most practical thing of all."[29]

There is a further connection between the two practical forms of knowledge. In fact, both of them require human decision or choice. The poet needs to decide about the fate of his protagonists on a case-by-case basis, selecting the particular story line which will be able to show the universal in the particular. Aristotle also provides a rather detailed account of how the practically wise person chooses. Practical wisdom is, in fact, the ability "to deliberate well" in—as we would say—difficult cases. "The unconditionally good deliberator, however, is the one capable of aiming at and hitting, in accord with rational calculation, the best for a human being of things doable in action."[30] The *phronimos* (the practically wise person) is able to deliberate well, because he possesses the virtue of character or deliberate choice (*prohairesis*), which enables him to find the correct desire and the true reason for that choice. While theoretical thought is purely either true or false, in the case of non-theoretical thought, which is either practical or productive, "the good state is truth in agreement with correct desire."[31] Hence, in Aristotle's view, in order to make good choice, a human agent needs both to know the world correctly, but also to desire correctly as well—and these might be regarded as the objective and the subjective criteria of choice.

Choice, then, is crucial in both practical and productive thought. Aristotle assumes both of them to have the same structure. This is also true of the early modern teaching on moral and aesthetic judgement, which was also Aristotelian in its inspiration.[32] The third Earl of Shaftesbury, for example, claimed that there was a sense of right and wrong, which enabled human beings to judge the affections other people have—those affections which determined the quality of the actions those people were engaged in.[33] Shaftesbury was also interested in the way we make aesthetic judgements, that is to say the way we judge whether something, someone or some activity is beautiful or not. It is also important to note that, as he saw it, both moral sense and the sense of beauty are born with us, but at the same time both of them require education, through which they can be refined.[34] This education is meant to be carried out both at the level of the individual and at the level of a community, with a multi-generational dimension as well: "Taste or Judgment … can hardly come ready form'd with us into the World… Use, Practice and Culture must precede the Understanding and Wit of such an advanc'd Size and Growth as this. A legitimate and just Taste can neither be begotten, made, conceiv'd, or produc'd, without the antecedent Labour and Pains of Criticism."[35] This is important, because it foreshadows the way that the general term "culture," or more precisely "cultural tradition," as proposed by the German Enlightenment, will play a major role, both in moral (practical) judgement and in the judgement of taste.

Cultural relativism, however, leads to radical subjectivism, to the idea that each well-developed and educated person will have her own standards of moral goodness and aesthetic quality.[36] In the field of politics, the equivalent of this radical moral and aesthetic relativism would be a radical libertarian position, stressing the individual's autonomy, as far as her political judgements are concerned. Some conservative theories come close to this position—arguably, among them is Oakeshott's own view, emphasised by his famous metaphor that politics is like a voyage on the sea, without harbour. Scruton, however, argued for a kind of natural law, which operates as an external control over the standards of different political communities, and this made it possible for him to counterbalance relativism, and to criticise standards even from within that very tradition.[37]

Plato on Beauty, Poetry and the Divine

There was another ancient Greek thinker who made a great impact on both Oakeshott and Scruton. And that, of course is Plato. Plato's *Republic* and *Symposium* both address the relationship of politics and poetry (or art, in more general terms) in respect to philosophy. Although Plato did not influence Scruton's political thought directly, his philosophy of beauty, which he developed—among other places—in *Symposium* might be considered relevant for an understanding of Scruton's understanding of beauty as something which leads human beings towards the metaphysical dimension.

One should recall in this context Socrates' story in Plato about the prophetess Diotima. Perhaps the most interesting and famous part of her narrative concerns the rise of the soul towards absolute and pure beauty. Plato in the *Republic* criticises the poet, because he leads us away from the truth. Yet Socrates' teacher of love, Diotima, presents the case differently. Diotima reminds us that *poiesis* in the most general sense means to produce or create: "poetry is more than a single thing. For of anything whatever that passes from not being into being the whole cause is composing or poetry" (205b–c).[38] Poetry in the narrow sense is only one kind of production, which is connected with music and verse: "a single section disparted from the whole of poetry—merely the business of music and meters—is entitled with the name of the whole. This and no more is called poetry; those only who possess this branch of the art are poets" (205c). In Diotima's teaching, the relationship between producing in the general sense and producing in the narrow sense is compared to *eros*. There is a general sense of *eros*, wishing the Good and happiness, "all that desire of good things and of being happy" (205d). At the same time one should not forget about the narrow sense of *eros*, which we use about those whose wish is to have the Good and happiness in a specific way, "all those who pursue him seriously in one of his several forms obtain, as loving and as lovers, the name of the whole" (205d). The tricky thing of Diotima's tale is that she does not simply draw attention to the same logical structure between the general term and the specific sense of it, of *poiesis* and *eros*. She also connects poetry and *eros* substantially. She claims that lovers, in other words those who wish to have the Good for ever with them, act in a specific way: they create something beautiful. Love, the wish to have the Good, is "begetting on a beautiful thing by means of both the body and the soul" (206b). Diotima defines begetting as "the conjunction of man and woman is a begetting for both" (206c). Procreation is divine in a certain sense, because it is the *poiesis* of what is immortal, "an immortal element in the creature that is mortal" (206c). Moreover, the divine cannot take place in the ugly, because that would be discordant. Thus, Diotima also proved that the wish to have the Good for ever for ourselves leads us to the immortal: it is also the search for the divine.

The next stage is to show that this procreation can take place not only in the body, but also in the soul. In this connection, Diotima mentions both poets and statesmen. Both of them conceive and bring forth something that is proper for the soul. And prudence and the virtues are surely proper for the soul. That is why both the poet and the statesman are prudent according to Plato. Considering everything we know about the virtues, it becomes clear that "of these the begetters are all the poets and those craftsmen who are styled"—in Diotima's narrative—"inventors.

Now by far the highest and fairest part of prudence is that which concerns the regulation of cities and habitations; it is called sobriety and justice" (209a). This suggests that poets and statesman are aiming at the same things: to have the Good for themselves. To achieve this, they "create in the soul," surpassing their own selfish interests, and through that activity they eventually become prudent and virtuous.

After showing how close poets stand to statesman, Diotima, the teacher of Socrates in Plato's dialogue, identifies different kinds or levels of production. Sexual procreation itself is regarded by her as a natural form of *poiesis*. A higher level of beauty can be achieved by creating that which lasts for ever than can be attained by creating mortal bodies. "Homer and Hesiod and all the other good poets" created poems to "procure them a glory immortally renewed in the memory of men" (209d). But an even higher form of immortal beauty is that created by the lawmakers and those who govern cities (209e).

It would seem, then, that statesmanship is at a higher level of creating beauty than natural procreation or poetry. The highest level of beauty, however, is achieved only by those who confront not one beautiful body or soul in the material, particular world, but "a province of beauty," the "beauty in the mass" (210c). This realm is only discovered by the philosopher, who contemplates "the main ocean of the beautiful" (210d). It is the philosopher who will be able to achieve "a certain single knowledge connected with a beauty," which is akin to a metaphysically inspired aesthetics. He catches sight of "a wondrous vision, beautiful in its nature" and this is "the final object of all those previous toils." The object he contemplates is "ever-existent, and neither comes to be nor perishes, neither waxes nor wanes" (211a). This is, of course, the vision of the divine being, which is the realm of the theologian in European culture. In other words, the hierarchy which Diotima argues for, includes, in ascending order, sexual love, poetry, politics, philosophy (together with aesthetics) and finally theology. As we shall see, Scruton's philosophy in these fields was indeed strongly influenced by this vision of the hierarchy of forms of knowledge and of the love of beauty.

Practical Life and Contemplation

Happiness or *eudaimonia* meant something more substantial to the ancient Greek than it means to us. For Aristotle, it is that unspecified thing which humans strive to achieve in and by their life. Among the ways to achieve *eudaimonia* the second best seems to be "the life in accord with the other virtue," while the happiest is contemplative activity (*theorein*).[39] As we have seen, practical life can be active or productive, and relies on the forms of knowledge identified by Aristotle as *techné* and *phronesis*. Both of these activities make humans happy, yet it seems that contemplation is of a higher order, as it requires less of external conditions, which means that it is more self-sufficient, and in that sense less vulnerable to that which cannot be controlled.

Aristotle does not seem to decide the issue with enough clarity to end all disputes. However, his argument in *NE* X8 ends with a description of the wise man ("whose activity is in accord with understanding (nous))."[40] In this sense, the philosopher turns out to be both closest to the gods and the one living the happiest life.

In order to show how this conceptual pair (practical life–theoretical life) would go on to be discussed throughout European intellectual history, let me refer to two phases of its later history. One is the context of the Roman empire, the other that of the medieval Christian cloister. In Roman discussions of happiness what we find is a return to the conceptual pair of *otium* and *negotium*. The Romans, too, wavered when it came to evaluating the term *otium*. Epicurus promised *otium* as a quiet bliss. More influential, though, were the views of Cicero, who wrote about a worthy leisure, *otium cum dignitate*.[41] This was how he portrayed his own life after his withdrawal from public life due to the vagaries of political fortune. In *On Duties* Cicero considers a retreat to the countryside a good option when politics becomes too hot in the city. In *Pro Sestio* there is a precise description of *otium cum dignitate*: "That which stands first, and is most to be desired by all happy, honest and healthy-minded men, is ease with dignity."[42]

The term retained its significance in the medieval Christian context too. First of all, that period saw the emergence of the concept of *otium philosophandi*, once again connecting contemplation and leisure. At a time of political cataclism, Augustine praised for a life of peaceful retreat as indeed something to be wished for. Yet this concept was also adopted by the system of Christian monasteries, where monks were expected to live a life of withdrawal, peace and intellectual activity.[43] This is how this life is described by medievalists: "in its essence the monastic life is a *vita contemplativa*... And the essence of this *vita contemplativa* is not to do or act, but to contemplate, meditate upon God and the human soul."[44]

Taylor emphasises that one of the examples which this Christian concept was built on was precisely the theoretical life of Aristotle. However, he finds that a more important concept for this was that of Christian love, describing a mutual emotional attachment between God and the human being, created by God. The use of a somewhat surprising expression, "Christian ecstasy" explains that this idea can in fact be understood as a Platonic element in the medieval frame of mind. After all, the concept of ecstasy, *ekstasis*, means "to be or stand outside oneself." It was famously used by Plotinus, perhaps the most important Hellenistic inheritor of the Platonic legacy, who explained ecstasy as follows: "an expansion and accession of himself, a desire of contact, rest, and a striving after conjunction."[45] This is also the aim of the medieval monastic life: to enable its participants to concentrate on, and if possible, to achieve, the highest level of human perfection, that of enjoying the presence of God.

Interestingly, when the humanists formulated their increasingly sharp criticisms of the medieval ideal of monastic life, what they regarded as a sinful form of seclusion, they too, relied on the distinction which, as we have seen, came from ancient Greek philosophy.[46] Already in Petrarch's writings there is a conflict between what can be regarded as his Christian calling and the aspirations which led him to write. He strived to achieve a balance between the two *vitae*, while his long-lasting fame was based on the perfection of his creation, which was, once again, about a perfect life, lived through the love of beauty, and through that, the love of God.

An even more explicit case of the presence of a double standard, that is, the effect of both the ideal of the *vita activa* and that of the *vita contemplativa* is characteristic of the thought of Coluccio Salutati. The combination of "legal knowledge, political cunning and diplomatic skill, but also... psychological penetration, a gift for public relations, and unusual literary skill" made him famous not only within the city but also far beyond its walls.[47] Salutati's master and example was the Roman orator, man of letters and statesman, Cicero, from whom he learnt the relevance of rhetorical abilities in political life. Yet he learnt from his masters in Latin poetry, Virgil and Petrarch, that the greatest human achievements are the achievements of the intellect, even if he had serious doubts, "a broad scepticism about the capabilities of human reason in divine matters."[48]

Vita activa and *vita contemplativa*—these two patterns of intellectual life remained constant in modern European culture, spawning a long line of reflections on the role of the intellectual in politics, and the virtues of living in an ivory tower of humanistic studies and self-reflection, popularised by examples like that of Montaigne.

Art and Politics

As we have seen, Aristotle presented *techné* and *phronesis* as two different forms of knowledge. *Techné* relates to *phronesis* as art does to politics. Art is the sort of activity which produces what we call works of art, while politics concerns action for the common good. If we wish to explore the connection between the two, we might take the public nature of art as an example. Both architecture and sculpture produce objects that will be enjoyed by all members of the community, as houses and statues are both on public display, in the streets and squares of the city. Similarly, ancient Greek theatre was a public form of cult, as members of the Athenian *demos* were expected to take part on the occasions of theatrical performance and were paid for their participation. In the same way, music was enjoyed by the whole community and even poetry of the Homeric kind was tied to public occasions, mostly to *symposia*, where pieces of literature were recited to entertain the assembled company. As the example of the Homeric epics show, these pieces were long narratives about the fate of the community, relating adventures and turning points in its life.

Taking the art world of the ancient Greek *polis* as a whole, it becomes clear that basically all of its forms, architecture, sculpture, theatre, music and poetry had a public relevance which made the artists themselves also politically relevant. Greek history writing has bequeathed to us the most illustrious names of these sort of activities. Of them, perhaps, Homer himself was the most prestigious, but if we mention the names of Iktinos, Phidias, Sophocles or the fictional Orpheus, representatives of all the major forms of art can be collected from the written remnants of Greek culture. Preserving the memories of the best among them from generation to generation, as they commemorated the great military leaders, legislators, rhetors or statesmen. Only the sports can compare to art as far as public relevance was concerned: sports festivities enjoyed the same popularity as cultural or artistic events, all of which were enjoyed by large gatherings of the community. Likewise, the erection of a statue or monument for public display was considered an important event in the life of the community, as were the festive occasions when a new public building was opened, such as a gymnasium or a temple.

Notable were the narratives which preserved historical events, including foundation myths—stories about the origins of the community. Besides recounting the significant events in the lives of the major political and military protagonists or heroes, they also invariably gave the audience (whether they believed what they heard or not) an insight into the life of the gods and semigods of the culture. In fact, the word "cult" itself shows that the origins of cultural events and productions or works of art can almost always be traced back to religious activity for the veneration of gods. Public occasions with artistic performance were regarded as partly liturgical, partly political festivities, which sometimes even allowed the citizens to have ecstatic experiences, like the Dionysian festivals (i.e. festivals to celebrate God Dionysos) that were described poetically by Nietzsche in his work *The Birth of Tragedy from the Spirit of Music* (1872).

This account of the genealogy of Greek art and its classification was also considered important by Scruton, as he often referred to Nietzsche, while Wagner was one of his favourite composers. Interestingly, for the nineteenth-century German thinker, the Dionysian was far more relevant and valuable as a form of art and thinking than the Apollonian, even if he made good use of both registers of human consciousness. As he saw it, poetry and music were more original, while rationality in all its forms was only a secondary form of consciousness. Nietzsche preferred art, which helped the human being to accept himself and his life. In general, he famously claimed: "We possess art lest we perish of the truth,"[49] suggesting that we should learn from artists "how to make things beautiful, attractive, desirable for ourselves when they are not."[50]

The relationship between modern art and politics was not ideal. Since at least the Enlightenment, and certainly in the age of Romanticism, artists in the empire were often regarded as subversive trouble-makers, and the politics of the age considered the relationship between art and culture as politically dubious or downright suspicious. Nietzsche himself was not able to find his place in the cultural policy of Bismarck's Germany, and his writings were to inspire radical political ideas in the early twentieth century.

Just as in the age of Pericles in ancient Greece, Florentine humanism had a long-lasting effect on the modern understanding of the public role of art. Royal courts and great urban centres competed in a Europe-wide rivalry of sponsorship of the arts. From the fine arts to theatre, from architecture to music, from literature to rhetoric, artists and intellectuals could establish their reputation by contributing to the unashamed praise of their own political leader or the community. Art, from the Renaissance onwards, became well known as the best support of a political power's fame and reputation, among the best statesmen and their advisers in the rich courts of the continent, as well as in the most thriving cities of Europe. This was the contemporary form of what came to be called soft power, the use of art and culture to raise prestige and earn public recognition.

Politics and Philosophy

Yet it was not only artists who were useful to a republic, state or city. Since the earliest times, rulers also employed philosophers. Not so much in order for them to praise their rulers, but rather to give advice, to educate their children and help them write their speeches.

The philosopher in the service of a ruler was known already to the Greeks. Plato travelled as far as Syracuse to advise his friend, the local tyrant, Dion. Aristotle returned to Stagira, to the court of Philip II of Macedon, to take up a position teaching the future conqueror, Alexander the Great. Certainly, one can question the actual political effectiveness of an education led by a famous philosopher. Still, both rulers and republican communities seemed to be inclined to have in their entourage political advisers, who often had philosophical erudition, besides a knowledge of the theory of rhetoric.

In the European history of the somewhat risky relationship between ruler and adviser, once again, Renaissance Italy stands out. If you ask someone to name but one philosopher who was employed as a political advisor, the most obvious answer is Niccolo Machiavelli. Indeed, Machiavelli's oeuvre is almost exclusively composed of political advice. Florence was a famous centre of artistic and intellectual life in late medieval and Renaissance Italy, yet the political conflicts between rival groups of the citizenry threatened to tear the city apart, causing constant political turmoil.

This was the political context of the activity of Machiavelli. Unlike Plato or to some extent, even Aristotle, Machiavelli was not an idealist in his political convictions. On the contrary, he was probably the earliest theoretician of politics who publicly defended a political theory of realism dividing his readers according to their morals, religious convictions and political experiences. The ancients, too, had their realist authors, notably the famous historians Thucydides, Polybius and Tacitus. Certainly, Machiavelli was inspired by them. Yet Machiavelli was also directly involved in political matters throughout his life. He held important positions during the republican period of his city, collecting firsthand experience of its actual workings. His surviving texts prove his competence as a political thinker who exercised a profound influence.

The most vexing question of the Florentine thinker's oeuvre is that he seems to give contradictory pieces of advice to different clients. In spite of the fact that he had his own political preference, probably for a republican form of government, his most famous work, *The Prince*, is a rather clear-headed advice-book for an authoritarian or even tyrannical ruler.[51] Machiavelli remained the paradigm case of a thinker who looked into the abyss of practical politics and gave a realistic picture of what he saw there. Like his ancient Roman forerunner, Cicero, whenever he was not actively involved in political machination, he was ready to write about his own experiences or the political past of his city, and drew from those narratives what he regarded as rational conclusions. As his biographer put it: "For Machiavelli there is no question which life is more fulfilling or more fit for an intelligent and capable man. Ironically, he makes his most passionate case for the vita activa even as circumstances forced him to adopt a way of life more in keeping with the opposite."[52]

Machiavelli's case foreshadowed the relationship between political power and the intellectuals in the twentieth century. This relationship was also indebted to the consequences of the Enlightenment and the age of Romanticism. The French *philosophes* reordered the connection between politics and ideas. While the theories of Locke and Hume were influential in the American movement of independence, it was some of Rousseau's wilder ideas which seem to have inspired the French revolutionaries in Paris. In the nineteenth century, too, the ideas of thinkers like Tocqueville, Mill or Kant had a political impact. The distinguishing mark of the twentieth century was the breakthrough of what Hannah Arendt called *Totalitarian ideology*, leading to the brutal regimes of Communist Russia, Fascist Italy and National Socialist Germany. All of these ideologies were based on the a priori theories of intellectuals. It is very disillusioning to examine more closely how intellectuals related to the centres of absolute power. There was a wide variety of how intellectuals reacted to the temptation of power. Examples range from George Orwell, who after a period as a Marxist in his youth, discovered the inner logic of absolute rule, and towards the end of his life became a sharp critic of totalitarian impulses in European politics. Yet other highly intelligent thinkers, like Carl Schmitt or Martin Heidegger on one side, George Lukács, Jean Paul Sartre or the Cambridge Five on the other, could not resist the attraction of Totalitarian power centres, and for some time became their servants and apologists.

Between critics of Totalitarian power, like Orwell, Koestler, Solzhenitsyn or Sándor Márai, and the unambiguous supporters of these regimes, there is a grey zone which is perhaps even more interesting. Intellectuals were always inclined to gravitate towards the magnetic centres of power. The reigning power very soon realised that in order to sustain oppressive regimes it is necessary to cultivate ideology, in other words, propaganda art and culture, and artists were ready to serve particular political interests.

Twentieth-century intellectuals were easily able to delude themselves that they could fight one type of oppression by serving the other one. Each needed to disguise its similarity to the other.[53] The Communist regime possessed an especially powerful ideological engine, and made great efforts to win over public sympathy in the West by finding support among Western intellectuals. While there were those who saw the deceptive nature of this temptation, like the philosopher Hannah Arendt, or the historian John Lukacs, some of the leading voices of intellectual life remained for a long time sympathetic to the Communist bloc, notably the thinker Jean-Paul Sartre and the members of the Frankfurt school, including Horkheimer, Adorno and Marcuse. It was easy to remain external supporters, so called fellow travellers of Communist regimes. Inside of these systems intellectuals had much less elbow room to keep their distance from the political authorities. Even the most authoritative voices, like the poet and public intellectual Gyula Illyés, László Németh or Tibor Déry, had to make compromises in order for their works to continue to be published in Communist Hungary.

The large camp of fellow travellers in the West and the domination of the party over the public sphere in the East illustrate the poisonous effects of Totalitarian ideology on intellectuals. This impact has been immortally expressed in the works of Arthur Koestler, Czesław Miłosz or Václav Havel. Some of the best tried to keep their moral integrity intact, like the philosopher Béla Hamvas or the political thinker István Bibó, once again in Hungary. As we shall see, these examples of opposition were formative influences on Scruton. To be sure, as the poet Mihály Babits argued, in the context of modernity, no intellectual can avoid defining his relationship to power: "because he who is silent is an accomplice of the guilty ones, / brother is called to account for the deeds of his brothers."[54] If you are politically a traitor, or at least a fellow traveller, these compromises will poison your ideas, too. Both Heidegger and Sartre have to be interpreted by taking into account their relationship to Nazi and Communist rule, respectively.

Art and Philosophy

To answer the question of the relationship between art and philosophy, the third logical relationship in the triangle of politics, art and philosophy, one must first define one's concept of philosophy.

Philosophy underwent a rather unfortunate divide in the twentieth century, between analytic and Continental philosophy.[55] We shall view them here as two different traditions within modern (and postmodern) philosophy, where tradition is the way one is educated as a philosopher—determining what to read, how to define a philosophical problem, and what styles of thinking are adequate to tackle those problems.

Scruton himself was well versed in both of these traditions, or rather he made deliberate efforts to bridge this divide. Educated in Cambridge, England, his first commitment was to analytic philosophy.[56] After his years in Cambridge, he spent some time in France, which gave him the opportunity to look into the background and cultural context of the Continental tradition, and Scruton was keen to read about and immerse himself in that tradition. And even if his philosophical instincts never denied his analytic allegiance, by the time he became a mature philosopher his intellectual profile also contained family resemblances with the Continental tradition.

Philosophy, for Scruton, is a form of reflective intellectual activity which tries to make sense of the human condition. It is defined, therefore, by having a specific subject matter: like the natural sciences, which, as their name suggests, deal with the natural world, for Scruton, philosophy deals primarily with the human being, with the whole complexity of this phenomenon.

If philosophy is about the human condition, then it cannot be far away from the arts. In fact, philosophy thus understood is a major pillar of the humanities, a specific form of understanding, which Continental philosophy saw as an alternative to science. As we shall see later, for Scruton it is crucial that the human being can be only understood from an internal point of view, instead of the external perspective of natural science.

Scruton made this meta-philosophical choice very early on, while retaining his interest in the natural sciences. Art turned out to be a natural ally of his philosophy. What else is art, as understood in the post-Kantian paradigm, but a way to depict or portray the specifically human phenomenon? Aristotle used the word "mimesis," or "imitation," to describe this aspect of poetry in *Poetics*: "Epic poetry, then, and the poetry of tragic drama, and, moreover, comedy and dithyrambic poetry, and most flute-playing and harp-playing, these, speaking generally, may all be said to be 'representations of life'."[57] In other words, the artist is interested in showing us what is relevant in our life. In a drama, to take a specific example, "living persons are the objects of representation," in particular, "they present people as doing things."[58] Understood this way, drama represents the active life. When we go to the theatre, the point is to become involved in other people's life, as acted out on the stage by the actors. While in poetry in the narrow sense, it is only through words that the representation takes place; in a theatrical performance actors embody the represented figures. Not all kinds of action are represented on stage, however. This is his famous definition of tragedy: "Tragedy is, then, a representation of an action that is heroic and complete and of a certain magnitude—by means of language enriched with all kinds of ornament, each used separately in the different parts of the play: it represents men in action and does not use narrative, and through pity and fear it effects relief to these and similar emotions."[59] In other words, theatrical representation relies on both words and acts. The distinguishing mark of the action represented on the tragic stage is that it is "of a certain magnitude," causing a certain "pity and fear" in the audience, which helps to purify their soul of "these and similar emotions."[60] We know that in Athens participation in theatrical performances was obligatory for the citizens, to remind them of their duties. Ancient Greek theatre had an exceptional civic urgency.

Plato wanted to keep power of artistic representation under political control. His critical attitude was due to what he called "an old quarrel between philosophy and poetry."[61] Interestingly, however, the texts of the Platonic dialogue manifest something different from what he claimed in his explicit, "official" theory of the relationship between the two. Plato's philosophical prose, itself, has a certain poetic power. And if we accept the insights of the linguistic turn in twentieth-century meta-philosophy, we have to admit that the way a claim is presented has an impact on its truth.

A specific form where poetry and philosophy meets is the philosophical dialogue. Scruton seems to have taken this form of philosophical expression very seriously, and he produced philosophical dialogues himself. The question arises as to why this genre of philosophical writing was important to him. It may well be because from very early on, Scruton had the conviction that art can convey truth in a very convincing manner.

The philosophical dialogue uses a specific technique: it enables the reader to change perspectives, by confronting the views of the protagonists. They share with the viewer their different accounts of the object, and this helps the viewer to sense the three-dimensional nature of the object. Like the operation of the eyes, which allow us to see things in space by watching them from two slightly different positions, two alternative views in a dialogue can reveal the spatial nature of the object under debate. Or to take another picture: as a result of the stereo high-fidelity effect of a recorded music, our two ears sense slightly different things, and our mind puts these different perceptions together in a way which allows for a richer auditive effect.

The author of the philosophical dialogue offers a narrative, and with that the experience of motion and change: our point of view is itself transforming during the process of reading the text. In other words, narration serves to bring us from a beginning to the end of the story. While Aristotle's analytical discourse offers us only the effect of a two-dimensional photograph, Plato's philosophical dialogue gives the effect of a three-dimensional motion picture, recorded by cameras that are viewing the object from different angles, and that are themselves moving.

Besides the effects of opacity and perspectivity, the third feature of this type of text is that it allows us to feel a certain detachment. While in Aristotle's style we find a neutral description of reality, Plato's texts reveal the illusory nature of ideas. From Plato, you can learn important things about your own position, including about yourself, and not only about the object. To put it more succinctly, the philosophical dialogue's narrative embeddedness can lead to self-reflection. If you are informed indirectly, or in a delayed manner, this distance or delay gives you time to reflect—which means that you receive the information about the object together with your own thoughts and feelings about it.

A further difference: while in non-fictional prose the human presence (including that of both the narrator and the protagonists) is not pronounced, in a dialogue ideas are mediated by persons, embodied beings, taken from life. Ideas relate here to other embodied thoughts, as humans relate to other humans.

Finally, Plato's text is obviously written with the intention of having an aesthetic effect on the reader, while Aristotle was not so concerned about the aesthetic quality of the language he used.[62] For Aristotle, the medium of language is non-problematic. Wittgenstein's famous adage, of course, was: "whereof one cannot speak, thereof one must be silent."[63] Yet the post-Tractatus Wittgenstein himself was aware of the rhetorical and poetic function of language. In fact, he exemplifies how for a philosopher language is the most useful analytical tool. Scruton was raised in the sober analytical tradition, which claimed rhetorical neutrality. His discursive language most of the time is purely transparent.

Yet there is an awareness of language in his prose as well. The linguistic turn is crucial for a certain type of analytical philosophy. It helped to realise that language is not a private matter. As soon as we use natural language, its presuppositions will likewise prefigure our philosophical message. In this sense, analytical philosophers aim at a zero degree of linguisticity, together with a maximum awareness of rhetorical distortions, in their use of language, while they use ordinary language as their test course.

Following an inspiration of Wittgenstein, ordinary analytical philosophy analyses language, as a method of practising philosophy. By the time Scruton arrived in Cambridge, philosophers had grown less ardent or passionate about mediality, yet he, too, retained an awareness of the linguistic nature of philosophy, in his philosophical methodology. He seems to have shared the view that if you have a clear idea on a certain topic, a test of its philosophical validity (or truth) is whether you can express it clearly, in a way that non-professional philosophers can make sense of it. While he was one of the most refined and cultured philosophers of his generation, his language does not hinder the reader's understanding of his text.

Scruton's Triangle: Philosophy, Art and Politics

Let us summarise our findings so far. We shall approach Scruton's philosophy with an interest in his views on politics and art. To prepare the ground, I explained the interconnections between these separate fields of knowledge or enquiry. I also delimited a certain discursive terrain. Scruton's view of the human condition was determined by his having been brought up in the analytical tradition. Yet he did not share all the reservations of analytical philosophers concerning politics and art, topics which are difficult to address simply by an application of logic. Beyond the English language tradition, Scruton was familiar with much of Continental philosophy. But perhaps even more importantly, he cherished a conviction that to connect these two discoursive universes promises to be fruitful.

With its primary focus on politics and the arts this book has a structure resembling a catalogue or linear summary of Scruton's most important books concerning these matters. It was meant to be helpful in a general sense to those interested in either or both of these realms, enabling readers to take a first glance at one or more of Scruton's works in these two fields.

I referred above to two substantive convictions of Scruton. The first of these was that even if philosophy cannot do much to further the cause of politics, philosophers also have a duty to take part in the public discourse of their day. He thought that philosophy can be useful as a form of criticism, drawing attention to the potential dangers of what came to be called social engineering. Whatever one thinks about his political activism, one has to be aware that a large part of his political philosophy is simply the repeated pronouncement of cautionary remarks of the excesses of political passions.

He was aware of the dangers of propaganda: he also pursued political activity himself, especially, but not only, in Communist and post-Communist Central Europe. His political commentary on British politics and later also in the US made him a *bête noire* of large sections of the media and later also of academia.

Scruton's second substantive philosophical conviction is perhaps more positive than the first one. It concerns the philosophy of art, perhaps his most beloved form of philosophical engagement. As a person who seems to have had a natural inclination towards art, and in particular a passion for music and architecture, it is all too obvious that Scruton had an exceptionally strong interest in the philosophy of art. In his doctoral thesis he addressed the philosophy of the perception of art. He was tempted to cross the border between thought and art, and he tried to do so himself by writing and composing. He was convinced that through art we can in fact catch a glimpse of something which is beyond ordinary human experience, entering the realm of transcendence. Although for most of his career he seems to have remained agnostic, he kept searching for the meaning of life with an urgency which could not fail to lead him to the final question of divine existence. As a Kantian he was careful not to cross the strict border between philosophy and theology. Yet, arguably, his thought had a latent Platonic underpinning, just as Aristotle's had.

In this book I will argue that Scruton increasingly realised that through art we can indeed learn something about human nature which is of a metaphysical relevance. It concerns the human being as a *zoon politikon*, a being born into a community, and to a large extent determined by that same community. Roger Scruton's late philosophy of art also has a metaphysical dimension. His *vita contemplativa* flowed naturally from his *vita activa*.

To close this introduction, a final cautionary remark may be in order. Scruton had a holistic view of philosophy. He held that the different branches of philosophy were connected, and therefore as soon as you commit yourself to a position in one field, it has consequences on your views in other fields. Not only was there a connection between the beautiful and the good, but both of them led to the truth and to the one, as medieval Christian thinkers would claim.[64] He was well aware, therefore, that his concern with beauty and with what is possible in politics, had both preconditions and consequences in philosophical anthropology, epistemology, ecology, the philosophy of sexuality, the philosophy of culture, metaphysics and the philosophy of religion, among others. He knew that no one can fully develop a theory in all these fields, yet he kept stressing the interconnections and correspondences between these fields, outlining an amazingly complex, holistic view of the realm of philosophy.

Notes

1. For a short comparison of the two, see Oliver Letwin's piece: "Defenders of a shared culture", published in *The Critic* (May 2020) after the death of Scruton. Available: https://thecritic.co.uk/issues/may-2020/defenders-of-a-shared-culture/.

2. Here, too, I should express my gratitude to Anthony O'Hear and Bob Grant, for their detailed and deep comments on my first draft.

3. Oakeshott's major writings about the mode of experience called politics can be found in RP, while his work on poetry is already present in his early *An Essay on the Relations of Philosophy, Poetry and Reality* (1925), and then returns in his much acclaimed *The Voice of Poetry in the Conversation of Mankind* (1959). For writings on Oakeshott's handling of the modes of politics and art see Suvi Soininen, *From a 'Necessary Evil' to the Art of Contingency. Michael Oakeshott's Conception of Political Activity* (imprint-academic.com, Exeter, 2005); Elizabeth Campbell Corey, *Michael Oakeshott on Religion, Aesthetics and Politics* (Columbia, MO: Inv. Of Missouri Press, 2006); see also the present author's "A Brief Enchantment: The Role of Conversation and Poetry in Human Life," in *The Meanings of Michael Oakeshott's Conservatism*, ed. Corey Abel (imprint-academic.com, Exeter, 2010), 238–54.

4. Scruton uses the term "great tradition" in the title of his rather late book: *Conservatism. An Invitation to the Great Tradition* (New York: All Points Book, 2017). One should also note, however, that one of Leavis' book on the novel published in 1948 had in its title the expression "The Great Tradition".

5. In what follows I rely on Terry Nardin, "Michael Oakeshott," *The Stanford Encyclopedia of Philosophy* (Spring 2020 Edition), Edward N. Zalta (ed.), URL = https://plato.stanford.edu/archives/spr2020/entries/oakeshott/.

6. Michael Oakeshott, *On History and Other Essays* (Oxford: Basil Blackwell, 1983; reprinted with different pagination Indianapolis: Liberty Fund, 1999), 2.

7. Timothy Fuller (ed.), *The Voice of Liberal Learning* (New Haven: Yale University Press, 1989; reprinted Indianapolis: Liberty Fund, 2001), 38.

8. For his works, which distinguish poetry as an independent form of experience, see note 2 above. Politics is dealt with mostly in his *Rationalism in Politics and Other Essays*, new and expanded edition, ed. Timothy Fuller (Indianapolis: Liberty Press, 1991).

9. Wilhelm Dilthey, Introduction to the Human Sciences (Volume I), in SW.I, 47–242. For a short overview of his distinction, see Rudolf Makkreel, "Wilhelm Dilthey," *The Stanford Encyclopedia of Philosophy* (Winter 2020 Edition), Edward N. Zalta (ed.), URL = https://plato.stanford.edu/archives/win2020/entries/dilthey/.

10. Nardin, *Michael Oakeshott*.

11. In this respect, what Oakeshott calls a discoursive universe is comparable to what is called tradition by MacIntyre. See for example Alasdair MacIntyre, *Three Rival Versions of Moral Enquiry. Encyclopaedia, Genealogy and Tradition* (London: Duckworth, 1990).

12. Oakeshott, *Rationalism in Politics*, 488–91, 497.

13. Peter Simons, "Metaphysics in Analytic Philosophy," in *The Oxford Handbook of the History of Analytic Philosophy*, ed. Michael Beaney (Oxford: Oxford University Press, 2013). See also Emmanuelle Garcia and Frederic Nef (eds.), *Métaphysique contemporaine* (Paris: Vrin, 2007).

14. See the collection of essays about Scruton and religion, edited by Bryson with Scruton's own contribution in it: James Bryson, *The Religious Philosophy of Roger Scruton* (London, etc.: Bloomsbury Academic, 2016). See especially Robert Grant's contribution to that collection, which accepts Scruton's description of the sacred as real, but finds Scruton's notion of religion less convincing.

15. Scruton, *Conservatism*, 9.

16. *NE*, 1139b15.

17. *NE*, 1139b39.

18. *NE*, 1140a25.

19. *NE*, 1140b1–3.

20. *NE*, 1141a10.

21. *NE*, 1141a18.

22. *NE*, 1144a5.

23. The Project Gutenberg Ebook of Poetics, by Aristotle, trans. S. H. Butcher, release date: November 3, 2008 [Ebook #1974], last updated January 22, 2013. http://www.gutenberg.org/files/1974/1974-h/1974-h.htm.

24. Ibid.
25. See in this connection Samuel Johnson's formulation: Nothing can please many, and please long, but just representations of general nature. Samuel Johnson, *Preface to Shakespeare* (1755). I used the Project Gutenberg Ebook version of the text, which has no page numbers: https://www.gutenberg.org/ebooks/5429.
    I am grateful to Robert Grant for this reference.
26. Silvia Carlis, "Poetry is more philosophical than history: Aristotle on Mimesis and form," *The Review of Metaphysics* 64, no. 2 (December 2010): 303–36.
27. *NE*, 1141a15. Importantly, Reeve explains that a science which is prior to another, or more exact than another is so, because both its subject matter is prior to that of others, and the explanation of the subject is more exact as well. (See note 44 on p. 277.)
28. Aristotle, *Politics*, 1259a.
29. Note 447 on p. 279.
30. *NE*, 1141b13–14.
31. *NE*, 1139a30. Charles Chamberlain, "The Meaning of prohairesis in Aristotle's Ethics," *Transactions of the American Philological Association* (1974–2014) 114, (1984): 147–57.
32. For a description of the early modern classification of types of judgement, see the chapter on the significance of the humanist tradition for the human sciences in Gadamer's *Truth and Method*, as well as Alfred Baeumler's *Das Irrationalitätsproblem in der Ästhetik und Logik des 18. Jahrhunderts bis zur Kritik der Urteilskraft*. The present writer himself published a volume in Hungarian on aesthetic thought in the age of enlightenment (1650–1800), and specifically about what he calls the aesthetics of taste: Ferenc Hörcher, *Esztétikai gondolkodás a felvilágosodás korában (1650–1800)* (Budapest: Gondolat Kiadó, 2014).
33. Third Earl of Shaftesbury (Anthony Ashley Cooper), "An Inquiry Into Virtue and Merit," in *Characteristics of Men, Manners, Opinions, Times, 1699–1714*, vol. 2, ed. Douglas Den Uyl (Indianapolis, IN: Liberty Fund, 2001), 1–100., 16.
34. For some of his accounts of teaching what to feel, see Roger Scruton's *Culture Counts. Faith and Feeling in a World Besieged* (New York, London: Encounter Books, 2007, 2018).
35. Shaftesbury, *Characteristics*, 3.164.

36. The problem of subjectivism was addressed in a clear and influential way by David Hume, in his essay on "The Standard of Taste."

37. See for example, Scruton's chapter on natural law in his book *The Meaning of Conservatism*. The problem of comparing different traditions was systematically analysed by Alasdair MacIntyre, in his *Three Rival Versions of Moral Enquiry: Encyclopaedia, Genealogy and Tradition* (1990).

38. From now on, page numbers of Scruton's books analysed in a detailed fashion are given in the main body in brackets.

39. For a recent overview of Aristotle's concept of theoria, see David Roochnik, "What is Theoria? Nicomachean Ethics Book 10.7–8," *Classical Philology* 104, no. 1 (January 2009): 69–82.

40. *NE*, 1179a22.

41. Chaim Wirszubski, "Cicero's CUM Dignitate Otium: A Reconsideration," *The Journal of Roman Studies* 44, no. 1 (1954): 1–13., J. P. V. D. Balsdon, "Auctoritas, Dignitas, Otium," *The Classical Quarterly* 10, no. 2 (May, 1960): 43–50.

42. *Pro Sestio*, XLV., 98.

43. Henry Osborn Taylor, *The Mediaeval Mind, A History of the Development of Thought and Emotion in the Middle Ages*, in two Volumes, Vol. I. (St. Martin's Street, London: Macmillan and Co., Ltd., 1911), chapter 15. The Reforms of Monasticism. Mediaeval Extremes; Benedict of Aniane; Cluny; Citeaux's Charta Charitatis; the vita contemplativa accepts the vita active.

44. Chapter XV. As I used an online copy of the book, I cannot give page numbers.

45. The above quotes are from Wallace N. Stearns, *Plotinus and the Ecstatic State*, 356–61., 360.

46. Paul A. Lombardo, "Vita Activa versus Vita Contemplativa in Petrarch and Salutati," *Italica* 59, no. 2 (Summer 1982): 83–92.

47. Stephen Greenblatt, *The Swerve: how the world became modern* (New York: W.W. Norton, 2011), 123.

48. James Hankins, "Salutati, Plato and Socrates," *Coluccio Salutati e l'invenzione dell'Umanesimo, Atti del Convegno internazionale di studi*, Firenze 29–31 ottobre 2008, Rome: Edizioni di Storia e letteratura, 2010 [published in 2011], 283–93., 284.

49. This quote is taken over from Anderson, R. Lanier, "Friedrich Nietzsche," The Stanford Encyclopedia of Philosophy (Summer 2017 Edition), Edward N. Zalta (ed.), URL = https://plato.stanford.edu/archives/

sum2017/entries/nietzsche/. Who quotes from Sämtliche Werke: Kritische Studienausgabe (KSA), edited by G. Colli and M. Montinari. Berlin: W. de Gruyter, 1980 ff., according to the accepted form of the literature on Nietzsche.

50. Once again taken over from Lanier: Nietzsche, the source noted as GS 299, referring to The Gay Science, Walter Kaufmann (trans.), New York: Vintage, 1974 (1st ed. 1882, 2nd ed. 1887).

51. For a short overview of his oeuvre, see: Quentin Skinner, *Machiavelli* (Oxford: Oxford University Press, 1985). Robert Grant advised me to consider Machiavelli's *The Prince* as a satire on the long line of the pious literary genre called Mirror for Magistrates.

52. Miles J. Unger, *Machiavelli. A Biography* (New York, etc.: Simon and Schuster, 2011), 249.

53. This point was suggested to me by Robert Grant.

54. Lóránt Czigány, *A History of Hungarian Literature, From the Earliest Times to the mid-1970's*, available at: https://www.arcanum.hu/hu/online-kiadvanyok/MagyarIrodalom-magyar-irodalomtortenet-1/a-history-of-hungarian-literature-from-the-earliest-times-to-the-mid-1970s-lorant-czigany-47D8/chapter-xviii-the-writers-of-the-nyugat-i-4BEC/1-a-view-from-the-ivory-tower-mihaly-babits-4BED/.

55. C. G. Prado, ed., *A House Divided: Comparing Analytic and Continental Philosophy* (Amherst, NY: Prometheus/Humanity Books, 2003).

56. For his account of his apprenticeship in philosophy in Cambridge, see the chapter "Becoming a Philosopher," in his *Conversations with Roger Scruton* (London, etc.: Bloomsbury, 2016), 29–38.

57. Aristotle, *Poetics*, trans. W. Hamilton Fyfe, 1447a, available at Perseus, http://www.perseus.tufts.edu/hopper/text?doc=Perseus%3atext%3a1999.01.0056.

58. Ibid., 1448a. The footnote tells us, that literally, the term "Aristotle" used meant: "men doing or experiencing something."

59. Ibid., 1449b. Certainly, there are cruel acts in these stories, which happen off-stage.

60. Ibid.

61. The Republic of Plato, translated with notes and an interpretive essay by Allan Bloom, 607b5–6. (New York: Basic Books, 1968).

62. At least that is the case with the Aristotelian texts that we have, which some scholars claim to be simple lecture notes, taken by his students.

Tradition has it that there were Aristotelian dialogues, but they do not seem to have survived. Roger D. Masters, "The Case of Aristotle's Missing Dialogues: Who Wrote the Sophist, the Statesman, and the Politics?" *Political Theory* 5, no. 1 (1977): 31–60.

63. The famous final sentence of the *Tractatus*, connected by some of its critics with an understanding of communication, which is close to the mystical tradition.

64. I am grateful to Anthony O'Hear for emphasising this point in our correspondence about my work in progress.

2

The Emergence of a Philosophy of Art and Politics

Although the lives of the philosophers have been a legitimate object of study for centuries, it is a controversial topic in connection with an analytical philosopher. After all, this is a kind of philosophy which portrays itself as a neutral, depersonalised form of activity, or expertise. In analytical philosophy, the distinguishing mark of the philosopher's professionalism is that—as in the natural sciences—it can be detached from the personal life of the philosopher, which is assumed in this discourse to be a private affair. Hence, it should be emphasised here that one cannot make sense of the development of Scruton's philosophy on art and politics without embarking on an interpretation of his life. The classical tradition has always been interested in the life of its heroes. A prime example is the famous collection of philosophers' biographies, Diogenes Laertius' *Lives and Opinions of Eminent Philosophers*. From the post-classical period, one should recall the famous philosophical autobiographies, from the confessions of Augustine to Rousseau's Confessions. One can also refer to the biographies and memoirs of statesmen and artists: both of these professions had a longstanding reputation in European culture, which generated interest in the lives of their best-known exponents.

Scruton himself reaffirms and legitimises an interest in his own life. Not only did he write a short introduction to Kant and another one

© The Author(s), under exclusive license to Springer Nature Switzerland AG 2023
F. Hörcher, *Art and Politics in Roger Scruton's Conservative Philosophy*, Palgrave Studies in Classical Liberalism, https://doi.org/10.1007/978-3-031-13591-0_2

about Spinoza, but in both cases he provided detailed accounts of the life of the thinker. Moreover, Scruton was aware of his readers' interest in his own life. In his book *On Hunting* he ventured into autobiography. Later he was ready to make use of the genre of the memoir. The book *Gentle Regrets* was published in 2005, when he was 61 years old, at an age when he found it appropriate to give an account of his life. Explaining his reasons for writing it, he argued that it was the experiences he gained in his life that enabled him "to find comfort in uncomfortable truths."[1] He admitted that to make sense of the birth of some of his ideas we have to reconstruct their emergence in the context of his *Lebenslauf* and his *Weltanschauung*. He suggests that a description of what happened to him often has an explanatory power for why he came to certain views.[2]

This connection between his biographical details and the details of a philosophical position he assumes is apparently also connected to his conservatism. Conservatism emphasises the relevance of experience in one's life, and this is what Scruton is doing when he explains his efforts to write a narrative account of his life: "this book is not a record of my *education sentimentale* but an attempt to explain a particular conservative outlook."[3]

Beyond *Gentle Regrets*, a book with a very telling title, another source is *Conversations with Roger Scruton*, a book authored by him together with Mark Dooley, an Irish philosopher and journalist, and published in 2016 by Bloomsbury.[4] The preface of this book was written by Dooley, telling the reader that the book offers an external record of an internal view, its author being in conversation with Scruton, speaking about Scruton's life.[5] This is how the preface describes the product of three days' conversation: this book is "a broad-ranging and fairly intimate portrait of Scruton's life and career, one that sheds some new light on both."[6] As Dooley puts it, these conversations "often move from biography to ideas and back again," in order to "give the reader a greater understanding of Scruton's thought, but also of the unusual life that lies behind it."[7] The present volume similarly makes an effort to find the connections between the philosopher's life and his specific philosophical points of view.

Scruton is a conservative philosopher. This is perhaps the first thing that one comes across about his work and life. Yet what exactly does that mean? Is it a certain set of philosophical doctrines that will mark him as conservative, or is it something else, perhaps a way of life, a particular approach to the human condition? Oakeshott famously claimed that conservatism is first and foremost an attitude of mind or mental constitution, which has a direct impact on one's practical behaviour. As he put it in *On Being Conservative*: "My theme is not a creed or a doctrine, but a disposition. To be conservative is to be disposed to think and behave in certain manners: it is to prefer certain kinds of conduct and certain conditions of human circumstances to others; it is to be disposed to make certain kinds of choices."[8]

Yet Scruton—perhaps unlike Oakeshott—was not born conservative. He recognised his conservatism at a comparatively late age. As his own recollections reveal, his transformation was a reaction to the vandalism of the Paris student revolutions in 1968. The chapter on his conservative epiphany in *Gentle Regrets* was originally published a few years earlier in *The New Criterion*.[9] While the earlier version connected his impressions of the Paris events with his adventures in Central Europe, the later version in *Gentle Regrets* focuses instead on two other experiences within the world of British Conservatism, on his intellectual education at Peterhouse College, Cambridge, and on his own activity within the intellectual background of the British Conservative party. In what follows we have a closer look at these three episodes of Scruton's conversion to conservatism.

Paris 1968

This is how Scruton reports from the spot: "the students were shouting and smashing," "the plate-glass windows…slid in jagged fragments to the ground," "Cars rose in the air," "lamp-posts and bollards were uprooted and piled on the tarmac, to form a barricade."[10] This is what you expect in a revolution. Why did it shock Scruton so much? He presents himself in this recollection, reading the *Memoirs* of De Gaulle, against whom the angry young men rebelled in Paris, and in it the description in Paul Valéry's poem, the *Cemetery by the Sea*. The poet's own, state-funded funeral in post-war Paris was described in De Gaulle's *Memoirs* in moving words.[11] Scruton compared De Gaulle's view of France with Valéry's poem *Cimetière matin*, "that haunting invocation of the dead." In

Scruton's ideal world, the world of the poet and that of the statesman were not separated.

It is telling to consider how he presents the contrast between reality and ideal. On one side, the vision of the rebelling students, keen on the ideas of Antonin Artaud and his "theatre of cruelty," as well as on what Scruton regarded as the strong rhetoric of Michel Foucault, one of his key targets in his later book, *Thinkers of the Left*.[12] This is how Scruton judged Foucault's *Les mots et les choses*: "an artful book, composed with a satanic mendacity."[13]

On the other side, his own interest in de Gaulle, the statesman, and Valéry, the poet. Scruton presents his dilemma as an aesthetic choice between these two alternative visions. It was his own taste which led him towards the more solemn and less fearsome of the two. Instead of cruelty and transgression, he preferred the vision of peace and order: not only that of the Gaullist vision but also that of the English law and its major ideologue, Edmund Burke. Interestingly, when Burke argued against the French revolution he, too, used the same technique of comparing visual alternatives: he painted the picture of the revolution in fearful colours, and he set that in opposition to the more familiar composition of the world of the *ancien regime*.

Burke, like Scruton, started as a thinker on aesthetic problems: he, too, made a rather inspiring contribution to aesthetic theory as a young man. Scruton's choice in 1968 was an aesthetic choice, just as Burke's own one was in 1789–1790. This is how he himself describes his conversion: "Like Burke, therefore, I made the passage from aesthetics to conservative politics," adding, as the common denominator, his search for home: "in each case, I was in search of a lost experience of home."[14]

In his conversation with Dooley, Scruton made it clear that in those days he was definitely not a politically minded person, and therefore his conservatism was not based on a political choice. When describing the book of his political "coming out," *The Meaning of Conservatism*, he explains it as the output of "my sparse reading and my abundant sentiments."[15] The point of the book was to show them, believers in and ideologues of the free market, that conservatism was a philosophically defensible position, and not "what they believed it to be."[16]

Casey and The Peterhouse Right

Although there is no doubt that Scruton's first-hand experience of the culture of destruction and "repudiation" in 1968 Paris played a crucial role in his choice of political direction, there are further factors at work here, which played a part in his philosophical roaming on this uncharted territory. The intellectual influences he encountered at his postgraduate Cambridge college, Peterhouse, must have played a crucial part in his formative years. To be sure, he chose this college for his graduate work because of its conservative reputation. He characterised his own attitude in those days as a rebellion against rebellion—a description not too dissimilar to the attitude of Edmund Burke. John Casey from Caius and Maurice Cowling from Peterhouse were friends who had an impact on his way of thinking, together with David Watkin, also from Peterhouse. All three opened up a different field before the eyes of the young Scruton: Casey was an expert on literature, Cowling on history and religion, while Watkin introduced him to the fields of architecture and art history. These uncommon Cambridge intellectuals undoubtedly had a formative influence on Scruton.

John Casey

John Casey is claimed to be the mentor of Scruton, and undoubtedly was a crucial influence on his intellectual development.[17] In *Conversations* Scruton describes Casey as an English scholar, brought up with traditional Catholic views, "a very difficult and domineering person."[18] It was with him, as well as with Hugh Fraser, MP, that Scruton, Casey's former student, would establish the Conservative Philosophy Group in 1974.

Casey's degree was not in philosophy but in English.[19] He never identified, therefore, with the analytical tradition which was the mother tongue of Scruton. Casey rather connected philosophy with a number of broader issues of society, morality, culture and politics.

Covell describes Casey's overall position as that of an aesthete who started out from a position of "philosophical Leavisism," and arrived at "Hegelian expressionism."[20] Casey also took over something from the

Arnoldian ideas of poetry, criticism and general culture, combining them with Leavis' views on language and "practical criticism."[21] Of Oakeshott's traditional discourses his favourite one was poetry, the claims of which he regarded as superior when compared to those of science, philosophy or religion. He took further inspiration from Aristotle and Thomas Aquinas, as well as from Hume and Nietzsche—an extraordinary mixture of philosophical signposts.

Casey's doctoral thesis, *The Language of Criticism*, originally published in 1966, was concerned with what he regarded as the importance of practical criticism. His starting point was Wittgenstein, and his late concept of rule-following, as a public practice and as something which was framed by public conventions. In contrast to a kind of subjective emotivism, Casey went for a naturalism which was confirmed by his reading of R. M. Hare and Philippa Foot. This naturalism, however, was based more on our second nature, that is, on conventions, and less directly on nature itself. The world of language and institutions were crucial for him, and he agreed with attributing importance to education, too.

Casey adopted from Arnold the connection he claimed to exist between morality and art, a connection which would also remain, as we shall see, in Scruton's own mindset.

There was a strong Kantian line in Casey's way of thinking, in particular in his claim that aesthetic judgement was rational, if not scientific, and not irrational, like simple taste was. For him art was anti-utilitarian, and works of art were to be regarded as ends in themselves. This issue was further explored in a later essay entitled *The Autonomy of Art*.[22] In this piece, Casey criticises Croce, a contemporary authority on aesthetics. To understand a piece of art we have to grasp it as an expression of something. Yet his position was just as anti-Cartesian as Croce's, abandoning in this respect Wittgensteinism in favour of an idealist position. Culture becomes the key to human life generally. Casey is approaching Hegel, even if not directly the German philosopher's metaphysics, in a vindication of imagination and of aesthetic experience in general. To sum up: Casey connected Wittgenstein's public rule-following with a Hegelian idealism, while he connected art and morality, as he found it in Arnold and Leavis.

Based on this rather divergent mix of influences he built an aesthetics, which, in due course, led him to "an overall conservative doctrine."[23] Covell connects Casey's conservatism with four themes: education, Roman Catholicism, national politics and intellectual and cultural affairs. His views on the university were indeed conservative: he defended it as an institution of corporate autonomy, along Hegelian arguments. The same applies to his views on the Catholic Church itself. His religious convictions were conservative both doctrinally and politically. As for his views on national politics, his idol was Enoch Powell.

As an editor of the *Cambridge Review* from 1975 to 1979, Casey published a number of essays which were deliberately vague stylistically. He used an ironic strategy in his argumentation, pretending to defend himself before a court. Both his defence of Powellism and his Hegelianism made him suspect politically. Casey had no problem with the term "authority," as expressed in his essay *Tradition and Authority*, published in a collection entitled *Conservative Essays*, edited by Cowling.[24] It represented a defence of traditions and institutions against any potential utilitarian criticism. The individual had to accept his position in this objective social realm, only made possible by *pietas*, a virtue Casey derives from Aquinas: "our conscious loyalties to institutions, our conscious pieties, cannot be explained in terms alien to" the objective social order itself.[25] Casey disregarded notions of natural law or natural right. In other essays, however, like *Actions and Consequences*, published in 1971, and *Human Virtue and Human Nature*, published in 1973, he still left it undecided whether he finally argued for a Thomistic naturalism, or a Hegelian historicism.[26] All in all, his position remained closer to cultural conservatism and did not satisfy the stricter criteria of a more general conservative political philosophy.

Casey's essay "Emotion and Imagination" can be regarded as his mature position on aesthetics.[27] His standpoint here was an acceptance of the traditional view of literature, as proposed by Arnold, Leavis and Richards, based on general theoretical suppositions about what he called "the expression theory of art," which he attributed to Hegel and Collingwood. While he was keen to reject a didactic "function" of art, resulting from a short circuit between art and morality, he seems to argue instead for a connection between artistic sensibility and the practical knowledge of

Aristotle's *phronimos*. While Casey's aesthetics were easily applicable to nineteenth-century high culture, it remained uncertain how exactly culture can provide those loyalties and pieties to traditions and institutions, which his Hegelianism would have required. After all, aesthetic sensibility required a certain liberty and autonomy of aesthetic judgement, while his general point about the social role of culture required an acceptance of traditional values and conventional social roles, which makes him a traditionalist. The gap between his aesthetics and his politics could have been bridged by his ethics. In this respect, the crucial issue was the parallel between the operation of aesthetic judgement and the judgement of practical wisdom. It was that parallel which suggested that a "blend of Aristotelianism and *Sittlichkeit*" could actually be defended.[28] His efforts to make such a blend possible, in spite of the warnings he could read in MacIntyre's neo-Aristotelianism, was to be found in his lecture, entitled *The Noble*, published in 1984.[29] This presented an argument in favour of the aristocratic virtue of nobility, based on Aristotle and Hume, set against Kant's and Rawls' idea of selfhood. His analysis of nobility remained only an aesthetic ideal, and not a full-fledged political morality. Like his hero, Nietzsche, Casey could not convincingly substantiate his conservatism, which remained a complex but also contradictory blend of literary influence and social mores.

Maurice Cowling

A further influence on Scruton in those early days was the historian Maurice Cowling, a crucial figure of the Peterhouse Right. He had been a dominant voice in the college for decades. Cowling was, in fact, generally regarded as the central figure and intellectual leader of the Cambridge Right. He was a highly original thinker, yet one whose greatest debates were with himself. He embodied ideas which he could not satisfactorily express in words.

As Scruton, Cowling came from a lower middle-class background. He "was taught by the Anglo-Catholic priest Charles Smyth and came under the influence of Herbert Butterfield."[30] Besides Butterfield, he also met in

Cambridge Michael Oakeshott, the main representative of British intellectual conservatism.[31]

These influences on Cowling turned out to be crucial for his intellectual development. Charles Smyth's book *The Church and the Nation: Six Studies in the Anglican Tradition* (1962) can be considered a prelude to Cowling's three-volume magnum opus on the same topic. Herbert Butterfield, too, had an interest in religion, though his attitude was more turned against liberalism than turn towards God. Catholicism fascinated him, yet he himself claimed to have "a very Protestant mind."[32] It was Butterfield who, after Cowling's unsuccessful attempt to impress the world of politics, leading to his failed run for a parliamentary seat, helped him to get a permanent job at Peterhouse, in his capacity as master of the college. Butterfield is commonly claimed to have consciously collected talented young conservatives around himself. Michael Bentley, however, argues in a detailed analysis of the relationship between Butterfield and Cowling that the two did not become or remain especially close to each other, as Butterfield could hardly bear the unfriendly style of Cowling.[33] What is more, according to Bentley, Butterfield's book *The Englishman and His History* was not a Tory manifesto, but instead resulted from Butterfield wishing to argue that "Whig history was a bad thing qua historical science but a good thing in its political and constitutional effects… it helped Britain to value freedom and resist Hitler."[34] Finally, although "Butterfield had always disliked Marxists for their atheism and liberals for their sentimentality," he did not deliberately bring conservatives to Peterhouse, but only intended to invite those who had, as intellectuals, that intellectual "electricity" that Butterfield most adored in colleagues.

Cowling attracted a court of friends around him who were characterised by their brilliant minds and peculiar manners. He also made a great impact on generations of students at Peterhouse, Cambridge and elsewhere. In the rebellious 1960s he rebelled against the mainstream of history writing, exploring the history of political thought as well as social and economic history. He became a major force behind a kind of high Tory history writing. His major early writings included *Mill and Liberalism* and *The Nature and Limits of Political Science* (both published in 1963). In the first one of these books, he argued that the greatest icon of British liberal thought in the nineteenth century was a "moral authoritarian," providing a generalised "polemic against 'liberalism' and 'the liberal mind'."[35] The second work "was an Oakeshottian critique of the disciplines of political science and political philosophy."[36] Cowling's main argument in *The Nature and Limits of Political Science* was that the emerging new social science of the day, political science, was in fact non-sense, since without substantial philosophy and moral theology it did not have the means to say anything meaningful about the "complex motives behind human behaviour."[37]

In the second phase of his career Cowling published three works under the umbrella title *The Politics of British Democracy*. In these highly contested works he claimed that examining short and intensive intervals is more effective to grasp the real turning points of history. A crucial aspect of Cowling's methodological teaching was a focus on the minute, often personal details of high politics, which meant, in his period (from 1850 to 1940) scrutinising a handful of protagonists in British political life, instead of focusing on large forces such as classes or delving into the archival resources of unnoticed and unnoticeable authors. Finally, his last contribution to academic history was his multiple-volume work *Religion and Public Doctrine in Modern England*, published in 1980, 1985 and 2001, respectively. These volumes underlined his most important point as a historian, that religion played a major, yet underestimated role in the birth of modern Britain. His aim in this magnum opus was to conduct an "investigation on the broadest front possible of the complicated relationship between politics, religion, scholarship, art, literature and morality which has been the basis for all public doctrine in England in the past century and a quarter."[38] To be sure, his own religious stance was somewhat unorthodox: "I'm not sure of the depth or reality of my religious conviction. It could well be that it was a polemical conviction against liberalism rather than a real conviction of the truth of Christianity."[39]

There is no doubt that Cowling exercised a major influence on the young Scruton. He was much more critical, for example, of the ways of life some of the dons lived in Cambridge, and less convinced of the advantages of the conventional Cambridge-style, paederastic methods of teaching than some at Peterhouse were; he did have first-hand experience of the intellectual brilliance of Cowling and his circle. He did not accept Cowling's claim that conservatism was only "a political practice, the legacy of a long tradition of pragmatic decision-making, and high-toned contempt for human folly."[40] Yet it was crucial for Scruton, that Peterhouse was not only a bastion of brilliant historical scholarship but also the head-quarters of intellectual conservatism in Cambridge.

David Watkin

Of all the people at Peterhouse who influenced Scruton's thought the most important was probably David Watkin. Watkin was not as ardently involved in politics as the others. His main focus was art and decorum. His friend, Mary Beard characterised him thus: "(h)e was a clever archi-tectural art historian (of the neo-classical above all), a generous, kind and funny man, an enemy of some of my best mates, a working-class lad who spoke posh, and (he would know that I would say this) a frightful old conservative."[41] Scruton recalled later that he first met Watkin as a second-year research fellow at Peterhouse. Scruton describes the impression Watkin's private space in the college made on him, a room which looked like "the chambers of a Regency gentleman, with furnishings, prints and ornaments that might have been rescued from a great estate, and a great disaster." He adds: "It had the air of someone who had fallen from the heights of inherited affluence and who was struggling to maintain him-self in elegant decline."[42] As Scruton describes their first meeting, Watkin was "dressed in a double-breasted suit and starched collar," and he was not alone. He was accompanied by a mysterious churchman, himself "dressed in the style of an Anglican clergyman of Jane Austen's day."[43] This was Alfred Gilbey, who succeeded in winning over Watkin for the Church of Rome, and this, too, made a great impression on Scruton, himself much impressed by Catholic spirituality. The whole scene was basically anachronistic—and indeed Scruton perceived it as a great theat-rical scene, in which the two of them were "accomplished actors, who had chosen their roles and chosen to be meticulously faithful to them."[44] Just as the Monsignor, as Father Gilbey was referred to in the college, func-tioned as the spiritual leader of Watkin, so did Watkin serve as a mentor in Scruton's intellectual life.

This spirituality was the foundation on which Watkin built his professional interest in classical architecture. For Scruton, it was based on a heartfelt conviction as to the moral superiority of the age which had produced the works of art he dealt with. According to Scruton, Watkin recognised that "form needs proportion, that proportion needs boundaries, that boundaries need mouldings, and that mouldings belong to a complex grammar of detail that generates facades, doors, windows and colonnades in something like the way that the deep grammar of language generates the sentences that we speak."[45]

Watkin's posture was interpreted as a critical alternative to that of his own earlier supervisor, Sir Nikolaus Bernhard Leon Pevsner, CBE FBA, perhaps the greatest name in architectural history in Britain at that time. A German emigrant, he had a Russian Jewish family background, yet his most famous work was a comprehensive description of *The Buildings of Britain* (1951–1974). In spite of all his mastery of historical architecture, Pevsner was the prophet of architectural modernism, a teaching, or as Watkin would claim, an ideology, which was thoroughly "materialistic, secular and egalitarian."[46] As Scruton read it, Watkin's major professional breakthrough, his book *Morality and Architecture* (1977), was a polemic, indeed an attack on the progressivist ideology of modernism, and a defence of "ornament, excess and grandeur." He tried to show that modernism was, in fact, a credo, a quasi-religious confession, built on simplistic moralising, disregarding the formal logic of architecture. He also attacked the historical narrative of Pevsner, which was a simplistic exercise in retrospection, which understands the past as the preparation for the present moment, a method which unsurprisingly led to a Marxist vision of the victory of progress over the dark forces of the past.

Just as Pevsner felt compelled to defend the aesthetic ideology of modernism, so Watkin had no choice but to defend the classical tradition, including its late revivals, like that of the early nineteenth century. Watkin's publications on Cockerell and Soane were not simply works about great architects, but addressed the issue of urban design, a major topic for Scruton, connecting aesthetics to politics, in the original sense of the word, that is, to the affairs of the polis. From the very beginning, his interest in architecture was a question of how to defend the order around oneself in a chaotic world, given the eternal facts about human nature and the scarcity of resources.

Scruton readily admitted the great influence of Watkin over him in those years. He served as a role model for him of order and composure. For this reason, Watkin was for Scruton a "dissident, but not a rebel"[47]— revolution was part of the ideology of modernity, so if one disagreed with modernity, one could not become a revolutionary oneself. Furthermore, through the example of his friend, Scruton realised how behaviour and thought are connected. Due to the spiritual effects of Monsignor Gilbey, and through his conversion Watkin found a key to "creating and appreciating order in the midst of chaos,"[48] an idea which had a major impact on Scruton.

Certainly, he was aware of the artificiality of Watkin's self-fashioning, his snobbish adoption of a style. Scruton did not give in to the Evelyn Waugh-type worship of wealth and ancestry, either. Yet behind the mask of culture and sophistication he discovered "a deeply vulnerable person," for all his gestures of formality and civility. It was this affectionate vulnerability that he sympathised with, which added an extra dimension to the calm and cool classicism both of them came to admire.

Catholicism in this context was not simply about ancient ritual and pomposity, a formality in a time of formlessness, but also a very detailed teaching, which offered a language which allowed one to make sense of a world which seemed otherwise to oppress and overwhelm the human spirit. A key concept behind the package Scruton inherited from Watkin's endorsement of Classicism and Catholicism was the concept of beauty, understood as the order which exists even in the very formlessness of the world around us, and which is not impossible to find or to create even for such a fragile and imperfect creature as the human being. Hence, from the very beginning, Scruton's interest in art, aesthetics and architecture was motivated by a search for "dwelling," for a form of life, which is not simply a defence-mechanism against external threats, but a creative gesture, and through it, the source of a sense of joy about having the opportunity to feel "at home," as part of a greater whole.

Cultural Criticism

The most relevant body of critical enquiries into Scruton's aesthetics, the collection of essays entitled *Scruton's Aesthetics*, has an introductory chapter by him on the development of his aesthetic views. In that chapter he underlines the formal impact of F.R. Leavis on his thought.[49] As Andrew Huddleston summarises it in his review, it was this influence which explains the philosopher's basic approach to art and politics, which distinguishes him from others who work in analytic aesthetics. To be a Leavisite is not a praise in the context of analytical philosophy: Leavis has no great reputation among analytical philosophers. He was better perceived in English or comparative literature departments. Scruton's self-perception is that of an analytical philosopher and of a Leavisite at the same time: this is a rare combination and one which distinguishes his position from others.

F.R. Leavis

In his longish, biographical discussion with Mark Dooley, Scruton describes the figure of the late Leavis, "pottering in a slightly mad way around the streets" of Cambridge.[50] His figure was painted with vivid colours by others, too.[51] This figure had a certain charisma, which had an impact on the young Scruton, just arrived at Cambridge, preparing for studies in the sciences, but who promptly switched to Moral Sciences, as the undergraduate course in Philosophy was labelled there in those days. Here is an account of the distinguishing features of the "school" of Leavis in Cambridge, and around the country:

> Leavis and what Cullen calls "the Richards-Eliot axis in Cambridge" placed, Cullen says, "particular emphasis upon professionalizing English Studies as an intellectual discipline, one capable of groundbreaking innovation similar to that which their colleagues, Moore, Russell and Wittgenstein, had achieved in the Cambridge philosophy school. [T]hese Cambridge critics saw their task as one of de-aestheticizing literature so that it could take its place as a key component of cultural science.[52]

This recollection of Leavis' overall project explains it from the perspective of what came to be called later cultural studies. Yet the basic impact of Leavis on Scruton was his philosophical, or to be more precise, his moral philosophical interest in literature and the arts in general. It is due to this impact that Scruton's own approach to art would often shift to that of the cultural critic, who is interested in such general questions as human nature and modern culture, in connection with works of art.[53] He read Leavis, together with T.S. Eliot, as the two major voices who had attempted in the twentieth century to "re-write the literary canon, and displace philosophy with poetry as the key to the modern condition."[54] Scruton writes in his own autobiographical recollections: "The severity of Dr Leavis appealed to me," adding that this father figure led him to the insight that "it is not life that is the judge of literature, but the other way round."[55]

The severity of Leavis' voice had a puritan overtone, but more importantly, it helped to shape Scruton's persona as a general critic of modernity. Leavis was a defender of what he labelled as the great tradition, and what might be identified with the humanist canon. He was not much interested in contemporary avant-garde art, although in *New Bearings in English Poetry* he defended Eliot, Pound and Hopkins. This is not exactly true of Scruton: he was genuinely interested in contemporary art, even if he was very critical of most of it, for aesthetic, moral or political reasons. Like Leavis, he thought that literature was indeed a mirror of life, and he had strong views on both. Although it is not always clear how exactly these two, literature and life, related to each other in his mature work, it is obvious that whenever he tried to make sense of a work of art, he was interested in what it told him about life and the human condition in general; and the reverse was also true: whenever he tried to explain the human condition, he relied heavily on works of art.

Studying the Law

There is one further element which played a role in Scruton's youthful turn towards conservatism, which is usually downplayed. This is his learning the law at the traditional institution, the Inns of Court. The Inns of Court were traditional English institutions: they emerged in the fourteenth century, as professional guilds where barristers were trained. The inns of the City of London were institutions, where those studying to become barristers under supervision were provided with accommodation, a library, dining facilities and a workplace. The inns were also institutions protecting the interests of their members, and they also had disciplinary functions. The reason why law was not taught at the universities was that it was regarded as a practical activity, one of the professions that should be learnt from practitioners of the guild.

A short text by Scruton recollects his major impressions when learning the law. In it, he recalls that he entered the Inner Temple in 1974. Written from the perspective of 2018, he saw that his legal studies "implanted in me a vision of the English law that I have never ceased to cherish, and which has profoundly influenced my philosophical outlook."[56]

Scruton made some major discoveries about the law during his studies. He recognised that "parliament is only one source of our law, and not the most important source." The content of the law is not the invention of the sovereign power, but the legacy of earlier "attempts made by the people of this country to bring their disputes to judgement." In the common law system, "the sovereign enforces the law, but does not dictate it." Scruton claims that the procedures were dictated by the "requirements of natural justice," as explained by Augustine, and as passed on by generations of legal practitioners: judges and barristers. As he saw it, a key maxim of his insights into the nature of English Law is that the law is "not uttered in the imperative mood, but in the indicative."[57]

Yet he has drawn some more conclusions, as well from his legal training. Among the principles which determine the operation of the common law system, *stare decisis* is crucial: it determines that precedents (i.e. the judgements of similar cases by earlier courts) should be followed unless a higher level court has overruled them. As a result, the common law judge works upwards, from the bottom up, in an inductive manner, starting out from a comparison of particular cases. Such comparisons are made easier by the *ratio decidendi*, the reason of the judgement, which is not always made (fully) explicit by the earlier judge, but instead may require interpretative work by the later one. Even if they do not find relevant earlier cases, judges do not devise the legal solution on their own, but have a procedure to follow to come to the right decision. If the judge cannot find the remedy for the complaint, there is a chance that a solution will be arrived at by turning to the other sphere of the common law, known as equity.

As Scruton summarised the wisdom of generation of legal practitioners, the law is "a summary of what is assumed, though not necessarily consciously assumed, by all of us in our free dealings with each other." It is not the will of the sovereign, but "the voice of its most important critic." As it accumulates precedents, English law has remained "concrete, close to human life and bound up with a given history." Importantly, it is the law which makes the sovereign, and not the sovereign who makes the law. The English law is not God-given, it is not the order of the Queen-in-Parliament, but represents an independent force, which is above even the sovereign. It is "the voice of a territorial jurisdiction," "the law of the land." This law has been implanted in human hearts by God.

In his overview of his political career, *How to Be a Conservative* (2014), Scruton claimed that through his studies at the Inns of Court, he "was granted a completely different vision of our society," than the one which became fashionable later, influenced by "the pollution injected by the European Courts" and by "the constitutional changes haphazardly introduced by Tony Blair."[58] The vision Scruton referred to was one of a community "built from below," guaranteeing justice for all who turned to the courts with their complaints "with clean hands." For Scruton, the English common law was nothing less but a "narrative of home." Also, it seemed to him to be a powerful safeguard against arbitrary power, of whatever kind, because of its characteristically plebeian, communitarian element: "the English law is the property of the English people, not the weapon of their rulers."[59]

Notes

1. Roger Scruton, *Gentle Regrets. Thoughts from a life* (London, Continuum: 2005), vii.
2. Which does not mean, of course, that it necessarily affects the cogency of those views themselves.

3. Scruton, *Regrets*, vii.
4. Roger Scruton and Mark Dooley, *Conversations with Roger Scruton* (London, etc.: Bloomsbury, 2016).
5. Dooley is the author of two other books, Roger Scruton, *The Philosopher on Dover Beach* (London and New York: Bloomsbury, 2009), and *The Roger Scruton Reader*, ed. Mark Dooley (London and New York: Bloomsbury, 2009 and 2011). The first is a monograph on Scruton, starting with a chapter on the connection between philosophy and the *Lebenswelt*.
6. Scruton and Dooley, *Conversations*, vi. It could be claimed that this book reveals more of the philosopher's life and its connection with his philosophy than *Gentle Regrets* or Dooley's earlier work did. This is to a large extent due to Dooley's technique of frequently returning to direct quotations.
7. Scruton and Dooley, *Conversations*, vi.
8. Michael Oakeshott, "On being conservative," in Oakeshott, *Rationalism in politics and other essays*, New and expanded edition (Indianapolis: Liberty Press, 1962/1991), 407–37., 407.
9. Roger Scruton, "Why I became a Conservative," *The New Criterion* 21, no. 6 (February 2003), 4.
10. Ibid., 33.
11. De Gaulle, *Mémoires de Guerre* is a three-volume grand narrative by France's most charismatic post-war politician published between 1954 and 1959.
12. Roger Scruton, *Thinkers of the New Left* (London: Longman, 1985). Second edition: Roger Scruton, *Fools, Frauds and Firebrands: Thinkers of the New Left* (London: Bloomsbury Publishing, 2016).
13. Ibid.
14. Scruton, *Gentle Regrets*, 39.
15. Scruton and Dooley, *Conversations with Roger Scruton*, 45.
16. Ibid., 45–6.
17. Charles Covell, *The Redefinition of Conservatism. Politics and Doctrine* (London: Palgrave Macmillan, 1986), 25.
18. Scruton and Dooley, *Conversations*, 25.
19. In the following description of Casey's position I will largely rely on the chapter on "Casey" in Covell, *The Redefinition*.
20. Ibid., 15.
21. Ibid., 16.

22. John Casey, "The Autonomy of Art," in *The Royal Institute of Philosophy Lectures vol. VI: Philosophy and the Arts*, ed. Godfrey Vesey (London: Macmillan, 1973), 65–87.

23. Covell, *The Redefinition*, 25.

24. John Casey, "Tradition and Authority," in *Conservative Essays*, ed. Maurice Cowling (London: Cassell, 1978), 82–100.

25. Ibid., 94.

26. John Casey, "Actions and Consequences," in *Morality and Moral Reasoning*, ed. John Casey (London: Methuen, 1971), 155–206.; John Casey, "Human Virtue and Human Nature," in *The Limits of Human Nature*, ed. Jonathan Benthall (London: Allen Lane, 1973), 74–91.

27. John Casey, "Emotion and Imagination," *The Philosophical Quarterly* 34, no. 134 (January, 1984): 1–14.

28. John Casey, "After Virtue," *The Philosophical Quarterly* 33, no. 132 (July 1983): 296–300.

29. John Casey, "The Noble," in *The Royal Institute of Philosophy Lectures, vol. xvi: Philosophy and Literature*, ed. A. Phillips Griffiths (Cambridge: Cambridge University Press, 1984), 135–53.

30. Michael Bentley, "Maurice Cowling—Political historian and Conservative controversialist who craved the limelight," *Independent* (Saturday 06 July 2013), available at: https://www.independent.co.uk/news/obituaries/maurice-cowling-8691679.html.

31. Jonathan Parry, "Maurice Cowling: A Brief Life," in *Crowcroft, The Philosophy*, 13–24., 15.

32. Naim Attallah, *Singular Encounters* (London: Quartet Books, 1990), 129–31.

33. Michael Bentley, "Herbert Butterfield and Maurice Cawling," in *The Philosophy, Politics and Religion of British Democracy. Maurice Cowling and Conservatism*, ed. Robert Crowcroft, S.J.D. Green and Richard Whiting (London, New York: Tauris Academic Studies, 2010), 85–107. According to Bentley, Cowling was difficult as a colleague, and "both men saw one another as cases of contrast rather than sympathy.", 90. According to the personal recollections of Robert Grant, Scruton himself thought him culpably "mischievous" and obstructive, and lost patience with him.

34. Ibid., 89.

35. Parry, *Maurice Cowling*, 16.

36. Ibid.

37. Richard Vinen, review of The Philosophy, Politics and Religion of British Democracy: Maurice Cowling and Conservatism, (review no. 1130), https://reviews.history.ac.uk/review/1130.

38. Maurice Cowling in the *Times Literary Supplement*, 3 June 1977, 680, reprinted in PPD, 343.

39. Naim Attallah, *Singular Encounters* (London: Quartet Books, 1990), 129–31.

40. Scruton, *Gentle Regrets*, 52.

41. Mary Beard, "A don's life. A tribute to David Watkin," *Times Literary Supplement*, https://www.the-tls.co.uk/articles/tribute-david-watkin/.

42. Roger Scruton, Professor David Watkin Eulogy—24 September 2018, Kings Lynn Norfolk, available at:… Scruton also published an earlier piece about Watkin: Roger Scruton, "David Watkin and the Classical idea," in *The Persistence of the Classical* (Cambridge, 2008).

43. Ibid.

44. Ibid.

45. Ibid.

46. Ibid.

47. Ibid.

48. Ibid.

49. Andy Hamilton and Nick Zangwill eds., *Scruton's Aesthetics* (Basingstoke: Palgrave Macmillan, 2012).

50. Scruton and Dooley, *Conversations*, 21.

51. "You became accustomed to seeing him walk briskly along Trinity Street, gown blown out horizontal in his slipstream. He looked as if walking briskly was something he had practised in a wind-tunnel." Clive James, *May Week Was In June: More Unreliable Memoirs* (London: Picador, 2009, [first edition: 1990]), 57.

52. Barry Cullen's "The Impersonal Objective: Leavis, the Literary Subject and Cambridge Thought," quoted by Dr Leavis, I Presume? by Brooke Allen, May 22, 2006, 12:00 AM, Washington Examiner, available at: https://www.washingtonexaminer.com/weekly-standard/dr-leavis-i-presume.

53. See his books: Roger Scruton, *Modern Culture* (London, New York: Continuum Books, 1998); Roger Scruton, *On Human Nature* (Princeton and Oxford: Princeton University Press, 2017). See also his collection: Roger Scruton, *Culture Counts: Faith and Feeling in a World Besieged* (New York, London: Encounter Books, 2007, 2018).

54. Scruton and Dooley, *Conversations*, 62.

55. Roger Scruton, *Gentle Regrets. Thoughts from a Life* (London, New York: Continuum, 2005), 5.

56. Roger Scruton, *The Law of the Land*—The Temple Church Sermon, 3 October, 2018, available at: https://www.roger-scruton.com/articles/548-the-law-of-the-land-the-temple-church-sermon-3-oct-18.

57. All the quotes above are from the essay "The Law of the Land."

58. Roger Scruton, *How to Be a Conservative* (London: Bloomsbury Continuum, 2014), 5–6.

59. Scruton, *How to Be…*, 6. Scruton here also adds that this perspective of British history and English law is not something that one can find in the history books of Hobsbawm.

3

The Political Philosophy of Conservatism (*Vita Activa*)

After the above review of the education and formative years of Scruton, the philosopher, let us now turn to the active part of his career, his involvement in ideological struggles, journalism and political activism. These elements define this part of his life as a *vita activa*, an active confrontation with the state of affairs in politics, and a rather courageous attempt to make an impact on the thought of his day by popularising the political thought of conservatism, which was at the time lagging behind both in the ideological competition and in the theory-building efforts of academia.

The Salisbury Group and the Salisbury Review

As we saw, influenced by the circle of John Casey, Maurice Cowling and David Watkin in Cambridge, Scruton drifted towards conservatism. This development was no doubt fostered by the intellectual atmosphere at Peterhouse, even if he had certain reservations about the specific image of conservatism that was associated with the college. His conservatism caused him difficulties in his later academic life, which by that time had been fatally infected by that post-1968 spirit, which was anything but tolerant towards alternative explanations of the world and society.

© The Author(s), under exclusive license to Springer Nature Switzerland AG 2023   **55**
F. Hörcher, *Art and Politics in Roger Scruton's Conservative Philosophy*, Palgrave Studies in Classical Liberalism, https://doi.org/10.1007/978-3-031-13591-0_3

Scruton seems to have deliberately chosen a road which made his academic life more difficult. Together with Casey and Cowling, he took part in the establishment of an intellectual workshop, the Salisbury Group, "a loose collection of reactionaries,"[1] and in the publication of its organ, *The Salisbury Review*. The group came together in 1976 and was named after Robert Gascoyne-Cecil, the Third Marquess of Salisbury, who famously pronounced that good government consisted in doing as little as possible. This is how he summed up his view of politics: "Whatever happens will be for the worse, and therefore it is in our interest that as little should happen as possible."[2] He was elected three times as the prime minister of the UK, altogether for a period of 13 years.

The Review itself, established in 1982, under the editorial responsibility of Scruton, aimed to criticise both leftist and liberal ideologies, and the Thatcherite programme of the free market as well. Instead of the latter, the *Salisbury Review* regarded itself as an organ of social conservatism. Scruton had to confront tremendous difficulties when preparing its publication: he needed subscribers and it was not easy to collect 600 of them, who would be enough to pay the minimum costs of editing and printing. On the other hand, authors were sometimes afraid of the prospect of a hostile reception for what was regarded as the subversive program of the journal. For some time, most of the material was written by Scruton himself, publishing pieces under various pseudonyms.[3] He was not a born political activist and his interest in politics was mainly intellectual, yet he was ready to make personal sacrifices in order to create a new forum for ideas to tackle issues which seemed to him crucial for the future of British, and indeed, Western society and culture.

Perhaps the most famous of the affairs surrounding the journal was that of "Ray Honeyford, the Bradford headmaster who spoke the truth about the folly of multiculturalism in our schools. Attempts to defend him led to libels and the persecution of other contributors although the resulting publicity increased (…) subscriptions. Speaking at universities during those extraordinary years could involve you in vicious physical attacks."[4] In *Conversations* Scruton summarises the events of April 1984, including the publication by the National Union of Teachers of a Press

Statement, in which they demanded that the local authority should immediately remove Mr Honeyford from his position. As Scruton viewed it in those days, the argument for such a dismissal was "totalitarian": if someone is critical about a policy of an authority, he should not be sacked, but instead his or her arguments should be heard and discussed.[5] Scruton, as the editor of *Salisbury Review*, defended his author, and therefore he was also labelled a racist. Although Scruton was even physically attacked at certain university campuses, he persevered, knowing that he was defending free speech and freedom of thought, basic values of British political history. This defence would, in the long run, win, and his reward came when he was invited to write the entry on Mr Honeyford for the *Dictionary of National Biography*. The charge of "scientific racism" was a real threat, but it had the benevolent unintended consequence that it generated increased interest in the journal. After all that adventure, Scruton gave up his academic job, and felt ostracised from official British philosophy. This latter charge was certainly not true literally, even if he clearly made a number of enemies in academic life, and huge crowds could feel hatred towards him. However, he always enjoyed exceptional academic prestige, proven by the fact that he left Birkbeck for a prestigious professorial job at Boston University, and that throughout his career he was invited to give some of the most prestigious public lectures, including the Gifford and Stanton lectures. Establishing the *Review*, he thought, was not a futile effort as it played a major role in forming the public debate in Britain and the English-speaking world.

Maurice Cowling famously argued that, unlike with other political ideologies, one cannot summarise conservatism in a philosophically convincing fashion, relying simply on abstract philosophical concepts. According to Cowling's argument, conservatism as an independent political teaching was "a political practice, the legacy of a long tradition of pragmatic decision making and high-toned contempt for human folly."[6] As Cowling saw it, it was only the naivety of Americans to think that the essence of it can be condensed, and construct a nice, neat theory about it. Scruton, however, came to the conclusion that his task as a philosopher was to venture such a summary.

Underground Teaching in Communist Central Europe

A further front opened by *Salisbury Review* was the publication of authors from beyond the iron curtain, from what was called Eastern Europe.[7] This was connected to Scruton's own adventures on the other side of the Iron Curtain, participating in a programme launched by a handful of mainly Oxbridge dons to help educate the youth of those countries in the great European tradition. He participated in the work of two organisations which served this noble task: first, the Jan Hus Educational Association, and later the Jagiellonian Trust. The first of these operated in Czechoslovakia from 1980 onwards. The Czech secret police deemed it a "centre of ideological subversion," and persecuted it. As a contemporary account reports, the initiative to launch this project came from Julius Tomin, a dissident philosopher from Prague and signatory of Charter '77.[8] As Scruton recalls it, the underground university was organised by Kathy Wilkes from Oxford, a friend of Scruton's, who invited him, along with Anthony Kenny, who was by that time master of Balliol College, Oxford, and famous as a co-founder of what came to be known as analytical Tomism. The second of these initiatives was established in 1984, with the target countries of Poland and Hungary, aiming to support dissident movements there. It was Jessica Douglas-Home who organised this effort with Scruton himself and with Caroline Cox, and its trustees included Dennis O'Keeffe, Agnieszka Kolakowska, Timothy Garton-Ash and The Baroness Cox. The Hus Association had to operate in a much harsher climate, in the late 1970s, while the Jagiellonian Trust worked "in completely different circumstances. It was much easier to get in and out of those countries," namely Poland and Hungary in the 1980s.

When thinking about Scruton's adventures in Communist Central Europe, one should bear in mind two things. First, it should be noted that a number of Scruton's colleagues participating in the support project were themselves left-wing intellectuals, with idealistic visions of the role of the public intellectual in history in general, and in politics in particular. This is exemplified by the French philosopher, Jacques Derrida, of whom Scruton ironically said: "In my opinion, the best thing that Derrida ever did was to get arrested in Prague."[9] As mentioned above, the young Scruton's own views were, for some time, not far from the mainstream progressive-liberal position and it took him years of intellectual development to see the whole enterprise from a genuinely conservative perspective. The process must have been extended further, as his friends in Central Europe themselves were mostly leftist intellectuals, belonging in Hungary to the small circle of "democratic opposition," who published *samizdat* journals, some of whom were the sons and daughters of the Communist elite. Scruton came to know Gáspár Miklós Tamás, a Hungarian philosopher brought up in Transylvania, in Romania. His mother was one of the founding members of the Romanian Communist Party. His mentor in philosophy was György Bretter, a reform-Marxist, who published a book entitled *A filozófus: Marx* in 1968. Tamás himself left Romania in 1978, to move to Budapest, and later to teach at Yale and other American and French universities. In 1983 he wrote the anarchist text *A szem és a kéz* (The Eye and the Hand) which was published underground. He had become a "liberal-conservative" by the time of the transition, later turning into and remaining until today an activist neo-Marxist celebrity. A man of high culture and somewhat exotic political views, Tamás and Scruton became such good friends that he became the godfather of Tamás' daughter. Later however, as a result of the ever intensifying culture wars, they were separated by the battle zone, and their friendship grew cold.

Beside the perseverance of leftist and liberal views in the flying universities, the second thing to emphasise is that for Scruton it was an instructive learning process. He gained first-hand knowledge about the region, its history, its conflicts with the West and its oppression by Russian communism. He became fascinated by the rich local cultures of these nations, including both folk and high culture. The achievements of intellectuals, like the playwright Vaclav Havel, the pope John Paul II and the philosopher Jan Patočka deeply touched and impressed him. Scruton would not be the same philosopher with the same remarkable ideas if he had not learnt his own lessons in Central Europe—partly through intimate relationships, friendship and love, partly through collecting experience in a fight against powerful centralised authorities.

Conservatism: Doctrine or Philosophy

It was Edmund Burke who famously claimed that conservatism is not a philosophy which can be worked out in an abstract form with the help of philosophical categories. It is, rather, more a practice, an implicit set of assumptions, which are followed in an almost unconscious manner, within the context of a specific way of life. This criticism targeted the abstract, philosophical language established both by the French Enlightenment and by the tradition of the social contract in Britain, since Hobbes and Locke. Arguably, though, Burke's cautionary methodological remark was taken too seriously, and this led to British conservatism lagging behind in the ideological warfare of the nineteenth and twentieth centuries. Its intellectual prestige is expressed by John Stuart Mill's cruel bon mot: "I never meant to say that the Conservatives are generally stupid. I meant to say that stupid people are generally Conservative."[10]

By the time Scruton came to formulate his own version of conservatism, a very powerful philosophical conservative stance was already on stage: the anti-rationalist political philosophy of Michael Oakeshott. Yet Oakeshott himself was not a professional philosopher. As an undergraduate he read history at Gonville and Caius in Cambridge, where he and Butterfield were both members of the same Junior Historians Society.

Unlike those two thinkers, Scruton was educated as a philosopher and remained one throughout his life. He was a Cambridge-educated, analytical philosopher, who had very precise views of what it means to be a philosopher. It is perhaps because of this that he set himself the task of articulating an up-to-date account of what conservatism actually meant in a philosophical sense. He admitted in the preface of his pioneering book that he owes a great deal to "conversations over several years with John Casey and Maurice Cowling," which indicates that the book can also be read as a summary of the ideas of the Cambridge Right, and that it is deliberately less of an abstract system, in the manner of John Rawls, and more an expression of common sense.

The Meaning of Conservatism (1980)

In the light of his self-perception as a professional philosopher it is somewhat surprising that in the first of his four efforts to deal with conservatism in a book-length text, entitled *The Meaning of Conservatism* (1980) Scruton is quick to announce that "(t)his is not a work of philosophy but of dogmatics."[11] This can, of course, be read as a piece of ironic self-criticism. Yet we saw that Scruton studied law in the 1970s at the Inns of Court. Dogmatics is a jurisprudential term: it means the conceptual elaboration of legal doctrine, in the light of existing legal practice. However, given the fact that in the common law tradition law was always bound to court practice, no legal doctrine could go on to live an autonomous life outside of the courtroom. Instead, common law dogmatics preserved a close connection to legal practice. Scruton's aim in *The Meaning of Conservatism* seems to have been to keep his theory of conservative politics as close to the political practice of conservatism as possible. As he explains in the introduction to that book, there are three levels of conservative ways of thinking. The most profound is "the philosophy upon which it rests"; the second is its dogmatics and finally there are the "policies which spring from it."[12] He is not engaged in either setting out those fundamentals, nor in specifying particular conservative policies. Instead, his aim is to outline its set of dogmas, which, he claims, are indeed "systematic and reasonable."

Before Scruton, conservative dogmatics was not often made explicit. This is due to two factors. First, conservatism stresses that human nature is a rather complex phenomenon, and no true description of it can be based on the abstract-utopian ideals of socialism and liberalism. While these latter try to provide a "deep description" of their respective politics, conservatives warned of the "danger in abstract thought." Instead, they cherish ideals, which have confirmed their feasibility. In order to deem them worthy of preservation, conservatives need to see the practical effects of theories, reflecting the way that the common law lawyer views the connection between legal principles and the actual daily operation of the legal system. The level of the philosophical reflection Scruton is engaged in is more abstract than the day-to-day policies pursued by conservative politicians, but less abstract and alienated from political practice than the philosophical systems of the liberals and socialists. He identifies this level as the level of dogma, which equates to "reasoned belief," comparable to what Burke called prejudice.

Another general observation about his intentions is that his approach to politics can be labelled as regulatory-institutional. This means that he sets out to provide an explanation of why an institutional order exists, and why it should exist. This institution-based approach is visible at the very beginning, in the chapter about the conservative attitude. There, Scruton distinguishes conservatism from liberalism, its major opponent in the modern party system. For the liberal, individual freedom is a universal value while for the conservative there is no freedom without the guarantee of an institutional order. The existence of this guarantee depends on "the authority of established government." (19) As he understands it, the major problem with the liberal idea of freedom is that it is ready to destroy the institutions upon which that very freedom depended. It also fails to take into account the notion of political authority. For Scruton, there is yet another, even worse approach to freedom, institutional order and authority: that of the Marxist teaching. The Marxist is an ideologue, always talking about power, which endangers freedom. In reality, Marxism is not of course, much interested in personal freedom, which may seem to them a bourgeois hangover. Instead of the neutral form of institutional order, characteristic of the rule of law, the Marxist prefers centralised authority, which can guarantee justice with the help of force. Therefore the Marxist centralised authority requires the monopoly of the use of power.

Unlike these destructive approaches to authority, the conservative seeks to conserve the common trust in an institutional order. Scruton takes a somewhat legalistic approach to conservatism in this book. Almost all the major concepts in this book are taken over from jurisprudence: authority, allegiance, constitution, law and liberty, property, the world of labour, establishment and the public world all belong to the vocabulary of jurisprudence.

For Scruton, to demand individual freedom it is necessary to demand its guarantees. Now the logical question is who or what can provide that guarantee? The answer is that if we wish to avoid arbitrary power, there needs to be an institutional order, which does not depend on arbitrary will. No institutional order can exist without the law which enshrines it. Order can only be enshrined by law if we accept its authority, even if it is disadvantageous to us in certain cases. In other words, one has to accept the rule of law instead of the rule of men, to prepare the ground for the guarantees of individual freedom. This is a longstanding conservative conviction, which had its roots in Aristotle's preference for custom as opposed to the rule of individual rulers, and which became the first political axiom of the British conservative: to defend individual liberty one needs to accept the priority of the law, and with it that of political authority, too.

The smooth operation of the law requires one further thing: certain forms of life. For as jurisprudence teaches us, there is no law without those who accept its rule over them. The acceptance of the rule of law establishes a form of life and a certain attitude towards the instituted order: this is precisely the conservative attitude, a way of life which recognises that there are institutions and other legal arrangements in society which will circumscribe and hence frame one's sphere of individual activity. "To put it briefly, conservatism arises directly from the sense that one belongs to some continuing, and pre-existing social order, and that this fact is all important in determining what to do." (21)

According to the conservative, allegiance is required for the survival of social order, and there is no bond of allegiance without a respect for authority. Scruton's Hegelian thinking approaches the phenomenon of authority and allegiance via the example of the family. As he sees it, the family requires or demands from the individual a respect and acceptance which determines the individual's sphere of decision. Certainly, liberals view with suspicion any argument that starts from a comparison of political power and the family—the most famous liberal opposition to this view was that of John Locke, who, in his *Two Treatises*, opposed the main thesis of Robert Filmer in *The Patriarcha*, that the example of the father explains the status of the head of the state. This idea was supported by the Christian tradition—as when Aquinas compared fatherhood and the monarchy in *De Regimine Principum*—and also had a firm historical foundation, as presented by James VI, in his *True Law of Free Monarchies*.[13]

Scruton, as a modern conservative, does not go back to Filmer or James I—only to Hegel. Besides his reference to the family as an example of royal power, he also draws a conceptual distinction between the state and society. Based on Hegel's philosophy of Right, Scruton distinguished the levels of family, civil society and the state.[14] Hegel also established in the *Elements of the Philosophy of Right* that human *Sittlichkeit* (roughly, ethical order) has three levels, the higher always construed as dependent on the lower level, dialectically. The human being is directly born into the family, which is the basic unit of community, where inter-subjective recognition is rooted in love. The next level is that of a market-based civil society. At that level all humans participate primarily as singular, autonomous individuals[15] who as such can freely decide to participate in social transactions, thus creating society. The social institution expressing the true nature of this level of social organisation is the market. Within that, human behaviour is to a large extent (but even there, as we saw in the note above, not exclusively) characterised by internal, egoistic motives. For the market to operate smoothly it is necessary to harmonise individual transactions, thus conventions are born among the players regarding the rules of the game. When properly operating, markets are able to harmonise human behaviour, by adapting supply to demand. Finally, the third, most complex form of human coexistence is that of the state, which preserves both of the earlier forms, including the love relationship, along with elements of the voluntarism of civil society, and its spontaneous order. At the state level, however, a new player emerges, the legal fiction of the state, which is necessary in order to ensure and guarantee large-scale human adaptation to circumstances, and the long-term survival of customs and social manners.[16]

Scruton can be regarded as a Hegelian thinker. He is ready in *The Meaning of Conservatism* to indicate the parallels between the family and the state, without reverting to a kind of patriarchalism. As Scruton explains, the child experiences both the love of the parents in the family, and their power over her at the same time. One of these attitudes presupposes the other: familial love does not exist without parental power, and vice versa. This analogy helps to explain the human being's relationship to her country: "it is a similar recognition of constraint, helplessness, and subjection to external will that heralds the citizen's realisation of his membership of society; in this recognition love of one's country is born."[17] (32)

Scruton explicitly refers to what he calls "(t)he Hegelian defence of the family," (202) making explicit the source of his philosophical inspiration. He illustrates the similarity between the experience of family love and the emotional attachment of the citizen to her country with the help of the institution of the monarchy. The monarch is able to embody in the eyes of the subjects the totality of the state, and in the subjects' affection towards the monarch we can encounter the love which connects the individual to her home country. There are no further rational reasons which could explain this attachment of subject to monarch, beyond the emotional engagement. In this respect, although Scruton does not make a direct reference to theology, this affectionate but rationally unfounded attachment resembles the believer's relationship to God. According to Scruton, expecting rational justification as to why the subject should be loyal to her monarch opens the way to doubt. The attachment to the monarch is not based on his or her personal qualities or character, it is simply the office itself which creates that relationship, of which the citizen is part of, and which demands her loyalty towards the person who embodies the office.[18]

Clearly, Scruton's explanation cannot satisfy rationalist liberals. According to Scruton, this is because the perspective of the liberal on the state is mistaken. In the Appendix of his book: Liberalism versus Conservatism he argues the following way: unlike conservatism, liberalism is characterised by a rather straightforward individualism. Scruton proves this point by an account of how the liberal and the conservative defends the concept of property. The liberal view is based on the assumption of the individual as an autonomous, rational and morally responsible agent, while for the conservative property helps the smooth operation of human cohabitation.

To appreciate the originality of Scruton's analysis of the nature of property in comparison to the standard liberal justification, one has to recall the fact that property is a crucial element in the founding text of English liberalism, Locke's *Second Treatise*. The argument starts from the claim that "every man has a property in his own person." Then, as soon as the individual performed manual, bodily labour, it transformed the object into something which belongs to him, his property.

Roger Scruton's account is significantly different.[19] His own starting point is the "social sense of man." The institution of property is the meeting point between nature and man. Through acquiring private property, the human being starts to liberate himself from the power of the external, objective world. By the act of institutionally establishing rights and responsibilities over things, the objects acquire certain mirror-like properties: they start to reflect the human being's way of thinking and in particular her social performance. The objects in closest proximity to her start to resemble and reflect the individual. "He is now at home where before he was merely let lose."

Home, meanwhile, is not characterised by an individualist form of human existence. Instead, it is the realm of the family. There is an internal connection between one's sense of property and one's sense of home. Within the space of the home, the individual property becomes shared by the members of the family. This is done without any formal acknowledgement and allowance, without any formal social contract. Rather, the existence of a common place of habitation for the members of the family presupposes viewing the private property of an individual member of the family as available for use by the whole family.

Finally, there is one more step in Scruton's account of the conservative understanding of the relationship between property and the family. If we accept the Hegelian point, we also have to accept the fact that the human beings' relationship to the objects around them in the enlarged community resembles their relationship to them in the family. Aristotle started from the concept of *oikos*, and the economic analysis of the polis was built by him on that of the primary unit of the *oikos*. Similarly, if the family is to be understood as the model of the social relationships of the state, private property exists in the state as well for the common good, just as is the case in the family. Without the institution of private property, it is difficult to conceptualise the flourishing of the political community. Western societies were all built on the assumption of private property, so it occurs in Western culture as a natural phenomenon, even if it was only historically grounded, and even if Westerners have always been aware of transactions which reach beyond it, such as gifts or sacrifices.

In the book's Appendix Scruton contrasts the "I" perspective of liberalism, in other words its individualism, with the third-person perspective of conservatism.[20] The first-person perspective only allows the individual to think in terms of his own self. It is only through a process of rationalisation that the human being will accept the fact that, since there are other "I"s in the community, they too may demand for themselves the right of having private property, and that this is a right everyone has to acknowledge. Individual rights are central to liberalism, as they are indispensable in order to defend the sphere of privacy for the individual. In contrast, the third person perspective establishes an external viewpoint, from where I myself get connected to the other members of the community. This external viewpoint creates the community. The state is the highest institutionalised form of the community, which—as we have seen—is symbolically embodied by the monarch. In the Hegelian *Sittlichkeit* the sphere of the community has primacy, instead of the individual's right to a sphere of privacy. "It is the 'ought' of piety, which recognises the unquestionable rightness of local, transitory and historically conditioned social bonds" (202). In conclusion, Scruton adds, the "I" perspective depends, in fact, on the third-person perspective: without the existing institutional framework of the community, the individual is unable to obtain personal rights. For example, private property is something that requires others in order to be accepted. In this respect liberalism presupposes conservatism: individual rights presuppose the existence of communal ones, that is, commonly shared norms.

Scruton's later thought would present a much more nuanced and elaborate interpretation of Hegelian perspectivism. He would soon realise that in order to characterise the specific nature of human communality, what needs to be explained phenomenologically is the first-person plural perspective, that of the "we." Let us see how Scruton develops his conservative political thought.

A Political Philosophy: Arguments for Conservatism (2006)

Scruton's second book-length study of conservatism is *A Political Philosophy: Arguments for Conservatism* (2006). Most of the material for this book was written after the Scrutons were coming under criticism for being paid by a tobacco firm, and while Scruton was writing about risk-taking and risk-management as an independent journalist. In his *Conversations* with Dooley he admitted that it was a "big mistake" to enter into a business relationship with JTI. When Dooley confronted him with the view that there is a conflict of interest between having a media relations consultancy and working as a journalist, Scruton accepted that criticism, although he claimed that he did not have to write anything which he would not have done otherwise. In any case, it was a big mistake, and they paid the price for it. As a result of the public scandal, he lost his contract with the *Financial Times*, his visiting professorial privileges at Birkbeck, and his contract for a new book with Chatto and Windus.[21] Perhaps even more importantly, they felt that the public hostility generated rendered it impossible for them to continue their life at home, and they decided to migrate to the US to start a new life there. They brought a plantation house in Virginia, and Scruton took up two part-time positions, one at the Institute for the Psychological Sciences in Arlington, Virginia, and another one at the American Enterprise Institute in Washington, in order to make their life sustainable there.

The book *A Political Philosophy: Argument for Conservatism* was meant as a reaffirmation of his basic position as an outstanding conservative political thinker. In this sense it was a decision to keep on swimming against the tide, and accepting all the consequences this had on his career and existential conditions.

The introduction to the book made it clear that his own relationship to certain circles of the intellectual elite somewhat resembled that of Edmund Burke, the arch-conservative: it raised intellectual animosity within the progressive circles of intellectual life. A further Burkean element in Scruton's position was to argue philosophically against the use of philosophy in politics. After all, what else distinguishes conservatism, if not the pronounced conviction that "custom should prevail over reason as the final court of appeal"?[22] His position was that of a conservative in the British tradition, where conservatism was even less intellectually respectable than in America. He himself argued that "British Tories are becoming notorious for the thinness of their philosophy."[23] One should not forget that the political context of the book was the era of Tony Blair, a long decade of Labour rule in the UK, extended even further by the three years of Gordon Brown—while in the US it was the presidency of George Bush Jr., leading to the breakthrough of Obama.

The novelty of the approach taken in this book by Scruton was to argue for the local relevance of conservatism, instead of regarding it as a wholesale ideology, as the neoconservatives behind the Bush administration did. The difference between the views of the Straussian American neocons and Scruton's own beliefs is illustrated by the orientation of the former to international relations and foreign affairs, while Scruton's real interest lay in the defence of local traditions.

Scruton also responded to the debate started by Douglas Murray in his book *Neoconservatism: Why We Need It*, also published in 2006. In it, Murray proposed adopting American neoconservatism, as the best strategy for British conservatives, too.

Scruton's own book did not directly address the issue of neoconservatism. He simply wanted to show that "conservatism is inherently local… In this book, therefore, I have tried to mount a qualified defence of the nation state."[24]

Yet on the long run, the book's most important conclusion was the decision made by the Scrutons to return home from the US, and to resettle in the British countryside. This decision was the conclusion of a practical syllogism in the Aristotelian sense. In a practical syllogism, a valid argument results in a practical decision, which you are ready to enact, as the outcome of the argument. Scruton's decision is even more characteristically conservative, as he decided to live the traditional life of an English country gentleman, only updating it with those intellectual activities that technology allowed them to do, besides cultivating the land. Subsequently and gradually, this return home became symbolic for Scruton, for his family, as well as for his readers.

A major theme of the book is the defence of the nation. The nation as it is understood here is a political community, connected to an institutional form, determining territorial sovereignty. It is due to this institutional form that strangers in society can trust each other, "since everyone is bound by a common set of rules."[25] In other words, this institution establishes trust. To achieve this, citizens have to identify themselves with the particular institutional arrangement.[26] Rules create links between them, as they all accept its power over them, most of the time in an unreflecting manner. These links may be financial, legal and fiduciary. Neither of them presupposes any personal tie—which is why the family comparison holds true only to a limited extent. The rule of law, which can be interpreted as the outcome of a specific kind of social convention, presupposes an attachment on the part of the members of the community to a common cause, in other words the existence of a "first-person plural."[27] Scruton is introducing here a further grammatical form, beyond the first- and third-person singular forms dealt with in the *Meaning of Conservatism*. He also cited figures from the history of political thought as originators of this idea. He referred to Burke's "hereditary principle" and Hegel's ideas about "non-contractual obligations," while he attributed the notion of piety, also used in this connection, to the French reactionary writer, Joseph de Maistre.[28] When writing about trusteeship, he mentioned Burke, Moser and Gierke, the latter two thinkers belonging to the German tradition of the *Genossenschaft*, an idea developed in the eighteenth and nineteenth centuries, on medieval foundations. It is here that the theoretical foundations of the nation touch upon conservatism. The sense of a common cause to maintain the trust among strangers is an important part of the meaning of *Genossenschaft*.[29] The institutional framework is the legacy of past generations, and therefore the present generation has to take care of this legacy as a good steward, in order to pass it on to the next generation. This community of the dead, the living and the unborn is crucial for Scruton, for securing the survival of trust among strangers in the nation state.[30] The conservative thinker is, of course, aware of the threats to this vision of intergenerational solidarity, which he proposed earlier in his eulogy to the nation, *The Need for Nations* (2004) as well, as he did in his literary hymn about the nation: *England, an Elegy* (2000).[31] The concept of *oikophobia*, a theoretically supported rejection of homeland, is introduced in this work—a concept which would lead Scruton to create its positive counterpart, the term *oikophilia*, to signify his type of conservative local attachment. Below we shall return to this term, which became one of Scruton's characteristic ideas of homeliness.

Another term which was crucial for him came from Aristotle. *Equilibrium* was a term that Scruton used both in the social and in the ecological context, claiming that "the maintenance of the social ecology" also requires a stewardship of nature. It is also Scruton's ideal in his description of the interpersonal relationship of marriage. Marriage became politicised with the outbreak of the culture wars. Although progressivism fought a successful campaign in 1968, leading to the victory of both the civil right movement and the student rebellion, the fight has not ended. The rights of social minorities remained on the leftist agenda, including those of racial, sexual and other cultural minorities, who were claimed to be oppressed by the majority society.

Scruton regards marriage as a social institution, which can be interpreted from both an internal and an external perspective. Its significance is recognised by most societies, and not only from an internal, but also from an external perspective. While in most Western societies it also had a religious dimension, with the birth of the administrative state, it was transformed into a civil law concept,[32] turning it into a contract which can be cancelled if one of the partners wishes to do so. As Scruton understands it, this development signalled a major shift in the public perception of the role and nature of marriage. In his view, "marriage has ceased to be what Hegel called a 'substantial tie'."[33] Scruton views this as only one step in a downward spiral which will inevitably "downgrade and ultimately abolish the marriage tie."[34] This is to be understood, Scruton claims, as "a retreat from the world of 'substantial ties' to a world of negotiated deals."[35] This development is due to the left's critique of social cohesion, understood as domination, and a threat to individual liberty.

Scruton also offers an analysis of the erotic foundations of marriage, based on his book-length study of sexual desire.[36] He connects the transformation in the social imaginary of the role and function of marriage in human life to the birth of a postmodern way of thinking, which erodes the traditional values of society, to replace them with its own, transitory and relativistic ones. By relativising the marriage tie, Western societies jeopardise "social reproduction, the socializing of children and the passing on of the social capital."[37] Scruton, in this respect, is quite pessimistic: he thinks that the movement to demolish religious sacraments such as marriage, is too powerful, enjoying as it does the protection of the state administration, of the academia and the media. It has acquired powerful institutional sponsors such as the US Supreme Court, whose decisions led to the acceptance of the right to gay marriage, having earlier defended pornography or abortion, both of them part of the sexual revolution, a crucial battlefield of the culture war.

As we have seen, Scruton himself was not a devout believer, but as a conservative, he was aware of the religious significance of marriage, claiming that the civic union is a recent innovation of social engineering. He addressed philosophically the conceptual opposition between Religion and the Enlightenment. As he saw it, we were living in a post-Enlightenment age, and no post-Enlightenment culture can return to an earlier stage, unless there was a major social catastrophe.

Scruton himself was aware that his own thinking is partly the product of the Enlightenment. In this sense what he has to say can also be read as an effort of self-scrutiny. His position towards the Enlightenment was rather ambivalent: when comparing it with Islamic radicalism, he was proud of its achievements in Western culture. Yet when he viewed it as the opposite pole of (Christian) religion and the sacred, he was strongly critical. In his view, we are children of an earlier, more religious era but also the liberated individuals of the Enlightenment. Religion is conceptually opposed to the secular dimension of the Enlightenment. Scruton refers to Nietzsche and Wagner, in his account of religion, taking the opportunity to reflect on "the dark secrets of the human soul."[38] Nietzsche, and in his work *The Birth of Tragedy* (1872), in particular, described how religion works as a cult, while Wagner presented in his operas the case for religion as myth.

Scruton's association of religion with the dark spheres of the soul comes through the inspiration of the contemporary French philosopher, René Girard, and in particular, his book *La violence et le sacré* (1972). Girard's talk of "sacred awe" and forms of communal violence was quite influential in his own day. For Scruton, Frenchman's discussion showed that religion is not so much about transcendence, but about the possibility of the long-term sustenance of human communities, in spite of the fragile and fallen nature of human beings. While he identified himself partly by the heritage of the Enlightenment, Scruton claimed that there is a fundamental mistake in the conception of Enlightenment, in its deterministic tendency to try to get rid of the "false" suppositions of religion. According to Scruton, the dark side of the human soul remains with us as a reality, and we continue to require mechanisms to make communal life possible.[39] He claimed that art would take, or even has already taken over from religion the function of reflecting on those dark secrets. It is no accident, then, that Scruton's book ends with a chapter on Eliot and conservatism.

Before examining that final chapter, let us consider how he presents the unfortunate consequences of the Enlightenment's naivety, as far as the working of human community is concerned. In line with the argument of authors such as Adorno and Horkheimer, in *The Dialectic of the Enlightenment* (1947), and in Orwell's dystopian novel *1984* (written in 1948) Scruton connected the philosophical naivety of the Enlightenment and the political disasters of twentieth-century Totalitarianism. According to him, the birth of the totalitarian state is due to resentment, which leads to the destruction of safeguards against the misuse of power, including the law, property and religion.[40] These institutions were replaced by a centralised authority operated by the Nietzschean *Will* of a single individual. Orwell's masterwork explains the mechanism by which those units of human life are destroyed which allowed the human being to live a normal social and a safe private life, and how the human mind is captured, to use a concept popularised by the Nobel laureate Polish émigré poet, Czeslaw Milosz, in his revealing work, *The Captive Mind* (1953).

Scruton also made the bold claim that the totalitarian temptation survives in the institutional design of the European unification process, in spite of the fact that the founding fathers of the European Union meant the European institutional framework as an institutional device for providing safeguards against any totalitarian temptation in Europe, and in particular, in Germany. By pointing out the similarity between the bureaucratic language of European politics and the Newspeak of Orwell's *1984*, Scruton makes a convincing case that the totalitarian impulse remains there in the project. Scruton deals in a separate chapter with the Arendtian problem of the nature of evil.[41] In that, he draws on his own personal experiences of the operation of totalitarian power in Central Europe in the final years of Communist rule. He cites the canonical literature of the unofficial, democratic opposition to this rule. Besides Milosz, Scruton points to the work of eyewitnesses such as Solzhenitsyn, Václav Havel, Leszek Kolakowski and Arthur Koestler. The point he was trying to make was that there is a widespread illusion among Western intellectual, political and media elites that the egalitarian impulse, initiated by resentment, which provided the ideological weapon of the Communist rule, is basically right, and its justifiable demands can be satisfied only by the kind of centralised supranational agencies which appeared in post-1968 Europe, under the aegis of a never-ending process of European unification. Scruton's fears about the birth of a European superstate were in line with the scepticism of some Britons about European centralisation, which later led to Brexit, a cause which the philosopher supported wholeheartedly, as a reaction against the European superstate, taking over functions of national sovereignty from its member states.[42]

Scruton's own alternative to the EU project was not an isolationist British utopia, however. He suggests a cultural response to the impasse of the twentieth century he had earlier depicted in the last chapter of his book, on T.S. Eliot's poetry and its strong cultural criticism. As he saw it, Eliot was not simply "the greatest poet writing in English in the twentieth century," he was also a very innovative literary critic and a religious thinker.[43] His early poetry (*Prufrock and Other Observations*, 1917) and his early criticism (*The Sacred Wood*, 1920), established him, Scruton claims, as the major voice of modern poetry. In his essay *Tradition and the Individual Talent*, republished in *The Sacred Wood*, Eliot describes the happy mixture of tradition and originality, achieved by the creative artist, who remakes tradition by his creative acts. As a revolutionary innovator, Eliot would portray himself as "classical in literature, royalist in politics, and Anglo-Catholic in religion."[44] Viewed from this perspective, Burke was not captive of a backward-looking nostalgia but an innovative statesman who understood that it is only "a genuine tradition, which grants us the courage and the vision with which to live in the modern world."[45]

Eliot's great poem, *The Waste Land*, published in 1922, was his response to the disaster of the First World War, which he saw as the suicide of European civilisation. It is crucial for Scruton that Eliot was doing in poetry what Wagner, his most important modern composer, did in music. Yet he did something even more crucial, as an Anglo-Catholic religious thinker, in *Ash Wednesday* (1930), after his conversion in 1927. From that time, he devoted himself to becoming the conservative voice of his century.

Eliot's conservative stance was most explicitly formulated in two of his most famous essays,[46] *The Idea of a Christian Society* (originally presented in lecture form in 1939) and *Notes Towards the Definition of Culture* (first published in a journal in 1943). Surprisingly, Scruton criticises these pieces, arguing that neither of these essays was as successful as his great poem, *Four Quartets*, written approximately at the same time, which he believed was "the greatest message of hope that has been given to us."[47]

Besides characterising his verse drama, and commenting on the personal life of the poet, Scruton made a strong claim about Eliot's oeuvre as a whole. For Eliot, the task of the modern poet is not social repudiation but social reconciliation. As an arch-conservative, he was a critic of democracy, defending instead the aristocracy of social and cultural elites. For him, the poet and the critic had a mission: to sustain the authority of taste. Unlike others who did not have the courage to confront reality as it really was, these two, the poet and the critic, had the right habit of feeling and the necessary sensibility to talk about what they actually perceived to be true.

Yet art and literature in itself is not enough. Religion, in particular Christianity, is also crucial in order to overcome the deceit and self-deceit of Western modernity. Only the true believer will find her way "In the general mess of imprecision of feeling / Undisciplined squads of emotion."[48] The Christian believer connects modernity with the ages that have passed, with tradition. The Church is, in fact, the most enduring institution in Western culture. This is because "religion is the life-blood of a culture. It provides the store of symbols, stories and doctrines that enable us to communicate about our destiny."[49] It is by making sense of this package of culture and religion that the poet will become able to contribute to the revival of the tradition of the community. This insight explains Eliot's identification of the poet and critic with the religious martyr, the saint. The act of poetry, in fact, serves to "redeem the time."[50] The poet will be able to speak the language of that culture only when she joins the church and becomes a true, believing member of it. This is because "prayer is more / Than an order of words," and "the communication / Of the dead is tongued with fire beyond the language / of the living."[51] This is why "We are born with the dead."[52]

Scruton's language itself becomes rhetorically charged here: he seems to identify with Eliot and his position. It is through the poet that the experience of the continuity of the generations can be expressed, and hence what was only of local relevance can become true in a placeless and timeless sense that is, it becomes classical. The connection between the political and the cultural idea of tradition is thus established through the religious idea of tradition. In other words, both to become a legitimate conservative thinker and an authentic conservative poet requires a return to religion, to make sense of the human experience in the correct manner.

This is not, however, a simple task. The mission of the poet is, according to Scruton, to "embrace" modernity, but to do so both critically and self-critically. The poet is also a link in the chain which connects the past with the future, the mouthpiece of a culture, of a whole community.

In the context of culture, Scruton's claim is much bolder than what is normally required by a common-sense type of British conservative. His message here is beyond a political conservatism. Its "message is beyond politics, a message of liturgical weight and authority."[53] As he sees it, one needs to perceive and understand this message of poetry and religion, "if humane and moderate politics is to remain a possibility."[54] It is here that we can catch a glimpse of Scruton's political philosophy opening up to art and poetry.

We arrive here to the core of this book: to the connection Scruton supposes between politics and art, the distinguishing mark of Scruton's version of conservatism. For the late Scruton, the fact that culture is rooted in religion is crucial, even in a secular age. Although he himself had his limits in his religiosity, the religious dimension remains meaningful for Scruton's account of the relationship between politics and art. The major claim of this book will be that Scruton's cultural conservatism is based on this triangle of politics and art and religion.

How to Be a Conservative (2014)

As we saw, *A Political Philosophy: Arguments for Conservatism* was written at a time, which was both personally and politically hard for Scruton. *How to Be a Conservative* was published in 2014. The first decade of the new century was hard for Scruton. As we saw, he even had to leave England for a while. That decade was part of the 13 years of Labour governments, characterised by Blairism, a Left-wing version of Thatcherism.[55] Scruton eventually came back home from the US, and made great efforts to re-establish himself and his family in the English countryside. Conservative rule also returned to Britain in 2010. It was in this personal and political context that his next summary of the conservative cause was written and published in 2014.

Scruton dedicated the book to his second wife, Sophie, and their children.[56] Obviously, Scruton felt relieved to find himself and his family a safe home. Also, living in the English countryside might have caused him to mellow somewhat in his political philosophy. And still, his position remained more or less the same. The book was meant as a "valediction forbidding mourning."[57] He used the term in the preface and that expression would dominate the last chapter, entitled: "A Valediction Forbidding Mourning but Admitting Loss."[58] By both lamenting loss, but also preparing the soul for hope, Scruton sought to continue, but in a different key, his beautiful book: *England, an Elegy*, which seemed to be a kind of capitulation before the powers of destruction.[59] In this new defence of conservatism, Scruton aimed to show the vigour and stamina of this worldview.

He addressed this book to his audience in the English-speaking countries.[60] This is because he claims conservatism, as he understands it, was born and preserved in this context, even during and after "the traumas of the twentieth century." As in his first book on the topic, here, too, he starts by lauding the common-law legal tradition, because, as he claims, this lies behind the Anglo-Saxon notion of politics as a conservative enterprise.[61] It is in this tradition, he argues, that the most relevant institutions defending freedom grew naturally.

We should also keep in mind, that at the time he became befriended by Maurice Glasman, Baron Glasman, the founder of the Blue Labour movement, the ideology of which is based on pre-1945 Labour values, emphasising grassroots, small community and local organisations. Baron Glasman is a believing religious Jew, for whom the Jewish traditions are also a major source of inspiration.[62] Scruton's own conservatism was also inspired by the blue labour perspective.

He distinguishes between two kinds of conservatism in the Preface of his book: one type he calls metaphysical, the other empirical. The first strand is more elevated, dealing with issues of sacredness and desecration. The second type is more down-to-earth, dealing with the everyday reality of politics. Most of this book is concerned with this second, empirical version, only the last part addresses the metaphysical dimension of conservatism. This was a deliberate choice by the author, because he hoped that it might make his story more easily palatable for non-conservatives as well. He proclaims that the survival of all the well-known principles and institutions of safeguarding liberty, so characteristic of the contemporary Anglo-Saxon world, against the trespasses of the state, in fact comes from what we can call tradition, perhaps the most important concept of conservatism.

Scruton's conservatism is based on the following simple truth: "good things are easily destroyed, but not easily created."[63] This claim became a slogan by now, the truth of which can be accepted even by non-conservatives, if they value "peace, freedom, law, civility, public spirit, the security of property and family life," the values of down-to-earth, empirical conservatism which Scruton defends in the greater part of this book.

Although by this time Scruton had already published his autobiographical recollections, *How to Be a Conservative* also has a chapter on his own intellectual development, entitled "My Journey." This is important for him, as an intellectual conservative. For an intellectual conservative it matters how you arrive where you stand. His upbringing, his *education sentimentale* turned out to be crucial in this respect: he was not born into conservatism, he had to find his own path to it.

According to Scruton, to become an intellectual conservative these days requires one to swim against the tide. This is because his age is dominated by Leftist thought. He is right: according to most statistics, in the Anglo-Saxon world a large and growing majority of the academics working in the humanities and the social sciences identify themselves as belonging to the left.[64] This majority tends to supress alternative worldviews, labelling those, the majority of non-academics, who identify themselves as conservatives, as "reactionary, prejudiced, sexist or racist."[65] This is the state of affairs that Scruton was attempting to counterbalance by writing this book. And this is why he thinks that it is interesting how he concluded to identify himself as one belonging to the Right. By the time of his writing the book, the others labelled anyone who was not leftist as belonging to the Right. This was the first sign of an awakening cancel culture in politics.

Scruton identifies his own family background as lower middle-class, as most of the Peterhouse Right in Cambridge belonged to that social stratum, only "playing" the role of the conservative blue-blooded. Scruton's father was not only lower-middle class, but also a Labour sympathiser. By the time he was grown up, however, Scruton was ready to accept his legacy, as he had discovered his father's deep-seated love of the country, and even more of the countryside. As he interprets it, his father, too, had his own conservative inclinations, covered however, by the social teachings of the Labour movement.[66] Scruton admits that his father's grievances about social injustice were well-founded, only finding his solutions to be utopian. He claims that even his father honoured habeas corpus—a sign for Scruton, that his father loved his home country and even cherished its traditions.

Scruton also reveals that his father was anti-intellectual, even though he worked as a schoolmaster. The realm of life where he himself really felt at home was that of culture, including philosophy, art, literature and music, rather than politics. As we saw in an earlier chapter, his was, a rather unusual route to conservatism—through culture, in particular through the culture of F.R. Leavis and T.S. Eliot. His own study of the English past originated in his reading for the bar, where he learnt the history of common-law justice, which was a "narrative of home."[67]

While, for Scruton, the 1970s seems to be identifiable as the period when a culture of repudiation spread across the West, the 1980s was a much friendlier environment, due to Thatcher's government in Britain. Scruton claims that he found Thatcher's motives sympathetic, even if he did not become a "court philosopher," one of those intellectuals around the prime minister serving the government as backroom boys. This was largely because, as an intellectual conservative, Scruton harboured suspicions about intellectuals who were so fascinated by power that they could not help taking part in power games. Moreover, Scruton regarded Thatcherism as a kind of caricature of the conservative stance. It was to counterbalance this that he wrote his book *The Meaning of Conservatism*, published in 1979. While Thatcher famously relied on the individual's own initiative, Scruton, in contrast, built his own conservatism on the idea of a society built up of smaller communities.[68]

Scruton's conservatism was reaffirmed by his experiences in Eastern Europe, which he wrote about in his late novel, *Notes from the Underground*, published in the same year as *How to Be a Conservative*.[69] To the present writer, who was born and brought up in Communist Hungary, Scruton's vision of Eastern Europe in this novel always seemed to be somewhat caricature-like, a Romantic expressionist, or a Freudian world of dark instincts and repressive political power. This might be the consequence of a deliberate artistic choice, but it may also be the result of his own subjective impressions in those countries before the fall of the Iron Curtain.

Parallel with his struggle in Eastern Europe, he also battled at home, with his journal *Salisbury Review*. He finds it important to recall the affair of Ray Honeyford, a conscientious educator, who was unjustly and brutally attacked after he published his views in the *Salisbury Review*. Scruton, too, was constantly under fire for his opinions, and by 1989 he had decided to leave academia. While working in Central Europe after its liberation from Soviet rule, Scruton's interest turned towards European and global affairs. He was quite critical of the European adventure, noting that the foundational document of the EU denied its Christian past, and that the bureaucratic machinery in Brussels had a tendency to erode democracy. Because of his travels in Lebanon, Scruton also learnt that the radical political-ideological version of Islamism represents a real threat to the world. With this insight came the conviction that Western civilisation, like any other, needs to be defended in its traditional form, by defending the idea of national boundaries.

The final page or so of the autobiographical chapter of *How to be a Conservative* is about the spiritual values, which make up Western civilisation, including confession forgiveness, acts of sacrifice. Add to that the idea of accountability, as well as of respect for the law and public spirit— and you have the major pillars of this civilisation. All this comes from our Judeo-Christian tradition, and all of that is jeopardised and almost forgotten by what he calls the "anti-Christian turn" of the EU. This insight leads Scruton to the conclusion that a transcendental background to his conservatism is vital. Yet he finishes the chapter on the final note that his book will not be about those transcendental values, but rather about the way we live in the empirical world.

A story with great explanatory force of the modern malaise concerns the unintended consequences for society of the activity of the man of self-interest. For example, in the account offered in Adam Smith's *The Wealth of Nations* there is a market mechanism which helps to sustain the whole set of human activities, based on the motivation provided by individual self-interest. Yet Smith himself admitted that this system can only work properly if a whole range of values are cherished in the given society, including sociability and consequently social and moral virtues. These are values that can only be inculcated in human minds if traditions survive in those societies.

Human beings need cooperative drivers of human action, beyond mere egotism. Liberal theory from Locke to Rawls tried to explain the existence of these latter motivating forces as the result of a social contract. Arguably, the founding documents of the American Republic show that such social contracts can work effectively in the empirical realm of politics. The same example, however, also shows that there was a need for a pre-existing social cohesion in order to create those documents: they are written, after all, in the name and interest of "we, the people." It is also true, however, that a new form of a sense of cohesion and togetherness was created by them, which overwrote an earlier form of a somewhat spontaneous belonging.

Instead of employing the explanatory tools of the theory of *homo oeconomicus*, Scruton proposes his theory of *oikophilia*. This is a concept based on emotional attachment to a certain geographical location, an impulse which is present in most of us. It is through this sense of local attachment that we become "stewards and guardians of our common inheritance."[70] Scruton also utilises the Aristotelian concept of friendship, as explored in a new literature of neo-Aristotelianism, including the works of MacIntyre and Nussbaum. He also draws the important distinction between *otium* and *negotium*, the idea that relaxation and leisure is not necessarily asocial. In this respect he seems to rely on the work of Oakeshott, in particular on his book *On Human Conduct*.

Oakeshott was, of course, Scruton's forerunner, writing about an inbuilt conservative inclination in human beings. Yet Scruton's description is original, relying on the view of human nature provided in art, music and literature. To explain our original disposition, Scruton refers to a novel by Stefan Zweig, *The World of Yesterday*, originally published in 1942, after the writer's suicide, committed together with his wife. Scruton interprets this book as an indirect, but rather powerful criticism of the ideology of progress and transformation, present in all major new ideologies of the age, including the left- and right-wing variants of totalitarianism. All these ideologies relied on the assumption that humanity needs to rearrange the existing social order. When proposing and enforcing radical changes, the ideologists of these new creeds discount the costs and risks of transformation. In contrast to modern totalitarian ideologies, which aim to cut away human ties from their local roots, Scruton describes conservatism as "the philosophy of attachment" and preservation.[71]

Scruton, however, does not present conservatism as superior to all the other major ideologies of modernity. Instead, he tries to make sense in the book of the different ideologies' contributions to the well-being of human societies. In the subsequent chapters of his book he analyses the values of nationalism, socialism, capitalism, liberalism, multiculturalism, environmentalism and even those of internationalism. It is only after reviewing the comparative advantages of these modern ideologies that Scruton once again turns to conservatism. For him, conservatism is simply a corrective and auxiliary of those other ideologies and in no sense a replacement for them. This is because all of these ideologies have important truths to teach. In Scruton's view conservatism can help understanding the actual motivational forces behind cohesion in human societies.

When explaining human nature, which is vital to provide a firm foundation for his political theory, Scruton returns once again to Hegel, and his work *Phenomenology of Spirit* (1807), a nuanced historical reconstruction of how forms of human cooperation rose, of the birth of institutions of politics, law and education. Hegel played a major role in some of his other writings, including *Hegel as a Conservative Thinker*, published in his important volume of essays *Philosopher on Dover Beach*.[72] He regards Hegel's thought crucial for conservatism. As opposed to the view of man expounded in economic theories of human nature, Scruton finds human beings "home-building creatures, cooperating in the search for intrinsic values."[73] Among the fatal misdeeds of the totalitarian regimes, including the Soviet occupation of Central Europe after the Second World War, was that they destroyed the local tissue of society. Scruton explicitly refers to the example of the sins of the Hungarian Communists, and in particular, of János Kádár, who ruled the country for a quarter of a century, and who exerted political pressure to disrupt the web of associations, which had thrived in the civil society of this nation until 1948.[74]

One might call this the Tocquevillian moment of Scruton. As Tocqueville stressed the importance of the firm foundations of civil society in the US, so Scruton argues for the necessity of a powerful realm of civility in any free society. In his view, there are certain civil values, without which the cohesion of that society is unimaginable. This is why Communists wanted to destroy the traditional ties of civil society, while creating the possibility for individuals and small family units to survive. The idea was to create an atomised society which would be unable to sustain an alternative hierarchy of values. One can argue that the difference between the impact of the dissident movement in Poland and Hungary was because in Poland civil society remained intact and therefore more resistant, partly because of the influence of the Church, and its legal, as well as illegal institutional framework.

Alongside the Tocquevillian inspiration in this part of Scruton's argument, there are references to Hayek's notion of spontaneous order and Oakeshott's concept of the art of conversation, in his idea of civil association. In this context, the concept of leisure also resurfaces. While leisure is also crucial in Catholic thought, see for example Josef Pieper's work on that topic, Scruton links Oakeshott's notion of civil association with the Aristotelian concept of the contemplative life and friendship as an alternative to a world of material production.[75] Scruton refers to leisure as the foundation of social values, connecting the idea to Aristotle: "Leisure, for Aristotle, was a community-forming arena, in which we enjoy the friendships and virtues through which happiness dawns."[76]

Contrasting it with the official materialist ideology of the Soviet sphere, he also recalls the Schillerian account of human *Bildung* in the famous *Letters on the Aesthetic Education of Mankind* (1795). Scruton's claim that Schiller strove to show the relevance of art and culture in human life, as a form of human fulfilment is clearly a tribute to the thinker who had connected art and politics before Scruton. Schiller's reference to the ancient Greek custom of the public enjoyment of art reminds Scruton of the Hegelian notion of recognition. Explicitly mentioning the famous dialectic of the master-slave relationship in Hegel, Scruton argues that recognition is a universal engine of human communication and cooperation.[77] His Hegelian reconstruction of the politics of recognition paralleled the fashionable critique of alienation in the critical Marxism of the day, including the work of Adam Schaff.[78] In this respect, Scruton is aware of the ideas of contemporary leftist thinkers including Charles Taylor, for whom recognition is indeed one of the great legacies of the Hegelian philosophical oeuvre.[79] The concept of recognition seems to be quite useful for Scruton—after all, it can be countered by a return to art and friendship, in accordance with the Oakeshottean vision of civil association.[80]

Having taken up the notion of civil association, it is not surprising that Scruton examines the importance of religion and the institution of the family for civil society. He views both of these as crucial for what he calls "the mutual interaction" of people.[81] Art itself, and its appreciation, are activities in which we can experience this commonality of human beings. It is here that Scruton, the cultural conservative, is at his best. Drawing on his predecessors such as Matthew Arnold and T.S. Eliot, he very convincingly argues for the political relevance of the enjoyment of art, by political meaning here human as well as humane interactions. In this regard he quotes Eliot's expression, the "common pursuit of true judgement," a term which recalls, of course, the famous expression of the Declaration of Independence, the "common pursuit of happiness."[82]

Art in this sense is a communal achievement: something to be enjoyed together with others. Every culture has its canon: a selection of artists and their works regarded as the best and most perfect of their kind. Canons are the result of common judgements, or judgements made by the most perfect critics (a rather dubious and debatable category in real-life situations, perhaps) in the name of the community. It is the task of education to initiate students into the ever-changing canon—not only letting them know the actual content of the canon, but teaching them how to select the most perfect works of art. Schools teach students to acknowledge the best art and learn how to recognise the masterpieces.

Modernity experienced a revolt against beauty, the main carrier of the message of our common tradition. Artists of the avant-garde claimed that beauty turned into kitsch, and therefore the mission of modern art is to show that what is regarded as sacred by the tradition is, in fact, nothing like of the kind: in other words, they aimed to desecrate the sacred. The rebellion against beauty had its own theorists, including Arthur Danto, who presented the case for and the history of the "abuse of beauty."[83] He took his key term from one of the first rebels against beauty, the poet Arthur Rimbaud, who famously wrote: "One day I sat Beauty on my knees, and found her bitter, and I injured [abused] her" (*A Season in Hell*). Although Scruton admits that there is a desire in human beings to desecrate beauty, he continues to appreciate those artists, like the writers Saul Bellow and Seamus Heaney, the composers Henri Dutilleux and Michael Tippett, and the architects John Simpson and Quinlan Terry, who defended the experience of beauty against these challenges. According to Scruton, this defence is a truly conservative gesture on their part, in the sense of defending the foundations on which our culture is built. He refers to a range of eighteenth-century philosophers, from Shaftesbury to Kant, who sacrificed some of the basic assumptions of our culture, including religious orthodoxy and political authority, in order to achieve their aim of the liberation of the self. Yet even these representatives of the Enlightenment acknowledged the eternal in the transient phenomenon of the artwork. It is, in fact, this last defence-line, that the conservative, and in particular the cultural conservative, seeks to defend.

In the final chapter Scruton returns to the initial idea of his book: that conservatives should admit their losses while not giving in prematurely into mourning. By this point, Scruton had succeeded in demonstrating that conservatives had indeed lost many battles; now he suggests that to regain their self-assurance they need to admit these losses, for example, in the realm of religion, as a vital part of public culture. For Scruton, who views religion primarily as a source of membership in a community, this is a great loss, and one that might prove to be fatal to our civilisation. Yet he identifies heroes, who have succeeded in preserving something from that tradition. Arnold, Eliot and Rilke are the examples he gives of those who did more than just lament the losses: they tried to preserve the proper order of things, against the pressure of chaos that takes the place of organised religion in our communities. They knew, according to Scruton, that by preserving the order of things they had inherited, they could "preserve a common dwelling place – the place that is ours."[84]

Scruton enumerates some of the foundational elements of the English heritage, including parliament, the monarchy, the common law, the old universities, the Inns of Court, the county regiments and even the Anglican Church. None of them is perfect, but that is not the point. What is important about them is that this is the heritage, which identifies this particular community, allowing its members to feel at home in their vicinity. This is what makes these heritage sights so precious in spite of their occasional artistic imperfections. He further claims that after the loss of a public culture of common religious belief, the way to preserve our sense of home is to maintain our ability to appreciate works of high art. This has become quite a challenge since the advent of Romanticism and avant-garde art, but the demand is the same today. After the "death of God," cultural conservatism became the first condition of a politics of conservatism. This is Scruton's conclusion in this book, relying on Nietzsche's famous dictum, "we have art so that we may not perish of the truth."[85]

Conservatism: An Invitation to the Great Tradition (2017)

Scruton's fourth attempt to capture the essence of conservatism with the help of philosophical analysis regards conservatism as a great tradition.[86] This is quite a daring enterprise at a moment when the internet, and in particular the social media, has subverted social life and whipped away most of its institutional safeguards.[87] Due to an ever-increasing isolation of individuals, conservatives are in a difficult position if they want to keep their conviction. Scruton's narrative refers to the fact that the totalitarian regimes of the twentieth century drew conservatism once again closer to liberalism, as both defended free speech and freedom of expression. Yet in the age of globalisation they seem to have forgotten the local attachments. In an age of the four freedoms they experience difficulty if they want to assert their localism.

Scruton is critical of certain parts of the legacy of Thatcherism within conservative thought in the age of Brexit. He is in favour of a conservatism which is philosophically much more sophisticated than ordinary British conservatism used to be. He claims that politics as we know it depends on settlement, admitting the need of human beings to be connected to a place and an appreciation of the customs of that place and its inhabitants. This local attachment is a universal condition of humans as political animals—and this anthropological fact explains the use of the first-person plural in connection with politics. The rootedness of humans in particular local cultures requires that they keep the traditions which feed those cultures intact and alive. His belief of the rootedness of humans draws the contemporary conservative into alliance with nationalists, against the globalising and universalising aspects of the neoliberal agenda. Although British conservatism made for long the ideology of nationalism unnecessary, the European unification process and other pressures to globalise have made conservatives realise that local attachment is a *conditio sine qua non* of a healthy political life.[88]

These late developments in Western politics turned Scruton's own philosophical interest towards a localist conservatism. In *Conservatism: An invitation to the Great tradition* he defends the idea that there are certain pre-political conditions of political loyalty. While theorists of liberalism are blind to the communal dimension of British or American liberty, it is the mission of conservatism to remind people of the reality of this cultural precondition in an age which tries to wash away all the particularist engagements, in order to allow a global free market to gain dominance. Moreover, leftist ideologies require the creation of a global public, by enforcing the trans-national adoption of political correctness and cancel culture. For such leftist ideologues, global capitalism is an enemy, yet global corporatism is most welcome, as a means to achieve a globally "just" society. According to Scruton, these ideological demands threaten the very foundations of our civilisation and encourage conservatives to defend their civilisation's laws, institutions and high culture.

Scruton certainly does not share the anti-modernist agenda of Strauss and the Straussian neoconservatives. Yet his reconstruction of the origins of conservatism goes back to the age of Aristotle, as the pre-history of the Great Tradition crucial for his cultural conservatism.

The narrative strays as far back to the topics of cultural anthropologists like Sir James George Frazer, author of *The Golden Bough* and historical sociologists like Émile Durkheim. Both of them wrote about the need "to sustain the networks of familiarity and trust on which a community depends for its longevity."[89] Yet because of the disruptive drives of rivalry and competition, which can often overrule the dictates of reason, human societies require firmly rooted customs and institutions in order to survive. The rise of science, and its background, Cartesian and Enlightened philosophy, made it necessary for all political regimes to provide rational accounts of their legitimacy. Together with this demand, in the British context the power of the parliament grew to counterbalance the arbitrary rule of the king. Beyond this control over the monarch, the Enlightenment popularised yet another idea, namely the separation of state and church. Scruton draws attention to the fact that conservatives fought against it, as exemplified by Richard Hooker's attempted compromise in *Of the Laws of Ecclesiastical Polity* (1594).

Scruton's premodern narrative also depicts a quarrel between the moderns and the ancients. The avant-garde of enlightened individualism and secularisation was represented by innovative thinkers like Hobbes, Locke and Montesquieu, theorising the English constitution as the "mirror of liberty," in particular a reflection of modernist, individual liberty. But Scruton calls attention to critics of Enlightened reason, including Sir William Blackstone, David Hume and the critic and poet Samuel Johnson. This trend of thought led to conservatism understood as an attitude and way of life based on human sociability and civility as well as a knowledge of the wisdom of the forefathers.

It is important to note that in Scruton's narrative Hume belongs to the prehistory of conservatism, while Smith's and Burke's theories contributed directly to the birth of philosophical conservatism. Their impact is explained by two great contemporary events: the foundation of the US and the outbreak of the French Revolution. While these two events are usually interpreted as the most important challenges which conservatism had to confront, Scruton's narrative distinguishes between them. While the French Revolution was a dangerous innovation which provoked a conservative criticism in the work of Edmund Burke, one of the great founders of the American constitution, "Jefferson was a conservative in the manner of Blackstone."[90] The common ground between the two of them was the importance they attached to the continuity of the rule of law, defending it against arbitrary power. Certainly, Jefferson's personal practice of slavery makes him subject to criticism today. Yet he discovered an important motive which has recurred in American conservatism ever since: and this is the significance of the land in the life of the political community, and in particular, "the art of settling it."[91] Part of Jefferson's legacy was his practical activity in his own estate as well as his great founding act of establishing the University of Virginia. Jefferson insisted on a classical humanistic educational programme, which meant to preserve and develop the way of thinking characteristic of the culture of the old continent.

Scruton's further heroes from the same period are naturally Burke and, somewhat surprisingly, Adam Smith. He refers to Smith's moral theory, as expressed in *The Theory of Moral Sentiments* (1759), and especially his critique of the idea of social contract, so characteristic of the Age of Reason. Scruton finds in Smith an awareness of sociability which recalls Aristotle's own views on it. Sociability is explained by Smith with the help of the sentiments of sympathy, and the imaginative device of the "impartial spectator." Sociability is naturally implanted in the heart of the human being, but it is further polished over generations to achieve the perfection characteristic of the commercial society of Britain. This topic had already been addressed by Hume's *History of England* (1754–1761); Smith transformed this political history into a history of institutional growth and of legal and cultural refinement.

Scruton is prepared to advocate Smith's other major work, his *Inquiry into the Nature and Causes of the Wealth of Nations* (1776), as also representing an important element of the conservative tradition. Here, his key concern is the social effect of the market economy, as described by Smith. Markets allow each and every individual or company free participation in market exchanges, producing values which thus help to stabilise interpersonal relationships in the long run. The opposite of market economy is the French model of the state's control over the economy, which was to some extent already present in the absolutistic rule of the French court during the *ancien regime*, but which became explicit during the French Revolution and under the reign of Napoleon.

While both the law and the market were the results of long-term processes, and contributed to the stabilisation of social order, the language of
abstract universalism, which was introduced in the French *Declaration of
the Rights of Man and the Citizen* (1789) disregarded the long-term experience of groups of ordinary people, and was based instead on the logical,
idealistic but impractical theories of philosophers. In this context,
Scruton's hero, naturally, is Burke, and the main target of his criticism is
the theory of Rousseau. Burke's *Reflections on the Revolution in France*
(1790) was a storehouse of conservative observations of the workings of
practical wisdom in human societies. Instead of the social contract, which
he found unconvincing, Burke's own thinking relied on trusteeship, as
the key element of how coordination between generations and within a
large scale population is possible, as well as on the "little platoons" of
society, held together by "affection and trust."[92] The most important idea
in Burke's work, however, is the view that social knowledge is preserved
in the form of a traditional reverence for the past. Each individual also
has to play his or her part in the transmission of the social capital of
knowledge, he claimed, educating the next generation into their manners
and ways of life. Burke's theory of education emphasised nurturing, imitation, customs and precedents. Burke's criticism of Enlightened educational models leads Scruton in later chapters to Oakeshott, Hayek and
T.S. Eliot.

Before that he discusses Continental conservatism, and once again the
relevance of culture for conservatism. As we saw above, Scruton began his
story of conservatism by citing Anglo-American authors of the age of
Enlightenment. His heroes from that period of the Continental tradition
are Kant and Hegel. He regarded Kant as a defender of the French
Revolution—at least in its initial phases. He also points out that Kant
favoured a version of the social contract in his political philosophy. Not
so Hegel, who was, of course, almost half a century younger, and therefore confronted political reality in a different political milieu. He found
Kant's Enlightenment philosophy unsatisfactory in politics—it seemed
to him not much more than a theory of abstract rights.[93] According to
Scruton, as Burke critically reordered the ideas of Locke, so did Hegel
reorder some of the ideas of Kant, but this time the philosophical criticism was more metaphysical. He also adds that Marx was similarly

inspired by Hegel, but the younger thinker drew novel ideas from the Hegelian way of thought. Scruton regards Hegel as the most systematic defender of the conservative order, while Marx's theory, of course, was the quintessential revolutionary ideology.

Hegel in his *The Phenomenology of Spirit* (1806) offers his famous analysis of the master-slave dialectic.[94] This is helpful as a means of explaining how an ordered society is step-by-step established. Its dialectic of conflict, domination and recognition proves that freedom is not simply free choice, but also the recognition of the rights of others to freedom.

In Hegel's *Elements of the Philosophy of Right* (1820) Scruton's major theme is once again human sociability. Hegel's threefold structure includes those of the family, of civil society and of the state. It is through these steps, each growing in social complexity, that human societies arrive from *Sittlichkeit*, an ordinary "ethical life" at a complex form of politics. Beyond the "substantial tie" of marriage, the second and the third levels of social complexity consists of civil society (*bürgerliche Gesellschaft*) and the state. Drawing on the example of medieval civil associations, Hegel argues that civil society is a net of civil associations, all of which rise in an unreflected manner, as the result of "the cunning of reason," which is Hegel's version of Smith's invisible hand. While civil society is more or less the sphere of practical and conventional order, the state is a legal order and a corporate personality. Hegel's version of the rule of law is based on the specific German legal-political tradition. In a brilliant way, Scruton relies on this Hegelian idea, to distinguish between the totalitarian state and the rule of law. While the totalitarian state is an impersonal machine, he claims, Hegel's idea of the state as a corporate personality would be a guarantee against such alienation.[95]

Hegel's notion of the strong state competes with the understanding of the role of government in the British tradition of conservatism. Scruton identifies Hegel's position as one which is critical of democracy but which defends the representative parliamentary system. As he understands it, Hegel takes a position between the individualism of classical liberalism and the collectivism of socialism. Scruton's staunch critics have often criticised his Hegelian inclinations, because due to the impact of Popper, Hegel's position is often interpreted as a preparatory phase to totalitarian thinking.

No doubt, Scruton provokes his English-seeking readers. Besides Hegel, he mentions three French authors whom he regards as significant in nineteenth-century Continental conservatism. Two of them, Chateaubriand and de Maistre, are in fact reactionaries. The third of them, however, de Tocqueville is usually regarded as holding views which were closer to liberal conservative position. Scruton admits that de Maistre, the author of the *Essai sur le principe générateur des constitutions politiques* (1809), was a "réactionnaire," characterised by a certain remorseless extremism, "lamenting what he saw as the Devil's work."[96] Scruton calls attention to the religious dimension of nineteenth-century French conservatism.

The other father figure of the French conservative tradition is Chateaubriand, a writer and poet, author of the *Génie du Christianisme* (1802). He advocated not only the Christian faith in an age of growing secularism, but also "a kind of aesthetic and spiritual renewal."[97] Chateaubriand had a major impact on the Gothic Revival, a movement which would go on to become crucial for Conservatives in Britain, generally, and for Scruton's understanding of cultural conservatism, specifically. The combination of religion and art which characterises Chateaubriand's way of thinking would return in later authors of conservatism, who stressed the Christian tradition in poetry, architecture and also in music. Scruton's adventures in French culture played a major role in the birth of his concept of cultural conservatism in the British context, too.

Tocqueville takes his place in Scruton's story as a third example of the French self-criticism of the Enlightenment. He points out that the author's famous treatise, *Democracy in America* (1835) provides a defence of American localism and the institution of township, which he identifies as a safeguard against both the concentration of power in the centralised government and the tyranny of the majority. His major late work, *The Old Regime and the French Revolution* (1856), is a criticism of the French aristocracy, which, unlike its English counterpart, did not understand the spirit of the age and therefore had to fall.

While Scruton is quite familiar with the Continental affairs, unsurprisingly his real strength is in the analysis of the British conservative tradition. He regarded modern British conservatism as primarily a cultural issue. His nineteenth-century heroes were poets such as Coleridge, art critics like Ruskin and cultural critics like Matthew Around, who all drew attention to the loss of values in the cultural field as a result of the changes in lifestyles brought by the age of industrialisation. Scruton made no effort to defend their political ideas, which he found both nostalgic and unrealistic. He appreciates their diagnosis of cultural decline, as a result of the birth of mass society and the deconstruction of social hierarchy and its accepted norms. The only politician who is included by Scruton in this nineteenth-century gallery of British cultural conservatism is Benjamin Disraeli, also a novelist, who in the prefaces to his novels also gave a biting criticism of the age. His remedy, the political ideology of "one nation" conservatism, is the first conservative ideology applicable to mass society and general suffrage.

Scruton's chief heroes, however, are two twentieth-century men of letters, T.S. Eliot and F.R. Leavis. Eliot wrote the most influential English-language poetry of the century, including *The Waste Land* (1922), interpreted by Scruton as a diagnosis of the loss of direction in Western culture after the end of the First World War. Eliot's powerful language, and the spiritual nature of his art, served as an encouragement to engage in high culture for those who had lost their sense of security in social and political life. Even if it is the most rebellious modern poetry, it also draws on long traditions of artistic thought and practice. Scruton appreciates Eliot's existential choice to stay and settle in Britain, his religious conversion, his advocacy of the social role of culture and in his theoretical reflections on modern literature, as in his famous essay *Tradition and the Individual Talent* (1919), a powerful defence of tradition at the moment of its loss.

Scruton also makes the courageous move of including F.R. Leavis in his short overview of cultural conservatism, despite admitting that Leavis was never ready to identify himself as a conservative. Neither was he a religious person. Leavis was, however, quite influential as a critic. His educational programme, communicated through his journal, *Scrutiny*, as well as in his books, like *Education and the University* (1943), was based on the assumption that the "Great Tradition" (*The Great Tradition* (1948)) of English literature should be studied so as to find a way back to—the widely shared ideal of—"the organic community" which had been destroyed by the "technologico-Benthamite" way of thinking of modernity.[98]

Leavis' idea of defending the Great Tradition points towards America, where Scruton identifies two, rather opposing cultural directions. The Southern Agrarians' manifesto, *I'll Take My Stand*, dates from 1930, and it is regarded by Scruton as an important sign that people there too had experienced a sense of loss and cultural decline. He criticises their failure to capture the reality of the day, and their inability to "come to grips with slavery and its legacy."[99] He was aware, however, of the output of this tradition, exemplified by the work of Allen Tate, Eudora Welty, Flannery O'Connor and Robert Penn Warren.

An opposite, and outspokenly more urban direction of what Scruton regards as cultural conservatism was linked to the school of Leo Strauss, a European émigré of Jewish-German background, who succeeded in renewing political science in the US. His conservatism was a mixed baggage, consisting of his characteristically esoteric understanding of Plato and Platonism, the Jewish hermetic tradition, German idealism, and the traditional discourse of natural law and natural rights, leading him to his own, idiosyncratic understanding of the US constitution.

The next phase in the historical overview of Scruton's narrative is the Cold War. His main argument about this era is that, in the sphere of political theory, classical liberals united with Burkean conservatives in order to fight the threat of totalitarian socialism, inspired by Russian communism as well as by the Chinese revolution. To prepare the ground for one of the major figures of this movement, Friedrich von Hayek, Scruton pays tribute to the conservative Nachlass of the literature of the dying Habsburg empire, mentioning Stefan Zweig (*The World of Yesterday*, 1934–1942), Robert Musil (*The Man Without Qualities*, 1940) and Joseph Roth (*Radetzky March*, 1932). As he sees it, Hayek, an Austrian émigré in London, was connected to this subculture, although his Anglophilia led him to his groundbreaking work *The Constitution of Liberty* (1961). Scruton explains why Hayek added an appendix to that book entitled "Why I am not a Conservative," with the unexpected success of the anti-Communist coalition of classical liberals like Hayek and British type conservatives, such as Michael Oakeshott.[100] While Scruton locates Hayek's work in the context of the school of Austrian economics, he also discovers in his thought the remnants of the ideas of Burke and Hegel. Hayek's great contribution was the idea of "spontaneous order" or "catallaxy," which manifests itself in the smooth, because politically unhampered, operation of the market. The common law had a similar foundation, and it also grows in a natural and spontaneous manner. Scruton claims that the political result of Hayek's self-regulating market and precedent-based and "judge-discovered" law is "a mitigated conservatism."[101] On the other hand, he finds Hayek's early work, *The Road to Serfdom*, published in 1944, as a major document of anti-communism, an "imperfectly argued" book, which nevertheless had a major impact on the thought of the day. Smith and Burke are in the background of the major voice of post-war British conservatism, Michael Oakeshott. Scruton regards Oakeshott as less of an anti-Communist advocate, and more a finely tuned cultural conservative. While Scruton is not impressed by Oakeshott's sense of real politics, and criticises what he regards as his neutral position towards religion, he fully endorses Oakeshott's stress on the importance of non-political social activity. He especially welcomes Oakeshott's reference to "conversation, friendship, sport, poetry and the arts" as activities directed towards "things of intrinsic value," which reflects Scruton's own advocacy of the *vita contemplativa*.[102] Scruton also recognised the circle of like-minded thinkers at the LSE politics department around Oakeshott, which thus developed into "a centre of conservative resistance."[103]

Although Scruton's last book on conservatism is confined to a historical narrative, its final chapter addresses the present. It touches upon two of the recurrent themes of present-day conservative discussions: political correctness and religious extremism. In connection with the first of these topics, he refers to Orwell's classic *1984* (1948), a somewhat surprising reference to a left-wing intellectual in a conservative narrative. Yet Orwell had become one of the most powerful critics of the totalitarian state by the end of the Second World War. Scruton's other example is Allan Bloom, a disciple of Strauss, and his book *The Closing of the American Mind* (1987). The author, like Hayek before him, never accepted the label of conservative as a description of his way of thinking. Instead, he preferred to present himself as an advocate of the contemplative life.[104]

Scruton is careful not to forget two near-contemporary circles of conservative thought, in order to show that there were exceptional cases when and where conservatism could organise itself. We have already touched upon one of them, the LSE circle of conservatives, gathered around Oakeshott. Scruton explicitly mentions in connection with this circle the name of Elie Kedourie, the Iraqi Jew, a critic of "the creeping culture of liberal guilt in his *The Chatham House Version, and Other Middle Eastern Studies*, 1970) as well as the Hungarian-born Peter Bauer, and Kenneth Minogue, an immigrant from New Zealand, an Ortega-like critic of democracy."[105] In mentioning these figures, Scruton arrived at his own days, to his own personal friends and acquaintances.

It was in this context that he mentions Peterhouse conservativism as a second nest of near-contemporary conservative thinking. We referred to Scruton's personal attachment to this Cambridge college. His hero was Maurice Cowling, the historian, "a trenchant critic of liberalism," encouraging him and other younger colleagues to be "more forthright in declaring our dissent from the left-liberal orthodoxies of the day."[106] In that obituary, Scruton had connected Cowling to the tradition of British cultural conservatism, including authors like Coleridge, Arnold, Ruskin and Leavis. What is somewhat more surprising is that he connected Cowling's intellectual history first to a "defector from the left," the historian Paul Johnson and then to a number of his younger colleagues, including Niall Ferguson. He also compares him to the historian of the custom-based constitution of Britain, to F.W. Maitland, the author of *The Constitutional History of England* (1908).[107] The point he wanted to make was that conservatism reclaimed English (not British!) history from leftist narratives, including Whig historiography just as much as the Marxist theory of history.

The pantheon of the great masters of conservatism finishes with a pair from the US and an international triumvirate. The American pair is, of course, William F. Buckley Jr, a devout Roman Catholic and witty critic of establishments, and Russell Kirk, who first helped Buckley to establish the *National Review* in 1955, but who later established his own platform, *Modern Age*, in 1957. They published powerful summaries of their respective positions. Buckley's book, *God and Man at Yale* (1951) was an attack on his alma mater, for its loss of direction, betrayal of the American idea and lack of spiritual guidance. Russell Kirk's *The Conservative Mind* (1953), on the other hand, is often regarded as the Bible of American conservatism.

Finally, Scruton named the triumvirate, proposing himself, together with Samuel Huntington in America and Pierre Manent in France, as the contemporary embodiments of cultural conservatism. The three of them share a common message that "Muslim immigration poses a challenge to Western civilization, and that the official policy of 'multiculturalism' is not a solution but part of the problem."[108]

With these forbidden topics, Scruton arrives at the present-day concerns of conservatism, turning his historical account into a contribution to present-day debates on the clash of civilisations. In the culture war, politics and culture meet in a rather specific way. Although Scruton was not a culture warrior, his professional acquaintance with the philosophy of art, aesthetics, together with his practice of political philosophy turned him into a key protagonist in the debate.

After this overview of Scruton's main publications on conservative political philosophy, let us turn to his work on patriotism and his concept of *oikophilia*.

National Attachment

British conservatism is embedded in British history. British history is dependent on the birth of an empire, an effort in which England united with Scotland and Wales. Because of this constitutional structure, the nation was not a priority in the nineteenth century. British conservatism itself was primarily British, and not English.

Given this prehistory of British conservatism, it was surprising to see that in the last two decades of his life, Scruton turned towards England and Englishness. His work in this direction anticipated the rise of a specific version of conservatism, called national conservatism.[109] In what follows we shall deal with two of Scruton's book-length efforts to build a theory of national belonging.

England. An Elegy (2000)

The elegy is a specific literary form. In Ancient Greek, *elegeia* meant a poem written in elegiac couplets. It could concern a wide range of topics, one of which was the epitaph, or short poem lamenting the loss of a beloved or famous person.[110] By entitling his book as an elegy Scruton explains the paradox inherent in this choice of topic with Hegel: "The owl of Minerva spreads its wings only with the gathering of the dusk."[111] The elegiac tone here is in Coleridge's sense of the word. Scruton's intention was "to pay a personal tribute to the civilisation that made me and which is now passing from the world."[112] He refers to the genre as both a memorial address and a funeral oration, and recalls the twentieth-century prehistory of the genre in English literature. Scruton regards his own specific contribution to the genre as a philosophical account of an ideal which England furnished to her sons and daughters, an attempt to describe the "gentleness, amiability and civilised manners" of the English people. By describing it he wants to prove that "ideals are important."[113]

In what follows I will not be able to do justice to the overall panorama Scruton provides in his book the nature of community, religion, law, society, government, culture and countryside. His story finishes on a note concerning "the forbidding of England."[114] Instead of attempting a comprehensive account, I will concentrate here on two elements which connect the political and the cultural aspects of this tribute: on Scruton's account of the gentleman, and on his interpretation of Shakespeare. These are, of course, topics which no author can avoid when talking about Englishness, but Scruton's way of handling them is characteristic of his own approach.

The first mention of the gentleman, discussed along with the lady, comes in this book in the chapter on the national character, together with virtues such as courage, reserve and law-abidingness. He compares the notion to the Polish concept of the *szlachta*, but he finds a major difference between the English and the Polish terms. The criterion for being an English gentleman is from the beginning emphatically not a question of "birth and blood" or material advantage. As he understands it, the gentleman is a moral category, "defined independently of lineage and wealth."[115]

In the society into which he was born, social titles and all the material attributes of exceptionality were dependent on certain criteria of manners which he identifies as belonging to the essence of the notion. As he describes it, in English society, any man could aspire to the status of the gentleman. Scruton's conception of "gentle"-ness constituted an exceptional position emulated by the character itself becoming gentle, to retain "the ability to deal kindly, distantly and humorously with others."[116]

He also admits that the concept of the "genteel" is still there in the term. Scruton makes his case with an illustration taken from English literary history, about the character of Mr Pooter from the Grossmiths' *Diary of a Nobody*.[117] Mr. Nobody wants to establish himself in society by being both "gentle" (ordered and reliable) and "jaunty," having *dignitas* in his way of behaviour. In the story Mr Pooter, the nobody becomes somebody "because he had made himself a home."[118] As we shall see, acquiring for one's family a home will prove crucial for both Scruton's philosophical anthropology and for his conservative political philosophy.

The philosopher returns to the notion of the gentleman later in the book. He recalls some further literary examples, taken both from English and from European literature. He argues at this point that despite its being a social or class barrier, it was not understood as a moral barrier. He refers to Chaucer's *The Canterbury Tales*, and in particular to the figure of the knight, an "archetype of the English gentleman," characterised by his "courtesy, nobility and chivalry."[119] The other members of the group deferred to the knight, because he was able to defend them. Scruton connects this relationship to that described by the historian David Cannadine in the First World War. There, too, officers were still recruited from the upper-middle class and upwards, because they had a special affinity with their particular army units, often local regiments, and because they were ready to die for their troops.[120]

In this context, too, class distinctions were based on achievement and performance. In this sense Scruton could say that "the ideals of lady and gentleman" were available in some measure to everyone. One could become an "honorary member of the upper class" by acquiring their levels of learning and behaviour. The standards of excellence were clearly defined, if not by Chaucer, then by Henry Peacham, at the latest, in his *The Compleat Gentleman*, published in 1622. This was a manual which

explained the particular common code of conduct one had to appropriate, a code of how to act in emergency situations—an essential skill for
subjects of the British empire by the time they were governing a substantial part of the world.

The gentleman was not defined by his chivalry, which meant the use of
violence. Scruton recalls Cardinal Newman's famous definition of the
gentleman, which describes him as "a paragon of sympathy, fairminded-
ness and cultivated ease,"[121] quoting even the famous sentence: "It is
almost a definition of a gentleman to say that he is one who never inflicts
pain."[122]

Surprisingly, Scruton also draws two literary examples from the works
of foreigners—from authors coming from East-Central Europe. One of
these authors became a naturalised Englishman: Joseph Conrad. The
novel writer identified the virtues of the typical English gentleman with
those of English merchant seamen and English colonists. His particular
example is Gould, an Englishman by ancestry, and his English-born wife,
in his novel *Nostromo*. They both possessed the character traits of being
and remaining calm and graceful "in the midst of decay."[123]

More surprising than Conrad is Scruton's second choice: it is Karel
Čapek. It is in Čapek's *Letters from England* (1924) that Scruton, who had
a special taste for Central Europe, finds the ideal description of the
English gentleman. Scruton quotes Čapek's—no doubt, somewhat
ironic—definition as a verbatim catalogue of the specific repertoire of
manners: "A gentleman… is a measured combination of silence, courtesy,
dignity, sport, newspapers and honesty."[124] Scruton assents to the sub-
dued irony and humour, because it fits the tone of his own narrative as
well. He also accepts Čapek's examples of English decency and politeness:
the club-waiter, the booking-clerk and the policeman. All of them
belonged to lower social classes than Chaucer's knight, or Cannadine's
army officers, which he took as proof of the broader applicability of the
term in the twentieth century. All of these figures are useful members of
what Scruton labels as "the society of strangers," the members of which
"you can trust without reducing the distance between you."[125]

Finally Scruton takes as an example of the gentlemanlike quality of
character even a lady: Kathleen Vaughan-Wilkes. The irony lies not in the
fact that she, a childhood acquaintance and the object of the author's

early adoration, is a female representative of the gentlemanlike character, after all, according to Scruton "the ideal has nothing especially to do with sex."[126] The irony is that she was a born aristocrat, turned into a philosophy don as well. In other words she was a class traitor. While she left her class in order to become the defender of the lower classes as an Oxbridge leftist intellectual, Scruton himself left his lower middle-class background, which he identified here as "proletarian," in order to rise to the position of a "sceptical conservative" philosopher, equipped to defend the ancient manners of his culture.

The ideal of the gentleman, in Scruton's reading, is a normative category, both in its political and its cultural dimension. The political dimension of the ideal of the gentleman defines him as a "born leader," one who is able to assume his social responsibility and fulfil his social role as a member of the elite, capable of defending others in conflicts. However, governing or ruling is not primarily about "inflicting pain." On the contrary, it requires the acceptance of a special code of conduct, which can be traced back to the chivalric ethos of the medieval Christian knight. The gentleman, too, needs to acquire a form of behaviour, which involves decorum. This system of norms has its origin in the specific manners of the knight. As opposed to the individualist ethos of the modern liberal, the gentleman is defined as a trustworthy member of his society, one who is aware of his role and duties, as a reliable contributor to the well-being (common good) of a society of strangers. The decorum of his style is not empty style and formality, and does not exist simply for its own sake—it is an external sign that the person who is identified by it is a carrier of social values.

If a cultural element defines the perfect gentleman, it is not surprising that Scruton takes so many examples from literature. His methodology, using literature to identify real Englishness, returns in his use of Shakespeare.

Scruton claims that Shakespeare is not only the greatest, but also the most English of English writers. In each national culture one can name the most outstanding representative of it. In his view, Shakespeare is to English culture what Goethe is to Germany and Baudelaire to France. His oeuvre embodies the essence of English culture—in this sense, Shakespeare is the embodiment of England itself. Scruton is brave enough to characterise Shakespeare's Englishness with the help of four points, which he thinks together are also able to define English culture itself.

Significantly, he starts his list of character traits with Shakespeare's view of the common people, his use of the traditional figure of the Everyman. This is the great paradox of Shakespeare's art: that his plays are the highest culture, while remaining stories of ordinary people. Unlike Molière's court theatre, The Globe was basically a pub, where ordinary people met, drank and enjoyed themselves while they watched the performance. Shakespeare remained in the realm of popular culture, in spite of the fact that his art belongs to high culture, touching upon the most important themes of the human condition, including love and jealousy, marriage, family life, power and obedience, treason and loyalty, war and peace, sacrifice and heroic death. Scruton regards Shakespeare as representing the Everyman tradition in English culture, which predates Shakespeare (it is already there in the work of Chaucer, Langland, Wycliffe and Tyndale) and which will survive him too, in the works of Milton and Bunyan, Hogarth, Dickens and Orwell. Look at the role played by ordinary people in his tragedies. They are given the last word on stage: think of Falstaff, Yorick or "the fickle crowds in Julius Caesar."[127] Shakespeare's dramatic art takes Everyman as "the test against which morality and ideals should be measured," in order to let us recognise that it is in fact part of our ordinary condition to have "freedom, guilt, judgement and responsibility."[128]

If Everyman is the representative of the general public on stage, Scruton's second topic about Shakespeare is its exact opposite, the theme of the individual. Dramatic art allows us to see real people. But Shakespeare's realism is more than just making use of the opportunity of the stage to confront us with the human figure. Although one of Shakespeare's sharpest weapons is language, with which he can always cast a spell, his dramas are full of actions. His complex stories do not give the playwright much time to characterise his heroes. Yet he produced such a repertoire of great and real figures, including Lear, Hamlet and Leontes, Rosalind, Juliet and Portia, Coriolanus and Cleopatra that the stage is sometimes not large enough to host them all. Shakespeare's greatest stories are full of dramatic turns and breath-taking moments. Yet someone he is able to show us the inner essence of his figures as well, their naked self or selfhood. Although Shakespeare was definitely not a philosopher, he was able to show the duality of human nature, by showing us the innermost core of individuality tested in the extreme situations of his dramatic world.

The third Shakespearean theme for Scruton is England itself, as a historical entity. Shakespeare's great individual heroes play a certain role, evaluated by the "audience," the people of England. The history plays "dramatise the English constitution," presenting the Crown as the symbol of a mysterious corporate person which unites the ruler with the people. For Scruton, England as a historical entity is presented on Shakespeare's stage as the eternal struggle to turn power into authority, the wish of the powerful to be accepted by the ordinary man and—at the same time—an illustration that without loyalty to lawful power England would not keep its position on the stage of history. To achieve the right distance, and the right balance between the powerful and the ordinary members of the public, those in power need to possess that extraordinary quality which we call charisma.

Scruton's fourth and final Shakespearean theme is enchantment. While the art of a dramatist indeed lies in turning the stage into a place where exceptional events happen to magic figures, as happens in Shakespeare's *A Midsummer Night's Dream* as well as in *The Tempest*. The poet's greatest marvel is his ability to show the enchanted and enchanting in the ordinary forms of human existence. Shakespeare outshines even such great masters of poetry as Sidney and Spenser, who both present the ideal form of England. Shakespeare was able to achieve something more. In John of Gaunt's speech in *Richard II* England appears as "a place, a land transfigured by nature and history, and personalised and moralised by the Crown."[129] His art consists in showing that lawful and just, or in other words, authoritative and trustworthy politics can transform a place into our common home, and thereby merit our true loyalty. His art turns the stage into an enchanted land, which is England, the true object of our emotional attachment. Here lawful kings like Richard can be rotten, while perhaps usurpers make a good king. In two lines Shakespeare encapsulates the essence of Englishness: "This blessed plot, this earth, this realm, this England, / This nurse, this teeming womb of royal kings."[130]

Scruton found the link between the ideal of the gentleman and Shakespeare's art. The great English playwright is able to present in a perennial form both the chaotic history and the ideal order of England as a political realm, showing us its kings, its common people, and the gentlemen standing between the two. The artful manners of the gentleman turns power into a legitimate use of force, or authority. This power remains in the service of the ordinary members of the public, of the Everyman. His virtuous artfulness gives meaning to the *arcana imperii*, to the enchanted world of politics, turning the country, the teeming womb of royal kings, into the common home of the people, "this blessed plot."

The Need for Nations (2004)

While in *England: An Elegy*, written at the turn of the millennium, Scruton lamented the loss of the nation state, in particular the decay of England, in 2004 he published *The Need for Nations*, in which he "defends the nation state."[131] The "Foreword," written by the Cambridge-based economist Robert Rowthorn, who himself was a New Leftist in the 1960s, claims that the book is not easily located politically—it addresses both Left and Right. Rowthorn also stresses that Scruton is not a nationalist—in this label he hears an overtone of belligerence. Rather, he is a patriot, and his love of country is national loyalty. Patriotism is defended by leftist republicans like Viroli, as well. Yet it is not simply the opposite of nationalism.[132] Instead, Scruton simply distinguishes between two forms of national loyalties: one of them is a "natural love of country," the other is a pathological form of attachment. Patriotism is understood in this book as a kind of territorial loyalty of members of a law-abiding political community, or in the words of John Stuart Mill, the "principle of cohesion among members of the same community or state."[133]

Scruton's position is interesting for two different reasons. First, because, as Rowthorn indicated, it may be acceptable for left-wing patriots as well—in fact, in the notes he describes a lineage pointing in that direction. In other words, this book is not confrontative. Instead, its author tried to find a common ground between the left and the right. Secondly, compared to Yoram Hazony's 2018 book, *The Virtue of Nationalism*, one can argue that it is also less radical. Hazony does not mind to be identified as nationalist, arguing that nationalism is not a "pathological form" of loyalty.

Scruton, on the other hand, seems to accept the critical narrative that both French nationalism in the late eighteenth century and the German variant in the first half of the twentieth century were cases of "nations gone mad," warning his readers not to judge the normal, healthy and natural case by the standards of "the nationalist fever," or frenzy. He distinguishes between nationalism and patriotism with the help of Chesterton, who claimed that to judge national loyalty on the basis that some people went to war in its defence is comparable to judging love on the basis that some people committed murder in defence of their love. As opposed to Scruton, Hazony, writing his book somewhat later, claims that nationalism, in fact, is a virtue, and that the cruelties committed by the French and the Germans were carried out because they swapped their nationalism for their visionary dreams of empire. While Scruton remains an old-fashioned patriot, and not a fervent national conservative, he seemed to support Hazony's movement of national conservatism at the end of his own life, in the context of Brexit and Trump. He was pro-Brexit, but a sharp critic of Trump.

The book in question was published in 2004, the year when Central and Eastern European countries joined the European Union, and when Tony Blair still governed Britain. Thus, in making the case in defence of the nation state, Scruton is critical of its transnational alternative, because he fears, a European empire would be "disastrous" for both Europe and the world.

Scruton's basic thesis rests on a Hegelian criticism of contract theory. Contract theorists insist that our loyalty to the state is based on a social contract which creates the very membership itself. However, to make sense of a contract you need to presuppose a common ground, a common understanding of the concept of a social contract. Partners to a social contract are not made partners by that very contract itself. Instead, they are able to decide about their common future because they already trust each other, as part of a community defined by the use of the first-person plural. When it comes to national allegiance, a pre-existing form of cohabitation is merely formalised by the much-heralded social contract.

One is supposed to fight and die for the community one is part of as a citizen, and that is much more than what follows from a simple cost-benefit analysis, which is the basis of the mutual rational choice supposed by the idea of partners making contracts with others. Even if we assume the existence of the social contract as a founding act, Scruton claims it is only a single phase in the much longer history of an emerging community. The first-person plural is based on the common past of the members of the community. The basis of the trust and the security of the tie is traditional in its nature: national loyalty in this sense depends on the conservative idea of a tradition-based form of common practical knowledge.

In what follows I shall concentrate on three points Scruton makes in this work about the nation. First, I shall identify the particular form of nationalism that he wishes to defend. Secondly, I will examine his double loyalty to England and to Britain. Finally, I will consider the advantages of national loyalty for representative democracy, in opposition to the vague alternatives that critics of national loyalty can offer.

Scruton distinguishes national loyalty from two other drivers of communal organisation: "family love" and "religious obedience."[134] As he understands it, tribal communities are based on blood relationships, and in particular, on the idea of familial connections: the community is delineated by kinship. This is a natural source of alliance, but one which has serious constraints. Scruton identifies two of its drawbacks. The internal problem with the tribal principle is that this type of community tends to be hierarchical. As Scruton explains, a characteristic of tribal societies is that accountability is "running one way – from subject to chief – but not from chief to subject."[135] This is why a tribal form of association could never lead to "an impartial rule of law."[136] No stranger has the chance to become a member of the society, as she has "an incurable genetic fault," that is, that she was not born into the particular family that defines the particular community.[137]

There are also serious limitations of community life in the second variant, called by Scruton a "creed community."[138] Here, obedience is based on worship. In other words, one can only count as a member of the given community if one shares their religious beliefs, and follows the same rituals as they do.

Both tribal and creed communities are tradition-based societies, and lack the contractarian element in their sense of belonging. The idea on which the community is based for both of these types of community bond is very old, which gives it a prestige, and excludes the possibility that the present generation can easily and fundamentally change it. Moreover, both of these systems have a metaphysical underpinning. As Scruton puts it: "Creed communities, like tribes, extend their claims beyond the living."[139] The living and the dead are members of the same community, they "throng together in the great unknown."[140]

There are further problems with both of these types of community: they seem to be destined to generate enmity and conflict. This is connected internally to the strictly hierarchical nature of their internal structure, which does not allow any basic differences of views, and externally to the metaphysical as well as genetic underpinning of the community. Both metaphysics and genetics exclude the politics of compromises.[141]

What, then, is the basis of communal belonging, if Scruton excludes on the one hand the social contract, and on the other hand genetic and creedal forms of communal attachments as the foundational principles of communities? As we saw earlier, Scruton tends to attribute great significance to institutional settings and legal arrangements. Yet, as he points out, the development of English law, or what is generally referred to as common law, the primary institution of the British system of public administration, has a very powerful connection to a locality: it is the jurisdiction of a community that inhabits a certain territory, independently of the particular creed or family connections of the individuals concerned.

Scruton clearly commits himself to an explanation of national loyalty based on the territorial principle, adding to it the institutional-legal dimension. Here is his definition: "By a nation I mean a people settled in a certain territory, who share institutions, customs and a sense of history and who regard themselves as equally committed both to their place of residence and to the legal and political process that governs it."[142] This definition takes into account the particular form of institutional development which characterises European nations. It happened to be the case that in Europe the territorial monarchy gave way to the nation state, as a "territorial jurisdiction." This meant, in essence, the rule of law over a certain territory.

Given the fact that historical development plays such a crucial role in the legitimation of the nation state as a territorial jurisdiction, Scruton had to explain the genealogy of the UK, in other words, the relationship between his national loyalty (which connects him, as an Englishman historically to the English nation) and his loyalty to the particular historical form of the UK of Great Britain and Northern Ireland.

Given the fact that national loyalty is defined by territory, this form of attachment can be "multiple." By the notion of multiple national loyalty Scruton means that different ties of loyalty can "nest within each other without conflict."[143] He also calls this inclusion of one loyalty in another or others a "composite" national identity. The explanation for the particular British form of coexistence is this: when James VI of Scotland inherited the English throne, "the British nation... was an inevitable result of the juridical process."[144] It created a legal status quo, which was defined by the fact that the jurisdictions of the earlier territories of Scotland and England were united, just as had happened with England and Wales, and as was, much later, to be the case with Britain and Northern Ireland. These jurisdictions "aimed for harmony rather than assimilation."[145] By preserving the earlier jurisdiction within the larger framework of a new one, different levels of loyalty emerged. This was made possible by the fact that the British identity subsumed the "more deeply rooted identities" of Englishness, Scottishness, Welshness and Irishness. This subsummation was made easier by the fact that the system of government was and remained monarchy. In this system, the subjects belonged to the Crown, which was, according to its legal fiction, a "corporation sole," an "entity recognised only by the common law of England," but which now extended to include the inhabitants of the other parts of the territory of the Isles. Interestingly, this composite British national identity did not absorb the earlier, more deeply rooted ones; on the contrary, it still depends on them, except for those subjects of the Crown who come from other territories of the earlier empire, which lie outside of the geographic borders of the island(s). This allows for a remarkable flexibility concerning national and British loyalty, and Scruton is ready to accept Linda Colley's explanation of this, which is based on the assumption that the need for Britain was explained by the intention "to give credibility to the Union," in other words by an expansionist policy.[146] He is also ready to admit that, beside the local, tribal and religious dimension of political belonging, there is also an ethnic dimension to it. For Scruton, moreover, what is crucial is the fact that, just as the Scots, Welsh and Irish preserved their more rooted identity within the framework identity of Britishness, so too the English were able to preserve their sense of belonging to "England as a homeland and a territorial jurisdiction" within the inclusive identity of being British.[147] Similarly, the constructed identity of Britishness allows those inhabitants of the former empire, who adopted British nationality, to continue "retaining ethnic and religious loyalties forged far away and years before." He does not speak about the centrifugal aspect of this remarkably adaptable forged national identity, at a time of mass migration, ethnic and religious terrorism, culture war and Brexit. There are very practical, chronological reasons for this silence. He published this book in 2004, which predated the new wave of migration, domestic terrorism, the culture war and Brexit. Even now, at the time of publishing the present overview of Scruton's oeuvre, after Scruton's death, we cannot tell what exactly will be the consequences of Brexit for British identity. Yet Brexit, so far, has not destroyed the internal cohesion of the idea of Britain, even if the country paid a high price for it. But the same is true about the European Union, which however does not want to draw conclusions from the event. To this latter Scruton applied Bentham's term "nonsense on stilts."[148]

Finally, let us address the third question posed by Scruton in *The Need for Nations*: how does British-English national loyalty relate to the idea of representative democracy in comparison with more utopian, non-national concepts of political loyalty? Scruton's most daring chapter sees the nation state as a source of virtues. This is a challenge to the normal understanding of the nation among liberals, who typically claim that the nation state provokes hatred and aggression against other nationalities. Scruton's rhetoric does not address these allegations but instead employs an opposite strategy: it endeavours to show the virtues which derive from being a citizen of a state based on national loyalty. This strategy is taken one step further by Yoram Hazony. The title of his book is, of course, *The*

Virtue of Nationalism, setting out to turn the critical, negative term into one which one can be proud of.[149]

Scruton's chapter on these virtues starts out from a review of the advantages of the nation state compared to tribal and creed loyalty. First of all, unlike creedal communities, it offers freedom of conscience and worship. It can also unite all the people living in a territory, in other words it is not ethnically exclusive. This fact makes it possible for everyone living there to unite under a national banner and flag to defend a certain territory against its invaders. This non-discrimination along ethnic lines is defended by the law itself, making law-abidingness "the way in which the land is settled."[150] Its ideology is non-aggressive: it is not based on the hatred of others. On the contrary, the language and imagery of its ideology is peaceful, dependent on the character of the particular place. It also has an ameliorative, pacifying effect not only externally, but also internally: its ideology serves to reconcile the social groups and classes within the nation. Its key concept, the rule of law, permits the nation state to establish at least a minimal agreement among the members of the community, encouraging political processes based on consensus. Most importantly, it is a governmental arrangement which makes it possible for the rights of the individual to be respected by the community, a *conditio sine qua non* of lawful coexistence which has been severely damaged by modern totalitarian regimes.

Scruton focuses in this context on two particular advantages provided by the nation state, and in particular by the system of government prevailing in the British Isles: accountability and human rights.[151] His argument is that, ironically, these are virtues celebrated by those who believe in transnational governance, while these very virtues are only actually secured today by nation states. The demand for the accountability of political power is based on the age-old observation, recalled by Lord Acton, that power tends to corrupt. It is only natural that the community needs tools to enforce accountability on its rulers. This is feasible if the legal regime allows the free operation of an opposition, and even beyond that if the citizens are ready and able to defend the institutions of a free press and the rule of law, in general. The nation state offers a political arrangement in which people of diverse, often opposite political views can recognise a common interest—which is to have political institutions which enforce the accountability of whoever is in power. The effectivity of this arrangement is based on the assumption that individuals should remain the sovereign lords of their own lives, and this is provided by the sovereign state, and no other arrangement so far developed has been able to provide it. This is a basic innovation of the Western model, and the counterexamples are many in countries where the idea of the nation state is disregarded, like in Iraq, Syria and in Africa generally.

Yet even within the Western model, there are challenges today to the nation state. While in Africa subnational (tribal and religious) interests disrupt the democratic political process, in Europe a democratic deficit has resulted from the birth of a supra-national entity, the European Union. The fact that this is a supra-national entity makes it impossible to control those exercising power within it, who are basically bureaucrats, as well as their non-elected leaders. Besides the fact that the EU lacks the usual attributes of a national parliament, in which the pro-government parties can be checked by the opposition, it also lacks the participation of the European public, which could express public opinion to enforce the general interest even against those in power. This fact is the reason why corruption, sooner or later, takes over supernational entities, including not only the EU but also the UN, UNESCO, the WHO or the ILO.[152]

The second point of Scruton's criticism of supranational entities concerns the concept of rights. His argument is that individuals can only enjoy rights in regimes which have the means to enforce those rights against its critics. The very notion of universal human rights threatens to tear the notion of rights away from the legal machinery which secured their enforcement. As a pragmatic Englishman, Scruton is rather critical of all the high-flown language of the rights of man, as exemplified by the French Revolution, which was later used against innocent victims. Another egregious example is Communism, which also celebrated general human rights in the abstract, while in practice committing crimes against the population.

Tellingly, says Scruton, it is the nation state that provides for its inhabitants institutions against those in power in that state, if they violate the laws. His example is the Bill of Rights and "the medieval writ of habeas corpus," legal techniques provided by the common law of Britain to enable the ordinary person to find redress against abusers of political power.

This is made possible by the generally accepted axiom of that political regime, which claims that "the entity enforcing the law is also subject to it."[153] Scruton claims that this requirement only holds, so far, within the context of the nation state and in no other regimes, according to the testimony of history. This is because the nation state owes its existence to national loyalty, and therefore there is no guarantee to redress atrocities against human rights beyond this national framework. On the other hand, supranational entities are founded by international treaties whose validity and contents are beyond the ordinary people, who will thus be unable to keep in check the ones empowered by them. This is again an issue which concerns locality: power is beyond reach in supranational entities, while the nation state belongs to a specific territory which is controlled by its rule, and where its inhabitants are settled, who will therefore be able to demand redress from those in power over the territory, as long as the idea of national sovereignty is in use, which renders power legitimate only if it is supported by those who live there. In other words, the nation state remains the last bastion of the rule of law and a potential safeguard over those in power: "The state is accountable to all citizens since it owes its existence to the national loyalty that defines its territory and limits its power."[154]

The Concept of *Oikophilia*

As we have seen, in Scruton's view of patriotism, territory is the defining factor. It is, in fact, the first prerequisite of the rule of law, since law is defined both in the common law and in the Roman-law tradition as applicable to the inhabitants of a certain territory.[155] In this respect, territory can link the theory of the nation state with that of the rule of law, as shown above. Yet it has a further advantage. This theory convincingly refutes the allegation that nationalism is based simply on ethnic identity, in other words on blood relation, a theory of biological exclusivity, which would count in fact as racism. However, the principle of territoriality itself is hotly debated, in an age of global migration, as the effort to turn migration into a human right has shown.

Yet one can hardly deny that there is a natural link between long-term settlement and access to the fruits of the land. This presumption is based on the Lockean idea that a certain territory should be ruled by the local community who invested their work into its cultivation. Under most natural conditions communities can survive in a territory if they cultivate its soil, and through their labour many of their members produce the artefacts necessary for the meaningful life of its inhabitants. Clearly, some territories are contested, and most demarcation lines between neighbouring countries are among these areas. Here again historical rights prevail in most cases, reaffirmed in more straightforward cases by international bilateral or multilateral treaties, and accepted by the international community. However, as the period of imperial expansion by European powers showed, there are circumstances when technically superior civilisations set out to conquer less successfully defended territories. In these cases overwhelming power prevails. In fact, this earlier practice of imperialism on the part of European, and in particular Western nations was also legitimised by theories of lawful conquest. This practice of the system of imperial rule, characterised by control over a territory and its people by the rule of a state which lay far away from the given entity, based on its superior power, is rightly criticised. The fact that any neutral observer can easily agree with the natural injustice of such a situation shows that the presumption prioritising the settled political community's claim on the fruits of the territory is valid. It is on this natural basis that Scruton establishes his concepts of *oikophilia* and its polar opposite of *oikophobia*. Interestingly, however, this had not yet been worked out in his book on national loyalty. Instead, it was to be worked out in a more detailed fashion in his great work on nature conservation, entitled *Green Philosophy*, published in 2012. It is especially significant that one of his most influential political concepts, the idea of *oikophilia*, is to be found in his book on what might be labelled conservative ecology. It is an idea which has a complex meaning, fusing the insights of the modern natural sciences (e.g. the theory of communal adaptation) with conservative insights like that of Burke on the "little platoons" we belong to, or Hegel's account of the role of family and civil society in political communities.

This is Scruton's first description of the term:

> human beings, in their settled condition, are animated by an attitude of *oikophilia*: the love of the *oikos*, which means not only the home but the people contained in it, and the surrounding settlements that endow that home with lasting contours and an enduring smile. The *oikos* is the place that is not just mine and yours but ours.[156]

Evidently, this is an Aristotelian idea. We read in the *Politics*: "The community naturally constituted to satisfy everyday needs, then, is the household; its members are called 'meal-sharers' by Charondas and 'manger-sharers' by Epimenides the Cretan."[157] The quotations used here come from ancient sources, from the sixth and fifth centuries, which proves that Aristotle was in fact voicing an already traditional view, as represented by a legislator and a religious leader. He also refers to Hesiod, quoting from his poem: "First and foremost: a house, a wife, and an ox for the plow."[158] The basic conditions for the human community, marriage, the family and the village, are already present in Aristotle, and these are the terms that were crucial in Scruton's understanding of the love of home as well.

His first description is followed by a long list of artists, novelists, painters, musicians and filmmakers who created works of art which can help us recall the first impressions we preserve from our childhood about our home. Just as Aristotle referred to the poem of Hesiod, so does Scruton refer to Hesiod and Theocritus, as the poets who stand at the head of that kind of European art which pays tribute to our sense of natural belonging. Scruton's language becomes rhetorically charged, rising almost to the point of the poetic, in order to help us sense what he has in mind: the sort of link which connects us to these early experiences of mutual love and support.

Beyond the literary references, he also makes use of the sort of phenomenological analysis which became so crucial for him in the final years of his career, when making sense of the human condition as the basis on which a realistic political philosophy can be founded. It is with the help of the Husserlian terms of a "surrounding world" (*Umwelt*) and a "lifeworld" (*Lebenswelt*) that he explains the vital importance of belonging in human life. He offers a whole set of key terms connected to everyday life, including "house, tool, friend, home, music; the noble, the majestic, the sacred; legality, politeness, justice," which, he claims, do not belong to the natural environment, but more to the interpersonal realm of human beings, the "I-to-I" relationship, without which we cannot give an account of political life.[159] As we shall see later, these terms would be crucial both in Scruton's understanding of the role and function of art in everyday human life, and in his account of metaphysics, based on his interpretation of the concept of the sacred. These terms were first grouped together in the language of phenomenological analysis, like in Max Scheler's work on shame and sympathy, St Edith Stein's thoughts on empathy and Heidegger's discussion of building and dwelling.[160] In particular, it is Heidegger and the tradition he invokes that Scruton relies on, even if he remained rather critical of "the outrageous claims" of his "armchair philosophy."[161] Scruton reinterprets Heidegger's reliance on Hölderlin. In his reading, "Heidegger's philosophy is a philosophy of settlement," based on a theme he finds in Hölderlin's poetry: the famous "turning for home" or *Heimkehr*. Scruton harshly criticises the German philosopher's political judgements, including the one which led him to a personal involvement in the Nazi political movement. Yet Heidegger's analysis of the homeland, or *Heimat* is not connected to his Nazi party membership. Scruton's account of the human attachment also relies on the findings of other phenomenologist and personalist philosophers, such as Scheler or Jonas. What gives depth to that analysis, according to Scruton, is the enlarged temporal scale of human communality, including in a description of it also the "respect for the dead" so characteristic of this kind of thinking. He refers in this context to T.S. Eliot's poem *Burnt Norton*, which explores the notion of personal time, leading Scruton to a reference to the future generation as well: "We come to see that this present moment is also past, but the past of someone else, who has yet to be."[162]

Scruton usually attributes to Burke the insight that there is a connection between the dead, the living and the unborn, but here this is attributed to this phenomenological literature, based on an analysis of German Romantic poetry, including Novalis and his strong sentence quoted by Scruton: "Philosophy is indeed homesickness, a longing above all to be at home."[163] However, this "homeward bound"—our enduring attachment to the place where we were brought up—and to the living and the dead and the unborn there, connected to that place, is not only philosophy's central topic, but also the theme of the great works of religion and art, both European and trans-European, including, according to Scruton, the *Torah* (as in the story of Moses and Abraham or that of the prodigal son), Homer's *Odyssey* and Augustine ("our hearts are restless, until they rest in You"), or even the *Bhagavad Gita*.[164] Scruton's analysis proves that the description of this natural inclination to one's homeland is deeply embedded into European culture and the Judeo-Christian religious tradition.

The attachment to a geographically determined location is based on your emotional fixations: you tend to love those whom you loved and who loved you when you were a child. The concept of the home connects a perception of a geographical location with your memories of all those who were important then. *Oikophilia* thus becomes an attachment to a personalised space, to "the ones you love and need; it is the place that you share, the place that you defend, the place for which you might still be commanded to fight and die."[165]

The conservation movement, the movement to defend our home, both in the form of natural conservation and in historic conservation, should, therefore, be based on *oikophilia*. It should also connect to two human attitudes which are related to each other, according to Scruton: "love of beauty and respect for the sacred."[166] To account for these drives, his first reference is to British and German Romanticism, to the work and thought of Burke, Kant, Rousseau, Schiller and Wordsworth. This is interesting because his favourite poet, T.S. Eliot was, of course, rather critical of the Romantics. Scruton did not favour Romantic art, either. He cites them here, in this train of thought, because in their mind the concept of beauty and the sacred was connected, as expounded by John Ruskin, a late Romantic, a Victorian thinker and art critic beloved by Scruton, who indeed viewed art as a secular religion. To understand *oikophilia*, that almost irrational commitment to a place and its people, it is important to understand that the psychological mechanisms which operate in aesthetic appreciation and in religious devotion are somewhat similar. In both, we attribute a specific, intrinsic value to an object—it is intrinsic because the value we attach to the given object does not depend on its utility and service to us. Scruton also compares this sense of value-attribution, so characteristic of both aesthetic appreciation and devotion to the sacred, to the Aristotelian theme of friendship, because in its highest, most developed form, Aristotelian friendship is also a relationship of "I-to-I," without calculations of its utility, one which cannot be replaced by anyone else. In *oikophilia*, inspired by our love of beauty and devotion to the sacred, we experience this "I-to-I" relationship: our cherished memories of a place have an irreplaceable intrinsic value for us.

By connecting the phenomenon of *oikophilia* to our experience of beauty and the sacred, in the sense that all three attach an intrinsic value to the objects of their devotion and loyalty, Scruton is not implying that this value is purely subjective, or that our sense of *oikophilia* is simply contingent and accidental. On the contrary, applying an understanding of aesthetic judgement, worked out by Hume and Kant, he demonstrates that there are solid, external reasons for such emotional investments. Comparing the high street of European cities and the ordinary American main street, he points out that the former is more often judged to be beautiful, because its growth depended on a kind of aesthetic attention which was lacking in the American case, where simple functionality prevailed over all other aspects, disregarding the intrinsic value of aesthetic beauty.

For Scruton, as Hume and Kant agree, aesthetic judgement has both a subjective and an objective component. The sense of beauty, which we are born with, but which we have to elaborate and refine, is an important component of human nature in this tradition, enabling us to find the beauty in nature, in human behaviour or in the arts. This is because, in the course of our education we learn what is to be appreciated, that is, we learn to interiorise those rules which define what is called beautiful. Even this common stock of knowledge is not arbitrary, however: instead, it is the result of long processes of trial and error, hence the results are in a sense tested. Scruton seems to accept the implication of this Humean and Kantian reference to an objective component in our assessment of beauty: beauty, in this sense, is "in accordance with nature."

If we forget and disrespect beauty, in the words of Milan Kundera, allowing the "uglification" of the world, we disrespect what is given by nature, and we go against the order of the human being's natural and cultural environment. Scruton suggests that we have to furnish our world in a way which harmonises with the natural conditions we encounter, and with our own nature. This is achieved by the typical street of the traditional European city, even if it was not consciously: "the main streets of European cities are the result of meticulous aesthetic decisions over centuries, in which the details aim to harmonise and nothing willingly obtrudes."[167] This order has been preserved because members of the *civitas* regarded themselves as attached to that particular setting and learnt and the local community worked out its conventions in order to live together peacefully: they were "guided by a shared tradition that makes aesthetic judgement central, and which lays down standards that constrain what everybody does."[168] Yet the fact that, when we analyse the beauty of different cities around Europe, we find similar elements of beauty, reveals that they had to take into account external standards as well, which were discovered and observed perhaps in an unreflective manner, by the sense of beauty. In other words, the sense of beauty also has an epistemic function—it helps us understand better both our natural and built environment and ourselves.

Aesthetic appreciation even teaches us something about the metaphysics of our world, as the example of the sacred shows. It also has a moral, or even political significance. Scruton takes the example of good manners. He regards manners as "continuous with aesthetic choices," but importantly, they are "an important example of a self-correcting tradition."[169] Through the manners it develops and which it expects from its members, a society works out and ensures the conditions of peaceful coexistence, by teaching the individual the strategies to cope with the requirements of society and to adapt to the environment. As the early modern literature on the behaviour of the ideal courtier showed, by acquiring the particular habits which our society regards as good manners, we learn the rules to follow, which always allow us a certain degree of freedom in our private sphere, while preserving society in the long run.

In Scruton's conceptual universe, beauty operates in a similar way to manners, "as a coordinating device, whereby individuals can adjust to each other and live on terms."[170] This is a crucial claim, because it suggests that beauty is not simply to be understood as a subjective choice of taste, or a wholly autonomous kind of value, entirely independent of the communal coexistence of human beings. Scruton here distances himself from a simplistic notion of *l'art pour l'art*. His own aesthetics rejects, or rather transcends the Romantic-modernist aesthetic, based as it was on a concept of art as self-expression, stressing the expression of the genius of the artist. For Scruton, the sense of beauty is a social virtue, which allows us to pay tribute "to our common habitat," "one of the instruments in our consensus-building strategies, one of the values through which we construct and belong to a mutually consoling world."[171]

At the same time that Scruton argues in favour of the social relevance of a sense of beauty, and of beauty as the pillar of social coexistence, he also connects it to religious devotion. Take his example of those simple rituals and customs we perform when we lay the table at home before we eat a meal. We follow strict rules, for example demanding symmetry and harmony. We learnt those rules from our parents and grandparents and we teach them to our children and grandchildren. We decorate the table to embellish it, to bestow a specific meaning on it, to mark the meal as a specific social occasion.

Yet these rules are not simply helpful because they turn the individual's existential need to eat and drink into a collective experience of being and acting together. There is "another continuity too, between aesthetic values and piety."[172] The properly laid table expresses the gratitude of the family for the food, and in fact constitutes an invitation for God to grace the event and even to join the family and their guests for this festivity. Think of the grace which religious people pray before they sit down and start eating together. Scruton is able to show that there is an unparalleled intimacy in the way a family celebrates its common meal, and this intimacy has an aesthetico-social and a pious-religious dimension to it. Recall the strictures about what you can and cannot do with bread. This is also related to a religious meaning: in the Christian liturgy the bread is a direct reference to the sacrifice of Christ for humankind. In this manner, beauty and piety are connected, helping us to establish and preserve our basic communities by establishing family rituals and customs. Similarly, *oikophilia* has a rather important, aesthetic, social and devotional dimension, too.

Scruton's efforts to connect the interpersonal, the aesthetic and the pious naturally led him from the intimate space of the family, its home, to the Aristotelian notions of the dwelling of the larger community of families, the village and the city, in other words, to the human settlement or habitat. The love of home applies not only to the individual home, the house, but also to the communal home, the settlement. As we make great efforts to embellish our daily family practices, so too a community is held together with the help of customs, rules and rituals which have an aesthetic, and often even a religious dimension. Obviously, to allow many people to live together in a confined area, very well-defined rules are needed. We can deduct from the visual pleasure of the cityscapes of such ancient cities as Rome, Siena and Istanbul, that the rules followed by the citizens of those cities also had an implicit aesthetic dimension. Importantly, these aesthetic demands—which are the demands of the community on each and every individual for the common good—are not imposed by the will of an individual power holder, an omniscient legislator. Instead, they emerge through the trial-and-error processes of long ages past, through the coordinated efforts of generations of citizens held together in a community.

Scruton was well aware of the work of urban theorists like Jane Jacobs, James Howard Kunstler, Lewis Mumford and the theorists of the New Urbanist Movement.[173] He quotes the great work by Mumford in which he refers to "the tightly packed and field-surrounded medieval city as his ideal."[174] This form of settlement was much more concentrated, and its beauty derived from the fact that its builders had to confront spatial constraints which are irrelevant for the planners of American cities. The defensive stone walls which encircle the medieval European city had strategic functions at a time of constant struggles between the city and its environment: they defended its inhabitants from unwanted invasion. Structurally, though, the walls of the medieval cities functioned like the frames of pictures: they encapsulated the whole city, and defined the whole. In America, the cities never experienced a similar threat, which accounts for the cult of the suburb (which would be the territory outside the walls in Europe) there, which has no well-defined end or limit, sprawling unchecked across the countryside, creating a grey, interim zone, which is neither an urban texture nor an undisturbed natural environment.

The distinction between the urban texture and the natural environment was made more pronounced by the New Urbanist movement. The key individual experiment in this regard is Léon Krier's and the Prince of Wales's conceptual urban quarter, Poundbury, in Dorset, England, a new quarter formed as an extension on the outskirts of the historic market town of Dorchester. The architect and urban theorist Leon Krier proposes the idea of the polycentric city. If people wish to move out from the urban centre, let them establish new urban centres, with all the major functions made available within an easily walkable distance. Only in this way can the inhabitants of a newly established settlement experience "the human community in a place that is 'ours', rather than individual plots scattered over a place that is no one's."[175] This is the essence of a lesson learnt from the historical precedents in Europe. London and the city of Westminster grew side by side until they were united, while the quarters of Chelsea, Kensington and Bloomsbury even today function as autonomous villages rather than suburbs around the city of London. To achieve this pattern of urban growth, what is required is less a voluntarist giga plan, created by a kind of planning superego, which marks out different urban functions on the map, and allows the functionally distinguished parts to grow like urban tumours, and more a "set of aesthetic constraints," which helps people, individuals and local communities alike to make the most suitable choices for their settlement's development.[176]

Once again, we arrive back to Scruton's major message that architecture and urban development prove that aesthetic norms are not for their own sake, but serve public functions. Aesthetic order and social order are visibly connected in the classical Western city, as described by Scruton's and Krier's theoretical texts. Roger Scruton had the opportunity in the last year of his life, as the chair, and later co-chair of the "Building Better, Building Beautiful" commission to translate these insights into practical advice on how to transform the legal regulations of urban development in Britain, in order to ensure that enough attention is paid to aesthetic concerns. The proposals of this independent commission, published at the time of Scruton's death, were phrased to be directly applicable by the British government.[177]

That a philosopher were offered such a public role, had its prehistory. The connection between aesthetic demands and the demand to turn human settlements into common homes had been promoted for a long time in the various natural and historical conservation movements in

Britain and the Western world, generally. In a chapter entitled "Begetting Somewhere" Scruton reviews the history of these movements, mainly in Britain but also considering major developments elsewhere in the West.

What Scruton sought, in both the urban and the natural context, is *homeostasis*, the ability of an urban texture to self-correct in response to destabilising change, and through that, to acquire resilience. His point is that the dynamic balance which guarantees long-term sustainability requires the existence of local affections, the sort of attachment human beings are able to feel for their settlement—their *oikos*—both as a built environment and as a natural landscape, together with a love of those who inhabit the place. This sense of attachment can be awakened and preserved by a sense of beauty, an aesthetic sensibility.

To prove this he points to the historical panorama depicted by Sir Keith Thomas, among others, and the historico-theoretical summary of Simon Schama.[178] He collects a convincing set of examples to show that modernity, in particular in the twentieth century, "the glory days of *oiko-phobia*," caused tremendous destruction both to the landscape and to the urban fabric.[179] He also points out that there is still a way back, if we turn towards those local attachments which are cherished all around our countries in the "little platoons," of "clubs, societies, sports leagues, churches, reading circles, pubs."[180] This new "sentimental education" should once again place beauty at the centre of our value system, and take seriously the established correspondence between the norms of beauty and well-functioning homeostatic systems.

Scruton suggests we learn from the counterexample of the devastating social and aesthetic effects of the state-controlled economy and urban planning in socialist Eastern Europe. He also stressed to appreciate that the social basis of sustainable development is to be found in the autonomous associations of civil society, so memorably lauded in the nineteenth-century American context by Tocqueville, and once again put on the agenda by Robert Putnam's analysis of the real social capital of contemporary Western society.[181] In accordance with the usual interpretation of British conservatism, Scruton connects Tocqueville's focus to the stream of eighteenth-century thought represented by Hume, Smith and Burke, labelling it "intellectual conservatism." According to Scruton, the Burkean tradition of attributing such a great significance to the "little platoons" makes sense in the context of the British tradition, as opposed to the state-centred notion of conservatism characteristic of Continental conservatism. Burke famously wrote:

> To be attached to the subdivision, to love the little platoon we belong to in society, is the first principle (the germ, as it were) of public affections. It is the first link in the series by which we proceed towards a love to our country and to mankind.[182]

This passage draws attention to the relevance of civil activity, independently of state, government and institutionalised politics. Yet it is obvious that Burke, who had his own political experience, did not mean to contrast civil association with the operation of the state which would substantiate the distinction between a British as opposed to a Continental understanding of the relationship of civil society and state. In fact, Burke connects the little platoons with the birth of "a love to our country," linking local patriotism and patriotism. For this reason, Scruton can claim that similar ideas also emerged on the continent, in the writings of de Maistre and Hegel, thus building a bridge from Burke to Tocqueville.[183] He applies the Hegelian dialectic of family, civil society (*bürgerliche Gesellschaft*) and state, arriving at a version of the famous Böckenförde dilemma. Böckenförde, a judge of the German Federal constitutional court, famously asked how future generations of citizens could continue to be actively engaged in common affairs, in a liberal state which should not involve itself in the private affairs of its citizens.[184] Scruton succeeds in connecting the British and the German medieval and early modern traditions of civil association, the "gatherings of people that exist for the sake of membership… conducting their affairs without interference from the state, and usually without the desire for political prominence."[185] He repeatedly emphasises that this is important for conservatives, because this is the guarantee of the renewal of society, independently of any state control. At the same time, one should be aware that the notion of civil association, a term used by Oakeshott, for example, does not allow absolute freedom; in fact, it requires obedience to the laws. In that sense, too, what is civil is also political.

The state-controlled soviet system, on the other hand, aimed to destroy the little platoons inherited from the past, and in fact went in the same direction as that diagnosed by Robert Putnam, whose analysis is repeatedly cited by Scruton. In Scruton's view, Putnam shows that the basis of *oikophilia* can be reconstructed even if it has been deliberately demolished, and that the Western world needs to attend to this, allowing the space for the rebirth of voluntary civil associations. A prime example in this respect is the Town and Country Planning Act of 1946. The success of the Act in defending smaller settlements (small cities and villages) depended on its trust in local governance and civil associations. The aim, therefore, was to increase the scope for civil society—as distinguished from lobby groups and ideology-driven NGOs—to relearn their lessons, in order to become able to judge urban developments, and in this way to acquire a sense of place and belonging. The conclusion is that right judgements in urban matters depend on connecting aesthetic issues with the love of one's local community. Britain, through its conservation movements, achieved unparalleled, even though still limited success in the twentieth century in defending traditional beauty both in the built and in the natural environment. While this is of the utmost importance politically for a conservative like Scruton, it is also important for our present topic, as it directs our attention to the immediate link between *oikophilia* and a common enterprise of aesthetic education, built on the human ability to enjoy, both individually and collectively, what is beautiful in our natural and built environment. This typical Scrutonian theme will be the topic of the next chapter.

Notes

1. Scruton, *Gentle Regrets*, 51.
2. Andrew Roberts, *Salisbury: Victorian Titan* (London: Faber & Faber, 2012), 328.
3. Scruton and Dooley, *Conversations*, 47.
4. Roger Scruton, *About the Salisbury Review*, available at: https://www.salisburyreview.com/about/.
5. Scruton and Dooley, *Conversations*, 54–5.

6. Scruton, *Gentle Regrets*, 52.

7. Natives of what are today called the V4 countries (Poland, Czechia, Slovakia and Hungary) usually dislike the denomination Eastern Europe being applied to their native country, as they regard themselves to belong to what is called Central Europe, or *Mitteleuropa*. For a famous article on the issues of the relationship between Central Europe and the West, see Milan Kundera, "The Tragedy of Central Europe," trans. from the French by Edmund White, 1 *New York Review of Books* 31, no. 7 (April 26, 1984).

8. Nicholas Hills, "Oxford dons battle Czech secret police," *The Montreal Gazette* (4 June 1980): 77.

9. Scruton and Dooley, *Conversations*, 73.

10. John Stuart Mill, *The Philosophy of John Stuart Mill: Ethical, Political and Religious*, ed. Marshall Cohen (New York: Modern Library, 1961), xxxiii/xxxiv.

11. Roger Scruton, *The Meaning of Conservatism* (London: Macmillan, 1980, 2nd edition, 1984), 10. I will use the page numbers of this edition.

12. All the quotes about dogma are from: Scruton, *The Meaning*, 11–13.

13. I am grateful to Robert Grant for these references.

14. I will summarise the Hegelian account of the hierarchy of human sociality with the help of the Hegel entry of the Stanford Encyclopedia of Philosophy: Paul Redding, "Georg Wilhelm Friedrich Hegel," *The Stanford Encyclopedia of Philosophy* (Winter 2020 Edition), Edward N. Zalta (ed.), URL = https://plato.stanford.edu/archives/win2020/entries/hegel/.

15. As Robert Grant reminded me, even in the realm of civil society, individuals also compete for the benefit of their families, and not simply for their own personal benefit. This is a difference of scale, between close, personal ties, and the relationship between the citizens.

16. For a more detailed account of the relevance of the Hegelian triad for Scruton, see: Paul T. Wilford, "Das Geistige Tier: Roger Scruton's Recovery of Hegel," *Perspectives on Political Science* 50, no. 2 (2021): 119–37, DOI: 10.1080/10457097.2020.1854015. It is worth noting that Charles Taylor played a major role in the renaissance of Hegelian scholarship, and in revealing its relevance for political philosophy. His monograph on Hegel was published in 1975 by Cambridge University Press. Scruton had a critical view of Taylor yet held him in high regard.

17. One should not forget about the lack of personal knowledge of the others in the case of one's love of one's country, which distinguishes this form of love from the love of friends or family members, based on close personal acquaintance.
18. This claim does not mean that the ruler's personal elements will not have an effect on the loyalty of the subjects—yet that effect is more of a sociological matter, and up to a certain point not a constitutional issue.
19. Scruton. *The Meaning*, 94–118.
20. Scruton adds here that utilitarianism, too, has a third-person perspective on human action.
21. Scruton and Dooley, *Conversations*, 142.
22. Roger Scruton, *A Political Philosophy: Arguments for Conservatism* (London, etc.: Bloomsbury, 2006), vii.
23. Ibid., viii.
24. Ibid., ix.
25. Ibid., 7.
26. Scruton refers to Fukuyama's famous book on trust: Francis Fukuyama, *Trust: The Social Virtues and the Creation of Prosperity* (New York: Free Press, 1995).
27. Scruton, *A Political Philosophy*, 8.
28. Ibid., 39.
29. Scruton certainly agreed with Oakeshott that this common cause of maintaining order does not require further common purposes—see Oakeshott's distinction of enterprise and civil associations. Once again, I am grateful to Robert Grant for this point.
30. He refers to it on p. 35. of *A Political Philosophy*.
31. Roger Scruton, *The Need for Nations* (London: Civitas: Institute for the Study of Civil Society, 2004), Roger Scruton, *England: an Elegy* (London: Chatto and Windus, 2000).
32. Scruton refers here to the historical overview of John Witte, *From Sacrament to Contract: Marriage, Religion and Law in the Western Tradition* (Louisville, KY: Westminster/John Knox Press, 1997).
33. Scruton, *A Political Philosophy*, 87, quoting paragraph 161 of Hegel's *Elements of the Philosophy of Right*.
34. Scruton, *A Political Philosophy*, 87.
35. Ibid., 88.
36. Roger Scruton, *Sexual Desire. A Philosophical Investigation* (London: Weidenfeld and Nicolson, 1986).

37. Scruton, *A Political Philosophy*, 95.
38. Ibid., 122.
39. To be sure, the exact mechanism how more communal violence can liberate the community from its own guilt is not fully explained.
40. Which does not mean, of course, that there would be no resentment in the latter, either.
41. Hannah Arendt, *The Origins of Totalitarianism* (originally published Berlin: Schocken Books, 1951).
42. Significantly, Scrtuton was not a strong voice in the pro-Brexit campaign.
43. Scruton, *A Political Philosophy*, 191.
44. T.S. Eliot, *For Lancelot Andrewes* (1928)
45. Scruton, *A Political Philosophy*, 194.
46. As a British thinker, Scruton does not pay, perhaps, enough attention to the fact that in the shadow of the Holocaust, both modern and late-modern conservatism have to make all effort, to detach themselves from any form of anti-semitism, a frame of mind which characterised historically, and keeps returning in the far Right. Scruton himself was also alleged to make anti-semitic remarks; these allegations, however, did not find evidence. His response to this charge, and a defence of free, uncensored discussion, is found in: Roger Scruton, "An Apology for Thinking," *The Spectator* (11 April 2019), available at: https://www.roger-scruton.com/articles/590-an-apology-for-thinking-11-april-19-the-spectator. After the debate which caused the government to withdraw Scruton from the position of the chair of a government position, the magazine, *New Statesman*, which published the allegation, apologised, and Scruton was reinvited as co-chair of the commission.
47. Scruton, *A Political Philosophy*, 196.
48. T. S. Eliot, "East Coker", *Four Quartets* (London: Faber and Faber, 1943), 182.
49. Scruton, *A Political Philosophy*, 204.
50. Ibid., 205.
51. T. S. Eliot, "Little Gidding," *Four Quartets*.
52. Ibid.
53. Scruton, *A Political Philosophy*, 208.
54. Ibid., 208.
55. Robert Grant tells me that Blair's successor, Gordon Brown went as far as to summon Scruton to give him political advice.

56. It is remarkable that three of Scruton's friends are also mentioned by name: Bob Grant, Alicja Gescinska and Sam Hughes, thus underlining that beyond the family circle Scruton had gathered by then an intimate circle of friends and allies, including, I am told, Robin Holloway, Marek Matraszek, David Wiggins, David Matthews.

57. Roger Scruton, *How to Be a Conservative* (London, etc.: Bloomsbury Continuum, 2014, 2019), ix.

58. Ibid., 173–84.

59. Scruton, *England* .

60. Scruton, *How to Be a Conservative*, vii.

61. He refers to a rather recent book in this context, Anthony Gregory, *The Power of Habeas Corpus in America* (Cambridge: Cambridge University Press, 2019), which explains the medieval legal historical tradition of the writ of habeas corpus, allegedly a specifically English invention, as the basis of American freedom.

62. I am grateful to Robert Grant for calling my attention to this personal connection to Baron Glasman.

63. Scruton, *How to Be a Conservative*, viii.

64. Neil Gross, *Why Are Professors Liberal and Why Do Conservatives Care?* (Cambridge MA: Harvard University Press, 2013); Neil Gross and Solon Simmons, eds., *Professors and Their Politics* (Baltimore: Johns Hopkins University Press, 2014).

65. Scruton, *How to Be a Conservative*, 1.

66. He identifies the mental landscape of his father with that painted of the English working class by George Orwell in *The Lion and the Unicorn*.

67. Scruton, *How to be a Conservative*, 6.

68. As Margaret Thatcher famously put it in an interview: "There is no such thing as society. There is living tapestry of men and women and people and the beauty of that tapestry and the quality of our lives will depend upon how much each of us is prepared to take responsibility for ourselves and each of us prepared to turn round and help by our own efforts those who are unfortunate." Douglas Keay, "Aids, education and the year 2000," *Woman's Own* (31 October 1987): 8–10, available at: https://www.margaretthatcher.org/document/106689.

The interview caused a large uproar, so No. 10 had to issue an explanation in the *Sunday Times* on 10 July 1988: "But society as such does not exist except as a concept. Society is made up of people. It is people who have duties and beliefs and resolve. It is people who get things done. She prefers to think in terms of the acts of individuals and families as the real sinews of society rather than of society as an abstract concept." Available as above.

69. Roger Scruton, *Notes from the Underground, a novel* (New York: Beaufort Books, 2014).
70. Scruton, *How to be a Conservative*, 25.
71. Ibid., 29.
72. Roger Scruton, *Philosopher on Dover Beach* (Southbend: St Augustine's Press, 1998).
73. Scruton, *How to be a Conservative*, 119.
74. Interestingly, the great criticism of leftist totalitarianism, Orwell's 1984 was also finished in the same year, 1948.
75. Pieper's *Leisure, the Basis of Culture* was originally published in German in 1948. T.S. Eliot wrote the introduction to its English translation, which appeared in 1952. Josef Pieper, *Leisure, the Basis of Culture*, trans. Alexander Dru, with an intr. T. S. Eliot (London: Faber and Faber, 1952).
76. Scruton, *How to be a Conservative*, 148.
77. One should not forget, however, that recognition can be accompanied by vulnerability to others.
78. Adam Schaff, *Alienation as a Social Phenomenon* (Oxford: Pergamon Press, 1980).
79. Although Taylor is not explicitly mentioned here, it is worth noting the conversation between Taylor and Scruton in "Roger Scruton and Charles Taylor on the Sacred and the Secular," in Bryson, *The Religious Philosophy of Roger Scruton*, 239–52.
80. Charles Taylor, "The Politics of Recognition," in *Multiculturalism: Examining the Politics of Recognition*, ed. Amy Gutmann (Princeton: Princeton University Press, 1994), 25–73.
81. Scruton, *How to be a Conservative*, 150.
82. Ibid., 159, referring to: T. S. Eliot, *On the Use of Poetry and the Use of Criticism* (London: Faber, 1933).
83. Arthur Danto, *The Abuse of Beauty* (Chicago and La Salle: Open Court, 2003).
84. Scruton, *How to be a Conservative*, 182.
85. Ibid., 184. The translation in *Will to Power* of this paragraph (822) by Kaufmann and Hollingdale is: "We possess art lest we perish of the truth." Friedrich Nietzsche, *The Will to Power*, trans. Walter Kaufmann and R. J. Hollingdale (New York: Vintage Books, 1967), 435. One

should also recall the fact that the Romantics attributed to art the knowledge of a superior truth.

86. Roger Scruton, *Conservatism: An Invitation to the Great Tradition* (New York: All Points Books, Horsell's Morsels Ltd, 2017).

87. He did not experience the socially disastrous effects of the Covid restrictions we ourselves have experienced lately.

88. One should note, however, the longstanding distinction between patriotism and nationalism, a distinction which is there, in Renan as much as in John Lukacs.

89. Scruton, *Conservatism*, 12.

90. Ibid., 33. It should be noted that Burke supported the American cause.

91. Ibid., 35.

92. Ibid., 46.

93. Ibid., 57.

94. *The Phenomenology of Spirit*, chapter 4, part 1. Hegel's expressions for these terms are: *Herrschaft* and *Knechtschaft*.

95. Scruton, *Conservatism*, 64–5.

96. Ibid., 70.

97. Ibid., 73.

98. Ibid., 94.

99. Ibid., 99.

100. It is worth recalling Hayek's famous self-identification, in the style of Edmund Burke, who never became a Tory himself: "The more I learn about the evolution of ideas, the more I have become aware that I am simply an unrepentant Old Whig—with the stress on the 'old'." F. A. Hayek, "Postscript, Why I Am Not a Conservative," in Hayek, *The Constitution of Liberty*, The Definitive Edition, ed. Ronald Hamowy (Chicago: The University of Chicago Press, 1960, 2011), 519–35, 531.

101. Scruton, *Conservatism*, 108, 111.

102. Ibid., 114–15.

103. Ibid., 115.

104. Allan Bloom, *Giants and Dwarfs: Essays 1960–1990* (New York: Simon & Schuster, 1990), 17–18.

105. Scruton, *Conservatism*, 130–1.

106. Roger Scruton, "Maurice Cowling's Achievement," *Open Democracy* (25 August, 2005), downloaded March, 2021 at https://www.opendemocracy.net/en/2783/.

107. Scruton, *Conservatism*, 134–5.

108. Ibid., 149.

109. For an overview of this position, see Yoram Hazony, *The Virtue of Nationalism* (New York: Basic Books, 2018).

110. See *The Oxford Handbook of the Elegy*, ed. Karen Weisman (Oxford: Oxford University Press, 2010). It has an entry specifically on ancient Greek elegy, Gregory Nagy, "Ancient Greek elegy" in Weisman, *The Oxford Handbook of the Elegy*, 13–45.

111. This famous quotation is from the end of the Preface of Hegel's *Elements of the Philosophy of Right* (1820).

112. Scruton, *England* , vii.

113. Ibid., ix.

114. This is the title of chapter eleven. See p. 244.

115. Both of the above quotations are from *England: An Elegy*, 65.

116. Ibid.

117. Ibid., 66.

118. Ibid.

119. Ibid., 157.

120. David Cannadine, *The Decline and Fall of the British Aristocracy* (New Haven, Yale University Press, 1990).

121. Scruton, *England*, 158.

122. Ibid., 158, quoting J. H. Newman, "Knowledge and Religious Duty," in *The Idea of a University* (London, 1852).

123. Scruton, *England*, 159. This is, by the way, the novel of which Scott Fitzgerald said: "I'd rather have written Nostromo than any other novel." Ian Watt, *Conrad: Nostromo* (Landmarks of World Literature) (Cambridge: Cambridge UP, 1988), 1.

124. Karel Čapek, *Letters from England* (1924), 172, quoted by Scruton, *England*, 158.

125. Scruton, *England*, 158.

126. Ibid., 159.

127. Ibid., 206.

128. Ibid., 206–7.

129. Ibid., 211.

130. Shakespeare, *Richard II*, Act II, Scene I.

131. Robert Rowthorn, "Foreword," in Scruton, *Need for Nations*.

132. Maurizio Viroli, *For Love of Country: An Essay on Patriotism and Nationalism* (Oxford, Oxford University Press, 1995).

133. J. S. Mill, *A System of Logic*, 10th edition (London, 1879), vol 2. 522.
134. Scruton, *Need for Nations*, 12.
135. Ibid., 11.
136. Ibid.
137. Ibid.
138. He takes the term from Spengler, and explains the idea in a more detailed fashion in his book: *The West and the Rest: Globalization and the Terrorist Threat* (Wilmington DE: ISI Books, 2002).
139. Ibid.
140. Ibid.
141. Scruton refers here, in this connection, not so much to the history of Christianity, which was eventually able to tackle the problem with the separation of church and state, but to Islamic history, which witnesses a proliferation of internal and external conflicts between rival religious groups, due to credal differences. Within that framework these conflicts seem to be impossible to resolve.
142. Scruton, *Need for Nations*, 12.
143. Ibid., 19.
144. Ibid., 19.
145. Ibid.
146. Linda Colley, *Britons: Forging the Nation, 1707–1837* (New Haven and London: Yale University Press, 1992). Characteristically, Scruton adds that this thesis was prefigured in Hilaire Belloc's *History of England* (London, 1915).
147. Scruton, *Need for Nations*, 21.
148. Ibid., 28.
149. Hazony, *The Virtue of Nationalism*.
150. Scruton, *Need for Nations*, 22.
151. Ibid., 23.
152. Scruton cites at this point examples of secondary literature about these mechanisms of corruption experienced in supranational entities.
153. Scruton, *Need for Nations*, 25.
154. Ibid., 28.
155. In this respect the American legal system is somewhat different: it does not exclude jurisdiction over issues arising outside of the realm of the territory of the state, in other words extraterritorial jurisdiction.
156. Roger Scruton, *Green Philosophy: How to Think Seriously About the Planet* (London: Atlantic Books, 2012), 227.

157. Aristotle, *Politics*, Book 1, Chapter 2., 1252b12–14.
158. Ibid., 1252b10–11. Hesiod's quote is from *Works and Days* 405.
159. Scruton, *Green Philosophy*, 229.
160. Ibid.
161. Ibid., 232–3.
162. Ibid., 235.
163. Novalis, *Das allgemeine brouillon, Materialien zur Enzyklopädistik* (1798/99), No. 857.
164. Scruton, *Green Philosophy*, 238.
165. Ibid., 239.
166. Ibid., 253.
167. Ibid., 259.
168. Ibid., 260.
169. Ibid., 261.
170. Ibid.
171. Ibid., 262.
172. Ibid., 263.
173. He explicitly refers to Jane Jacob, *The Death and Life of Great American Cities* (New York: Random House, 1961), James Howard Kunstler, *The Geography of Nowhere: The Rise and Decline of America's Man-Made Landscape* (New York: Simon and Schuster, 1993), Lewis Mumford, *The City in History* (London: Martin Secker & Warburg Ltd., 1961) and, of the representatives of the New Urbanist Movement he mentions Christopher Alexander, *The Nature of Order* (Berkely: Center for Environmental Structure, 2002), and Nikos Salingaros, *A Theory of Architecture* (Solingen: Umbau Verlag, 2006). It is also relevant for us that he refers to his own two books of aesthetic theory as his own contribution to the New Urbanist Movement.
174. Scruton, *Green Philosophy*, 269.
175. Scruton, *Green Philosophy*, 272. For a more detailed account of the Poundbury experiment, see the present writer's study: Ferenc Hörcher, "A léptékhelyes város dicsérete. A herceg, az építész és a filozófus beszélgetése," *Magyar Építőművészet* 20, no. 114 (2020): 63–9.
176. See Léon Krier et al., *The Architecture of Community* (Washington DC: Island Press, 2009).
177. *Living with Beauty. Promoting health, well-being and sustainable growth., The report of the Building Better Building Beautiful Commission*, January, 2020. Available at: https://assets.publishing.service.gov.uk/govern-

ment/uploads/system/uploads/attachment_data/file/861832/Living_
with_beauty_BBBBC_report.pdf. Part One of the report includes
chapters with the following titles: "Ask for beauty", "How do we want
to live?", "What should be done?".

178. Sir Keith Thomas, *Man and the Natural World: Changing Attitudes in
England, 1500–1800* (Harmondsworth: Allen Lane, 1983). Simon
Schama, *Landscape and Memory* (New York: Alfred Knopf, 1994).

179. Scruton, *Green Philosophy*, 350.

180. Ibid., 365.

181. Scruton refers to Alexis de Tocqueville, *Democracy in America* (originally published in 1835 and 1840), vol. 2, par 2, ch. 7. on p. 170,
n186. He also makes repeated references to Robert Putnam, *Bowling
Alone: The Collapse and Revival of American Community* (New York:
Simon and Schuster, 2000), who also took Tocqueville as his starting
point, diagnosing the disaster of civil society and advocating support
for its renaissance.

182. Edmund Burke, *Reflections on the Revolution in France* (1790), ed. with
intr. and notes by J.G.A. Pocock (Indianapolis, Cambridge: Hackett
Publishing Company, 1987), 41.

183. Scruton, *Green Philosophy*, 27.

184. "The liberal (German "*freiheitlich*"), [1] secularised state lives by pre-
requisites which it cannot guarantee itself. This is the great adventure it
has undertaken for freedom's sake. As a liberal state it can endure only
if the freedom it bestows on its citizens takes some regulation from the
interior, both from a moral substance of the individuals and a certain
homogeneity of society at large." Ernst-Wolfgang Böckenförde, *Staat,
Gesellschaft, Freiheit* (Berlin: Suhrkamp, 1976), 60. On the importance
of the Böckenförde-dilemma, see Ferenc Hörcher, "Prepolitical Values?
Böckenförde, Habermas and Ratzinger and the use of the Humanities
in Constitutional Interpretation" in Hörcher, *A bölcsészet-tudományok
hasznáról/Of the Usefulness of the Humanities* (Budapest: L'Harmattan,
2014), 87–101.

185. Scruton, *Green Philosophy*, 27.

4

The Theory of Art and Culture

While most of his readers have no problem classifying Scruton as a political philosopher of a conservative persuasion, his genuine interest in art is less well known to the general reader. It is therefore worth emphasising that his frame of mind can be better understood as fundamentally that of a philosopher of art and a cultural critic, while his conservatism is, in a way, only a side product, partly determined by his views on art (particularly on beauty) and on culture, and partly by his own political experiences in Paris, Central Europe and elsewhere. This thesis might seem to be somewhat courageous at first sight, given the political attacks against him during his life as a result of his conservative political views. However, the present summary of his thought is built on the assumption that his primary interest lay, in fact, in the arts and culture, while political philosophy was only of secondary importance to him.

Ecology, as we saw, with *oikophilia*, the love of place at its centre, is in fact a bridge which connects his political thought with his views on art and culture. His message was that to conserve nature we need a (self) education which enables us to acquire a sense of local beauty, either in the natural or in the architectural environment. He traced how the most important movements in Britain and the US to preserve nature and the historic urban environment were based on the special significance

F. Hörcher, *Art and Politics in Roger Scruton's Conservative Philosophy*, Palgrave Studies in Classical Liberalism, https://doi.org/10.1007/978-3-031-13591-0_4

attributed to beauty, or in general, to aesthetic value, as a sign of what is good and worth preserving in both the natural and the built environment.

By revealing the common ground in our perception in the fields of natural and historic conservation Scruton showed how a sense of beauty can help us to connect nature and culture, the natural and the built environment.

This chapter will concentrate on his views on art and culture, never forgetting the fact that for Scruton, all these endeavours had political implications. This is all the more interesting given the fact that, as a Kantian, he is ready to accept the autonomy of aesthetic judgement. In what follows I will start out from his theory of culture, progressing to his general aesthetics, and finally examining his particular views on architecture and music.

The Theory of Culture

That culture lies at the centre of Scruton's views was established earlier with reference to the influence of the literary critic F.R. Leavis on his thought. I argued above that in his account of the rule and function of art and culture Scruton remains a Leavisite, even if he is aware of the distance separating their respective views on politics. To be sure, as we have seen, his advanced conservative position was the result of a long intellectual journey. His Cambridge years started with a genuine interest in natural science, followed by a turn towards (analytical) philosophy, and arriving at a conservative position, with a special focus on art and culture—before turning towards religion and the sacred in the last years of his life. One could, in fact, conceptually distinguish a philosophical, a cultural and a metaphysical phase in the direction of his thought.

As all his autobiographical recollections made clear, culture became crucial for the young Scruton as a strategy to handle his discomfort at home, but partly also to make sense of the world in the sensitive years of his adolescence. He turned particularly to books and music to find consolation in those years. This interest in art, which apparently remained crucial for him ever after, explains his genuine interest in Leavis, and the role of the cultural critic more generally. Leavis was his first idol in cultural theory, and he remained loyal to him—lifting him into his pantheon of cultural conservatism, as pointed out above.

While Scruton continued to publish various collection of essays on culture throughout his life, no doubt at the invitation of different publishers, we shall concentrate here on two of these selections. The first one bears the title *Modern Culture*, and was published in 1998, with further editions in 2000 and 2005.[1] As the title suggests, this collection aimed to offer an overall account of his view of contemporary culture. The second collection of essays, *Culture Counts*, was first published in 2007, with a second edition appearing in 2018.[2] This volume mounts a defence of high culture, "in a world besieged." I will not attempt to convey the full richness and every nuance of these books.[3] Instead, I will try to assess Scruton's general views on culture and its role in human life, specifically in the late modern conditions of his own, Western cultural context.

Achieving this aim is made easier by the fact that both of these collections start with a chapter which addresses the very same question: What is culture?[4] This is Scruton, the analytical philosopher: before embarking on a certain topic one needs to define and delineate it. Moreover, if both books, published nine years' apart, start with the same, definitional problem, it might be a sign that Scruton felt that the results of the first effort were not wholly satisfactory. In what follows I show how his ideas of culture evolved by first analysing his account of it in the earlier work, then seeing how it was reconceptualised in his second essay on the topic.

Modern Culture (1998)

The book *Modern Culture* takes as its epigraph a telling line from Larkin's poem *Church Going*: "What remains when disbelief is gone?"[5] While clearly a pessimistic poem, it is still one which preserves something of Eliot's influence. Written in 1954, when Eliot was still alive, and Scruton only 10 years old, Larkin's poem describes a visit to "another Church" in the countryside. The poem is, in fact, a testimony to English culture, as it was perceived for centuries, but found dead after the Second World War. The poet's public persona had much in common with Scruton: cultured and intelligent, not accepted by his profession, pessimistic and highly critical, conservative in his inclinations, an admirer of church architecture and fond of music, and even decades after his early death he numbered among the most popular post-war British poets. Yet Scruton does not make more detailed reference to Larkin in this book, and the poet's name does not feature in the index of the book. So why is this half line the motto of the book?

The essay itself presents two paradigms of the concept of culture originating from German philosophy. While Herder's concept, adopted by the Romantics, regarded culture as "the defining essence of a nation, a shared spiritual force," the idea of culture proposed by Wilhelm von Humboldt, that of high culture, is a culture shared by a European or Western elite.[6] While the philosopher does not deny the relevance of such "common culture," the version attributed to Herder and the anthropologists, his references to some of the most influential English critics, namely Arnold, Eliot and Leavis in connection with high culture shows that he is specifically interested in the Humboldtian concept. This lies behind his admission that "as an educated person I sympathise with Humboldt and Matthew Arnold."[7] This is, in fact, a defence of an elitist tradition which was rejected by modern thinkers, and to a large extent destroyed with the emergence of cultural studies.[8] Williams is presented here as the founder that new discipline, an approach to culture which Scruton does not want to follow. Yet Scruton's own elitist sympathies are themselves moderated by his acceptance of a further logical step, which identifies a common root behind both elite and common culture. He first admits that "(a)s an old-fashioned Englishman I lean towards Herder," and then he arrives at the main point of the essay where he identifies at least one of his reasons for writing the book: "One of my motives for writing this book is a sense that these two sympathies are fed from a common source."[9]

It is at this point in Scruton's argumentation that Larkin features prominently. In the second essay, after this first, introductory one, Scruton tries to substantiate the rather bold claim he had made in the preface, and with which he starts the second essay. Its title *Culture and Cult*—referring to the etymological connection between the two words—is a fitting one. His bold claim is that: "The core of common culture is religion."[10] The boldness of this claim derives from the fact that it is declared in the context of an emphatically secular age. By now, religion had lost all its credibility and relevance in public life. In his second essay, Scruton presents an anthropological account of the way religion contributes to the survival of the community, or the tribe, as he calls it here. What he offers in five steps is an anthropological account of a pattern which is there in Hellenic, Judaic and Christian teachings alike, of communal devotion, consisting of a ritual and a sacrifice. He does not mention it directly here, but in later works he admits that his theory of communal rites is rooted in the theory of René Girard. According to the French thinker's account of the birth of culture from cult, the first step is an affirmation of communal belonging by a congregation at the shrine, which is the spatial focus of the community's dwelling. It is there that the individual feels encouraged to admit the experience of pollution. This might stem from a sense of moral guilt, but not necessarily, as it can simply be the "original sin," which is inherent in human nature, or it can be caused by the mimetic desire. To cleanse oneself of the pollution, the individual must make an act of sacrifice, an offer to the God(s) of something valuable. This offer becomes a custom, in other words something which the community takes care of. In the act of offering a sacrifice, the object of the sacrifice turns into something holy, in accordance with the commands of the ancestors, who demand sacrifice from the individual. The final act in the ritual is a reversal: the sacrifice offered, that is, the killing of the victim, turns into a sacrament in a miraculous fashion, which has the effect of purifying the individual, thus helping the individual find his way back to the community, and in this way also reaffirming and reintegrating the community itself.

All these communal rites are repeated in a cyclical manner, in accordance with the rhythm of nature and of human life, but also in accordance with the ordinances of the ancestors. Importantly, they can be performed on the spot, in a particular, concrete place or told in the form of myths, creating a world of communal mythology. In both variants, the function of rites is to make human life meaningful, to help the individual make sense of human life and to enable the individual to participate in the life of the community, if the need arises, even by sacrificing his or her own life for the common good. The ability of the individual to make such a sacrifice is strengthened by the rites, both when acted out and when reinforced in the narratives of myth.

Scruton makes it clear that when he speaks about the religious roots of culture, what he has in mind is closer to myth than to theology. He compares myth to art: "we find a parallel to the mythic consciousness in art, and many of those (like Jung) who have noticed the parallel have used it to explain the experience of beauty."[11] It is crucial for Scruton that this affirmation of communal belonging, and through it, turning individual human life into something public and meaningful, happens in the context of intergenerational dialogue, where "a common culture binds a society together," by "an altogether peaceful method… by dedicating them to the past and future of the community."[12] The individual discovers that she is not alone, and becomes a generational bridge of her community. The present generation of the community itself is not alone but is preceded and followed by other generations, who come, one after the other, in a natural order. Furthermore, even this procession is not isolated, as it is part of a natural order.

Besides this generational structure of a common culture, Scruton also endeavours to explain the operation of high culture. Like his account of religious rites and intergenerational communal myths, his account of the relevance of high culture is based on the assumption that community is reaffirmed through culture. While in his anthropological description of communal cults he described an unconscious procedure; when discussing high art, he proposes the use of an explicitly reflective educational process. The foundational assumption is that through different forms and manifestations of creativity (including art, literature, history and music) we acquire a form of knowledge which is crucial for us. The philosopher differentiates between three different kinds of knowledge: "Knowledge that, knowledge how and knowledge what."[13] "Knowledge that" refers to knowledge of facts, and this is the form of knowledge of natural science. To know how means technical knowledge, something that the artisan or the craftsman needs: to know the methods, the procedures and the technique of how to create the objects he wishes to create. Scruton's real interest, however, lies in the third form of knowledge, which is knowledge what. Here he relies on an Aristotelian insight: "Knowing what to do, Aristotle suggested, is a matter of right judgement (*orthos logos*); but it also involves *feeling* rightly."[14] High culture provides this sort of moral education, which allows us to feel properly, in accordance with the nature of things. This is also closely connected to acting properly, since, as Aristotle points out in *Rhetoric*, we act as we are inclined to, under the impulse of our emotions. In other words, our moral judgement and our sense of responsibility are based on feeling properly, and through high culture we are educated in that regard.

Now, the final question might be raised: what exactly is the relationship between the two notions Scruton explores in this essay? On the one hand, he argued that there is a common culture, based on communal rites. Communal rites of sacrifices, inherited from the forefathers, strengthen the community. With the help of these rituals the individual can be cleansed and purified, and as a member of the community the individual can reintegrate into the community. On the other hand, there is the sentimental education of high culture, which, as in Jane Austen's novels, teaches us how to feel, and through that it can "encourage us to know ourselves and to judge others rightly."[15] In a healthy culture both of these functions are required, therefore cult and culture operate in conjunction. Scruton emphasises that: "In no genuinely religious epoch is the high culture separate from the religious rite."[16] Scruton proves this point by referring to the Athenian theatre. He makes the convincing claim that in Athens theatrical performance was indeed just as much a religious act as it was a moment of high culture. Ancient Greek tragedy recounted narratives about heroes who were somewhat above the members of the audience in their social standing, and who had to accept the rule of poetic justice as a consequence of their mistaken judgement. The hero's fall by the end of the narrative caused a catharsis in the members of the audience, who identified with him, and who therefore were also able to experience a sudden emotional shock in their imagination. The members of the audience were ultimately reaffirmed in their sense of communal belonging, experiencing "a sense of the restored community, into which, through death and transfiguration, the erring hero is (also) reabsorbed."[17] Athenian dramatic performances, and in particular the ancient Greek tragedy, provided not only a religiously provoked purification of one's self, but also an experience of sentimental education, learning how to feel properly, and therefore learning the proper way to judge. They were also events of political participation which citizens expected or even demanded to take part in, in order to ensure that they went through this experience. As this example amply shows, in Scruton's view, religious cults, the experience of high culture and political education went hand in hand and fit together in traditional societies. This is because "the connections between common culture and high culture are deep," as they stem from the same "psychic need – the need for an ethical community into which the self can be absorbed."[18]

Importantly, this is a crucial connection even in a post-Enlightenment culture, where the common experience of cult is no longer present. If anything, in such a culture literature and art, and indeed all forms of high culture become not less, but even more important, as they have to take over many of the functions of religion, as far as the social function of reintegration into the community is concerned. This has to be done in opposition to the main "spirit" of the age, which both through alienation, and through an almost religious cult of the individual, preached by liberalism, cuts the individual off from the community. The community thus restored by high culture in the process of the proper reception of the artwork by the members of the audience is an imagined community, but according to Scruton, this imagined consolation can also have real life effects. Art can enter our life.

Culture Counts (2007)

Once again, in *Culture Counts*, a book which is subtitled *Faith and Feeling in a World Besieged*, Scruton places high culture alongside the religious cult. In his introductory essay, once again, he provides an overall definition of culture. He employs a concept of high culture where it includes the canonised classics, "the accumulation of art, literature and humane reflection that has stood the 'test of time' and established a continuing tradition of reference and allusion among educated people."[19] He does not seem to mind that this culture is "the creation and creator of elites."[20] He seems to suggest that there is a "social need to define and conserve a shared way of life."[21] He refers to the conceptual pair of civilisation and culture, an opposition he attributes to Herder, and in a somewhat different context, to Spengler. He does not see an unresolvable contradiction between the two terms. Instead, he claims that civilisation is an umbrella term which also covers culture.[22] Culture, in this context, turns out to be that through which a civilisation "rises to consciousness of itself and defines its vision of the world."[23] Apparently, it is no problem for Scruton if that specific function is brought about by an elite—so far as membership in that specific elite is open to everyone who would be interested joining. It is important for him, however, that the elite should remain loyal to this function.

It also follows that not all cultures are equal—they are largely determined by the specific needs of the civilisations they serve. Yet they share certain common elements, as they all are in the service of human nature, which is common to all. Moreover, they can have an impact on, or even converse with each other. Western culture, Scruton's own culture and the one to which—with a somewhat different experiential horizon—the present author also belongs to is, for example, "the fusion of Christianity with the law and government of Rome."[24] Its exceptional ability to assimilate other cultures is its specific distinguishing mark. This ability needs to be preserved and maintained, and this can only be done as long as the elites perform their role, and through their conflictual readings offer the community their interpretations of their particular civilisation.

To achieve this, members of the elite need to learn something crucial—the virtue of judgement. Scruton makes a somewhat bold claim when he connects culture and judgement in the following way: "culture issues from judgment."[25] As Scruton uses it, the term "judgement" is rather vague and ambiguous. However, Scruton is happy to use that vagueness for his own purposes. Although when applied to culture, it is most probably a reference to aesthetic choice, Scruton is obviously aware that the term is also used in the context of everyday moral (or even logical) choice. He makes the following comparison: "Just as customs emerge over time, from the countless efforts of human beings to coordinate their conduct, so do cultural traditions emerge from the discussions, allusions, and comparisons, with which people fill their leisure hours."[26]

Both the concept itself and the ill-defined way Scruton uses it are taken, as he readily admits, from the eighteenth century with its profusion of discourse on taste.[27] Within that historical context, he distinguishes between two paradigms: the earlier, English language literature used the term "taste" to refer to a sense of the human intellect, which works like a separate rational faculty, enabling humans to pick out what seems to be relevant to them. In order to define this sort of relevance more precisely, however, the Germans began to use the concept of aesthetic judgement, originally introduced by Baumgarten, and reinterpreted by Kant and later Schiller. Scruton admits, in his short genealogy of the term, that neither taste, nor the German concept of aesthetic judgement (*Aesthetische Urteilskrft*) was helpful in clearly defining the specific scope of this judgement, by distinguishing culture from science, religion or morality. On the one hand, this semantic confusion is helpful for Scruton as its vagueness allows him to point out the connection between aesthetic and moral (or for that matter, even political) judgement—a connection which is made even in Kant's *Critique of judgement*, where the philosopher assumes that the beautiful serves as a symbol of morality, in the sense that it makes moral ideas visible.[28] On the other hand, he has to struggle hard to refute those views which claim that we cannot prioritise one judgement over another in an objective manner. This aspect of leaving the door open for the sceptical relativist, who will claim judgement is ultimately subjective, is deeply worrying for Scruton. A culture turns out to be vulnerable when doubt takes root in it, compromising its ability to transmit correct judgement from generation to generation.

Scruton makes an effort to clarify the social aspects of both moral and aesthetic judgement, in a similar vein to eighteenth-century writers, comparing judgements of artistic performance to judgements of jokes. This was a recurring topic for both Shaftesbury, Addison and Hutcheson, all of whom argued that through telling jokes and witticism, in fact interpersonal ties are strengthened in society. Jokes can be misjudged in two ways: either by not appreciating the humour in them, or by exaggerating them, and thus displaying "bad taste." One has to find the via media between these two ways of missing the target, and if one is able to do so, one will be recognised as a sociable being. While all of us have the capacity for this sort of judgement, making and understanding jokes properly is actually something which has to be learnt.

Scruton makes use of this analogy to argue that in our judgements of the aesthetic merits of works of art we are engaged in a similar process. As with jokes, works of art are not a "natural kind," and therefore their standards are not objective. On the other hand, neither are they purely subjective, as social control makes itself felt in their use.[29] Here, although he does not refer to it directly, Scruton seems to make use of the argument of David Hume, in his famous essay *Of the Standard of Taste*.[30] Although art is a functional kind, and therefore cannot have objective grounds like natural science has, dealing as it does with natural kinds, neither are its values simply voluntaristic. He refers to a certain "aesthetic interest" which is activated when we look at the objects of our enquiry with an interest in the world as it really appears to our senses. In other words, we mobilise our sensory experience and our intellect—together with the imagination. Looking at objects with the use of our imagination needs to be learnt, however. We acquire this skill by imitating the example of others. We do so in order to become better integrated into our community and its traditions. We thus become bearers of a common culture. If we also acquire an even more refined technique, we can become carriers of high culture, as well. Once again, Scruton's example is Greek tragedy, contrasted with the practice of the Roman games. The latter practice was morally deplorable, and becoming an expert in judgements concerning that practice did not help one to acquire good taste. On the other hand, through watching Greek tragedy Athenian citizens learnt how to get integrated into their society. Scruton is suggesting by this that bearers of high culture, that is, members of the cultural elite, are able to judge works of art, and in this way solidify the canon of their culture. Drawing in this respect on Matthew Arnold and T.S. Eliot, he argues that the practice of aesthetic judgement helps us to understand both the natural world and the life of society, "each other and ourselves." This is sentimental education in the original sense of the word, and Scruton's analysis helps to reveal the cognitive and moral functions of both moral and aesthetic judgements. He does this without claiming that there is necessarily a direct correlation between aesthetic judgement and moral judgement. The counterexamples of that correlation are the "evil aesthete" and the "philistine philanthropist." In the first case high culture is combined with the cruellest behaviour—Scruton's examples are twentieth-century totalitarian rulers like Lenin, Hitler, Stalin and Mao. In the second case a lack of culture is combined with the warmest heart and the most beneficial way of life for others. An example of this is the ordinary saint, who may not be familiar with the classics of culture at all, but who still will do what is morally the best. Scruton goes on to ask whether these examples do not prove an "a priori disconnection between 'aesthetic education' and the moral life."[31] In other words, the question is whether these examples are not proof that culture does not count morally.

Scruton's answer to this question is that culture cannot exclude the threats of the worst potential of the human character being realised. The dark instincts which draw us towards the morally unacceptable are often too strong for culture to counteract, and this is why the latter cannot guarantee that these dark motives will be overcome. As Scruton sees it, normal human behaviour, which enables the survival of humankind, is based on "a thin crust of normality," beneath which "is the dark sea of instincts… sometimes erupting in a show of violence."[32] As he describes it, human nature is fragile, but in itself it enables humans to achieve normality, peace and order in their societies, even if it is not predetermined that they will. Human nature cannot prevent for once and for all the eruption of that abnormality—evil—which each of us is prone to. If it does not provide that safeguard, what exactly can be seen as the socially beneficial moral achievement of culture? The answer, according to Scruton, is that humans need "the light-filled air of thought and imagination" which can help them to learn to see and feel with the eye and heart of the other, a prerequisite of any social contact beyond the purely egotistic. Through its stories of good and bad, of examples of heroic deeds and evil misdeeds, culture enables the individual to step out of the narrow confines of individualism, and survey the public scene from the point of view of the common good. Ordinary people cannot maintain such an elevated viewpoint for very long, but society should keep alive these chances to rise beyond fragile particularism. Culture is a vast reservoir of outstanding achievements, of stories of human beings that we are interested in. Through these narratives it teaches us how to feel about events in human life, thus ensuring that even if we commit the sins which we are destined to, we should be aware of our moral failures. Culture, in other words, is "the ongoing record of the life of feeling."[33] Of course, there are those who do not need it, and those who will still remain sinners, in spite of all their thorough acquaintance with high culture. Generally, great stories have public functions. It is enough to consider the great novels of the twentieth century telling the stories of the inhumanity of totalitarian regimes, from Mann and Orwell and Koestler, to Milosz or Solzhenitsyn, to see how culture itself alerts us to the dangers of the figure of the "evil aesthete." Or, as Scruton suggests, examples like "Hardy's Tess, Wordsworth's Michael, Péguy's Jeanne d'Arc," allow us to "understand the full force of the objection that tells us that such people are admirable beyond the reach of cultural freaks like you and me."[34]

In the final analysis, Scruton sounds convincing that these exceptions, the exception of the evil aesthete and of the "philistine philanthropist" do not constitute proofs that there is no socio-moral effect of high culture. Although they prove that culture cannot exclude evil from human lives, and the lack of it does not by itself, exclude their opposite, human perfection from happening, Scruton succeeds to show that culture "should conserve, through whatever troubles, the message of something higher: the image of a world of human feeling which is also a proof of human worth."[35]

In summary, Scruton's counterexamples are not strong enough to deny his claim about the socially ameliorative effects of high culture. However, one can bring forth yet another, more sweeping criticism: that high culture might be systematically connected with moral corruption. This argument has traditionally been exemplified by the Roman empire: as soon as it became culturally refined, the Roman empire was on the way to moral decline. Even contemporary critics formulated this criticism, of a decline which was caused by the disappearance of ancient virtues and untainted human relationships, arguing that the fall of the empire was caused by luxurious consumption, and by the delights of a refined culture. Indeed, this was the claim made by both Cato the elder and Cato the younger, whose stoic disgust of the new Roman manners and of the turning away from Republican virtues seemed a little exaggerated to Cicero, himself a prime example of Roman high culture, but also a propagator of the citizens' active involvement in public affairs.[36]

Later ages in Europe kept returning to the ancient examples, using for example the Roman narrative of moral corruption as a cautionary tale for their own age. This rhetorical strategy can be seen in the age of the Enlightenment, used by Scottish authors, or by Rousseau, or, for that matter by Gibbon, the author of the most widely known history of

Roman decline. The narrative of his opus magnum was once again built on a simple opposition of ancient pure morals and later cultural refinement and decline.[37] The recent grand narrative about Gibbon by Pocock, the six-part series entitled *Religion and Barbarism* (1999–2015), itself an opus magnum, showed that Gibbon took his storyline from a long line of authors, worked out the details of a traditional criticism of corrupted Roman manners and the loss of ancient warrior mentality. For Pocock, Gibbon paradigmatically represents a position of civic humanism, a latter-day version of a defence of moral virtue as a criticism of modern culture.[38]

Such criticism of the corrupting effects of refined culture in modern Europe was closely connected to the Protestant cause, and in Britain, specifically, also to puritanism. Scruton's real grasp of this position, however, was the result of his experience of his father's working-class mentality, including a defence of Old England, and a criticism of the culture of consumption in late capitalism. While we know how tense the relationship between Scruton and his father was, it should be recalled that in his old age Scruton found his way back to his father, and wrote an eloquent defence of his father's position of localism and his sharp criticism of modernist urban developments. The philosopher's autobiographical recollections include a balanced judgement of his father: "My father was an old-fashioned socialist of the English school, who hated revolutionaries," but he also "rejected the monarchy, the Empire, the class system and the Anglican Church. He admired Oliver Cromwell and John Hampden, who in his version of events had tried to reclaim our country from the toffs who were destroying it." Finally he makes the following comment on his father's cultural patriotism, and especially of his practical opposition to modern urbanism: "His vision of architecture sprang from the same Roundheaded attitude as his politics."[39]

Certainly, Scruton did not share this Roundheaded mentality, nor his father's radicalism. He did, however, share something of his passion, and of Jack Scruton's sweeping criticism of the corrupting effects of what the Scottish Enlightenment called commercial society and its value hierarchy. Sir Roger's final retreat to the country estate that he bought was itself an expression of his critical attitude towards the cultural industry and the institutional framework of contemporary academia, both of which play, as he saw, their parts in the degeneration of manners and morals. It was also a reaffirmation of the traditional values of Old England which had also been cherished by his father. This mentality had a natural inclination towards the rustic, favouring the way of life and mindset of the country people. Sir Roger, of course, was also a fully urbane phenomenon, aware of the discrepancies between his own petit bourgeois urban upbringing, Cambridge education and his final choice of rural England, but he was able to accept as his joint inheritance a combination of his father's severe ideal of ancient virtues and his own conservative advocacy of a naturally grown high culture without a sense of social superiority. His was the mentality of a British conservative, whose move to the countryside allowed him to pursue an ecologically more responsible way of life, while also following a career as an author and a public intellectual. Although he remained a member of the academic elite, he made an effort to adjust his own and his family's specific way of life to the lifestyle of a country household. In other words, he tried to maintain a harmony between the traditional common culture of the place which he chose as his home and his own ability to practice and enjoy high culture. This harmony of lifestyle and vocation can be called an aesthetically tuned conservatism.

The Theory of Beauty

Scruton's interest in high culture entailed a parallel interest in the arts, history, politics and philosophy. This is a wide range of interests, all of them typical of a guild member of the liberal arts.[40] One of his prominent aims was to construct a philosophically convincing account of beauty, as according to his anthropology beauty permeates the whole of human life in all its aspects and dimensions.

Beauty (2009)

His book, completed in 2008 and first published as *Beauty* in 2009, and later as *Beauty, a Very Short Introduction* in 2011, by Oxford University Press, works out an argument that beauty is "a real and universal value, one anchored in our rational nature, and the sense of beauty has an indispensable part to play in shaping the human world."[41] He intends to challenge the sceptical postmodern view that all subjective judgements of beauty are of equal value, and that there is no natural order among them. By arguing for a naturally given hierarchy of judgements of taste, Scruton argues for an aesthetic education to form people's sense of judgement. He aims to show that it is not true that anything goes, and that beauty itself plays a crucial role in human life, ordering it and giving shape and meaning to human aspirations and endeavours.

In order to lay a stable foundation for his theory, he first provides an account of aesthetic judgement. This issue had already been tackled in his PhD dissertation, later published in an edited form as *Art and Imagination: A Study in the Philosophy of Mind* (1974).[42] His supervisor at University of Cambridge was Dr M.K. Tanner, a young music critic and expert on Nietzsche, and the famous analytical Thomist Catholic Philosopher and disciple of Wittgenstein, Professor G.E.M. Anscombe.[43] The dissertation had three different layers: the first one drew an outline of the mechanism we call aesthetic judgement. Secondly, it embedded this aesthetic judgement into aesthetic experience. This layer described the intellectual faculties involved in aesthetic judgement, leading to what he called the aesthetic attitude, the attitude which enabled the individual to make proper aesthetic judgements. Finally, he presented the specific form of aesthetic judgement concerned with works of art, as determined by what he called the experience of art.

In *Beauty*, he again starts out from the act of judging beauty. Although he is emphatically not interested in making a historical reconstruction of reflections on beauty, Scruton refers to such diverse authors as Aquinas, Shaftesbury, Kant and Wittgenstein.[44] They were, of course, among his favourite aesthetic thinkers. His starting point is that, as soon as one realises that in order to discuss beauty there is a need for a judgement of beauty, problems will arise. These problems include the following questions:

* What is more important, the object judged or the subject who makes the judgement?

* Is beauty indeed transcendental like truth, and what exactly is its real ontological status?
* How is beauty related to our "desire for harmony, fittingness and civility";[45] is beauty an end in itself, or should it be seen in connection with the useful?
* How far is beauty a part of the everyday life of every human being?
* What are more involved in the judgement: our sensory capacities or our intellectual faculty?
* Is the judgement of beauty connected to moral motives, or can one really be disinterested when one is judging the aesthetic quality of something or someone?[46] and finally,
* How far is the judgement of beauty subjective?[47]

He does not aim to solve all of these questions, but he is ready to identify his own position. The Kantian aesthetics is quite close to him, yet he adds to it a specifically British flavour, relying on a notion of aesthetic common sense. Since architecture is crucial for him, he is more interested in everyday beauty than the elevated, indeed sublime beauty of nature or that of a work of art.

This interest in the everyday aspects of the human experience of aesthetics explains why this book contains separate chapters on human beauty, the sublime in natural beauty and what he calls everyday beauty. All three are connected by Scruton's insight that beauty plays a much more prominent role in our daily lives, even outside of the realm of art, than is typically acknowledged.

Scruton takes human beauty as his starting point, considering the Platonic problem of the erotic overtone of our interest in human beauty (the desire to unite with its object of desire). When we refer to Platonic love, however, we tend to dissociate it from the love involved in erotic desire and in the sexual drive. This brings Scruton to his other beloved author, Hegel, and his notion of the beautiful soul, referring to the asexual, contemplative, and—not least—moral aspect of human beauty.[48] Through this analysis, Scruton returns once more to the issue of the sacred aspect of our aesthetic interest. Through two specific conditions of the human body, childhood and virginity, he approaches the elevated realm of that human beauty, "which places the transcendental subject before our eyes."[49]

In the same way, when discussing natural beauty, Scruton starts out from our everyday experience of beauty in nature. This ordinary aspect of it, apparently drawing on Addison and Hutcheson, is crucial for him in the context of the human being's need for home. The beautiful (as distinguished from the sublime) leads human beings to the realisation that they are in fact at home in this world, that "this world is a right and fitting place to be – a home."[50] On the other hand, the sublime leads him again beyond this world, to the experience of the sacred, as well as to the Kantian idea of "purposiveness without purpose."[51] This is the thought that the beautiful has a teleological dimension: if we recognise beauty, we cannot help enquiring what is it for. We look at parts of nature as a work of art, as if it was created by someone. This means that it has an obvious intentionality: it refers back to its creator's intention. The late Scruton addressed this problem, as we shall see later.

The third form of non-artistic beauty analysed by Scruton is everyday beauty. Here his primary example is the garden, which he identifies as a mediator between our human world and the world of non-human nature. He takes the examples of industrial design, handiwork, and even the simple practice of laying the table in an aesthetically satisfactory manner for an ordinary common meal in our home with guests. In this regard, the notions Scruton use are harmony and fittingness, searching for what "looks right." These terms remind him of the cognitive dimension of aesthetic judgement. This cognitivist motive seems to be a Thomistic element. Yet in his analysis of everyday beauty a social dimension is also evident. For example, people cannot help judging the aesthetic character of a building. Architects, therefore, aim to build aesthetically appealing buildings. As Scruton phrases it, there is here a "coordination problem."[52] Each house has to fit into the order of the other buildings around it. Such an adjustment calls our attention to the existence of a language in architecture: builders need to take into account a certain vocabulary and even a grammar of the architectural environment. When a new building is built, the new inhabitants want to "elicit the spontaneous approval of others."[53] There is a common order of houses, partly defined by the building regulations of the place, partly by local practice or what is called the vernacular—the way master builders in a given area tend to solve practical problems. Through this often spontaneous effort of harmonising the newly built house to the order of pre-existing houses, the inhabitants of a certain locality will "build a shared environment in which we can all be at home, and which satisfies our need that things look right to everyone."[54] This aesthetic feature, the particular manner in which a technical problem is solved, in other words, the architectural style followed by the builders of a house, will then assume a social relevance: it operates as "a guide to our shared environment."[55] The order of the buildings of a street, square or a city quarter emerges out of these small adjustments which particular builders are ready to make in order to make the new house fit in, to bring it into line with an already existing pattern.

This leads Scruton to the notion of local style, or the vernacular, in accordance with the often unpronounced local rules, the accepted taste or fashion of solving technical questions. This whole process of trial and error is based on an implicit, indeed a "covert pursuit of consensus."[56] This is the social relevance of aesthetic judgements: they ensure that what is built will be accepted by others. Aesthetic character thus mediates individual preferences, and helps to create a common set of standards. These standards, together with the fittingness achieved by them, achieve an order which is pleasing to the eye, and the latter lends to the scene that sense of familiarity which we call home. This is the way that everyday beauty operates, identified by Scruton as "minimal beauty."[57]

Scruton's primary interest in the role that everyday aesthetics plays in solving coordination problems in societies, and his explanation of how and why it is achieved, also explains and defines his approach to art as a whole. Art, for him, constitutes a specifically intensive moment of the aesthetics of ordinary beauty. The master builder learns his craft by following the examples of others and in this way develops his aesthetic judgement, his sense of what counts as beautiful, that is, what is fitting or in accordance with general expectations. However, even the strictest local architectural vocabulary and grammar leaves a certain amount of leeway for making decisions freely. It is here that individual creativity can find its way of expressing itself. Even if a builder wishes to be accepted and to conform, and therefore meets all the pronounced and unpronounced requirements of a locality, there will remain moments in the creative process when decisions have to be made without any guidance from the common stock of local customs. It is here that individual talent can show itself: through "the thinking that begins when the rule-following stops."[58] Scruton gives two examples to illustrate his point.

The first is the "serenity and solidity" of the Parthenon. (ILLUSTRATION) At first sight, this building conforms to the requirements of the architectural grammar of ancient Athens. Yet the fact is that our eye prefers it to other solutions solving similar architectural problems. In other words, this building distinguishes itself, drawing our attention to itself, and this demands an explanation. Why do we prefer its appearance to that of other contemporary temples? Scruton's answer is that there was in this case an element of extra creativity, a freely added perfection in the way its details are put together, in "the scale, proportions, detailing."[59] In other words, the builders enjoyed the freedom they had in solving those problems, and they injected into those details their idea of perfection, their own personal preferences and their own style. This does not mean that they dismissed the requirements of their age and milieu, or that they blundered when considering them. Neither did they rebel against local habits. On the contrary: they remained within the demands of decorum and propriety. They simply succeeded especially well in applying a logic, a coherence or consistency in their solutions to particular problems within the field of what is allowed. Observers cannot fail to perceive the internal logic, stylistic repertoire, individual grammar of the work of art, even if they fail to identify the particular details which are responsible for that particular effect.

The manner in which this was achieved by the builders of the Parthenon is explained by Scruton with a reference to Schiller's description of the connection between art and play. It was in his *Letters on the Aesthetic Education of Man* that Schiller wrote that it is the achievement of art to transport "us out of our everyday practical concerns, by providing us with objects, characters, scenes and actions with which we can play, and which we can enjoy for what they are, rather than for what they do for us."[60] The artist is comparable to playing children, when they say "Let's pretend!" In their playful, dramatic scenes children are able to imitate real-life situations, and thus they learn the emotional impact of certain situations. In these dramatised situational improvisations children are able to reconcile their reason and their sense, by relying on their imagination. The same happens in art: by leaving behind the constraints of our practical life, we are able, as members of the audience of a work of art, to reconcile reason and sense, and in this way to see "a vision of human life in its wholeness."[61]

At this point in the argument, Scruton takes one further step. Relying on Hegel's contrast between classical and romantic art, as well as on Burke's distinction between the beautiful and the sublime, he compares the artistic intentions of the artists of the Parthenon with those of the planner of the Laurentian Library, in Florence. (ILLUSTRATION)[62] While the artists of the former managed to abide by the rules, and only played freely where the rules left them room to do so, Michelangelo straightforwardly disregarded the rules, and instead of applying them he created his own rules, which were only valid for that particular design of the steps and the façade of the building. In fact, Michelangelo's daring innovation constitutes no less than a mocking of the rules. Similarly, sublime events in nature, which destroy or simply disregard the essential living conditions of human beings remind humans of the power of their creator, who is also the creator of nature. When a sublime effect is achieved in art, the artist, in most cases a Romantic artist, imitates the power of God over the created world, by conveying the overwhelming effect of the work of art over the audience, bringing their state of mind to catharsis, a release from strong emotions, like pity and fear. To achieve this, the work of art subverts our mental conditions, and fully engages our imagination.

Something very similar to this second kind of artistic effect (achieved by such diverse artists as Michelangelo, Shakespeare or Tchaikovsky) happens in the erotic experience. This latter is "a kind of crux in the human condition, a mystery with which our earthly destiny is entwined, and from which we cannot escape without sacrificing some part of our nature and our happiness."[63] Although Scruton addresses this issue in a much more elaborated form in other works, going into the greatest detail in his huge volume entitled *Sexual Desire* (1986), it is also relevant here in connection with his efforts to show the metaphysical dimensions to which the work of art points. In real love (as opposed to pornographic imagination and joy), we imaginatively confront the other in his or her totality, and the other fully captivates our desire, which urges us to fully own him or her, both bodily and mentally. As this takeover cannot happen in practice, due to the confines of our bodies, sexual desire can never be completely satisfied, and it leads us beyond the bodily engagement with the other into a realm which we cannot control rationally. The same happens in the experience of beauty. The experience of the great work of art is comparable to a kind of ecstasy, involving an experience of stepping beyond our own natural borders into the realm of the unknown and uncontrollable. When encountering the beautiful, we experience the impossibility of satisfying our imagination, as we are never able to overcome the distance between our self and the object of aesthetic apprehension. This aesthetic experience of perfection without appropriation is a complex and demanding one, but it has a purifying existential and moral effect, described in Aristotle's notion of catharsis.

Since Scruton finds this experience crucial in human character formation, he is rather critical of those artistic trends which, he claims, flee from beauty, best exemplified by modern, and even more by postmodern art. Eliot's essays and his *Four Quartets*, as well as the works of Pound, Schoenberg or Pfitzner, still seek redemption for our souls. As the philosopher puts it, the goal of the modern artist is not "a break with tradition," but "a recapturing of tradition."[64]

On the other hand, as Scruton explains in his analysis of a postmodern performance in Berlin of Mozart's comic opera, *Die Entführung aus dem Serail*, postmodern art seems to be afraid of the subversive power of art. The postmodern artist scorns the human desire for beauty and perfection, and that way commits desecration. The contemporary artist does not confront the experience of awe in the presence of the sacred. The postmodern artist is not interested in the emotional upheavals of the Romantics or that of Shakespeare, whose best scenes of love present "an almost ritualistic reverence."[65] Most probably those who scorn this form of love, or the subversive effects of great art, in general, are afraid of this overwhelming experience of awe and reverence. This is why postmodern art prefers scorn and turns even to desecration, as a substitute for catharsis. It offers instead idolatry and profanation, a cheap and easy way of satisfying our emotional household, like the bodily gratification of sexual desires in pornography or the search for harmony and peace of mind by the shortcut of kitsch, which Scruton regards as a disease of faith, and identifies as a form of desecration.

At the conclusion of this work, Scruton denies being a Platonist. He does not attempt to argue that beauty is a feature of Being. He simply strives for more than just a subjectivist account of the aesthetic experience. As he understands it, aesthetic experience is a specific kind of experience, mostly evoked by works of art, themselves objects of a functional kind, which are meant to be perceived in an aesthetic manner. The detached attitude which characterises the viewer of a work of art enables her to enjoy in it, beyond the perfectionist application of certain rules, that particular game we mentioned earlier, the game of creating freely. The discovery of this free play will liberate the imagination of the viewer, and allow her to have an experience of things which is beyond the ordinary. She enjoys the experience of stepping out of one's own self, allowing her to have a look at the realm which is beyond both the human condition and the physical nature. The experience of encountering a work of art, therefore, offers an opportunity to sensually apprehend what is beyond our ordinary mental horizon, the dimension of the transcendental.

In Praise of the Vernacular: Aesthetics, Politics and Architecture

Beyond a general interest in the functioning of culture, and a general theory of the role and operation of artistic beauty in human life, both in its ordinary forms as well as in the realm of art, Scruton also had a special interest in the particular forms of art. As we have seen, in his late childhood and youth he spent much time under the spell of music and literature, due to certain friends and acquaintances. No doubt, as in many other cases, art opened up an escape route for the young Scruton, both from family conflicts—including an oppressive father and the serious illness and eventual death of his mother—and from the usual problems of the spiritual complexities of adolescence. Unlike most youngsters of his age and generation, he was neither absorbed by sport nor taken over by youth subculture, and in particular, by the pop and beat music of the late 1950s and the 1960s. On the contrary, enjoying an intellectual autonomy and having a somewhat rebellious nature which led him to spiritual dissidence, he plunged into the enchanted world of classical music, and into the enthralling sphere of books. These basic areas of interest were later supplemented by the visual arts, including architecture, the fine arts and photography.

This chapter will specifically concentrate on architecture, which over time became his primary interest within the realm of art. Although Scruton remained a man of the humanities throughout his life, as we have seen, in his youth he spent a rather intense period of studying the natural sciences, and especially the physical and biological sciences. This interest was later again complemented by an interest in the theoretical questions of politics. His philosophy merited a lot from his earlier study of the sciences. His approach to architecture was that of the generalist, as distinguished from that of the professional. Already during his time at Cambridge he had the time and the resources to study architecture in detail. This interest was supported by the rise of architectural theory in that era, and also by the heated public debates on modern urbanism in Britain, and specifically in Cambridge. But perhaps more consequential than any of these other influences was his close personal link with David Watkin, a key exponent of architectural theory within the profession of art history, and a great rebel himself. I described above both Watkin's extraordinary character and the nature of Scruton's relationship to him. Let us concentrate here on Watkin's little book, *Morality and Architecture* (1977), which not only caused great perturbation in his own age, but also directly influenced Scruton's approach, not only to architecture, but even to political theory.[66] Scruton's interest in architecture was always connected to his general enquiry into human nature, and into the forms of communal life. Interestingly, Watkin's book was critical of the modern phenomenon (ranging from the eighteenth to the twentieth century) of burdening architectural practice with too strong social, philosophical or (quasi)religious theories, a criticism which was based on the close link between abstract theories of urbanism and the uncompromising demolition of architectural remnants of the past, mostly in city centres.

The Example of Watkin

Watkin was only three years older than the philosopher, and yet he was already a don. Unlike Scruton, Watkin remained in Cambridge, which made his career more straightforward and linear, lacking the twists and dead ends of Scruton's own path. He established himself as a teacher both in Peterhouse, where Scruton got a research fellowship, and at his own faculty. It was also relevant that, while Scruton always remained a philosopher, even when he dealt with the arts, Watkin was trained as, and remained truly a historian of art, and within that a historian of architecture. Also crucially, he was a student (as well as an ardent opponent) of Sir Nikolaus Pevsner, one of the most interesting figures of the scene, and certainly the most influential one in the profession in Cambridge—and a champion of modernism.

Watkin left no doubt that he wrote *Morality and Architecture* under the anxiety of influence. Having been a PhD student of Pevsner, this was a kind of Oedipal effort to free himself of his influence, which had, however, the opposite effect: his rebellion connected his achievement to that of his master for ever. Watkin's revolt against the revolutionary ideology of modernism was a very important point in the history of reflections on modernity, and it had a deep impact on the development of Scruton himself.

As he admits, the topic had concerned Watkin since 1964, when he started to teach art history to undergraduates at Cambridge. His book was based on the lecture notes of a course he taught from 1968 onwards. It crystallised into a single theme: to establish (a critical) sense of modernism in art theory, through understanding the prehistory which had led to it. This was a somewhat self-contradictory exercise: Watkin used a historical method to show the ahistoricism, or—as it were—the historical determinism of the modernist venture. It was, however, a powerful attack which was partly due to its refined historical method. This method followed the pattern of the historiographical theory of Sir Herbert Butterfield, as Watkin acknowledges in the prefatory note. Butterfield famously attacked the Whig historians who believed that "there is an unfolding logic in history, a logic which is on the side of the Whigs and which makes them appear as co-operators with progress itself."[67] Watkin argued that the modernist programme is based on the same sort of historical determinism, based on Marxist inspirations, but also present in various forms of "prophetic" writings on art since the early nineteenth century. Watkin's story, in fact, starts with Pugin's *Contrasts*, published in 1836, and leads to Pevsner's *Pioneers of the Modern Movement* in 1936.[68] The two figures apparently have nothing in common, and there is no obvious logical chain leading from one to the other. While Pugin was the spokesperson of a nostalgia for the medieval world and its way of thinking, including its religiosity, one of Pevsner's heroes, Walter Gropius, is the modern architect *par excellence*, who introduced a form of design which departed radically from earlier styles and formal vocabularies. Watkin's original idea is that the two of them are related, and to show this he connected their names with the help of other names. What is common to Pugin and Gropius, he argues, is that both of them belong to a tradition of disregarding style as the most important element of architecture, and of making sense of architecture by means of external explanations, including either "religion, politics, sociology, philosophy, rationalism, technology, German theories of space or of the spirit of the age."[69] He focused on three specific types of external determinants on architectural theory: the first being either religious, sociological or political, all of which are characteristic of the English way; the second referring to the spirit of the age, which he identifies as a typical German modernist discourse of architecture; and finally, a rational or technological justification, the French approach.[70] Of these, the first approach can be traced back as far as the work of Winckelmann in the eighteenth century. The major explanatory power in this mentality is a reference to truth: works of architecture in some loosely defined way can lie or can be true. Moral criteria can be used to judge a building, and the task is to find such criteria and judge the moral status of the building with the help of them. This intention to connect art and truthfulness is present in such diverse intellectual movements as "the French rationalists," "the English Art and Crafts theorists" and "twentieth century propagandists."[71] Beyond Pugin and Pevsner, Watkin mentions the names of Viollet-le-Duc, Morris, Berlage, Frank Lloyd Wright and Le Corbusier.[72] All of them tried to interpret architecture with the help of an external standard, whether it be morality, politics or religion.

The second type of external explanation refers to the spirit of the age, as a universally applicable explanatory tool. In this vein, Watkin reconstructs a German-Swiss tradition, connecting Burckhardt, Wölfflin, Giedion and Pevsner. All of them, according to Watkin, viewed the architect as an expression of an immutable spirit of an age. Human nature is able to adapt, in order to meet the demands of the age. Yet, if new buildings do not harmonise with that spirit, it will be judged mistaken.

Finally, the French way of architectural thinking starts out from the particular technological repertoire available in a given period. The architect needs to solve particular problems, and this repertoire will serve as a toolkit to find the single best solution. There is a need for a certain architectural function, and technology will determine how to answer that particular need. According to Watkin, the need answered by a building is arbitrarily chosen, and its demand can be so urgent that it can lead to "the large-scale destruction, socially and architecturally, of a historic environment."[73]

All three of these external explanatory mechanisms commit the same type of mistake, Watkin claimed: they disregard the internal logic of the tradition of architecture, forcing instead external standards on it. A reliance on "taste, imagination, and scholarship," which has traditionally characterised architectural thought, is replaced in this scheme by what he calls "a scientifically plotted Utopia," leading the "tamed collectivist man" to a new environment in "some gigantic rationalistically constructed beehive."[74] As is evident from the rhetoric of this criticism, Watkin was in fact accusing the modernist venture in architecture of bringing alien, non-artistic, and in particular, political-ideological arguments into the debate. He drew parallels between these figures and the crusader of the medieval age, comparing religious zeal in its earlier form with their later, political-propagandistic fervour. In all these cases the energy is basically destructive, and rejects the traditional ways of thinking about architecture. The vocabulary Watkin uses betrays that he suspects a political motive behind all this, including a powerful strand of social criticism, and a voluntarist political intention to rearrange the status quo. As he sees it, it is a major mistake to bring into the debate on architecture external discourses, and to rely on political value judgements.

It is also telling that at the point where he mentions the "scientifically plotted Utopia" of the architectural theorists, he is referring to a text by Scruton. Scruton wrote a powerful critique of Stalinist architectural thought, published in the Cambridge Review.[75] It is not surprising that Watkin and Scruton start out from similar assumptions, one mobilising art historical and art theoretical considerations, the other one showing how far architectural thought had become ideology driven. Instead of that, both of them would prefer to see taste and imagination as helps to make proper judgements about architectural quality.

In other words, the revolution against the dominant influence of the modernist credo, as embodied by Pevsner, is criticised here by his student, Watkin, for its use of political argumentation. This is, however, a catch-22 problem. As soon as one seeks to criticise someone for using political arguments in a non-political debate, one arguably commits the same mistake: bringing external arguments into an aesthetic debate. This was the criticism Watkin had to confront: that he held partisan views when he objected to the use of partisan views in aesthetic debates. The point he made was a simple one, however: that the views of modernist architectural theorists were based on the assumption that "modern man should build a new collectivistic society based on a universally accepted moral and social consensus," where striving for an acclaimed, but deliberately vague notion of "architectural truth" excluded reliance on taste and imagination "either in the creative process, or by the critics."[76]

Watkin was indeed quite critical of his earlier supervisor, Nikolaus Pevsner, whom he took as the embodiment of the new direction of architectural thought. His surprising story of the origins of modernism served the final aim of criticising Pevsner. The fact that he showed the structural parallels between nineteenth-century forerunners, who operated within a religious frame of mind and Pevsner's collectivist left-wing radicalism only served to underline the quasi-religious nature of Pevsner's political conviction. In this sense, Watkin's criticism is in fact a political theological one, in the sense that he demonstrates how political ideology has the same structure as the ideology of a religious revival. This is all the more interesting given the fact that Watkin himself was a practising Catholic, and his architectural theory was not absolutely independent of that fact either. In other words, Watkin's criticism has a Catholic, theological dimension: he criticises both the revivalist Catholicism of Pugin, accusing him of committing what he calls a "curious materialist heresy," and Pevsner's quasi-Protestant criticism of architectural Catholicism. It is this latter criticism which we shall now turn to.[77]

First of all, it is important to note that Watkin was directly attacking his doctoral supervisor in this book. Certainly, in an ideal world of scientific research, it does not matter who formulates a particular view, and one's account of it should simply depend on the worth of the criticism, independent of its author. If that were true, there would be nothing strange about criticising one's supervisor, after one had defended one's own thesis. Also, obviously, Watkin is very generous with Pevsner, whom he happened to know personally so well. His attack is not a criticism of his character. Still, there remains something awkward about the act of the disciple turning against his master, if for no other reason than because of the Oedipal element in it. It is worth recalling in this context Bloom's reference to anxiety of influence. Apparently, Watkin felt an urge to "murder" his master in order to liberate himself from his tutelage.

In his detailed account of Pevsner's fallacy in art history Watkin is careful to show that Pevsner is part of a German-language tradition of writing about the history of art, and in a way this lineage already predestined him to committing his characteristic methodical mistake. Referring to Burckhardt and Wölfflin, he claims that Pevsner took from the former the idea that his own discipline, art history, is "an aspect of cultural and social history," and from the latter his reliance on the *Zeitgeist*, "the spirit or style of the age," which determines the art of individual artists much more than their own individual talent and personal choices.[78] Analysing Pevsner's critical writing on Baroque art, he points out that Pevsner's reconstruction of Jesuit thought in the seventeenth century is prejudiced and therefore distorts the historical facts, due to his "lack of familiarity with the customs and doctrines of the Church he is writing about," and that this distorted intellectual history is "transposed" "arbitrarily" by Pevsner to the field of artwork in order to criticise artistic practice as well.[79] Watkin perceives in all this a typically Northern, protestant misunderstanding of Mannerism, Jesuitism and counter-reformation thought.

Besides Burckhardt's thesis of the essentially anti-religious direction of the Renaissance, which evidently contradicts the facts of Christian humanism, Watkin attributes Pevsner's idea that the modern world is basically Protestant in spirit to the effect of Max Weber, and hence the ideologist's religious defence of modernism represents a "resounding pan-egyric on Protestantism."[80] Beyond that mistaken judgement, Watkin argues, Pevsner commits a methodological mistake "familiar in nine-teenth- and twentieth-century political philosophy," which is to rely on an ideological account of the age.

Watkin's criticism, however, becomes really biting only when he turns to the second phase of Pevsner's career, which was devoted to the defence of modern and modernist architecture. He asserts that the work which best defined Pevsner's position is his *Pioneers of the Modern Movement from William Morris to Walter Gropius* (1936). Pevsner constructs his story in that book in such a way that it takes the form of a genealogy lead-ing from the social prophets of the nineteenth century to the designers of twentieth-century architecture. As a result, Pevsner's own attitude is that of a "progressivist harbinger of the earthly new Jerusalem."[81] His descrip-tion has the major handicap that it is not open to falsification, contradict-ing Popper's requirement of a scientific theory. Instead, Pevsner's story of the new art of modernist architecture is like a prophetic announcement, and not accepting its "truth" is a form of high treason against the spirit of the age. As Watkin sees it, Pevsner already developed his deterministic theory while working at Göttingen University where he taught in 1930. Watkin does not make much of the early alleged sympaties of Pevsner for elements of the Nazi ideology, which play a major role in the award-winning biography of Pevsner by Susie Harries.[82] He mentions the term "totalitarian," which Pevsner applied to describe what he took to be the genuine style of modernism.[83] In the original edition, however, Watkin passed up the opportunity to make a generalisable claim about Pevsner's brush with totalitarianism, which played such a major role in the critical accounts of the relationship of intellectuals to totalitarian power by writ-ers from Raymond Aron to Czeslaw Milosz. In the 2001 edition of the book, which the present author has not seen, Watkin refers to Pevsner's flirtation with National Socialism, a most disconcerting theme for the Pevsner cult in England. Watkin makes much of the art historian's relationship to Wilhelm Pinder, his dissertation supervisor, who remained an advocate of Hitler even in 1939. Since then a whole literature has been written on the fatal attraction for Pevsner of the National Socialist ideology, a topic addressed in both of the detailed biographies of him by Stephen Games, and later by Susie Harries.[84] It seems to be an established fact by now that Pevsner did indeed harbour great expectations in connection with Nazism, and even if he had good sense to leave the country, he remained somewhat naïve about the fatal event of the century. Boyde White recalls "the continuing sympathy that he expressed in 1933 and 1934 for the politics of his oppressors, Adolf Hitler's National Socialist German Workers' Party (NSDAP)."[85] Games quotes a conversation of Pevsner from 1933, in which he explained: "I love Germany, it is my country, I am a Nationalist, and in spite of the way I am treated, I wanted this movement to succeed. There is no alternative to chaos…There are things worse than Hitlerism."[86] The nature of this relationship resembles a kind of Stockholm-syndrome. It is hard to understand today, but it had to do with the complexities of the psychological reaction to the social standing of a German Jew, of Russian origin, who was forced into exile in England. What is even less easy to make sense of is Pevsner's professional belief—though it did not last too long—that the Nazi revolution would endorse the modernist turn in art and especially architecture which he was an enthusiast of. As Boyd Whyte puts it: "For Pevsner, the National Socialist revolution was not an endorsement of sentimental historicism, but the promise of youth, rejuvenation, and advanced technology."[87] Although, as mentioned, Watkin does not make much of this Nazi sympathy, he refers to an appreciation of "a collective spirit," and uses metaphors taken from the language of theology to describe Pevsner's engagement, including "the gospel," "a mission," etc.[88] In Watkin's reading of Pevsner's *Pioneers*, the book aims to identify the British predecessors to the modernist movement, and in particular to Gropius, finding William Morris. As he interprets Pevsner's genealogy, it is based on the concept of artistic honesty (a concept of which Watkin is rather sceptical), on the idea of the growing relevance of technology, and also on the glorification of youth. Yet Pevsner's position is unclear, or even ambiguous: he enthusiastically hails Morris as a prophet revolting against the false gods of the Victorian era, while Pevsner himself would become the Chairman of the Victorian Society. In the same way, his enthusiasm for Morris is also limited by the fact, as pointed out by Watkin, that he did not love machines. This is the reason why the real pioneers of the movement would be for him Otto Wagner and Adolf Loos, in 1890s Vienna.

Watkin returns to the collectivist dimension of the ideology he finds in Pevsner in connection with the German art historian's insistence on the importance of the youth movement. It is in connection with this recurring theme in Pevsner that Watkin finally connects collectivism with both kinds of twentieth-century totalitarianism: "The suppression of the individual in favour of the collectivity which alone has permanent validity is, of course, as characteristic of the political rhetoric of the socialistic and Communistic radicalism of the Weimar Republic of Pevsner's young manhood, as it was of the National Socialism which succeeded it."[89] The continuity between the two (the left and the right wing) totalitarian regimes' principles is reaffirmed, according to Watkin, by their common dislike of ("onslaught on") style, which is based on taste. Watkin refers in this context to the architectural history of Miller Lane, who claimed that "The Nazis inherited a political view of architecture from the Weimar Republic."[90] Weimar architecture was influenced by Bauhaus, an organisation which was certainly hunted and persecuted by the Nazis. However, as the architectural historian points out, the Nazis took over elements of the architectural doctrines from their victims, which they found fruitful for their own purposes. This takeover was based on the assumption that architecture is not simply a moral dilemma: it is also an issue of political dominance. If that is true, then architects themselves have a public mission, as "the right guides and promulgators of social and political ideals."[91]

To be precise, for Pevsner, it is not the architect who can "guide and promulgate" social and political ideals. The architect is in fact merely a mediator. The real guide and promulgator is the *Zeitgeist*, which restricts by a process of historicist determinism the architects' potentially innovative ideals. This historicism decides what can be truly built in an age, and what will not be true in a period. The final trick of this historicism is that in the end, the demand of the *Zeitgeist* will be to kill itself: the historical demand of modernism is to forget about history, and remain trapped in the moment. An architect is never again allowed to turn back to a historical style: he will always have to remain encapsulated in his own time. No revivalism is possible, not even the revival of classical modernism, as "all reviving of styles of the past is a sign of weakness."[92]

It is a double irony of history that Pevsner was unable to see that with all these extreme demands, amounting to a denial of the right to recall the past, he is himself a victim of historicism itself, as defined by Popper and Mannheim. As Popper put it in the *Poverty of Historicism*: "historicism claims that nothing is of greater moment than the emergence of a really new period."[93] In 1936, Popper's aim was to show that if we claim that there are unstoppable forces in history which can determine our thoughts, we are in fact denying the autonomy of our own ideas, because we are only allowed to be mouthpieces of history and our own time. Watkin refers to Gombrich, too, for whom Popper's analysis "derived its urgency from the menace of totalitarian philosophies which nobody at that time could forget for a moment."[94] In other words, Watkin plays both Popper and Gombrich against Pevsner's views on historicism and the spirit of the age.

Following this critical reconstruction of Pevsner's failure to liberate his own architectural history and theory from the fashionable—mainly Marxist—methodological strictures of his day, Watkin draws a general conclusion about the historical or historicist determinism of modernist ideology. In this mindset he discovers the same mistake as in Burckhardt's treatment of Michelangelo. Burckhardt tried to make sense of the age by uniting all its forces under the umbrella of a single "idea." He could not do much, however, with the stark originality of Michelangelo's architectural innovation in the Laurentian Library. He simply claimed that it was "an incomprehensible joke of the great master."[95]

This example, once again, reveals the continuity between Watkin's and Scruton's ways of thinking. As we have seen, Scruton, too, dealt with Michelangelo's architectural masterwork, showing the originality of it, in its daring decision to go against the demands of the day. For both Watkin and Scruton, a great architect's freedom is one of her most valuable assets, which she should never give up, just to accept the enforced rules of a political, social, philosophical or religious order. On the other hand, through style and taste, the architect can always accommodate his or her own works to the order of the city.

The Aesthetics of Architecture (1979)

Scruton's own early architectural ideas appear to have been formed in an exchange of views with Watkin. This certainly is true of his first great venture in this field, *The Aesthetics of Architecture*, published in 1979. It is the product of the self-confidence of a philosopher who was sure that he would be able to contribute to the debate about contemporary architecture, by his enquiries into aesthetics, itself an autonomous field of study. His precise intention for the book was "to introduce the subject of aesthetics to those who have an interest in architecture," and in particular to outline the notions of aesthetic taste and aesthetic judgement.[96] The novelty of the approach lay in the fact that, as we have seen, the modernism prevailing at the time opposed traditional concepts of taste and style, introducing instead a functionalist and social approach to architecture. This made Scruton's return to the aesthetic aspects of architecture a kind of rebellion against this modernist inclination, an anti-revolutionary gesture in itself. He presented himself as a mediator between different disciplines—between that of the philosopher and those of the architectural critic and historian. This was achieved by a procedure of (hermeneutic) application: The book applied general aesthetic concepts to the description of buildings. However, one can reverse this logical relationship, and claim that the author is illustrating his general aesthetic claims with architectural examples. He is careful to remain in the field of philosophy, where he feels safe, even though his use of architectural terminology is compelling. The fact that his main interest is philosophy makes his potential mistakes in architectural details less of a problem. In fact, he admits freely that: "Architectural critics and historians may disagree with some of my interpretation, but this should not matter."[97] To be sure, if one wishes to mediate between philosophy and art theory, mistakes in the interpretation of details may have far-reaching consequences. The correctness of the author's aesthetic judgement is always relevant. Yet he makes it sure, that the main part of his narrative will remain within the discourse of philosophy. Scruton is brave enough to remove from the text what he calls the "technicalities of modern philosophy."[98] Yet he could be sure that, without a real familiarity with the language and cast of mind of the philosopher no critic would find a catch in it.

Scruton mentions John Casey and David Watkin as sources of inspiration for his work. Yet there is a long list of further references in his text. It includes Ruby Meager, a philosopher from Birkbeck (and earlier from Oxford) who was also interested in aesthetics, and David Pole, of King's College, London, a philosopher with a wide range of interests, including the late Wittgenstein, as well as the classics. The fact that the friends and colleagues referred to in the Preface are mainly philosophers reveals Scruton's own focus, and proves that his intention in writing this book was to bring philosophy closer to public discussions of contemporary architecture and not the crossing of professional boundaries.

Yet he has difficulties with defining the main themes of his book. Scruton understands philosophy in a Wittgensteinian way: its task is to make explicit the tacit knowledge we have of a given subject. In this case, it is to make explicit what we mean when we judge individual buildings or ensembles of buildings—he does not aim at a complete and systematic aesthetics of architecture. Scruton's distinction between architectural theory and architectural aesthetics seems to refer back to Kant's division of the mental faculties in his famous system of "critiques," where he distinguishes between the sense of beauty, what he calls judgement (*Urteilskraft*), understanding (*reine Vernunft*) and practical reason (*praktische Vernunft*). All of these define a specific way of thinking. Kant's systemic idea was to connect the realms of pure and practical reason with the help of aesthetic judgement. Scruton found this division somewhat arbitrary, and one of his main aims in this book is to show with the help of examples of architecture that the connection between practical reason and aesthetic understanding needs to be redefined.

A further preliminary issue concerns the position of architecture on the palette of the arts. Kant's third critique was not directly or solely interested in art; natural beauty and the natural sublime were even more important for him. Yet aesthetics as a discipline was built on Kant's system, and in particular on the Kantian assumption of the autonomy of aesthetic judgement. Scruton also had a deep knowledge of Hegel's philosophy and classification of the arts. Applying the Hegelian classification of the arts, he stresses the differences between architecture and the other art forms, including literature, music or painting. Also taking into account the neo-Hegelian work of Collingwood, he distinguishes between representational and abstract arts. This latter category includes music and architecture: the two forms of art which Scruton was most familiar with.

It is on these foundations that he builds the main features of architecture. The first of these features for him is function: the idea that the building has to serve certain needs and desires—most importantly that of sheltering human beings. This functional aspect makes architecture fundamentally a *synthesis* of art and craft. It is a mistake to overlook this nature of architecture, and an excessive focus on its artistic attributes would push architecture towards a sculptural understanding of it.[99] Yet modernists are inclined to go to the other extreme and overestimate the significance of function, disregarding the aesthetic quality itself.

A further feature of architecture is the fact that buildings are embedded into a particular environment. They do not stand on their own, and thus they are experienced visually together with other buildings or structures, and their joint impact on the onlooker will be crucial for their appreciation. To appreciate the relevance of the aspect of locality, we need to take into account the human being's sense of place, which helps us to make sense of the building's relationship to its environment, determining whether it is in harmony with it. The fact that our aesthetic appreciation involves an appraisal of the harmony between the building and its direct and indirect environment leads Scruton to his account of a sense of style, which can help us make comparisons. As we shall see, stylistic sensibility in fact plays a crucial part in Scruton's theory of architecture. To appreciate stylistic differences, however, one also needs to have an understanding of architectural technique. Scruton is also aware of the fact that to arrive at the correct judgement one should also be able to view architecture as—at least partly—a decorative art. Technical perfection and decorativity are two aspects of architecture which Scruton did not link directly, but which both emphasise the crucial importance of craftsmanship.

Seemingly, the most significant feature of architecture for Scruton is that buildings are public objects. This means that unlike the objects produced by the other arts, which are connected to specific institutions of art such as museums, galleries, music halls and theatres, buildings surround us during our daily activities in the open air, and as such we cannot help seeing them, unlike the products of other forms of art, which we generally only see if we decide to look at them. Products of architecture by definition have a "public voice."[100] The terms which Scruton makes use of to describe this emphatically non-subjective dimension of architecture are determined by tradition—in other words the continuity of certain manners of architectural form used in a given community—and the vernacular. The vernacular means "native to a country, domestic, home-born," derived from Latin "vernaculus."[101] As we shall see, the vernacular will remain crucial for Scruton, describing the style of architecture which is characteristic of a certain locality, just as a certain dialect, way of dressing and manners can be specific to a region, according to ethnography or cultural anthropology. This was to remain important for him as a counterpoint to the international style of modernism, probably the result of the globalising tendencies of finance, economy and progressive ideology. While most of the other arts are also easily conceived of as forming part of this globalising movement, architecture should contravene this pressure, because a building has to fit into its local surroundings.[102] If we seek a usable criterion for assessing architectural works, we need to work out an "aesthetics of everyday life," taking into account local variations.[103] This can only be done if we give up the post-romantic notion of high art, and if we entertain an interest in "common practical wisdom."

Practical wisdom is the term usually used to translate the Latin virtue of prudence, an equivalent of the Aristotelian notion of *phronesis*, which in the sixth book of the *Nicomachean Ethics* is listed as one of the forms of knowledge, together with science and theoretical reason, among others.[104] Practical wisdom is the ability to make proper judgements in one's moral life, and Scruton aimed to show the connection between these and judgements about artistic merit. However, it is also important for him to distinguish the aesthetic judgement of architecture from a scholastic form of moralising, which, as we have seen, lay behind the severe tone of modernist theory—having grown, as Scruton points out, out of the moralistic language of Pugin and Ruskin in the nineteenth century.

Scruton explicitly refers to Aristotle's (and, remarkably, to Wittgenstein's) attempt, "to clarify the distinction between theoretical and practical knowledge."[105] The point he wants to make in connection with this distinction is that architecture should not be seen as a theoretical activity—and in this way he divorces it from both scientific endeavours and from those universal claims of social engineering which were made by the Enlightenment, mostly criticising earlier forms of particularism. Within the realm of practical understanding, Scruton is keen to make a further distinction, focusing in this book on that part of the practical understanding, "which is affected and determined by the aesthetic sense."[106] Yet Scruton's interest in this aesthetically tuned practical understanding also means that an aesthetically coloured practical judgement cannot be made without a reference to the telos of human life.[107] Scruton refers explicitly to Aristotle's concept of *eudaimonia*, usually translated as flourishing life. In other words, like the Greeks, Scruton's aim is a full philosophical understanding of human nature. This ancient Greek philosophical scaffolding will turn out to be crucial, leading Scruton to an appreciation of classical architectural theory. Vitruvius is more interesting for him than Le Corbusier. His real hero is, no doubt, Alberti, the Renaissance master-builder and theorist. The British philosopher learnt from the Renaissance return to ancient Greco-Roman ideals that one needs to "reinstate aesthetic values at the heart of the builder's enterprise," and to focus on the "style of life" which a particular value is connected to.[108]

Scruton feels it necessary to distinguish himself from later and contemporary forms of architectural theorising, including functionalism and theories of space, together with the methods of German-style *Kunstgeschichte* (also criticising Pevsner), including references to the *Zeitgeist* and to *Kunstwollen*. Neither is he satisfied with art historians' references to proportion in Vitruvius and Alberti. A theory of architecture based on proportion is misguided if it tries to understand proportion as simply being based on certain mathematical truths, as was proposed by the Pythagoreans. Through references to different examples of ancient Roman architecture, Scruton demonstrates that proportion is not a final source of explanation, since, to understand the aesthetic relevance and workings of proportion we need to understand further concepts such as "harmony, fittingness, appropriate detail and order."[109]

The connection established between what can be perceived in a building by the senses and our perception of it by intellectual cognition brings Scruton to a discussion of the role of experience in aesthetic judgement. In his chapter on experience, Scruton cites his own work, *Art and Imagination*, where he discussed the role of sensation and perception in the reception and interpretation of works of art.

Scruton also emphasises the role played by intellectual pleasures in the process of making sense of a work of architecture aesthetically. This does not mean, however, that he would exclude the concept of imagination from his analysis. On the contrary, he stresses that, from Kant to Collingwood, imagination played a major role in aesthetic theory. How imagination actually works in the perception of architecture is described by an appropriation of some of the ideas of "phenomenology," with reference to the works of Husserl, Sartre and Merleau-Ponty. The skeleton of the argument is this: a being can use his imagination only if that being is self-conscious.[110] Self-consciousness allows us to reflect on our own experience, the major act of our imagination. In order to have aesthetic experience, we need imagination, and to imagine requires self-consciousness. A phenomenological description of aesthetic experience will also give an account of our own perception of it. What is more, to give a phenomenologically valid description of aesthetic perception, we also need to be able to give an internal account of our reaction to it—in other words, of how it felt to experience the particular work of architecture. To do so, we need to be able to remember and to recall that specific feeling—and this recollection itself is only possible with the help of the imagination. The recollection reconstructs a complex mental activity, involving a "literal" perception of what happened, but it also involves a recollection of the mental activities which attended that perception. Scruton takes the example of music. Unlike birds, which only have a direct perception of the bird song, and will react to it immediately, without associating something more with that perception, when a human being hears a melody, she will also hear it imaginatively—hearing in the succession of noises first of all musical sounds, and in the succession of sounds musical movement, which itself will have certain characteristics, to which we unconsciously react: we will associate with the musical movement emotions such as sadness, grief or joy, as well as more complex packages of feelings "expressed" by this emotional vocabulary. Anything that goes beyond what Scruton calls "literal" perception involves the ability to "transcend the immediate," an act which requires self-consciousness, which will enable us to imagine noise as musical sound, musical sound as musical movement in a musical space, and thus to imagine emotional and other cognitive contents in those movements themselves. To be sure, there is nothing moving in a musical movement, except what we imagine to be in it, a result of our second-order perception of what is happening outside ourselves. Yet Scruton's description of the whole process of perception makes it clear that there is nothing esoteric in the workings of our imagination. When we try to describe it phenomenologically, what we are doing is not a kind of introspective psychology. We simply look for expressions that can be used to describe them metaphorically. We are aware of the aesthetic reaction to a phenomenon, but we also know that the reaction has to be described with the use of a public language, and the meaningfulness of this description depends on our success in bringing together elements of the perception with particular elements of the phenomena perceived. We need to be able to show that it is because of this change in the melody, this unexpected shift in the rhythm, this musical phrase that we experience this feeling and have this imaginative reaction.

The same way, we can employ the same phenomenological language to describe buildings. We employ it to describe the impact of buildings on our imagination, if our imaginative capacities are accustomed to perceiving them as a result of our aesthetic attention. He illustrates this point with examples of how we perceive the line of columns in classical renaissance and mannerist buildings. As soon as we notice that the distance between neighbouring columns in a colonnade changes, we realise that we are being invited to look at them in a playful manner, noting the differences. For example, when looking at the columns of Peruzzi's Palazzo Massimo alle Colonne we can see either four pairs of columns or three pairs, depending on whether we opt to concentrate on the shorter or the longer distance between the neighbouring columns. Similarly, Palladio's Villa Cornaro invites us to ponder the differences between the distances, playing a game of sorting or pigeonholing columns. In other words, the arrangement of the columns on the plane of the façade operates as a proposal for those who perceive them to look at them one way and later another, and to bring the onlooker to the realisation that by shifting their attention they can perceive things differently. Accordingly, the architect can teach us to use our visual faculty in a certain manner.

Scruton provides further examples to show that the particular design of a building invited the observer to become involved in making sense of her own experience of it. What we learn in such a process of becoming acquainted with architectural intention, by looking at different buildings, and by comparing their specific parts, is that we can reflect on our perception, and hence our perception can itself become a secondary object of attention. The specific form of experience we acquire is one in which the imagination is directly addressed by our perception: we look for aesthetic enjoyment even before we actually start to perceive the particular details of the building, and this makes our experience different from our non-reflective perceptions.

This way of connecting primary perception and a secondary imaginative evaluation of that perception can be learnt, developed and perfected. It is this learning process which changes our way of looking at buildings, and which turns it into an exercise in taste and aesthetic discrimination. Yet Scruton is not only indicating the educational process which leads to the proper perception of works of architecture. He also expands the actual experience, beyond the visual interpretation of a plane surface, the façade, and encourages us to be aware that the object occupies a three-dimensional space. He also stresses the significance of audible experience. Furthermore, there are also tactile and even smell-dependent layers of an architectural experience, which all need to be taken into account.

The imaginative attention required to obtain a full and correct impression of the aesthetic qualities of a building is not, however, all that is expected from the observer. A second step in the process of becoming fully acquainted with the building is required after the sensual perception has happened: an effort to understand what is at stake in the building. As the philosopher points out, "it is one of the most striking features of imaginative attention as I have described it, that experience and understanding follow each other."[111] Understanding, in the sense of an intellectual grasp of something, needs to occur as part of the process of "learning" a building and is closely dependent on the sensory apprehension of it. The significance acquired by this operation of our understanding needs to feed back into and affect "the act of imaginative attention."[112] It is due to this role of understanding in making sense of our full sensation of a building that the result of our judgement of a building's aesthetic qualities can be debated, that is, their virtues can be argued for or against. It is the role of understanding in judging that Scruton next turns to in architecture.

Scruton wishes to emphasise two important points which run counter to our habitual assumptions about the workings of taste. One is the element of rationalising the experience, and the other is the role of education. To show what Scruton means by the notion of rational calculation in the process of active and imaginative perception, he offers the example of a church. This is a description, by Geoffrey Scott, of S. Maria della Salute in Venice (ILLUSTRATION):

> In silhouette, the statues serve (like the obelisks of the lantern) to give a pyramidal contour to the composition, a line which more than any other gives mass its unity and strength… there is hardly an element in the church which does not proclaim the beauty of mass and the power of mass to give essential simplicity and dignity even to the richest and most fantastic dreams of the baroque.[113]

The same building, of course, could be described in a different manner by another observer. John Ruskin found the same building of Longhena to be not much more than a meaningless ensemble of rather massive parts, which do not aggregate into a larger whole. The difference is not in the training of Scott's or Ruskin's eyes. It is rather that one of them concludes in the process of understanding that the relations between the parts are convincing while the other one was not persuaded of the success of this effort of unification. It is perfectly possible that the same sort of experience may lead to a different overall impact on the observer, given her own personal intellectual reservoir. In other words, in order to enjoy the beauty of a certain building, one's active involvement is required, together with the exercise of one's intellect. In this context, Scruton refers to Plato, and his concept of aesthetic pleasure, which involved an "ascent from the lower to the higher realms of the mind."[114] Plato is especially prone to stressing the higher intellectual elements in aesthetic pleasure.

Scruton also cites Aristotle, who showed that an experience can, in fact, lead to a conclusive argument. In other words, an argument can lead to a conclusion about an experience or it can miss that function—this element of intellectualism turns up in Aristotle's own account of experience. Yet one should be careful not to misunderstand the point—there is still nothing deterministic in his account of judgement: there is no strict logical necessity in the process of making judgements. The process of building the connection is intellectual, cognitive and imaginative.

What, then, is the importance for Scruton of this ancient Greek emphasis on the role and function of the intellect in making sense of aesthetic experience, to turn it into a proper judgement of taste? The point that he is trying to make, I would suggest, is this: a full aesthetic judgement includes critical discrimination, which is more than just the sum of sensory apprehension. It also requires an "imaginative transformation of experience," in the "search for the true standard, the 'correct' experience – in short, the cultivation of the 'appropriate' in all its form."[115] The full significance of terms like discrimination, correctness and appropriateness will be explained only later in Scruton's book, but it is already obvious that for him an aesthetic judgement will certainly involve more than simply a subjective and intuitive response to sensual impressions. It will require the contribution of the intellect as well.

An element of primitive aesthetic response is clearly present in an impression, and the urgency of this reaction excludes the possibility of successfully applying "scientific" theories like psychoanalysis or Marxist theory to explain the aesthetic phenomenon. This is because such "scientific" theories cannot be involved in a bodily element of choice. The same is true of the interpretative strategy of looking at architecture as a sign language, in which each type of component has a well-defined meaning, just as words and grammatical elements play their roles in coding the message. Although master builders, too, resort to generalisations, the actual process of building often disregards those norms. In fact, the quintessence of architectural originality is to play with those rules, to generate meaning by ignoring and transgressing them. In this respect, we can compare architecture with poetry. The poet's use of language similarly follows rules and has customary methods of composition and rhetoric, yet it is ready to transgress those norms intentionally, in order to acquire extraordinary significance.

This comparison between architecture and the artistic use of language brings us back to the assumption that style in architecture can encode meaning into the body of a building. But style is not logical argumentation. Its form of persuasion differs from logic. When the architect applies stylistic devices, what she has to bear in mind is not simply the rules of application, but the unity, harmony or propriety of those parts when viewed together. Scruton uses the example of the Ashmolean Museum in Oxford. Its designer, Cockerell, applied various elements of the classical stylistic repertoire, but the genius of the building is how he succeeded in harmonising its very different parts: "Roman half-columns, Greek capitals, Palladian windows, Vignolesque cornices, Greek frets and mouldings, baroque pediments and Michelangiolesque window frames, together with many an original invention of his own, all in one of the most harmonious of English buildings."[116] He achieves order apparently without heeding the master builder's usual cautionary remarks, such as the one which warns not to rely on dissimilar stylistic elements. Paradoxically, this is order achieved by breaking the rules and creating a personal architectural "grammar."

Scruton rejects the idea of a simple correspondence between how architectural elements are deployed and the coding system of the grammar of natural languages. He also refutes simple theories of expression and abstraction which seek to explain the operation and nature of architecture. He discusses the possibility of attributing imitative or representative functions to buildings, while stressing the difference between the meaning of these two terms. The example he gives in this regard is the internal design of Michelangelo's Medici chapel (ILLUSTRATION). According to Scruton, Michelangelo was more interested here in the art of sculpture than in architecture, and all the architectural elements surrounding the sculptures serve as parts of a monumental frame, "a frame carried round into a complete space like a four-sided niche."[117] He points out that even the ground plan of the chapel imitates a quite elaborately processed frame of a picture. In other words, Michelangelo, as a mannerist artist, is able to add certain expressive values to the spaces that he designs, just like the best Baroque masters succeeded in evoking emotions or even passions by architectural means. Scruton's example of the latter is the space arranged around Bernini's sculpture representing St Teresa's extasy in the Cornaro Chapel (ILLUSTRATION). The effect of the rather unique combination of architectural elements which play a part in the composition of the sculpture is quoted from Pevsner's description of it, which is close to an *ekphrasis*, itself.[118] Scruton's point is that architecture does, indeed, allow such specific ways of generating meaning and value, but that the task of the critic is to identify the particular stylistic repertoire applied in each case, in this example the mannerist and Baroque architect's engagement with the human being's emotional resources, as the specific tools of exerting influence on the onlooker.

In other words, the philosopher asserts that, like other arts, architecture, too, has certain expressive qualities. He draws attention, in this context, to the anthropomorphic characters of buildings. Facades, for example, the faces of buildings, have special relevance. Scruton explains why he focuses on facades thus: "A building does not so much express an emotion, as wear a certain expression."[119] This expression, he claims, is intransitive. It does not point at something outside itself, as works of art in representational art forms do. Instead, buildings have recognisable characters, and our relationship to them is connected to our decoding of that particular character. However, it is not easy to grasp conceptually the character of specific buildings, or of various architectural styles. The architectural critic, employing his rhetorical, or even poetic talent, is faced with a challenge: how can he "translate" the sum of those discovered character traits into the vocabulary of natural language? Scruton gives an example of his own interpretation of such characters: "The Georgian townhouse has a graceful and convivial expression, the baroque palace is stately, proud but genial, the high-rise block is cold and estranged."[120] This metaphorical description of the character of certain types of building is helpful: we can easily imagine the buildings themselves when we read these descriptions of them, which is a sign of the expressive quality of both the buildings described and of the natural language the art critic used to describe the character of those buildings. Scruton's description resembles the way children try to characterise the melody and other musical qualities of different languages: they abstract from their expressive values, and focus on the sounds which are there to carry the meaning, and make an effort to describe, for example, the feminine character of French, and the masculine character of certain dialects of American English.

Obviously, the expressive qualities we encounter in connection with buildings are rather different from the expressive functions of other arts such as poetry, music or dance. For most art forms, what we are interested in is establishing the connection between the objective details and their subjective perception, with the help of those particular experiences which we directly go through during the process of making sense of an artwork. We perceive things in a specific way, when we see, touch and move in buildings. We make an elementary adjustment to what could be called the general atmosphere of a building. A primitive choice, based on primary impressions, described above, gives way to a critical judgement, consisting of further, more intellectual activities of interpretation.

Scruton's book addresses the issue of the critic's sense of detail, as an important element in the process of architectural criticism. From the very start the philosopher emphasises that attending to the details of a building is not only a necessary part of our perception of it, but also something which we constantly do in our everyday life as well, including the case when we enter a building. He also refers to the traditional wisdom that what we do when focusing on details is to find the relationship of the details to each other, and to the whole. However, he is iconoclastic in relation to that point: he claims that there is no objective harmony (*concinnitas*) between parts, in the geometrical sense of the term. He admits, however, that our sense of beauty operates together with our ability to bring together and combine our impressions of different details, to see if we sense an adequate correspondence between the different parts or not. This will decide our final aesthetic verdict of the building.

For Scruton, it is the experience of the observer that matters and that will attribute certain aesthetic properties to the building, like grace or humanity—and impressions can be formed even if the particular details which evoke these reactions from the viewer are objectively or geometrically not perfect.[121]

The example Scruton gives is the motif of the scallop. This was a motif of ancient Roman architecture, and belonged to its established vocabulary. Renaissance architects adopted it from the ancient examples. Yet the way they used this motif is different from how it was used later, for example in Baroque style. Scruton compares the use of the motif in Bramante's Tempietto and how it was used by Borromini. Bramante uses this decorative element to make a contrast with the strong and stout Doric columns. Borromini also placed scallops in alcoves but did so within a different architectural framework. The motif recurs in different forms in his church of San Carlino in Rome, one of which similarly makes contrasts with stout columns, but in the other, this contrast has gone. Even in the first case, the contrast is not as explicit, since the distance and therefore the amount of space between the strong columns and the niche is different, and therefore it looks like "an articulation of the wall rather than a niche cut into it."[122] We make sense of Bramante's decorative element in comparison with the Roman prototypes, while Borromini is in a sense competing with Bramante's approach. Bramante wanted to achieve perfection, making use of the elements of the niche and the column, both elements of the classic vocabulary. Borromini intentionally spoils Bramante's invention, in order to let his own intention shine, which stresses movement and light, a flame-like quality, instead of classic harmony and ideal proportion. What Scruton wished to stress with this comparison was to show us the development of how a single motif was treated by the Romans, in the Renaissance and in the Baroque. He also stressed that the discovery of this development to a great extent depends on us. If we are able to notice the motif, and are ready to compare its relationship to other elements within a larger framework of the building, we shall be able to make similar observations. It all depends on our ability to realise that the architect is prepared to corrupt a perfected ensemble, in order to achieve an altogether different effect, when compared to its original. We should be open to seeing in this an artistic achievement, in spite of the fact that we realise that the perfection itself is gone.

What this last example showed was that the same meaningful sign can be interpreted differently in different contexts. It is this exercise of hunting for the meaningful details in order to learn something about the intentions of the architect—the one who determines the details of an architectural ensemble—which will lead us to a full aesthetic appreciation of a work of art in architecture. In Scruton's account, this search for the meaningful detail acquires exceptional relevance. He does not pretend, though, that this method is his invention. Instead, he reads the historically inherited tracts on architecture with the eye of a philosopher, and with a cultural background, which helps him to relate his readings to each other, and to different architectural masterpieces. He finds, for example, that Alberti is less interested in a general concept of beauty, and more in "the idea of the 'appropriate' (*aptus, decens, commodus, proprius*)," and beauty itself being merely a consequence of the latter.[123] Alberti's views on the art of the appropriate are of some significance for Scruton. He republished an essay on that topic, which he first published as an article in the Times Literary Supplement in 1977, in his later collection on (mainly classical) architecture entitled *The Classical Vernacular*.[124]

Concluding his discussion of the aesthetics of architecture, he returns to ancient practical philosophy. As he understands it, the notion of the appropriate is essentially the reasoned "fitting together" of details in the creative process itself. The architect does not simply want to find the best solution to a practical problem. What he looks for is an ordered arrangement of details, which will appear as a harmonious whole, and which has a recognisable style. An architect with a style distinguishes herself by the fitting deployment of details.

Since ancient times, human personality has been distinguished by character. Such character manifests itself in the taking of specific practical choices—in other words through style. As we know it from Buffon, his style defines a man. Through his practical choices about how to put together from small details the whole of a building, the architect reveals a lot about herself as well. While denying the full subjectivism of aesthetic choice, Scruton does not deny the connection between aesthetic choice and the particular character of the individual who makes it. On the contrary, he returns to Hume and Kant. He seems to accept Kant's claim that one's personality is more than simply a bundle of impressions, beliefs, etc., as Hume had thought. Instead, Scruton accepted Kant's transcendental unity of the self, although he claimed that this unity cannot be fully known by the individual herself, because it cannot be formulated in propositional form. Self-knowledge lies, rather, in practical knowledge, in other words, in action, in our choices. "The knowledge of myself as a unity is inseparable from a certain stance towards the world, the stance, as one might put it, of 'taking responsibility' for the acts, feelings, perceptions, and so on which I designate as mine."[125]

To this quasi-Kantian description of what self-knowledge consists of, Scruton adds a further, Hegelian element. If we assume that its form of expression is action, this also implies that self-knowledge is public—it happens in front of the eyes of others, who will judge it for themselves. As Scruton sees it, the human being is "construed as a complex form of social activity"; the fulfilment of this sociable being, the perfection of her life, depends on finding her place in a larger whole, finding herself "at home in the world."[126] The human being is a being, who is able to make sense of herself and the world through understanding signs: it is in a meaningful world that she feels at home. The aim of both the architect and the observer is to find meaning in the building. The architect aims to make the right choices, which will result in details that hang together, and through that mutual interdependence the building will have a meaningful unity, thus creating the circumstances for its users to feel at home in the building as a meaningful whole. As soon as the observer is able to recognise the unity of the details of the building, she will find it meaningful, and will find herself at home in it.

This connection between external objective order and an internal subjective sense of harmony is present, according to Scruton, in the way we perceive and understand a street. "Our aesthetic understanding of the street embraces a relation between interior and exterior, between content and façade."[127] Moreover, it is a fatal mistake, as he sees it, that modernist urbanism demolished the street, and created the phenomenon of the housing estate, with its isolated buildings, which have no characteristic façades, and which are not connected by meaningful streets, but only by empty space, which has no meaning at all to the inhabitants or the visitors.

Scruton's philosophy of architecture presents the activity of being an architect, therefore, not only as an engagement in the exercise of self-knowledge, of self-expression through public action, but also as an arrangement of the details of a certain segment of the public realm, of a part of the external world. The architect engages in an activity akin to tidying up what is chaotic. His activity is, therefore, a kind of realism. Yet while Scruton is ready to admit the close connection, and in certain cases even the overlap between a practical moral judgement and an aesthetic choice based on taste, he rejects the claim that the architectural theorist can find a magic formula, with which to define the intricate relationship between morality and artistic taste. As he puts it, although our aesthetic choice might "contain an intimation" (and note here the Oakeshottian phrase used by Scruton) "of the moral sense (the sense of ourselves as social beings, tied to an order greater than ourselves)," the inference does not work in reverse: "moral values do not in their turn contain any intimation of their aesthetic embodiment."[128] The one-directional nature of the relationship between moral sense and the sense of the beautiful is not a problem for Scruton, however. In fact, that is the safeguard of artistic freedom—that there is no obligatory connection between moral standards and aesthetic choice.

Scruton does not shy away, however, from identifying at least two of the constant features of what he regards as the architectural ideal growing out of the reservoir of "accumulated critical judgements."[129] These two elements are the moulding and the façade. The moulding is an architectural means to give accent to horizontals and angles. It is a tool in the hands of the architect, by which she can dress up the sheer surface. Without mouldings, it is very difficult to attach meaning to architectural details. Similarly, the façade helps to give external public expression not only to the internal space, but also to communicate the idea of that building. The façade is indeed the face of the building, in two senses. First, it is concerned with giving character to the building, uniting its details into a meaningful whole. Second, it is the public side of the building, fulfilling its public responsibility, by taking part in the formation of a street or a square, the public realm of the human settlement. Through its mouldings and façade, the building fits into its environment properly. Scruton accepts the wisdom of the ancient Greeks, as summed up by Sir Denys Lasdun—successful architecture depends on "a sense of belonging to time, place and people and being at home in the world."[130]

The Classical Vernacular: Architectural Principles in an Age of Nihilism (1994)

The two books by Scruton on architecture are worth comparing. Published 15 years apart, the views expressed by the author certainly differ. *The Aesthetics of Architecture* was the product of a young man, whereas *The Classical Vernacular* is that of a mature author, who is more aware of both his strengths and shortcomings. While the first one was written from the outset as a comprehensive study, the aims of the second one were more modest. It was simply a collection of essays on a loose array of thoughts, united by their topic, architecture, an undying love of the author. By the time he published this second volume, his hunger for success had already been satisfied by books like *The Politics of Culture* (1981), *The Aesthetic Understanding* (1983) and *The Philosopher on Dover Beach* (1990). Yet, apparently, he wanted to return to architecture.

In *The Classical Vernacular* Scruton was more concerned with helping the reader than in the earlier monograph, where he still struggled with his own thoughts. The title of the book is itself a provocation. The two terms in the title appear to contradict each other. As architectural historian Carroll William Westfall explains, "Tradition guides both the vernacular and the classical that anchors the opposite ends of the spectrum of buildings."[131] While there are different forms of the vernacular, the classical in European architecture remains the same: the language of architecture inherited from ancient Greek and Roman architecture, and its renaissances in European history. Scruton suggests that we can look at the classical itself as a form of the vernacular, albeit a special one.

The book's subtitle is also telling. It recalls Scruton as a combative public intellectual—who by the time of publishing the book, had given up his university position, and with it, his academic career, because of the sharp ideological confrontations he was involved in. This subtitle pulls no punches: Architectural Principles in an Age of Nihilism. Again, it sets up an opposition, this time between the worthless and hollow nature of the present moment and a principled way of building. The point here is that in spite of the decadence and decline of culture, it is still possible to discuss and indeed defend principles in the realm of architecture.

Besides the title, the other metatextual guidance for the reader is the Introduction, which is surprisingly short—although the whole volume is slim, running to no more than 150 pages. Taking into account the 55 pictures that illustrate Scruton's arguments, one cannot charge him with verbosity. In a condensed book such as this, the Introduction, even if it is only seven pages long, takes on a specific significance. Here, Scruton presents a short version of his philosophical anthropology, a topic which he addressed in a number of further writings, including his book *On Human Nature*. He starts out from the assumption that human societies are governed by fashions. Scruton, the highly critical aesthete, cannot help connecting his criticism of modernist architecture with a biting criticism of the planned economy of the post-war world: he views these two phenomena as embodiments of the public policy of the age.

A second preparatory note describes the institutional conditions, which led to what he calls the diseducation of architecture: according to Scruton, the decline is the effect of the misguided tuition delivered at the schools of architecture. Scruton believed that modernism would not have had such a major impact on our built environment if architects had not been educated in schools of architecture. When they decided to bring professional education into architectural schools, instead of the earlier workshops of the various handicrafts, the curriculum itself changed. Instead of the initiation of the apprentice into the skills of how to build in a proper style and form, students of these schools had to learn theories—the doctrines of modernism. This is why contemporary architects are not aware of the function of the façade, the relevance of the street, or how buildings should fit into their environment of a real or ideal community. They do not respect the distinction between the public and the private realm, which is the major dividing line for buildings. They tendentiously underestimate or miscomprehend the nature and significance of ornament and detail. Instead, they are well versed in ideology and utopia.

Scruton was not satisfied with simply making a sweeping criticism of modernist architectural education, however. He aimed instead to offer a real foundation upon which to build an understanding of the classical vernacular. He outlines a philosophical anthropology tuned to preparing the ground for architecture. He distinguishes two sides of human nature, the biological and the social. The biological elements of human nature include the following: (1) we orient ourselves in the world primarily visually; (2) we stand upright; and (3) we seek shelter from extreme weather conditions. All the three have effects on architecture. The same is true of rationality, the major source of human sociability. As free beings, the values and obligations we recognise motivate us. We have moral, aesthetic and religious criteria for evaluating actions and thoughts. They are the sources of our inclination to judge, which in turn leads others to judge us. Our activities cross each other, creating a community among us. We need stability, as well as ongoing transformation, to adapt to our ever-changing environment. Together we thus create a common set of values.

From these two sources of human nature Scruton moulds the major building blocks of his aesthetics of architecture. The starting point is the aesthetic sense, which helps us searching for and evaluating aesthetic worth, mainly in the visual realm, but also imaginatively. It enables us to embrace certain forms and materials, while rejecting others, leading to the creation of a characteristic human environment, defined by an aesthetics of design and order. Human beings create objects meant to carry meaning and aesthetic quality, and to be sources of gratification for the eye, the mind and the soul. The architect is able to create an object, which merits study for its own sake, through the sort of contemplation, which brings satisfaction with human rationality. In the traditional educational process, we practice evaluating buildings from this perspective as well, which helps us to acquire "taste, judgement and criticism."[132] The work produced by architects, the realm of common habitation in the city is the object of communal consideration and exchange of views.

This communal aspect of architecture, which sets it apart from other arts, is a recurring theme in Scruton's essays in *The Classical Vernacular*. It reveals the connection between the art of architecture and politics, in particular the politics of the city. To prove that we focus on two of the essays more closely, where Scruton directly connects his interest in architecture with his interest in politics.

The essay entitled *Public Space and the Classical Vernacular* was first published in 1984. The starting point of it is the concept of public space itself, including a definition of the public. To understand the notion of the public, one has to examine it with its opposite, the private. When we talk about the private sphere, we are referring to human relations which are both intimate and which involve involuntary obligations for a close circle around us, most often for our family. To be in private usually means to be within one's comfort zone, where one feels safe at home. On the other hand, to be in public means moving out of one's comfort zone, into an area where one needs to take into account the behaviour of unknown others, moved by motives that may be difficult to fathom, and to which one has to accommodate oneself flexibly. While the private sphere can be identified with the family, in Hegelian terms, the public sphere is that of civil society (the *bürgerliche Gesellschaft*).[133] When one tries to make progress in the public realm, one has to distinguish between those who seem to be friendly to the aspirations of the individual, and those who seem to oppose them.[134] Scruton associates the family with the human relationships of piety, respect, love and obedience, while the latter, civil society is characterised by choice and contractual agreement. While the private sphere is basically a world which is well-known and therefore friendly for the individual, the public sphere is unfamiliar, and the starting point there is a lack of trust, which needs to be earned by compacts, to which we adhere and which are guaranteed by institutions. The most important and powerful guarantee of these is the state itself, which, according to the model established by Hobbes in and by the *Leviathan*, is there to ensure peace, and to resolve conflicts among the participants in the public realm. In a well-functioning state, the aim of government is justice, securing a fair deal among people, which enforces mutual honour. Here Scruton relies on one of his favourite Kantian terms: in society there exists a demand to take the other not only as means to achieve one's own intentions, but as ends in themselves.

Justice can have institutional guarantees, but the ancients thought that it largely depended on the individual's virtue. Scruton also refers in connection with it to individual qualities: to what he calls "good manners" or "civility," "the formalised expression of the ruling virtue of civil society – the virtue of 'respect for persons'."[135] As he sees it, without civility and good manners there is no chance to have a sustainable civil society. Architecture can play a major role in establishing and enhancing the

virtue of civility, a virtue which has often been associated with an idealised British culture.

Scruton claims that the distinction between the private and the public
sphere is a political one. And architecture is the most obvious way of
physically separating the sphere of privacy from the public sphere.
Scruton refers to Ruskin, who in *The Seven Lamps of Architecture* (1849)
called it the most political art.

The other part of the concept analysed by Scruton in the essay is, of
course, space. The distinction in this respect distinguishes architectural
space from the physical space defined by geometry, or the personal space
which belongs to the human being, which is the theme of phenomenology. Space in architecture is defined by "perceived boundaries," meaning
the walls built by human hands, to mark the territory claimed by an
individual owner, or a human community. The public spaces of architecture Scruton is discussing here are not the church, the market or the
square, however. Instead, he concentrates on the street. The opposite
term which allows us to pin down the meaning of the street is the park,
the favourite exterior space of the modernists. Referring to Jane Jacobs,
Scruton claims that when the modernists took the park as the paradigm
case of the public, they forgot about the primary form of public space in
the city, the street.[136] "The street is the most important of the open public
spaces, and the task of constructing a street is the most important that
any planner may face."[137] With the shift in the architect's interest from
the street to the park comes a shift away from the political, which also
means a shift from the public. Interestingly, Scruton attributes the recognition of the importance of the street to the ancients. The examples he
provides, Ephesus and Pergae, were Greek cities. Yet it is in the Romans'
art of building streets that Scruton finds an expression of good manners,
as a result of the civic virtues, producing a harmony between the public
and the private.

When discussing the way in which a street can keep in balance the
exterior and the interior through windows and the façade, he returns to
the modern discourse. He refers to Hayek's influential ideas about spontaneous order, a major achievement of a flourishing society. Referring to
an interpretation of Hayek by John Gray, published by Scruton in the
Salisbury Review a year earlier, he identifies a sort of "tacit knowledge" of

a society, which is of primary importance when assessing the architectural qualities of a city.[138] The spontaneous order of a society is the unintended outcome of the practical knowledge of its members, including their skills and other intellectual and moral virtues. Yet Scruton manages to infuse an Aristotelian element even into his account of Hayek's notion of spontaneous order. It was Aristotle who emphasised the significance of practical knowledge (*phronesis, prudence*) for the smooth operation of the polis. Scruton makes use of this distinction between practical and theoretical knowledge in the sixth book of the *Nicomachean Ethics*, when he contrasts practical knowledge with rational planning. Hayek's major reference point is the market, as a social institution which can achieve spontaneous order, but which itself is never the result of a rational plan. In this argument, of course, one can also sense the influence of Oakeshott on Scruton: it was he who devoted so much energy to criticise the rationalistic impulse in social organisations, so characteristic of the centralising, bureaucratic tendencies of the twentieth century. He does not explicitly mention Oakeshott here, however. Instead, he refers to Burke, and his defence of prejudice, as his inspiration in this matter.

Scruton takes the example of riding a bicycle, used both by Hayek and by Oakeshott, to illustrate the difference between practical knowledge, which does not require reflection, and theoretical knowledge, which does not necessarily help in practical execution. We learn how to ride a bicycle by a trial-and-error method, following example, but most importantly, conditioning our bodies how to keep the balance. The theoretical knowledge of the physics of that balance might be useful to create a better bicycle, one which is easier to control or which can be faster and therefore better used in a bicycle competition. Scruton's point is not a contrast for its own sake between two forms of knowledge, but rather to point out that the two can cooperate very well, in fact. Once again referring to Ephesus and Pergae, he finds traces of conscious efforts of planning in these cities. What he finds counterproductive is not such planning in itself, but the planning mentality, which starts out from abstract principles, and strives to realise them, no matter what price is to be paid for it. At this point, Scruton might have had Eliot in mind, who famously wrote in *Notes Toward the Definition of Culture*: "[O]ne thing to avoid is a universalised planning; one thing to ascertain is the limits of the plannable."[139]

Developing a city, one should not underestimate the significance of practical knowledge that directs our lives, and the planner should not succumb to the hubristic belief that he knows better what is good for the inhabitants than they know themselves. What is relevant for a particular community cannot easily be determined from the outside, and therefore planners can make serious misjudgements when they try to prioritise the ends served by their plans. The façades of buildings, or streets in a city are not only functional in the sense that they allow purposeful activities to take place—they are valuable assets in themselves. A street is not only there for people to pass from point A to point B. It can also be enjoyed for its own sake by the neighbours who lodge nearby or by visitors to that part of the city.

The street where one lives can help one to feel at home, or even can contribute to the formation of one's identity. Scruton, as we have seen, was well aware of the significance of the place we have become accustomed to, or to which we are attached. Earlier, I mentioned his concept of *oikophilia*—which could be translated as the love of home. This love relates to the place, but also to the people living there. People who live close to each other are connected to each other by an invisible bond: they share the same horizon of memory, each playing their part in the same story.

Scruton keeps emphasising the relevance of boundaries in connection with the sense of feeling at home. As he sees it, walls and facades create the space in which we feel at home: "The classical idiom is devoted to the perfection of civil boundaries."[140] Once again, Eliot is a reference point, as he too felt that places define us, in the sense that they set the limits of our settled form of existence. Certainly, Eliot's own case is somewhat extraordinary: although he regarded himself a traditionalist, he in fact lived his life quite far away from the place where he was born. This is, of course, explained by the fact that the Anglo-American culture was, and remained to a certain extent, as an undivided whole, coextensive.

In order to feel "gemütlich," one should design the walls in a friendly and human manner. The façade is a wall made friendly and human. Describing the street where he lives in London, Scruton talks about "facades that stand politely beside one another."[141] He reinforces in this description of well-defined boundaries the idea that, in fact, boundaries help to create spaces which feel safe and homely. He recalls the idea of enclosure: a defendable area, which is human in scale, and which its inhabitants can keep under their control. When he claims that the enclosed spaces of his street relate to each other in a polite manner, he teaches a civic lesson. "The politeness of style… reminds one constantly of the ideal condition of society, in which people seek to co-operate, and in which conversation takes the place of command."[142] Here again, Scruton is drawing a parallel between architectural order and social bonds. The expression used by Scruton is once again Oakeshottian: conversation was Oakeshott's favoured term for describing the sort of encounter desirable in human community instead of aggression and violence. Scruton's classical wall, with its scales and standards, can teach people how to live side by side: "The classical wall, which is humanly proportioned, safe… reminds the pedestrian that he is not alone, that he is in a world of human encounter, and that he must match the good manners of the wall which guides him."[143]Once again, the philosopher calls attention to a connection between architecture and communal manners.

Another chapter of the book which also concerns the interaction between politics and architecture, and which is entitled "Architecture and the Polis," consists of numbered paragraphs—suggesting a manifesto. This is a specific genre in twentieth-century architectural and art history: it serves to sum up in an exemplary manner the basic truths about a chosen topic. Scruton's chapter tells the story of human settlement. When the term to *dwell* appears, it is in italics, to show the specific sense attributed to it—that it has been drawn from the Heideggerian vocabulary. For Heidegger the spatial aspect of the human individual—or of the community, for that matter—is crucial. Dwelling occupies him already in *Being and Time*, but receives even more attention in the later influential text, *Building Dwelling, Thinking* (1954). It refers to that specific aspect of being which is related to the home, to having a place.[144] To dwell is the result of a communal act of settlement, and the place chosen for that purpose has a specific significance: it will be regarded by that people as a sacred place. Here Scruton explicitly refers to Durkheim, but I think that he may also have in mind *The Ancient City* (1864), by Numa Denis Fustel

de Coulanges. Fustel regarded religion and cult as the sources of the institution building approach of the Greeks and Romans. Scruton also stresses
that a settled people attributes religious significance to the place it has
chosen to settle, and that it will erect religious buildings at the centre of
the place—in fact, the primary form of building for a settled people will
be sacred architecture. In order to live a peaceful life, and to acquire the
potential to grow, the community also has to make explicit its guiding
norms, in order to let the members of the community as well as visitors
know the requirements of the community. For that reason people living
together will establish their laws. Scruton recalls the Biblical story of
Moses receiving from God at the Mount Sinai not only the Ten
Commandments, or the basic laws of his people, but also the plan of the
temple they had to erect.

Just as the public buildings of religious worship defended the gods, so
private homes were seen as the main defence of the individuals, united
into families. The law prescribed the worship of God, but it also prescribed the protection of the private life of the individual. The conceptu-
alisation of the person in Judeo-Christian thought relates to the
understanding of the idea in the Old Testament: "the human life, sancti-
fied by the law."[145]

Scruton attributes special significance to the fact the temple is not
simply an enclosure but a precinct. This latter is a form of boundary that
is permeable—God leaves the building open to allow newcomers join the
community. They are, in fact, as new members of the community,
expected to enter the building to perform their cultic acts of worshiping
God. Beyond this lies an internal part of the temple, the inner sanctum,
which only those who have some specific role to perform in religious rituals are allowed to enter, with the most important task that of making a
sacrifice to honour the God.

The permeability of the building is made clear by architectural means.
The temple consists of columns, a colonnade and steps. Of these, columns are of primary importance. Columns hold up the roof of the building. They are erect in form so as to perform this function, and they are
therefore comparable to human beings. But they are also signposts to the
God. This humanlike and God-serving nature of the column led to the
birth of the statue, an important part of sacred architecture, later

acquiring an autonomy of its own, by decorating and lending symbolic meaning to the public space. Columns, too, have a posture, and their different parts have separate functions. These parts relate to each other, creating the internal proportions of the column. Finally, a column is not only the raw material of the stone(s) it is made of, it is also the form cut out of the stone, able to receive light, and to cast shade, through the fine elaboration of its surface.

Columns are placed in line, forming a colonnade, on a stepped platform. Building a colonnade, instead of an external wall, results in a permeable kind of building. Members of the community can enter it by taking the steps which lead them through the colonnade into the building. These steps serve to raise the citizen to higher ground, above the plane of ordinary life. Through its permeability the temple becomes an organic part of the city: its God is, as Scruton puts it, "the universal god of citizenship."[146] The architectural elements of column, colonnade and steps make whoever arrives at the temple feel at home: its scale is attuned to the human form. This human proportionality of the architectural form of the temple ensures that both the gods and humans feel that it is appropriate for them. The domestic God of the Greek temple mediates between the community and the divine sphere. The domestic God is "the god of justice and law," "the bringer of law, peace and compromise."[147]

The Greek temple is, therefore, not only a sacred site, the dwelling place of the God of the city. It also expresses and embodies the settlement, as the common good of the whole community. Its form includes three different layers of harmony: the harmony between the community and its gods, the harmony of law and politics under divine protection and the visual harmony of the building, which is expressed, pars pro toto, by the column, taken together with the stylobate and the architrave.[148] The temple collects the different dimensions of the city together. It is both the location of religious rituals and a political-legal entity, a geographical location, providing a home for the whole community and its gods in a physical environment, which has its own special aesthetic attributes. In this sense, the temple is more than a functional unit. It also needs to have an aesthetic standard of its own. Its beauty is nothing less than the public demonstration of the community's legal and religious convictions. The most relevant feature of this building is the orders of the columns, opening up the space to all the members of the community. The temple is built to embody religious permanence, even eternity, the exact opposite of the kairotic moment, so important in the political life of the community. Yet the architect can also employ the classical orders for rather different purposes, as it is a nicely adaptable architectural tool, with which basic problems of building design can be solved. The column played different roles in various kinds of buildings in ancient Rome, including religious sites, covered or open areas of public activity—political, military-defensive, entertainment and commercial interactions—and private homes. The orders of columns allowed architecture to interact with those who entered the building, in other words, architectural forms could begin to carry meaning, as expressed in the concept of "implied order," suggesting the harmony of what is visible, and what is beyond the visible. The pattern-book became a translating tool, the dictionary used by both the builder and the observer to make the reading readable and to encode and decode its meanings. As I mentioned earlier, Scruton's favourite signs in this sign-language are the mouldings and cornices of the façade, providing the expressive functions of the building.

Scruton eloquently proves the central position of the classical Greek or Roman temple in architectural history. It served as a prefiguration of the Gothic cathedral of the Middle Ages, which leads humans out of the world of everyday experience, in order to raise their soul up into a space of metaphysical and supernatural abstraction. He convincingly shows that elements of temple architecture would be used in private houses, where the idea of an implied order helps the functional building to obtain homelike attributes, enabling our private sphere to provide a decent form of cohabitation both for the members of the family and their guests. The language of the pattern book taught humans, builders and inhabitants alike, the social-political virtues of civility, good manners and decency.[149]

While both the medieval Christian church and the ordinary apartment house of the medieval city preserved certain architectural elements of the classical temple, neither of them can be seen to be as central to the architectural vernacular of European culture, as the temple was in the ancient polis. The home of the individual is built to enable him and his family to live meaningful lives as members of the community, if it is correctly proportioned. If art is overdosed in its architectural form, as in the Gothic cathedrals, or neglected as in the modernist functional building, architecture misses its point: For Scruton, both of these extremes miss the human scale, and therefore the actual building cannot properly achieve its task of connecting the members of a family to each other, or the community to the sacred. If the implied order is turned upside down, the architectural form does not serve the purposes of the settlement. Of these two possible mistakes, the modernist scandal of desecration is all the more devastating, as it can result in a way of life without standards. On the other hand, the effort to transplant the ideas of the Gothic cathedral to private buildings, suggested by Pugin, is just as disproportionate, and therefore mistaken. The idea is whimsical, as a "grand" style is mistakenly used for ordinary purposes. In fact, for Scruton, the two extremes are linked: the disproportionate, out-of-tune nineteenth-century neo-Gothic style was the gateway to modernity's loss of touch with the sacred, and its destruction of a balanced form of cohabitation. Scruton conceptually differentiates collectivity and community: while the first term refers to an inorganic relationship between the part and the whole, the second represents a balanced relationship between the individual and her private and public community, including her family, her city and her God.

After considering these two examples of illustrating how architecture relates to politics, finally let us examine Scruton's presentation of an individual artist, architect and thinker. As well as discussing modern masters, architects and theoreticians of architecture, Scruton devoted an essay to Leon Battista Alberti, the humanist architect and architectural thinker. Alberti is generally considered as one, whose ideas of architecture was collected in a set of humanist writings, inspired by the rhetorical ideals of Cicero, but also directly influenced by the ancient Roman architectural theorist Vitruvius. His humanist approach encouraged him to write about architecture, an activity he himself practised in Mantua, where he designed two churches. In these works he had to address not only technical questions like how and in what order to build certain parts of the building but also more substantive ones like how to live.[150] In other words, the discourse of Alberti, as a humanist, was one which covered such diverse fields as engineering, aesthetics and moral philosophy. For that reason, the author has difficulties to introduce such a thinker to the postmodern reader. Scruton decides to do so with the help of his unfinished project, an index of the terminology used by Alberti.[151] This methodology is reminiscent of the conceptual history practised by some German historians of ideas, like the project of the *Geschichtliche Grundbegriffe* of Kosselleck, or that of the *Historisches Wörterbuch der Philosophie*, edited by Joachim Ritter.

Scruton's interest is not in methodology, however. Rather, he aims to show that in a humanist context expounding the right way of building necessitated addressing the issue of the right way of living. In other words, his aim here is to surpass the strictly art historical approach to Alberti's work, and to look at the full range of its significance, making use of a philosophical analysis of his vocabulary.

Scruton is also eager to show that a simple identification of Alberti's concept of beauty with mathematical proportionality is misleading. He thought it important to show the way Alberti approached the problem of proportions. If we look at his list of vocabulary, we shall see at once, he argues, that the Renaissance master employed a whole range of terms to describe proportion, and the term most often mentioned, *concinnitas*, is in fact not the most important one among them.[152] His list of terms referring to proportion include *aptus, commodus, decens, dignus, integer, numerus, proprius*, all of them sharing the meaning of what is "'appropriate', 'measured', and 'correct'."[153] In other words, when thinking about beauty, Alberti came to the conclusion that whatever we regard as beautiful might also, in fact, be termed "appropriate" or "fitting." These terms cannot be substituted by simple mathematical formulae, but rather should be understood as identifying what is visually reasonable, or acceptable to the observer's eyes. Such visual acceptability depended on the proper (Scruton uses the term: "apt and significant") selection and arrangement of the building's details. In his interpretation, the humanist finds the choice of a detail appropriate, whenever it can be attributed to a person whose ideas seem to have borne the test of time. The appropriate choice of detail is evidence of a way of thinking which is aware not only of the technical problems confronted, but also of human nature. The architect's task is to choose the details that satisfy the eye, by searching for what seems to be agreeable to rational beings. We, as human beings, have "a sense of ourselves as creatures who endure," and who are able to recognise in the architect's choice of details "symbolic appearance," because "(t)he pursuit of such appearances is the pursuit of a certain style of life."[154] To choose the proper or fitting action is a practical, moral choice. In other words, the choices made in the building process are not simple functional choices. They are also subject to aesthetic appreciation. This second aspect of the choices of the architect is why an aesthetic education plays such a major role in the humanistic approach to architecture. To undergo an educational process is itself a choice of life. He appreciates Alberti's rich culture acquired in the best schools of the day, in Padua and Bologna.

Scruton is also eager to explain Alberti's definition of beauty: "harmony (concinnitas) of parts, fitted together with just reflection in such a way that nothing could be added, diminished or altered but for the worse."[155] As we noted earlier, the concept of harmony is crucial to this way of thinking, as it results in what is decorous (*decus*). Yet harmony is not simply a certain mathematical or geometrical quality, but something felt by the observer, whose sense of beauty is applied to the parts of the building, and who discovers this harmony in the "fitting" or "appropriate" concordance of details. The discovery of that sensual perception is made by a comparison of details, in other words by a rational exercise of deliberation. Scruton quotes Alberti on this: "non opinio, verum animis innata quaedam ratio efficient," which translates as "not determined by opinion, but rather by an innate faculty of the mind."[156]

The choice, then, is made through a thought process, including both the exercise of a sense of beauty and a rational justification. This second part of the process requires a langue, or style, which attributes meaning to the particular parts: to understand their relationship is like understanding a linguistic utterance by an analysis of its grammatical form and vocabulary, which on its turn will determine its style. However, the result of the thought process, as in Aristotle's practical syllogism, is not a theoretical conclusion, but a sense or feeling of something being coherent and right. When searching for the correspondences between or among parts, we depend on our own sensory impressions: we learn to listen and react properly to what we experience in our inner self, by perceiving the meaningful external elements.

The difficulty of understanding Alberti's conception of architectural beauty lies in the fact that he does not separate, conceptually, the aesthetic and the functional elements in the architect's choices, or in other words he does not distinguish explicitly between the technical (*techné*) aspects of it and the aesthetic side, which is also connected to practical choice (*phronesis, prudentia*). In this discourse, of course, Scruton applies Aristotelian terminology. But he also learns from Heidegger, from the specific way he interpreted Aristotle, when he described *phronesis* as a practical concern with one's life.[157] The crucial aspect of the plan (conception) of the building, for the observer, is its form and appearance. Architecture as an art enables us "to appoint to the edifice and all its parts an appropriate place, exact proportion, suitable disposition and harmonious order."[158]

Scruton does not refer to Heidegger when pointing out the connection between aesthetic and moral values. He simply explains that Alberti does not use a purely aesthetic terminology. When searching for his sources, Scruton tries to link Alberti's terminology back to the practical reasoning to be found in classical Roman moral and rhetorical writing, especially in Cicero's *Orator*. *Concinnitas* is a term which was also used by Cicero, he claims. Furthermore, he points out that Alberti uses the same language in his treatise on architecture as he did in his Ciceronian book on the family.[159] This was an early work by Alberti, in which he had searched for "the harmony and grace intrinsic to civilised behaviour."[160] This is not accidental, according to Scruton: throughout his life Alberti tried to keep aesthetic taste and practical (moral) reasoning together, to enable us to see the connection between the sense of beauty and moral judgement. This was a crucial point for Scruton, for a number of reasons.[161] It was partly because it is in harmony with Watkin's understanding of the moral aspect of architecture. Even more importantly, though, it was because it helps him to criticise the modernists, who, he claims, moralised their theories, while in their practice giving in to a totalitarian impulse. Modernism, in this vision, not only contradicts itself in this way but is revealed to be aggressive, as opposed to the "mildness and modesty of Alberti's discourse." Scruton himself becomes quite critical at this point against modernism, and supportive of the terminological harmony of Alberti. Of course, there is nothing surprising in Scruton's argument. In a certain sense, he is simply repeating the commonplace assumption of humanism: that art should be made appropriate to the human being. While the moderns were well aware of this ancient postulate, their practice disregarded the particular human beings, and focused instead on satisfying mass demand. For Scruton this turns out to be a crucial moral failure, one which has aesthetic aspects.

Scruton's analysis, at this point, once again builds a bridge to connect the two parts of his philosophical interest: art and politics. The thought of Alberti, the humanist artist, who revitalised the ancient Roman ideas of decorum and propriety, as analysed here, served as a role model for Scruton as a philosopher. Cicero's ideal of decorum and Vitruvius' own approach to architecture both connected aesthetic appreciation with moral worth. Alberti and his contemporaries revived this ideal, and they themselves became practitioners of a range of arts and sciences, supposing that some central notions of order and proportion were applicable to all these practices. Finally, Scruton, too, tried to become such a generalist, acquainting himself with the theory and practice of a number of arts and sciences, in order to be able to say something relevant about human nature and the human condition as well as about the failure of politics in the days of totalitarian ideology.

New Urbanism, Poundbury and the Building Better Commission

Scruton's fascination with architecture, as a way to build a house, as a form of design, and as a form of creating a community and a home for people, that is, in the form of urbanism, remained with him throughout his career. Although he did not publish any more monographs on architecture, he kept writing on the topic, mostly in the form of rather critical pieces about the ideal and reality of modern urbanism. In a way his criticism of contemporary architectural design and practices became just as iconic as his opposition to the twentieth- or twenty-first-century manifestations of left-liberal thinking. He became public enemy number one in this field as well, hated by many of the intellectual elite and the political class of the country (often even in the circles of conservative governments).

In a certain sense, however, he became a champion of the ordinary people, as a result of his unhesitant condemnation of inhuman practices, both in the political realm and in the realm of (mostly public) architecture, by the end of his life. He even became a cult figure, who succeeded in symbolising a form of learned resistance against all expressions of the centralising impulse, or against synchronised global efforts to achieve social engineering which disregards the interests and opinions of the ordinary local people, and which boasts of creating new ways of thinking *ex nihilo*, but in fact simply destroys old and proven institutions, practices and ways of life.

In the final part of this chapter on Scruton's architectural thought and activity, we shall discuss three forms of his engagement with contemporary architecture. First, we shall explore his role in a contemporary movement. Secondly, we shall look at a specific manifestation of his support. Finally, we shall review his achievements as the chair of an independent enquiry into the regulatory background of the construction sector, which supported bearing in mind local norms to control urban investment.

In a short text published by the American Enterprise Institute, Scruton published a manifesto for a new movement in architectural design and urbanism, called *New Urbanism*.[162] This happened in 2012, when the movement was on the rise, mostly in the US. Apparently, however, it lacked a coherent theory on the conceptual level. Scruton seems to have been approached to provide a concise body of reflections on the basic ideas which could serve to support this new movement, by offering the rational argumentation behind its policy criticism and its own suggestions about an alternative direction to take.

This is all the more remarkable, as the movement was based on the ideas and publications of such stars of twentieth-century architectural theory as Lewis Mumford and Jane Jacobs. By this time Scruton seems to have reached a level of public recognition comparable to that of these great critics of contemporary practices and ways of thinking in architecture.

The movement behind this initiative had already appeared in the early 1980s in the US. In his encyclopaedia entry on New Urbanism, Siddhartha Sen claims that "New urbanism or neo-traditional planning/design, is the most influential postmodern design paradigm for American suburbs. Developed by architects and urban designers since the early 1980s, it attempts to address the ills associated with urban sprawl and post-Second World War suburban development."[163] The movement's institutional basis is the Congress for the New Urbanism, established in 1993. Its foundational text, the Charter of the New Urbanism claims:

> We advocate the restructuring of public policy and development practices to support the following principles: neighborhoods should be diverse in use and population, communities should be designed for the pedestrian and transit as well as the car; cities and towns should be shaped by physically defined and universally accessible public spaces and community institutions; urban places should be framed by architecture and landscape design that celebrate local history, climate, ecology, and building practice.[164]

Although the Congress and its charter had managed to exercise great influence among practitioners as well as policy- and decision-makers, and a new conceptual tool had also been created in 2009, entitled the *Canons of Sustainable Architecture and Urbanism*, the movement clearly felt it had to further strengthen its conceptual credentials. It was most probably for this reason that Scruton was approached by the movement.

Scruton's message is clear, and in tune with his thought in other fields of philosophy. In his argument, he starts out of the assumption that Western culture is a culture of cities. He quotes Hayek to verify this point: "Civilisation as we know it is inseparable from urban life."[165] Certainly, Hayek's fascination with the age of the Scottish Enlightenment is connected with the fact that it was called the age of politeness.[166] Whenever there is a flourishing period in our history, our cities are crucial to it, and whenever the latter are decaying the whole of our culture is in decline as well. He points out that we have witnessed a flight from the cities, especially from the centres of cities, and the growth of the urban sprawl, a process where whoever can afford to builds her own little realm of privacy, disengaging from the community. The question which follows from all this is this: how can the city centres be revitalised? This question is an urgent one, and one which is especially difficult to answer in the US by a conservative thinker. This is because the American right traditionally trusts the markets, and distrusts central authorities, be they federal, state or municipal authorities. The American conservative prefers freedom to the will of an impersonalised agency or other power centres. Yet the depopulation of city centres is difficult to keep under control by traditional market means. But state subsidy is quite alien from the American political and business community. The market seems to reconfirm the tendencies of individual choices, favouring the suburb instead of the overloaded centres. Yet, in the long term, there is an unresolved problem of sustainability here: logically, there is no suburb without the urbs.[167]

In search of a solution to this disappointing phenomenon, Scruton seems to accept as a starting point Jane Jacobs' criticism of zoning in urban planning. Jacob famously criticised the artificial segregation between different functions of the city, a practice which assigns to each function a different zone, or quarter of the city, and which was one of the major innovations of modernist city planning. Scruton does not, however, take that insight by Jacobs to launch a general attack on central planning. As he points out, a number of great cities grew out of human plans, including the capital of the US, Washington, DC, or, going back further in history, medieval cities grew under serious legal constraints, which limited the freedom of choice of individual builders within the confines of the city, and especially in the city centres. His example of the success of such constraints is Venice, where city authorities did not hesitate to prescribe certain technical details of new buildings very early on.

Scruton finds the core of the problem in the fact that it is big business which takes over the city centre, and therefore the middle classes leave. The costs of apartments in centres rise (in terms both of price and of crime), and people are prepared to commute or use their cars on a daily basis, in return for living outside of the pressures of a great city. This is how the downtown plus suburbs model emerged.[168]

Loyal to his historical approach, Scruton recalls earlier critics of this development, including Joel Krotkin and Robert Gruegmann, or James Howard Kunstler's popular book *The Geography of Nowhere* (1993) and *The Long Emergency* (2005). He traces this critical strand back to its sources: to authors like John Ruskin, William Morris and others, up to Lewis Mumford. These authors provided the inspiration for New Urbanism, a movement which gained popularity recently both in America and in Europe.

In order to suggest a way out from this impasse Scruton recalls Britain's Town and Country Planning Act of 1946—the influential idea of Clough

Williams-Ellis. The aim behind this legal norm was to secure a green belt around British towns, in other words to check the growth of sprawl, or simply to preserve the countryside. In making this reference, Scruton also proposes to introduce certain measures to reverse the unwanted trend of emptying city centres.

As Scruton presents the case, the city centres are the heart of cities. They provide occasions for personal encounters between inhabitants as well as encounters with outsiders. One of the imperatives of why to live in cities is precisely to enjoy such encounters. Forms of pastime, which turn human beings into sociable creatures, in constant interaction with each other, requires the multifunctional use of space characteristic of centres. To experience peaceful but dynamic social interaction requires certain environmental conditions, including architectural density. City centres attract people, and that is not possible, if those who build them disregard a human criterion for being attracted: beauty. American modernism forgot about beauty, as it was too engaged in meeting the functional demands of investors and builders. Scruton's manifesto draws attention to the central significance of beauty in our experience of the city, and most importantly, in our impressions of the city centre. It requires special attention and care to shape or configure a place in such a way that people will feel good there. Even if most conservatives prefer unguided, organic growth, there is a need for appropriate standards in cities to sustain them. Without coordinated standards, no settlement can function properly.

Scruton takes Paris as his example of how a city can grow while keeping its vigour and vitality. This might seem a bit unfair, as Paris' history was indeed troubled, and its present physical form is due to that troubled history. History is lacking from most American downtowns. Yet Scruton succeeds to draw conclusions from the historical example of Paris to show how to encourage developments towards a beautifully built environment. One feature of the success of Paris is that the ordinances of the authorities did not contain ends to be achieved, but only those requirements which had to be fulfilled (the side-constraints), if people wanted to build: "Limits on height and scale, materials, and architectural details are laid down to ensure that whatever is built or renovated will conform to its surroundings."[169] These are the requirements which ensure that a newly built architectural product will fit in, and will seem to be embedded into its surroundings.[170] Accommodation to an environment depends on the building's chances to fit in. The appeal of the building's appearance depends on its aesthetic quality.

The second conclusion Scruton draws from the experience of Paris is that the constraints on building need to be unashamedly aesthetic in their nature. With the right sort of aesthetic side constraints, the end product—which is itself always changing—will be part of the face of the centre, which is recognisable and enjoyable, with an aesthetically pleasing appearance. And views and cityscapes which are enjoyable will very soon attract people: for they feel good in an urban environment which has aesthetic appeal. At this point Scruton adds an unashamed praise of the bourgeoisie. For it is the well-to-do middle classes who are ready to devote extra energy to turning their surroundings into a settlement, a home.

> The centripetal city is the city of the bourgeoisie, the city that attracts into its center the prosperous and adventurous middle classes who are not only the catalyst of economic life but also the ones who will invest in public order, rescue the schools from collapse, support the life of the theater and concert hall, fill and endow the universities.[171]

Scruton's main message in the manifesto, his suggestions about how to counteract undesirable recent developments were to be tested in the last year of his life, when the conservative government made him the chair (and later co-chair) of an independent commission convened to give advice on how such aesthetic constraints should actually work nationwide.

The UK government's Ministry of Housing, Communities and Local Government set up the body with the provocative name of the Building Better Building Beautiful Commission (BBBBC) in November 2018. The Secretary of State James Brokenshire provided a threefold explanation of the goals of the commission:

1. To promote better design and style of homes, villages, towns and high streets, to reflect what communities want, building on the knowledge and tradition of what they know works for their area.

2. To explore how new settlements can be developed with greater community consent.

3. To make the planning system work in support of better design and style, not against it.[172]

Sir Roger Scruton was an obvious yet courageous choice to pick as the chair of the Commission.

To promote beauty in architectural and urban design by administrative means was to challenge the earlier status quo. Yet the government was on firm ground, as there was obvious popular, common-sense support behind the idea that design should aim at beauty. Also, the initiative explicitly referred to local knowledge and tradition. But that should be a natural part of the conservative agenda, as Scruton himself has shown. Moreover, this agenda also had a general appeal throughout the country and across party lines. The government also added a democratic, others would say populist, element to this aesthetic programme: the expression "greater community consent" meant to give a chance for locals to participate in the process and have their say in the designing and building process.

The invitation for Scruton to chair the commission, of course, provoked an immediate outcry. The architectural and design professions, as well as the building sector of British industry felt that their professional privileges were being attacked by this initiative. The Commission had a very strong intellectual background, however, and a clear mandate. Its members included Gail Mayhew, a property consultant, characterised as "an advocate of community engagement in the planning process"; Mary Parsons, "the Chair and a trustee of the Town and Country Planning Association"; author and urban activist Nicholas Boys Smith; and Kim Wilkie, "a renowned landscape architect and environmental planner."[173] The work of the commission was also supported by a team of specialist advisers, including both professionals and academic research experts. While the commission and its experts were still working, Scruton was subjected to a politically motivated media attack, by the *New Statesman* magazine in April 2019. Having published an interview with him on a number of politically sensitive issues, a journalist portrayed Scruton in a social media post based on the interview he had conducted as a homophobe and racist, who used unacceptable language to defame Chinese people and Jews.[174] Without consulting Scruton, the government dismissed him from the position of the chair of the commission. It was another British current affairs magazine, *Spectator*, and the unstinting efforts of its polemicist Douglas Murray, as well as the release of the full text and audio of the interview, which changed the direction of the debate. From that, one could see the grave distortion of the views of Scruton by the journalist, deliberately taking statements out of their original context, unleashing a digital mob attack against him, characteristic of the cancel culture of the day. By July the journal apologised, Scruton accepted the apology and he was reappointed, now as co-chair of the Commission.[175]

In the meantime, the commission kept on working along its mandate. In July 2019, they published their interim report, with the title *Creating Space for Beauty*.[176] The work of the earlier chair until April 2019 is acknowledged in the report, and also the fact that Wilkie had contributed to it.

In defining its terms, the report identified three levels, or scales, which the commission searched for beauty at: that of the individual building, of the place that is created by the buildings, and of the way a settlement sits in the landscape. The commission presented eight proposals at the beginning of its report, namely:

* beauty first
* places not just houses
* regenerative development
* early collaboration not confrontation
* a level-playing field
* growing beautifully (which includes public sector bodies working collaboratively with local communities, mixed use and "gentle density")
* learning together
* making beauty count (including form-based codes and objective measure for wellbeing, public health and beauty, as well as nature recovery)[177]

The interim report reflected on the public discussion about its own role and function, explicitly admitting that it was due to its focus on beauty that most of the attacks had been directed against it. To defend its position, the commission arranged a large number of meetings with community and business leaders, professionals from the industries concerned and members of the public as well as representatives of public authorities in order to collect data and gather evidence of what people want. They found that "(t)here is a high degree of agreement as to what characteristics constitute 'a good place'," and around many of "the design approaches to achieve this."[178] The report presented the expression of what the general public wanted, mediating between the inhabitants of localities and the local and national authorities. Based on the commission's study trips, local hearings and consultations with all sorts of people interested in the business or who had just suffered the results of previous building developments, research and evidence-taking, the report presented the data it had collected, arguments it developed and a list of key themes on three levels of the search for beauty in the built environment. It tried to establish its own canon of intellectual authorities from the German philosopher Kant to the British poet laureate Sir John Betjeman, its major convictions and a terminology which enabled it to negotiate between the stakeholders and the general public. It was engaged both in the recollection of good practices and ideas from the past and in surveying present practices to find the most appropriate solutions to pressing needs and urgent problems. It was uncompromising as far as its mission was concerned, giving priority to beauty in all its renderings, and it even provided a glossary of terms in its Appendix, as the commission understood them. It offered 30 policy proposals (number one being: "ask for beauty" and number 30 "don't subsidise ugliness"). Even more relevantly it summarised its proposal in the following terms, arranged in a virtuous circle: "Beauty first and Places not just houses; Regenerative development and Growing beautifully; Early collaboration not confrontation and A level playing field and Learning together and Making beauty count."[179]

After Scruton's return to the commission, its work continued, leading to the publication of its final report entitled "Living with beauty; promoting health, well-being and sustainable growth" which was completed only a few days before his death and published posthumously on 30 January 2020.[180]

The well-designed cover page of the report shows urban details, including, symbolically, the tower of a traditionally built church and a public square.[181] These photographs were meant as a visual shorthand of the message the commission wanted to send to the government, the architectural and building professions and the general public. It can be read as the final message of the philosopher of whom the final report—speaking in the past tense—wrote, after having mentioned his ground-breaking work *The Aesthetics of Architecture*, that "(h)e ... endeavoured, through his popular writings, to raise public consciousness of the relation between the built environment and the happiness of human communities" (141). It also took its motto from its late co-chair: "Like the pleasure of friendship, the pleasure in beauty is curious: it aims to understand its object, and to value what it finds." (iii) This is a quote from Scruton's book *On Beauty*, from the chapter on "Judging Beauty," and the section "Disinterested Pleasure."[182] With this motto, comparing beauty to the highest Aristotelian moral virtue, friendship, the Commission made clear that it was dedicating the final report to the memory of Scruton.

The document summarised its message in an executive summary, to make the main message unmistakably clear. This executive summary had three very simple suggestions: its "new development and planning framework" aimed to "ask for beauty, refuse ugliness and promote stewardship." This is a tripartite requirement, the first part of which stipulates that beauty should be "the benchmark that all new developments should meet" (iv). It argued that beauty is connected to a "healthy and happy life," as well as to the notions of "place" and "home." It also referred to the term "somewhere," meaning home, taken originally from the musical *West Side Story* (1957), and popularised by both Scruton's *News From Somewhere: On Settling* (2004), and David Goodhart's ground-breaking book, *The Road to Somewhere: The Populist Revolt and the Future of Politics* (2017). It also pointed out the heavy social cost of improper planning and mistaken judgements which lead to ugliness in building. Ugliness of architecture was taken in this document as "unadaptable, unhealthy and unsightly," and they claimed that ugliness appeared whenever the new design did not fit into its environment. Ugly buildings "destroy the sense of place, undermine the spirit of community, and ensure that we are not at home in our world" (iv). The third of these exhortations, Promote Stewardship, is both a call for an ecological perspective, drawing attention to the fact that "our built environment and our natural environment belong together," and a reminder of transgenerational responsibility, in the style of Edmund Burke, "to ensure that we pass on to future generations an inheritance at least as good as the one we have received" (v). The ecologically sensitive message of the report is plain enough and expressed directly: "For too long now we have been exploiting and spoiling our country. The time has come to enhance and care for it instead" (v). The plain language of the executive summary made it an evocative text, with a rhetorical or indeed poetic effect. Its terminology was very powerful: the term "stewardship," for example, belongs to the terminology of the English common law, expressing its perspective. The original meaning of the term comes from the Old English word of *stiward* or *stigweard*, meaning "house guardian, housekeeper."[183] It has a special subsidiary meaning, when it refers to taking care of the property of others. Let us recall in this context how Burke's principle of intergenerational justice is connected to stewardship in this common-sense meaning of the term:

> [O]ne of the first and most leading principles on which the commonwealth and the laws are consecrated is [that] the temporary possessors and life-renters in it [should be mindful] of what is due to their posterity… [and] should not think it among their rights to cut off the entail or commit waste on the inheritance by destroying at their pleasure the whole original fabric of society, hazarding to leave to those who come after them a ruin instead of a habitation.[184]

The report proposed eight priorities, related to the following eight terms: planning, communities, stewardship, regeneration, neighbourhoods, nature, education and management. Each of the above items was assigned to a working group engaged in researching the theme, and in wording the policy proposal on that area. Some of the proposals might have sounded surprising, as they did not seem to fit the prejudices about conservative ways of thinking. Take for example communities: the agenda here was to increase the level of democratic decision-making. This is made explicit in the short summary of the proposal: "More democracy should take place at the local plan phase" (3). Another surprise was the emphasis on regeneration, the revitalising of areas which are left alone by industry or regarded as unfit for human habitation by the local people and authorities: "Government should commit to ending the scandal of 'left-behind' places" (3). The proposal included the setting up of a position within the government to take charge of regeneration, and in every local council, of "Chief Placemaker." While this issue was clearly connected to the notion of conservation, it had not been seen as part of the responsibility of the executive branch of government, as the conservative idea of the role of government was earlier less a vision of activism and responsibility for communal affairs, and more the running of a minimal state ensuring economic freedom for civil society.

The approach to architecture in the report was creative and innovative. It proposed a shift from planning and constructing "building units" to thinking instead in terms of "making places," which can host real homes and sustainable neighbourhoods. The text is aware of the difficulties of changing the public's and the authorities' perception of the function of investment in housing, whether it be private or public investment. Both this aim, and the aim of re-greening human settlements required a deliberate educational programme, and a reorganisation both structurally and in its approach of the "architectural syllabus" (4). The report introduced the idea of framework form-based planning codes, in order to avoid "subsidising ugliness."

The report also offered a kind of visual initiation into the set of insights New Urbanism arrived at, by offering photographic images of good practices, and examples to be avoided. It also suggested a vocabulary to frame its goals, including "townscape" (aiming at a "unity like an artwork") and "mixed-use," while also addressing the prospect of working from home, even before the subsequent experiences of the pandemic. It had both a social sensibility, emphasising "affordability," and a conservative strain, focusing on a "respect for heritage." As far as stylistic preferences were concerned, the report recommended accepting the value-judgements of local communities, in accordance with their aspirations. In fact, the study was rather critical of the taste of architectural professionals, and advocated heeding the value-preferences of ordinary town-dwellers and inhabitants of neighbourhoods. In the background of this was its criticism of the historical influence on professional taste of the views of Le Corbusier, the Bauhaus, and Russian constructivism, arguing that the tide was currently changing, as a result of the effects of Critical Regionalism and New Urbanism. The rhetoric of the report was very straightforward when it argued against the dictates of the architectural professions: "It should no longer be assumed that the people are to be led by the architects and the planners, rather than the other way round" (48).

The language of the document is pragmatic in nature, making proposals about the changes necessary in housing and building manuals, codes and various other local guidance. It also offered technical support in planning and laid the groundwork for establishing a new approach to housing by authorities, professionals and investors. Perhaps the most surprising part of the report was a detailed masterplan of the proposed change (*From Vicious Circle to Virtuous Circle*), with an exceptionally detailed roadmap, arranging for a division of labour among players, and drawing up the time-frame for determining when each of the protagonists bears the responsibility to act or to respond to the demands of the others.

The report was also rather self-conscious: it was aware of the problems of public bodies, and had a managerial approach to problem-solving, providing all the detailed tools required to check and verify that the processes it initiated were still on the right track, including the monitoring of the implementation of the report itself. To achieve its purpose, it required the setting up of an independent body besides the government, which was to give feedback to authorities and to the public on the actual standing of the project after the commission itself has finished its work. The actual outcome of the report remained, however, a question for the future. Yet it gave to Scruton's public career as an architectural theorist a fitting and worthy finish.

In Praise of Wagner: Metaphysics, Politics and Music

Besides architecture, the other kind of art in which Scruton felt at home was music, and especially classical music. During his lifetime, he kept returning to this theme, writing about what might be called the philosophy of music. Interestingly, the first time he directly addressed music in a book was comparatively late: it was a general philosophical account of music, his *The Aesthetics of Music* (1997). The next time was when he focused on Wagner in *Death-Devoted Heart: Sex and the Sacred in Wagner's Tristan und Isolde* (Oxford University Press, 2004). In 2009 he published *Understanding Music* (2009). Once again, he returned to Wagner in *The Ring of Truth: The Wisdom of Wagner's Ring of the Nibelung* (2016). His last, posthumously published work was also about the German composer: *Wagner's Parsifal* (2020).

Unlike in architecture, where he never crossed the dividing line separating theory and practice, in music he actually tried his hand at composing. He produced two operas, first *The Minister* (1994) and later *Violet* (2005), and both of them were put on stage.[185] If that was not enough, he himself was prepared to perform music publicly. In the last part of his life, he played the organ for the local Anglican service on Sundays in his local church.

The importance he attributed to music in his life is illustrated in the Afterword of *Conversations with Mark Dooley*. There he ends the conversation with the following remark, when asked about his would-be epitaph: "It should be on a gravestone in the grounds of All Saints in Garsdon, and it should say: The Last Englishman: Organist at this Church."[186] This personal wish is very telling: it is a story in which architecture meets music in the context of religion and national belonging. A gravestone in a churchyard is perhaps the simplest built object which has the function of reminding passers-by of the life of a human being. A gravestone should have letters on it, connecting architecture with language, and through that with literature and culture in general. The Last Englishman is certainly an exaggeration, and sounds like the title of a novel. It has a melancholic expressive force, however, referring back to the topic he addressed in *England: an Elegy* (2000). Scruton would want to be remembered as the last warrior on the battlefield, as well as an organist at this church, a rather unexpected role for a philosopher.

Scruton himself wrote about his being an organist at All Saints Church in Garsdon. He did this in the last chapter of his autobiographical work, *Gentle Regrets: Thoughts from a Life* (2005). Ten years before the writing of that book, the philosopher "went out of curiosity to our local church, no longer as a thief but as a penitent" (233). It was there that he learnt the fact, which can be found even today on the homepage of the church, that it cherished "the use of the Book of Common Prayer," "in whose idiom my prayers are invariably expressed." It was because of its continued use of this special liturgy that he decided to join the congregation and "volunteered to play the organ" for its evensong. He admits that, even there, engaged in the activity of the organist, his doubts remained with him: "Once we came before God's presence with a song; now we come before his absence with a sigh" (234). He resolved, however, that even if he was full of doubts, as he was, the singing of chorals should not stop. And that is why he kept playing the organ and singing the psalms in the old idiom. The last words of his memoir put this in the following way: "If, therefore, I am called upon to express my much-amended but nevertheless regained religion," it would be not in the words of poets like Eliot and Rilke, but "in the tranquil words of the Jubilate Deo":

> O be joyful in the Lord, all ye lands: serve the Lord /with gladness, and come before his presence with a / song. // Be ye sure that the Lord he is God: it is he that hath / made us, and not we ourselves; we are his people / and the sheep of his pasture. // O go your way into his gates with thanksgiving, and / into his courts with praise; be thankful unto him, and speak good of his Name. / For the Lord is gracious, his mercy is everlasting: and / his truth endureth from generation to generation. (239–40)

It is in this register, in the language of the Biblical psalms that Scruton thought about the function of music in human life. One of his favourite composers was Wagner, whom he analysed in this style. In what follows I will first concentrate on Scruton's interpretation of Wagner's operas, and in particular of Wagner's *Ring*. This will be followed by a subchapter on Scruton's general idea of classical Western music.

What follows, however, is a rather circumscribed endeavour: it will be a reconstruction of Scruton's writing on music, both on Wagner and on classical music in general, only so far as they concern his dual perspective on politics and aesthetics. One should not expect from the following pages a detailed account of Scruton's technical knowledge of music. Instead, this chapter will focus on practical philosophy and his account of human nature, as it shines through in the work of Wagner, and in classical music in general.

The Politics and Metapolitics of Wagner

There is no doubt that Wagner was a composer who kept challenging Scruton, the philosopher. He obviously had a special, intimate relationship with the rather specific world of the Wagnerian opera as a *Gesamtkunstwerk*, a total work of art. His engagement with this form of art did not allow Scruton to be detached in his description and analysis of the composer—yet he was undoubtedly a reflective fan, one who never lost his critical potential. Attachment in classical music largely depends on one's musical ability (usually abbreviated as having an ear for music) and one's schooling. In this respect, Scruton was really exceptional as a philosopher. His background knowledge in this field is only comparable to professional musicians and music critics. This refinement in musical connoisseurship explains Scruton's rich interpretation of Wagner. In what follows we shall concentrate partly on Scruton's general description of the Wagner phenomenon, but also on his explanation of how in the narrative of the *Ring* two of its main themes, love and power, relate to each other. This we shall do in the hope that through it we can explain how Scruton viewed the politics of Wagner's music, especially in his account of the *Ring* in his book *The Ring of Truth*.[187]

Scruton's approach to Wagner was made explicit in the very first sentence of his book, where he claimed explicitly that "Wagner's Ring of the Nibelung is one of the greatest works of art produced in modern times" (1). Clearly by making this claim he was admitting that his starting point was on the side of the Wagner fans. Yet the book is more than a summary of the delights to be found in Wagner. Instead, Scruton was interested in the present-day relevance of Wagner's work, and in particular its relevance for present-day debates in art and in political thought.

The greatest problem for Wagner-scholarship was Richard Wagner's own character, which Scruton described as "titanic," and "full of ambitions" (1). Scruton was not blind to the explicit character mistakes of his hero. First of all, he mentioned Wagner's anti-semitism, which was enthusiastically seized upon by the Nazis, turning the characters of his stories into an example of "the icons of German racism" (1). Scruton was painfully aware of the severity of the issue that Wagner became "Hitler's favourite composer"[188] (1). He made the anti-semitism in the thought of Wagner explicit at the very beginning of his narrative. He convicted it unconditionally and without hesitation. Yet he claimed that it did not provide the key to musician's character and work. Scruton did not want to interpret the oeuvre in the light of events which happened much after his death. According to Scruton, the specific views of German history and national identity at the centre of Wagner's own thought were unlike those of the leaders and ideological masterminds of the Nazi regime. The reason why so many recent commentators from Adorno to psychoanalysts read the former through the prism of the latter was, Scruton claimed, "the lamentable triumph of Hitler's view of Germany over Wagner's" in twentieth-century German history (3).

Scruton's own reading of Wagner's views on Germany was to a large extent based on Wagner's "striking" written autobiography. One should read it carefully, he noted, because it certainly involves an element of fabrication.[189] One cannot, however, discover in it a Nazi mentality, he argued, because for Wagner, as is evident in his *Die Meistersinger von Nürnberg*, Germany was not the new, post-1871 nation state, but the ancien regime, that of the Holy Roman Empire (3).

In Scruton's reading *Die Meistersinger* constituted nothing less than a political ideal of the autonomous medieval German city. Although Scruton did not mention the name of Otto von Gierke, his reference to the corporate character of the city, the order of which is maintained by autonomous communities like the local guilds, presented medieval Germany in a light which resembles how Gierke's masterwork,

Rechtsgeschichte der deutschen Genossenschaft, presented the Germany of that age. Gierke's famous book was published in 1868, about the time Wagner was at work on his memoir. Wagner himself, argues Scruton, intended his oeuvre to be a defence of the old Germany, and lamented its loss after the birth of the new nationalism in the age of and following Napoleon. The nostalgia for a golden age of civil society and the "ethic of renunciation" (4) characterised the ideology of the mature Wagner, as Scruton understood his work. It is in that context that Scruton criticised Wagner's revolutionary philosophy during his Dresden years, which most commentators tend to find behind his works, but which he dismisses as a mistaken sign of the composer's long-term intentions.

No doubt, Scruton's interpretation of Wagner was an original take. It certainly fitted in with his own philosophical attitudes. Take for example his suggestion of a symbolic figure, to explain Wagner's art: this is "the rediscovered father – a wanderer's attempt to come home" (4). This description could be applied to Scruton's own work just as much as to that of Wagner. There is, in fact, a tendency in Scruton's reading of Wagner to use it as a mirror, in other words to find solutions in it that are closely related to his own, partly philosophical, partly existential problems. The idiosyncrasy of this interpretation is a natural outcome of Scruton's rather specific philosophical approach, quite different from the way most professional interpreters of Wagner's work operate. The latter keep complaining about the "wrongdoings of his life," while Scruton, as a philosopher, and with a conservative pessimism, registered these missteps with a certain calm complacency and realism, as he did not find anything new or surprising in the idea of human fragility and character faults.

The result of Scruton's original approach to Wagner, the outcome of his mature philosophy, was the realisation that behind the smokescreen of the tales of powerful German heroes and demigods, he was communicating through complex symbols, which were meant to teach lessons such as that the "overcoming of the will to power demands sacrifice of a kind that love alone can accomplish" (7). The philosopher seems to have understood the composer's work. He admitted that indeed "self-sacrifice of the individual rearranges the world" (7). Scruton's original interpretation of the Wagnerian myth reminds the reader of Freud's novel tripartite interpretation of the psyche. He, too, identifies in that mythology three worlds: Nibelheim is the underworld, where power reigns; Valhalla is a Wagnerian Olympus, the place of the gods; while *Die Walküre* is the world in between, "the human world, in which love battles with law, and freedom with resentment" (7).

In what follows I will concentrate on Scruton's interpretation of Wagner's account of this human realm, the realm dominated by the never transcended conflict between love and power, or love and law, which leads to the admission that real love is only fully realised by an intentional act of self-sacrifice in human life, leading to human suffering. Here, again, we see Scruton the philosopher, in action. As mentioned earlier, here again he draws on the philosophy of religion of the French thinker, René Girard. It was with the help of his thought that Scruton arrived at the view that religion is built on the specific sacrificial exercise of the individual to save a community, confronting a crisis situation. Religion makes human sacrifice meaningful, a sacred act of salvation.[190]

Girard's explanation of religious ritual is of primary importance to Scruton, as it offers a clue to the relationship between individual and communal life. Scruton also cites Girard in his account of the *Ring*, in connection with Thomas Mann's understanding of Siegfried's sacrificial death. Starting out from the German writer's famous description of this meaningful event in *The Sorrows and Grandeur of Richard Wagner*, Scruton interprets this sublime act as an act of sacrifice, in the way that sacrifice is described in the great religious narratives of humankind.[191] The *Siegfried* of the *Ring* retells the story of Jesus Christ, the Saviour of Mankind, in the Christian New Testament. "Mann refers Siegfried's sacrificial death to the old legends of the god who is put to death to be reborn as a saviour" (284). Scruton, too, found Girard's understanding of this motif of self-sacrifice quite convincing. In his interpretation, Girard presents the "primordial experience of the sacred," making the case "for viewing the violent execution of a victim as the root experience from which the sense of the sacred derives" (284). The victim unites the community which would otherwise fall apart. Uniting the community is interpreted here in theological language, as a sacrifice which helps the community to reach redemption, or *Erlösung*. Redemption is a theological concept, which plays a prominent role in the Christian teaching of the life and Death of

Jesus Christ, the second divine person who became a human being to suffer death to take upon himself the original sin of man. Wagner's opera has its own myth, with its own lesson of the dying gods. Here too, self-sacrifice is important as a major step towards redemption, "that frees us from all the bad things that have beset us, by showing them to be necessary parts of an intrinsically valuable whole" (284). In an important sense, however, Scruton seems to be dissatisfied with Wagnerian redemption. While in Christianity, redemption leads to eternal life, in Wagner's universe this is not the case. In the latter there is no afterlife.[192]

Nevertheless, Scruton is able to rescue Wagner from his own philosophical criticism. In his interpretative work, Scruton is ready to pass beyond the Girardian explanation of sacrifice and redemption, which is meaningless if an afterlife is not possible. In the final analysis Scruton denies that Wagner's point was that the meaning of life is religious sacrifice. Instead, he finds a this-worldly clue to make sense of the self-sacrifice that was so characteristic of Wagner's world. As in Greek tragedy, and in particular in Antigone, which was the paradigmatic Greek drama both for German idealism and for Wagner, "life has another meaning than the pursuit of status and power" (306). It is precisely as mortal beings that we can arrive at a discovery of our innermost human capacity "to discount" our own personal interests, and by accepting death "stand up against the omnipresent forces of destruction" (306–7).[193] It is, in fact, this ability to oppose the temptation of power, which is the major threat of politics, in which Wagner's narrative finally excels. He offers a new way of approaching the relationship between art and politics in those moments when "individual sacrifice (or whatever) reverberates in the cultural community, obviously so in Meistersinger and Parsifal."[194] Crucial for this is the interaction between love and power, which Scruton finds at the centre of Wagner's *Ring*.

The English philosopher is willing to dig into the depths of the Wagnerian narrative, beneath the music which enchants and disarms the listener. His analysis of the Wagnerian world of *Love and Power* starts out from Schopenhauer's opposition of, or as he calls it, collision between nature and the demands of the will. Humans want love and consolation in a natural world which is devoid of it, and for this reason they crave power and dominion: seeking to grab it even if others do not want to give it up. Wagner's political economy asks the following question: what are the natural resources which help a human being to give up what is most important for human existence: individual freedom. For it is in love that humans lose their freedom to win something even more important. This political economy is the starting point of the *Ring*, the meaning of *Das Rheingold*. Surely, though, there is no commercial transaction the sum total of which could be real love and deep devotion. Scruton offers a critique of the classical political economy, with the help of Locke, Hegel and—perhaps surprisingly—Marx. The failure of Alberich's efforts shows that attempting to gain power through financial transactions leads nowhere. Alberich's forging of the *Ring* is counterposed by Siegfried's forging of the sword, which teaches him to forge ahead on his quest, without shortcuts, to arrive at self-knowledge and an acceptance of one's lot. Siegfried avoids the deadlock of financial deals, which captures Alberich's soul, resulting in his remaining loveless.

As well as Siegfried and his sword, Wagner counterposes the doom of Alberich in another way, by Wotan's "realm of legal order." This is again an alternative to the natural world, a realm which cannot be ruled free of charge. The currency in which Wotan is ready to pay is, again, love. The Giants are willing to build Valhalla only if they obtain in return Freia, the goddess of love. Once again, we confront Wagner's major, primeval opposition between love and power. To get the reward of love, one has to give up power, to grab power one has to sacrifice love.

Scruton's work on sexual desire prefigures his analysis of Wagner's message of love and power.[195] In that earlier piece, the philosopher also engaged in a delicate analysis of Wagner. As a result of that analysis, he found that jealousy certainly plays a major role in any account of genuine love, and of genuinely carnal love. However, jealousy is a poison, which kills the innocence of love. Love has another fatal attribute, too—another reason why it points towards death. Scruton's word for that in this book is Tristanism, a word he takes from Denis de Rougemont. Tristan's love for Isolde is of course, a forbidden love, and it can only be fulfilled by accepting death. Scruton made it clear in that earlier work that this is far from the ideal solution of love in a spiritual unification. After all, it unites the pair only in death—Shakespeare's Romeo and Juliet is a paradigm of this pattern and of its inadequacy as a story to teach youngsters how to secure love. Death cannot be the solution for a forbidden love. It is moderation, and in its purest form even chastity, the ability to abjure the violence of passion, that brings maturity to the human character, according to Scruton's own view on sexual desire. The fulfilment of love requires a more nuanced interpersonal approach, one which requires the full presence of both lovers. In other words, it requires a kind of balance. It is crucial to learn to renounce passionate love, if it is not balanced. Scruton's example of this is Hans Sachs from *Die Meistersinger*, who is able to renounce the fulfilment of his desire, when he realises that it is not reciprocated.

Intersubjectivity, reciprocity and responsibility for others are crucial terms in Scruton's analysis of love. But were they crucial for Wagner, too? Scruton finds a rather convincing analysis of erotic love in Wagner. It is presented as a blend of sexual desire and tender attachment (the composer identifies the musical motifs for both of these attributes of love in the theme he associates with Freia) (250). In other words, Scruton's Wagner assumes that real love involves the inclusion and active participation of the other's full personality, and that the partner is simply "irreplaceable" (250). The intentional act of offering oneself to the other is required, as it is evident in the loving relationship between Siegmund and Sieglinde. Through this offer of one's self the lover turns him- or herself into a "gift of the self."

The fact that we are mortal creatures will bring love to an end, which makes it by its very nature tragic: its end is unavoidable. In this sense, the nature of love is always to be tragic: it is composed of two opposing sides, the lover and the loved one, that can never be reconciled. This is true of all of Wagner's great works, from *Das Liebesverbot* to the farewell to erotic love in his last opera, *Parsifal*. Although the erotic element remains in most of its manifestations, the element of faithful attachment appears only in the love of Wotan's human children. Yet it is only this element which turns love into something meaningful which can transform the world and make unavoidable suffering itself worthwhile. In this experience of love's suffering the self is sacrificed—either in the form of becoming lost in desire, or by the offer to the other. Although these two outcomes are apparently equal, the meaningfulness of one's life is quite different in each case.

Scruton's account finds this unavoidable conflict of the two lovers at the centre of Wagner's account of our experience of love, because of his own metaphysics, which starts out from the Kantian description of the internal division of the individual human being into both a subject and an object. In the account of human nature sketched in the Kantian paradigm, the human being's animal nature (in which Kant is not much interested) will always be contrasted to the "transcendental" perspective of her as a rational creature. This dualist description of human nature had transformed by the time of Schopenhauer into the unavoidably tragic outcome of *the principium individuationis.* "The subject is locked in combat with the object, and is constantly overcome by it" (256). Although human freedom is real, it is compromised by our animal self, which stands poised to tear us apart anyway. This self-destructive animal drive— in which, once again, Kant is not much interested—can only be overcome by a voluntary surrender of that very freedom in the act of self-sacrifice. This "essentially compromised nature of freedom" is presented in the figure of Wotan. It is through self-sacrifice, the human act *par excellence*, one which Wotan can only arrive at by giving up his divinity and being reborn as a man (if that is indeed the case), that we can realise the real power of ourself over ourselves—this self-realisation is described in the vernacular of German idealism as *Selbstbestimmung*, to which an added value is attributed.

Human self-realisation is destined to have two dimensions: the internal-subjective dimension is identified by self-knowledge and is due to the will, while the external-objective dimension of it is identified with sovereignty and law. Wotan was originally the embodiment of both of these dimensions. His symbolic spear refers both to the rule of law and to the will of the individual which is required to uphold the former. Through both aspects, by self-realisation as well as by the rule of law the human being strives to achieve something which is beyond the human capacity—in other words the individual commits the sin of hubris—which brings to mind the dynamic of the ancient Greek drama form, tragedy, epitomised by Sophocles' *Antigone*. One should recall that there, too, the ability to engage in self-reflection, which leads one to recognise this as hubris, is itself a real personal achievement, hardly achievable for ordinary human beings. Human ambition needs to find its right scale, as classic Greek philosophy and art both taught, and Wagner wanted to prove the truth of that teaching in an indirect manner.

Wotan plays a central role in the Wagnerian mythology because he embodies the clash between the rule of law (objectified *Selbstbestimmung*), or the legitimate use of power, and love, the subjective *Selbstbestimmung*, which ultimately leads to self-sacrifice. Similarly to Plato's *Republic*, the rule of law, as an external aspect of the community, is paralleled in the internal drama of the individual human soul. Also like in Plato, the rationality of the former is complemented by the irrational power of the latter—resembling the two horses which pull in different directions in Plato's *Phaedrus*. And once again, as in Plato, an objective, scientific claim is always supplemented by a poetic one (36). This combination of the objective and the poetic has been illustrated by some of the best minds of European intellectual history, including Dante, Shakespeare and Goethe. Wotan's spear is a symbol. It represents a legal order, which not only determines interpersonal relationships, but also projects the internal order of the mind. However, both of these orders are prone to corruption, erosion and decline. Wagner reveals that this connection between the communal order and the individual psyche in the Germanic mythology survived. This link returns in the medieval Christian context, as pointed out, according to Scruton, by Rémi Brague's grand narrative.[196]

As in love, so in power, there are two conflicting elements. One is disruptive—sheer power, which enables one to have domination over others, taking away both their freedom and their possibility of self-determination. This aspect of power, which turns one into a demigod, controlling other people, is itself certainly a form of hubris, and therefore it needs a balancing element, a control mechanism. This counterweight is provided by the law: "from Tannhäuser onwards, the Wagner operas show a growing concern with law, as a social force that also shapes the inner life of those who honour it" (259).

The law in these works constrains the will of individuals, thus restricting their sphere of freedom. While the gods' association is a free association, that of the Nibelungs is certainly not. It is a political realm, and in politics no one is absolutely free. An association to be sustainable must be based either on contract or on love. Both contract and love constrains human activity. The difference between these two forms is that in a contract the terms of the association are stated or implied, while love has no such explicit terms. In both cases, the individual has to give up certain parts of her freedom. The paradox of human association is that, even if it is freely chosen, as in love, what you freely choose is a loss of freedom.

Though in love relations individual freedom is more limited than in a contractual relationship, love turns out to be a threat to the legal order, or at least a challenge to it. Wagner once again applies the paradigm of Sophocles' *Antigone*, reading it, like, Hegel, as a conflict between self-sacrificing love and the law of nature on the one side (Antigone's position) and the positive law of the political order on the other (Kreon's position).[197] In this conflict, however, the two parts also suppose each other. While Enlightenment philosophers (as well as their present-day heirs) had no problem assuming an easy and unproblematic flow from a state of nature to a legal order with the help of a social contract, the fact is that this process is necessarily a self-contradictory one: a contract requires the prior existence of a promise, which does not exist outside of a social realm, in other words, it is not to be found in a state of nature. One could claim that society precedes the establishment of a legal (i.e. state-run) order, yet Hegel's tripartite system in his legal theory shows that the existence of civil society presupposes two other forms of community: that of the family below it and that of the state above it. Of course, in the process of historical development, civilisation itself leads from the simpler form to the more complex one: from family to civil society, and from civil society to the state. The individual is born into the love-relationship of a family, and in order to free herself from it she becomes an independent personality freely taking part in the transactions of civil society. In order for the latter to operate properly, laws and law-enforcement are needed, which has an obvious effect on the sphere of individual activity: it constrains it. The law requires the existence of the lawmaker, the ruler and the judge, and it is through their interaction that obligations are created and enforced.

Wotan's spear is a symbol of the acceptance of the legal basis of rule, in other words, it is an expression of political authority. His dominion shows that law rules over the individual in a neutral fashion, which is equivalent to stating that law establishes justice. Through the institutionalisation of agreements, that is, through law, coercion and war are banished from society. But in order to secure its proper functioning, Hegel's state needs two things: the authority of the legitimate ruler, and the distance kept by the ruler or the judge from others. This latter is in fact created by the denial or replacement of love with procedural fairness, which is justice. Scruton does not mention here the Aristotelian proposal that there is a human social relationship which is less than love but more than law-abiding behaviour: that virtuous friendship which the Greek philosopher finds crucial in the polis. Certainly, Wagner's Nibelung mythology does not recognise such a relationship, but one would think that Scruton should reflect on its lack in this world characterised by the conflict of love and law. After all, in Aristotle's Politeia the civic virtue of friendship carries out much of the work of turning naked individual will into the sociable attitude of a social being.

Wagner's alternative to this friendship-model of human relationships under the rule of law, which Aristotle theorised on the basis of the experience of Athenian democracy, is to draw a clear distinction between a consensual order, one ruled by law, and a coercive order, ruled by "treachery and violence" (266). The place of love is extremely limited in a world "caught between these two orders, frequently defying the one and always threatened by the other." It is a "sphere of suffering," "which nevertheless contains the sole justification for the rule of law and the act of 'legitimate usurpation' (a term Scruton takes from de Maistre) by which the law is founded" (266). The containment of the realm of love, and the high price which the individual has to pay, and is indeed willing to pay for it, is proof of the unavoidable risks of human cohabitation, and a sign that indeed "everything we hold as precious, including love and law, rests on a thin crust above a seething magma of resentment" (266).

In fact, in Wagner's *Weltanschauung* the human condition is even worse than that. If love depends on the law, in other words, on the rule of Wotan, which is by its very nature prone to become corrupted, because it is in fact founded on theft (legitimate usurpation), there is no way to avoid tragedy. "With the collapse of the objective order of law, therefore, comes the collapse of the inner order of faith and trust" (267). In *Siegfried*'s victory over Wotan Wagner reflects on the possibility that love can indeed overcome law (once again we can recall Shakespeare's *Romeo and Juliet*), in the symbolic act of Siegfried shattering Wotan's spear. But in breaking the spear Siegfried also destroys law, because it cannot be sustained without the rule of Wotan. In other words, love turns out to be not only socially destructive, but also self-destructive: "love will inevitably destroy itself" (267).

Even if, on the empirical level, the "incurable tragedy of the human condition" (268) is in the long run inevitable, humans can experience individual moments of personal love, the only form of human salvation in Wagner's world. It is in love relations that humans experience moments in their lives, when the empirical order gives way to "transcendental" meaning. When a human being falls in love, just as when she witnesses the birth of a new life, or the death of a beloved, she suddenly realises a "rite of passage," or turning point in her individual life. Yet these moments are also, in some mysterious, unexplainable manner connected with "the survival and reproduction of the social organism" (269). These moments are windows of opportunity, through which humans can glimpse something which is more meaningful, but whose meaning the rational mind cannot fully grasp. The transcendental intimations lead one, as we saw earlier, in Scruton's philosophy, to the institutional establishment of religion, which—in spite of Christ's radical teaching—does not subvert the social order, but gives it what might be called a transcendental underpinning. This whole experience of the transcendental, which leads to the birth of institutional religion, is attached to those moments of insight, which we call moments of the sacred.

Wagner had a somewhat idiosyncratic understanding of the sacred. As we have seen, unlike in Christianity, which has an other-worldly dimension, in Wagner's world there is no place for a redemption, which promises peace to the individual after death. In his world, "Redemption does not consist in a release from death, but in the acceptance of death on behalf of a mortal love" (270). Wagner's story does not stop at the moment when he shows that the gods of his mythology are in fact dying: "the consciousness that killed the gods did not remove the sacred dimension from our experience" (271). The way to give meaning to human life in Wagner's this-worldly universe is by "free commitment," realising our real, and worthiest selves "in an act of self-giving" (271). The moment of self-sacrifice, which is the logical conclusion of one's love, turns out to be the moment of the sacred: "it is the moment that justifies my life, the moment that shows the absolute value of my being the thing that I am" (271).

Scruton refers to a line of reception, which leads from Wagner's thoughts on the sacred to the influential academic treatise by Rudolf Otto, *Das Heilige* (The Sacred) (1917). Obviously, however, there is a great difference between an artwork and a theoretical treatise. Wagner succeeds in vindicating the experience of the sacred. Members of the audience will indeed feel that there is such a moment of this worldly sacred. According to Scruton, the message of Wagner is to understand the relevance of sacrifice in human life, that it is an offering of the self in exchange for nothing, only as an expression of love, and that it is the greatest moment of human life, which should be regarded as sacred. Hence, understanding this message "is the most important step in understanding *The Ring*" (271). In the world of this opera cycle, the sacred is not a way to transcend the everyday life of the individual, but the moment when the transcendental enters the human being's everyday life, and turns it into something valuable and meaningful in itself.

The special significance of the human ability of sacrifice is due to the fact that Wagner recognises that the socially subversive element also exists in the human being. The narrative of the *Ring* and even more that of its musical *crescendos* show the destructive force of resentment, which is for him, as it was for Nietzsche, a creative force of human action. While Wagner strives to convince us of the reality of the moment of the sacred in human life, he does not hesitate to point out the miseries caused by the human being to others. In other words: "Wagner places implacable resentment at the heart of his drama" (272). Yet this is not a proof of the asocial nature of his art. On the contrary, it shows—together with the performance of the sacred—the reality of his art: that he is able to reveal, like Dostoyevsky, the evil force that lives within ourselves.

Scruton returns at the end of his analysis of the dynamics of law and love in human life to the topic of the Nazi concentration camps of the twentieth century. He claims that Wagner was able to foresee the unimaginable suffering that human beings would cause to others. He refers to the musician's *Autobiography*, where Wagner describes the point of absolute negativity in human life embodied by the figure of Bakunin, the anarchist. Scruton's Wagner, as presented in the conclusion of his analysis, is not a revolutionary himself, who turns the human world upside down. Yet he is able to show the dangers to human life of the potential negativity inherent in the psyche of Bakunin, a figure who insists "solely on destruction and ever more destruction."[198]

Although this was not the end of Scruton's analysis of *The Ring*, we shall leave his analysis of Wagner at this point. The philosopher managed to show that this music can bring to the stage both the deepest point of human political life and a this-worldly redemption of human suffering. The point Scruton made in his analysis was that he discovered in Wagner both a convincing symbolism of the sacred, of that special moment of this-worldly human life, and a fearsome image of the human potential to destroy and cause suffering to the other. Instead of continuing to trace Scruton's analysis of Wagner in the labyrinth of this oeuvre, let us step back now, and address the philosopher's general claims about European classical music and its connection to his own views on political philosophy.

Music as a Communal Experience

Whether one appreciates Wagner's world, including the powerful music, the weird mythological narrative, the characters on the stage of his operas, and all those elements which build up that world, is a question of taste. According to Kant, such aesthetic choices are made with the help of both the imagination and our rational faculty. In the final analysis, an individual's choice expresses her self, and that is not an issue about which one can easily argue. You are what you are, and your choice is, in a way, a conclusion about or derived deduction from your internal mindset. Scruton may make strong statements about why one should recognise the high quality of Wagner's music, yet he cannot convince one to love that specific world: it is the world of a powerful mind, but one about which one may easily confess that one does not like it. The present author, for example, does not like it.

In the second half of this discussion about Scruton's philosophy of music, we will leave Wagner behind. What we are interested in, rather, is how talking about music can turn out to be a discussion of society, or even of politics. The kernel of this idea is to be found in Scruton's Preface to the Bloomsbury Revelations edition of *The Aesthetics of Music*. Scruton there makes a sweeping claim about the parallels between the tonal tradition and the polyphonic character of European music and the kind of society that exists in Europe. He offers a description of that society which employs the terminology of polyphonic music: "Ours is a society of many voices, in which individuals are both independent and yet constrained by harmony." Following the footsteps of Mann, in his *Reflections of a Nonpolitical Man*, Scruton argues that this social development parallels the institutional framework of the politics of that society: "this is a fitting symbol of our greatest political achievement, which is that of individual freedom under a shared rule of law."[199]

Describing society in the musical terms of polyphony is indeed a powerful metaphor. But it is more than that. I would contend that it reveals the constant efforts on Scruton's part to connect in his thought the characteristics of classical music with his account of not only human nature in general, but of Western or European political communal life, in particular. In what follows I shall attempt to reconstruct this effort, by examining the ideas about culture he puts forward in the last chapter of *The Aesthetics of Music*.

The Aesthetics of Music presents the basic features of music, starting out from sounds, and finishing with performance. It offers fourteen such concepts, some of them used specifically only in discussions of music, some more general. He concludes this weighty tome with a general chapter on what he calls culture. In this chapter, Scruton returns to the topics of both high culture and popular music, comparing the two by drawing a political parallel: with the distinction between the tradition-based political world and mass democracy.

This comparison is based on an insight taken from Plato: "The ways of poetry and music are not changed anywhere without change in the most important laws of the city."[200] It is well known that the ancient Greek philosopher believed that the forms of art and the form of a particular political community correspond to each other. How is such a direct link possible between societal arrangements and artistic creativity? To discover this connection is one of the tasks of philosophy.

As we have seen, art is regarded by Scruton as an anthropologically defined phenomenon. It only appears in a society when the more urgent needs of its members have already been satisfied. Survival requires hard work, and when one is hungry and cold, one does not have the spirit and energy to do things which otherwise one likes and enjoys. The activities to eat, drink and clothe oneself and have shelter are not chosen for their intrinsic value—they are simply useful kinds of activity. Yet when these needs have been met, humans turn towards practices that they find internally enjoyable, "activities like sport, conversation, ceremonies, festivals, and art" (457). Taken together, these sorts of activities, in which humans find themselves "at home with" themselves, comprise culture, or more specifically, a culture. Scruton's definition is stylistically elevated, attributing to culture a relevance which was not supposed in connection with other topics: "by engaging in them we constitute the human world, transforming it from a system of means to one of ends, from an unchosen destiny to an elected home" (457). Interestingly, these activities, which he regards as intrinsically valuable to humans, are linked by Scruton to Schiller's concept of play, proposed in his ambitious work *Letters on the Aesthetic Education of Man* (1795).

The concept of play is a useful one for Scruton, as it can be contrasted with Marx's concept of work, a term which comes from exactly the same intellectual source. Work and play are conceptual opposites: when they are at work for survival, humans are not at home, not engaged in an activity which would express their true selves, while when they are at play they can overcome the experience of "alienation" characteristic of daily routine, and find the essence of themselves in the very act itself. While work is done with a certain purpose, play is purposeless. An example of this can be found in friendship, the most elevated human relationship according to Aristotle. Friendship needs to be purposeless, if it is to be seen as an elevated form of interpersonal relationship: you do not use your friend for a certain purpose, you simply enjoy her being there. Yet there is a further aspect to it, which Scruton identifies as its function: "friendship has a function: it binds people together, making communities strong and durable" (458). Scruton's point is not to say that people have friends in order to fulfil a function. The valid observation behind this point is this: none of the activities which humans perform because of their own intrinsic value, such as "love, learning, sport, and art," are solitary activities. On the contrary, in them, humans experience their sociability, their dependence on others, and their "political nature" in the original sense of the term used by Aristotle. Take the example of rugby in British public schools: it gives boys the direct experience of what it feels like to be a member of a team. Interestingly, these enjoyable activities, in which we can lose and forget ourselves, are not only public activities, but also connective ones: they lead us to each other.

This is true (to a certain extent), even today, of us, (post)modern European individuals. And it is particularly true of actions connected to music: when we sing, play a musical instrument, dance or simply listen to music in a concert hall, we are together with others, and our enjoyment is made the deeper by the fact that we are bound together by or through it.

Scruton likes to refer to these occasions of discovering the social aspect of our human nature, as the "first-person plural." But why are those elevated forms of enjoyment connected to this shared point of view? Apparently, in this regard Scruton drew on the findings of anthropology when explaining art and culture: "Art is the product of leisure; leisure the product of safety, and safety the product of friends" (458). Human societies are sustainable because all the individual members of the group are aware of the fact that all of them are ready to defend the group and each other individually. This mutual trust in each other's readiness to help in case of trouble fosters a sense of security, which allows the individuals to deal with other things beyond the acts of survival, thus meeting the major requirement that allows the birth of artistic activity.

Yet beyond this anthropological description of what might be called the natural community, another theory of leisure might be taken into account when attempting to reconstruct Scruton's intellectual orientation. It was Josef Pieper, a German Catholic thinker, who in his 1948 book *Leisure, the Basis of Culture* argued in favour of using the concept of leisure, if we want to understand the creation of great works of art and science. Starting out from the ancient Greek term *scholé*, his line of thought also contrasted free activity with work as we identified in Scruton's anthropologically inspired analysis. Pieper's effort to make sense of leisure is based on his analysis of the figure of Antisthenes, a friend of Plato and a disciple of Socrates. He depicts him as the first workaholic, a person who took work so seriously as to exclude non-work from his daily life. Pieper describes the devastating effects of such an attitude on one's own life:

> As an ethicist of independence, this Antisthenes had no feeling for cultic celebration, which he preferred attacking with "enlightened" wit; he was "a-musical" (a foe of the Muses: poetry only interested him for its moral content); he felt no responsiveness to Eros (he said he "would like to kill Aphrodite"); as a flat Realist, he had no belief in immortality (what really matters, he said, was to live rightly "on this earth"). This collection of character traits appears almost purposefully designed to illustrate the very "type" of the modern "workaholic."[201]

Although Pieper does not appear among the references of *The Aesthetics of Music*, Scruton was by this time well aware of his work. What is more, the influence Pieper had on his thought is well illustrated by the fact that he wrote an introduction to the English language edition of *Leisure*, republished in 1998, just one year after *The Aesthetics of Music*.[202] Scruton's introduction is extremely short, comparable only to the little book's own density. Interestingly, Scruton characterises the specific attitude to life introduced by the German thinker as "serene," and its proposition simple: "be still." It is worth recalling that both serenity and stillness are connected to the auditive aspect of the human experience: they express a meaningfulness achieved by the opposite of what Heidegger calls "idle talk" or "gossiping," or in writing "scribbling."[203] That experience of meaningfulness in silence is compared by Scruton to the effect of music on an audience, as well as to other distinguished sociable moments in an individual's life, such as eating together, or dancing together, when one is able to sense one's own exceptional position as self-conscious beings in the created world: "It is then, eating a meal among those we love, dancing together at a wedding, sitting side by side with people silenced by music, that we recognise our peculiar sovereign position in the world."[204] It is telling that two of the three occasions are connected to music. No doubt, for Scruton, too, music is the medium which can most easily bring us to the state of mind when we can make sense of what we are, human beings. In this sense, music is *par excellence* one of those forms of leisure which leads to self-knowledge, precisely in the way that it saves us from the hands of the monotonous slavery of work. The specific form of stillness of music makes occasions involving listening to music into celebrations and festivals. These words have clear connections with religious cult, through them Scruton once again connects music and religion. He talks about a meal with one's loved ones, but as we have seen, the same holds for occasions of common enjoyment of musical performance: "it is an offering, a sacrifice, and also – the highest instance – a sacrament."[205] What he describes is an exchange or interaction with the Unknown, which helps human beings to realise and even to express the exceptional quality of human life, by the ritual act, which is "a celebration and endorsement of our life here on earth."[206] This moment relieves us of the burden of survival which lies heavy on our animal self, and through "feast, festival, and faith" leads us to a momentary experience of insight, a form of reflection which will "endow our lives with sense."

It is through the work (and stillness) of Pieper that Scruton becomes ready to rejoice in practising his own profession, philosophy, which is connected in these moments of contemplation with "the divine command." Philosophy "reiterates that command as it came in a 'still small voice' to Elijah, and again to Pascal and Kierkegaard: in his own gentle way, Pieper tells us to 'Be still'."[207] This stillness is achieved, paradoxically, by the marvels of music, as Scruton understands it. In this case too, Scruton sticks to the original ancient Greek sense of the word. In that culture, music was the art of the Muses, the Greek term *mousiké* meaning the *techné* of the Muses. Likewise, one should not forget in this context that the original title of Pieper's book is *Musse und Kult, "Muße"* (leisure) itself being connected etymologically to the muses.

Even if he does not specifically analyse music, Pieper's understanding of leisure, as the moment of inspiration and creativity, can, of course, be traced back to the ancient Greek concept of contemplation. This is extolled in Aristotle's *Nicomachean Ethics* as the greatest source of happiness. Aristotle famously distinguished between three forms of life. The life of pleasure, the life of practical activity and the contemplative way of life. Although he obviously criticised the first one of these, it is not as clear, which one stands at the top of his hierarchy of values, an active, political life or a life of contemplation, both of which he presents as valuable in their own right.

Scruton's emphasis on the notion of friendship indicates that he had in mind the Aristotelian concept of a theoretical life. For indeed, the highest form of friendship for Aristotle has the same self-sufficiency as is characteristic of the life of contemplation. They both have an intrinsic value, of which Scruton writes: "intrinsic value, and the pursuit of it, are means to the highest human end: namely happiness – that elusive but abundant thing which we obtain only so long as we do not pursue it" (458). This happiness, of course, should be distinguished from mere sensuous pleasure, which is a bodily function, and which belongs to the shallowest form of life in the Aristotelian hierarchy of forms of life. The happiness of the theoretical life is *euadaimonia*, a concept of happiness which is connected to the highest aspirations of men, connected to their intellectual and spiritual powers.

In particular, Scruton connects this happiness to the fulfilment of the soul, which comes with religious belief. As we have seen, Scruton has a very specific understanding of the notion of religion. About religion, too, he keeps emphasising that it is basically a matter of "seeing the world through the eyes of a 'first-person plural'" (458). In other words, it is not so much the nature of God which determines the practice of religion. It is much more the sort of interpersonal ties which define a religious community, as he seems to understand it. This allows him to connect his anthropological interest and his Aristotelian emphasis on contemplation and friendship. He once again leads us through the calvary of religion along the lines Girard proposed, distinguishing four phases which are constitutive of religion as a communal phenomenon: "the experience of pollution, separation, or 'fall'"; "the sacrifice"; "the ritual"; and finally, "a wondrous inversion" by which "the sacrifice becomes a sacrament" (459).

The crucial aspect of religious experience, for Scruton, is its communal dimension. In religious rites we are not simply observers, but active participants, or even those who imaginatively take on themselves the burden of the sacrifice, in order to bring relief, as it happens when viewing a dramatic performance according to the notion of catharsis in Aristotle's account of the mechanism of artistic experience in the *Poetics*. Just as members of the audience in an ancient theatre shared with others the specific state of mind of passing through those phases of recognition and relief, as outlined in Aristotle's definition of catharsis, so too according to

Kant, we appeal to the common sense of implied others, or ultimately of humanity, in our aesthetic judgement of a work of art, including the enjoyment of a piece of music.[208] Once again, in a religious rite, we share the experience of our human condition not only with those who are present, but also with other, absent members of our community, even with those who are not members of our religious community, and even with "the dead and the unborn" (461). Scruton draws here, once again, on the work of anthropologists, who claims that customs and rites "seal the bond of membership," initiating the participants into a "common culture" (461).

The philosopher points out a parallel procedure whereby the example of the critic, which we follow in our aesthetic apprehension of the work of art, defines a small circle of the initiated, those who are able to see and hear, who are the initiated, the connoisseurs. The procedure to select the few experts has its origin in the recruitment process of the royal court in the early modern context, as described by Norbert Elias, among others. The small circle of art lovers at court later developed into the select society of the refined critics of the bourgeois salon. These groups were represented at the court by the intellectual aristocracy and somewhat later in the city by the *Bildungsbürgertum*.

The communal aspect remained crucial in these select circles, too. The judgement of taste of the expert critic also represents an effort to fit into society. "Our matching of thought to thought and image to image," and maybe even, perhaps, of certain notions of melody to other notions of it "is also a matching of person to person" (465). In other words, the implied community behind the judgement of taste is also a judgement of the moral worth of the other, a test of "what is appropriate, decorous, or revealing" (465).

Cicero's influence is obvious in this whole process: decorum lies at the centre of this early modern idea of the morally upright and sociable human personality.[209] The meaning of the term decorum is, essentially, maintaining good taste and propriety. The Ciceronian legacy remains preserved in European moral and political thought, from Renaissance and early modern authors, until Smith, Hume and the other authors of the Enlightenment.[210] Scruton brings up specific forms of the manifestations of the effort to maintain social propriety, including "games, jokes, ceremonies, and customs" (465). He specifically refers also to wit, a key element of the ruminations of the third Earl of Shaftesbury. He does not view wit as a sign of individual innovation—on the contrary, he regards it as a "sense of membership" (465).

It is on this basis that Scruton himself builds his own concept of classical art. Although starting out from philosophy and literature, he specifically focuses, in connection with this concept, on the arts of architecture and music. What others call the grammar or language of classical architecture, Scruton regards as tradition. "In the classical styles of architecture," he writes, "we witness a tradition, developing under the ceaseless impulse of the allusive sensibility." Tradition supports the community, "endowing the city street with the life and outlook of an imagined community of people"[211] (466).

In a similar vein, Scruton explains the operation of the effect of music on humans. He refers to Stravinsky, who claimed that the original milieu of music depended on what the French called *bon gout*, which was itself the product of aristocratic patronage. Scruton accepts the role and function of the aristocracy in supporting musical culture in the early modern court context, yet he is keen also to emphasise the role of the bourgeois, on whose actual provision of goods the aristocratic patronage depended. He seems to be convinced by the account of the birth of commercial society told by the conjectural historians of the Scottish Enlightenment, by authors such as Adam Smith, David Hume, Adam Ferguson or John Millar, from whom he borrows such socio-economic terms, as the market, the division of labour and economic cooperation. Unlike the textbooks of classical and neo-classical economics, which stressed the essentially egoistic or voluntary motivations of individuals, however, Scruton emphasises the sociable, Aristotelian-Ciceronian aspects of that development of the human condition.[212] As he points out, the appreciation of music is not simply the adoration of individual genius by the connoisseur. "A musical culture arises because people associate in order to make and listen to music" (466).

To support this notion, he makes a comparison between improvised musical performance and the essence of European urbanity. The communal performance and enjoyment of music is comparable to those processes of cooperation which resulted in the birth of the European city.[213]

The latter, too, can only arise and function properly, if individuals and communities are willing to harmonise their activity, by a constant flow of interactions among them. Scruton abstracts the mechanisms of the market, the major motor of urban life, when he explains the social mechanisms that harmonise the different trends of social dynamics. The market is an unintended human achievement, which helps partners to find each other, and organises the provision of supply and the meeting of demand. In this way, it helps people to come together and cooperate. "The town is the solvent of human differences, the only conceivable forum in which sympathies can be constantly enlarged" (467). Similarly, the social mechanism of music reminds him of the operation of the city: bringing people together, and thereby creating community.

Yet the connection between urban centres and the community built by music is not only abstract. Scruton traces the connection between the growth of an urban way of life and the institutionalisation of the music of Western high culture. Indeed, he convincingly shows that music is present in all the different fields of city life. City dwellers play music in "churches, assembly halls, ballrooms, and theatres," to which one could also add schools, guilds, religious and urban festivals, weddings and funerals. Scruton demonstrates that music did not remain a form of enjoyment of a distinguished elite, but became popular in an age of democratisation. Being "free from concepts," it is a "universal idiom," which can be learnt and shared by anyone (467). Scruton portrays the widespread use of music in the eighteenth to nineteenth centuries as a sign that Western "bourgeois civilization" was able to build up through music a "community beyond language" (467)—a narrative of the social function of culture which represents a substantial challenge to the Marxist paradigm of class conflicts, which leads to an interpretation of the oligarchic and discriminative nature of bourgeois society and even questions Schiller's and the Romantics' story of art as a form of total alienation of the lonely individual as a result of the inhuman by-products of a consumer culture, symptomatic of bourgeois capitalism and its inhuman procedures of market mechanisms.

Scruton does not accept Adorno's claim that there was a break between high and low culture at the end of the nineteenth century. In his view, this break only came in the twentieth century, with the birth of beat music from the genres of jazz and blues. He does not venture to give a full account why this happened, but he explicitly mentions among the reasons for it the technological invention of the gramophone, recorded music, and the radio, which spread music all over a given territory. Yet even the disastrous social effects of technology, diagnosed, among others, by Heidegger, do not suffice for Scruton as an explanation. Another prerequisite of it is the rise of the democratic man, demanding equality and the recognition of his simplified taste. The distance between high and low is not the by-product of bourgeois culture, but the result of the collapse of a way of life which sustained bourgeois culture, along with the customs of domestic chamber music and singing in choirs.

He also rejects Adorno's second consecutive claim that the only remedy for this schism dividing the two cultures of mass society is modernism, or the avant-garde. In fact, according to Scruton, the avant-garde simply guarantees the loss of the audience for art. Instead of being able to bridge low and high, the avant-garde turns against the culture of the bourgeois middle class, and its members—led by social solidarity—join the ranks of the proletariat. The modernist attempt is futile—it has abolished all those "customs, habits, and tradition" (471) without which no musical culture can survive, including the social basis both of amateur musicians and of the audience for professional musical performance.

Instead of the Romantic asceticism of Adorno's views of the modernist artist, the torchbearer of a new religion and the representative of a social revolution, Scruton turns to Wagner's *Meistersinger* in his search how to revive musical culture. Once again, he discovers in Wagner's art that synchronic movement of music and social life: "in the idealised bourgeois community of Nuremberg music serves as a *lingua franca*, uniting and harmonizing the many occupations upon which the life of the town depends" (473). There, the tonality of music becomes "the symbol of the broader harmony of the town, the invisible hand of cooperation which is the true gift of a bourgeois culture" (ibid.). Wagner showed that the way to revive musical harmony is not by throwing away its repeated, empty patterns, but rather to regain its social basis. Scruton offers here an ingenious musical summary of Wagner's solution to musical revival. Walther, dissatisfied with the shallow monotony and rule-bound nature of the musical life of the town, feels an aristocratic contempt towards what he sees as the marketplace of musical ideas, invoking the criticism of Hans Sachs, who shows him that there is no music outside of the community of listeners. While Walther is ready to accept this criticism and acquiesces, creating his own musical dialect, his melodies serve to fertilise the ossified layers of local music, and rescue it from exhaustion (474). Yet the combination which emerges from Walther's inventions and the musical performances of the community constitutes a revival of the old by resurrecting it with the new spirit of Walther's own musical inventions. Tradition survives and preserves the tonality of music.

It is in this Wagnerian spirit that Scruton deals with the theoretical challenge of explaining clichés and sentimentality in music, and of suggesting ways to handle this problem. As he finds it, the sentimental person is not captivated by her own emotions. Rather than "feeling something," she prefers to avoid it (486). Echoing Kant, Scruton criticises the sentimentalist, who treats the objects of her feelings not as ends in themselves, but as means for her own advancement. Following the example of F.R. Leavis, Scruton finds seduction and betrayal in the interaction between the sentimentalist and her audience (487). For Scruton, a work of art is sentimental when it offers a catalogue of clichés which are substitutes for the actual, rich tapestry of details of reality. Humans are tempted by sentimentalism, including sentimental art, because we cannot bear the burden of unadulterated reality for long. Hence, we tend to resort to collective illusions. In doing so, however, we are actually cheating and deceiving both ourselves and each other. It would be better, Scruton claims, if we choose the more difficult road of trying to confront reality, even if we fail in the attempt.

A crucial step in the process of the separation of classical music from everyday music was the moment when the human voice was no longer in the centre of it. While this was a sign that music did not play the same part in our lives that it had played earlier, along with "worship, dancing, marching, and as accompaniment to labour" (488), it also has a positive side effect. Instead of mirroring daily life, music becomes a messenger from an unknown realm, and an expression of the mysterious depths of the human soul. People saw in it a replacement for the functions of religion, creating a "spiritual and religious community" (489). This happened in the moment, when the traditional ties of society have dissolved under the oppression of a centralised state and a consumer culture. When music is heard in the concert hall, a quasi-community is summoned forth by the solemnity of the musical moment. This sense of music creating an "implied community" is reaffirmed by the fact that instrumental music is a "paradigm of order" and form, when social connections dissolve, and when the certainties of a well-ordered view of the world vanish. It is at this moment that music as an art form can assume the role of religion.

To achieve this function, in order to take over, at least practically, the redemptive function of religion, music as great art has to perform the "affirmation … of the actual" (492), in other words it needs to remain "life-affirming"[214] (494). That mission can only be fulfilled if music can preserve the perspective of the first-person plural: "art endorses life only through the 'we' of the implied community, which redeems the death and grief of the mere individual" (495).

Scruton underlines the difficulty of this task, describing the disintegration of the social element in the popular form of dancing. Traditional dances, which Scruton also calls "formation dances" had certain advantages when compared to the practices of dance today (which means the end of the twentieth century). First, they pursued well-defined forms, which had to be learnt by dancers, and to learn them required long hours of self-control, helping the formation of character and acquiring the virtues of patience, moderation and attention to the other.[215] This learning process taught the dancer "to fit his gestures to the movement of his partner and to the pattern of the whole" (498). Scruton thus presents dance as a symbol of the social tasks to be completed by the individual in a well-ordered society, where individuals similarly had to learn the appropriate actions to fit into their environment. A further advantage of the formation dance was that it taught certain values to the young mind. It was "a moral idea, a vision of peaceful community which serves to tame the sexual instinct and to overcome its impetuosity" (498). In contrast, the type of dance popular in contemporary Western society turns a social into a sexual occasion.

To be sure, Scruton seems to be somewhat naively idealistic, when defending the values of the past. Sexuality naturally accompanies the bodily movement which follows the rhythm of music. Yet his criticism of the sexual revolution of the twentieth century is in line with those of other cultural critics. Scruton's language turns sarcastic, when quoting a song by the rock band Nirvana, illustrating his well-founded point that contemporary popular "dance becomes a lapse into disorder, a kind of surrender of the body which anticipates the sexual act itself" (499). Yet his criticism of a lack of attention to the movement of the other in contemporary dance sounds convincing. The other seems to fall out of the picture, as the dancer is in fact taken over by a "kind of narcissistic excitement," exemplified by John Travolta as the dancing king of the discotheque (this is not Scruton's example). The problem here is that in popular music rhythm becomes all-important, pushing aside the relevance of melody and even more of harmony, the latter two surviving only in a compromised form.

Scruton, the idealist, paints a picture of music in the contemporary world, in which democratic political culture and an irreligious, or even an anti-religious impulse feed each other. Music, he claims, is just as much in decline as our social realm is impoverished. The individual is left alone, in her isolation not only from others, but also left alone by God, too. According to Scruton, the mistake Nietzsche committed was to find power relation in music, too. Power is the key to the social for Marxists like Gramsci and Lukács, and postmodern authors from Foucault to Bourdieu. Moreover, he underrates the social element in it (the creation of the *Erlebnis* of the first-person plural), as well as its connection to the sacred.

Instead of the democratic and irreligious present, Scruton proposes a world which is able to see and think in religious terms, thus also healing the wounds of society. Given human nature, differences of rank and social status between members of the group are unavoidable, anyhow. To regain these substantial functions of music, we need to return to tonal music. Take Wagner's *Meistersinger*. There, tonal music is expressive of a harmonious order of society, and listening to it can grant the listener the chance to join in a shared vision of life, a first-person plural perspective of the world. This is an enormous task, and it is characteristic of Scruton, that he can imagine such a redeeming act, which would allow a return to the music of a "sacral community" (506). Yet he is right: T.S. Eliot succeeded in returning poetry to a more fundamental concept of literature, without disavowing his own age. As Eliot's poetry was able to recll the power of language characteristic of Homer, the Bible or Shakespeare, an idealised composer would be able to return to that earlier notion of music, as soon as he could achieve a "rediscovery of the tonal language". This return would produce a music which is able to reinforce social cohesion.

Scruton's criticism of the damaged state of contemporary art, and the solutions he proposes for healing its wounds are remarkably similar for music as for architecture. In both cases, he makes repeated references to their social and sacramental dimensions. Moreover, in both cases, he searches for the solution, within the context of the city. It is the experience of the community of town burghers which helps the builder to build in a way to create home, and to play or listen to music in a way which turns music into a helpful guide for both individual and communal life, without turning it into an instrument of ideology.

Notes

1. I used the following edition: Roger Scruton, *Modern Culture* (London, New York: Continuum), 2011.
2. Roger Scruton, *Culture Counts, Faith and Feeling in a World Besieged* (New York, London: Encounter Books, 2018, second edition).
3. An earlier collection on the same theme was his book *The Politics of Culture and Other Essays* (Manchester: Carcanet Press, 1981).
4. Scruton, *Modern Culture*, 1–4., Scruton, *Culture Counts*, 1–15.
5. Philip Larkin, *Churchgoing* (1954, 1955) I do not address here the paradox that the poet's question concerns the decline of disbelief, and not that of belief.
6. Scruton *Modern Culture*, 1.
7. Ibid., 4.
8. Ibid., 3.
9. Ibid., 4.
10. Ibid., 5.
11. Ibid., 7. In the Bibliography, Scruton gives the following work of Jung: Carl G. Jung, *The Archetypes and the Collective Unconscious*, tr. R. F. C. Hull (London, 1959). He adds that Jung's work "brings the aesthetic and the religious together". (*Modern Culture*, 163).
12. Ibid., 9.

13. Ibid., 15.
14. Ibid.
15. Scruton takes this quote from Eva Brann's lecture entitled Jane Austen that she gave in 1975. A text from her with the title *The Perfection of Jane Austen* is available on The Imaginative Conservative website, containing the phrase quoted here by Scruton: https://theimaginativeconservative.org/2018/07/perfection-of-jane-austen-eva-brann.html.
16. Scruton, *Modern Culture*, 18.
17. Ibid.
18. Ibid.
19. Scruton, *Culture Counts*, 2.
20. Ibid., 1.
21. Ibid.
22. Certainly, the relationship of culture and civilisation differs in different national contexts. For an alternative understanding of the terms, see Thomas Mann's criticism of liberalism in his early *Reflections of an Unpolitical Man*, and the moderated critique of it by Settembrini, in *The Magic Mountain*. I am grateful to Bob Grant for this example.
23. Scruton, *Culture Counts*, 2.
24. Ibid., 3. Scruton is aware of the fact, that unlike Scottish law, British common law, as theorised by Blackstone and others, does not derive from Roman law, and that it has a bottom-up, evolutionary character, as opposed to the somewhat abstract, "principled" system of Roman law.
25. Ibid., 5.
26. Ibid., 5.
27. For a short history of the concept of taste in the age of the Enlightenment, see the present author's *Esztétikai gondolkodás a felvilágosodás korában 1650–1800 - Az ízlésesztétika paradigmája* (Aesthetic Thought in the Age of Enlightenment 1650–1800—the Paradigm of the Aesthetics of Taste) (Budapest: Gondolat, 2013).
28. See 2.8 Aesthetics and Morality, in Hannah Ginsborg, "Kant's Aesthetics and Teleology," *The Stanford Encyclopedia of Philosophy* (Winter 2019 Edition), Edward N. Zalta (ed.), URL = https://plato.stanford.edu/archives/win2019/entries/kant-aesthetics/, based on Paul Guyer, *Kant and the Experience of Freedom* (Cambridge: Cambridge University Press, 1993), and Paul Guyer, "Beauty, Freedom, and Morality: Kant's Lectures on Anthropology and the Development of his Aesthetic Theory," in *Essays on Kant's Anthropology*, ed. Brian Jacobs

and Patrick Kain (Cambridge: Cambridge University Press, 2003), 135–63; reprinted in Paul Guyer, *Kant's System of Nature and Freedom: Selected Essays* (Oxford: Clarendon Press, 2005).

29. See also Smith on the ideal spectator in Adam Smith, *The Theory of Moral Sentiments* (1759).

30. David Hume, "Of the Standard of Taste," in *Essays, Moral, Political and Literary* (1777), 226–49.

31. Scruton, *Culture Counts*, 42.

32. Ibid.

33. Ibid.

34. Ibid.

35. Ibid., 44

36. Nathaniel Wolloch, "Cato the Younger in the Enlightenment," *Modern Philology* 106, no. 1 (August 2008): 60–82.

37. J. G. A. Pocock, "An Overview of The Decline and Fall of the Roman Empire," in *The Cambridge Companion to Edward Gibbon*, ed. Karen O'Brien and Brian Young (Cambridge: Cambridge University Press, 2018), 20–40.

38. Pocock, "Between Machiavelli and Hume: Gibbon as Civic Humanist and Philosophical Historian," *Daedalus* 105, no. 3 (1976): 153–69.

39. Scruton, *Gentle Regrets*, 201.

40. Both in *Green Philosophy* and in his book *On Human Nature* he does not shy away from addressing issues of contemporary natural science.

41. Donald W. Crawford, "Review of Roger Scruton, Beauty [Book Review], *Notre Dame Philosophical Reviews* 12 (2009). Available at: https://ndpr.nd.edu/reviews/beauty/.

42. Roger Scruton, *Art and Imagination. A Study in the Philosophy of Mind* (South Bend, Indiana: St Augustine's Press, 1998 (1974)).

43. This context is introduced in the book's Preface. In the same way, the preface of *Beauty* shares with the reader the name of some of the experts he consulted (Malcolm Budd, an expert on natural beauty and the beauty of music, and John Hyman, a philosopher mainly interested in the visual arts), as well as his lifelong friends and fellow philosophers Robert Grant, Anthony O'Hear and David Wiggins, all three of whom are great names in their respective fields.

44. In his comments on the first draft of the present text, Anthony O'Hear claims that together with Spinoza, Scruton's favourite philosophers

were Kant and Wittgenstein. I do not have a strong view on that, but I would also stress his interest in the ancients, in Hegel or in Eliot, as well.

45. Scruton, *Beauty*, 12.
46. Robert Grant called my attention to his discussions with Scruton about Kantian disinterestedness, as a "thin" starting point of aesthetic worth.
47. These are questions which will return throughout the book.
48. One should not forget about Hegel's critical attitude towards the beautiful soul, though.
49. Scruton, *Beauty*, 53.
50. Ibid., 65.
51. Ibid., 78.
52. Ibid., 89.
53. Ibid., 90.
54. Ibid.
55. Ibid.
56. Ibid., 93.
57. Ibid., 96.
58. Ibid., 145.
59. Ibid., 145.
60. Ibid., 127.
61. Ibid., 128.
62. For a description of the Hegelian distinction, see: Stephen Houlgate, "Hegel's Aesthetics," *The Stanford Encyclopedia of Philosophy* (Spring 2020 Edition), Edward N. Zalta (ed.), URL = https://plato.stanford.edu/archives/spr2020/entries/hegel-aesthetics/. Burke's distinction is to be found in his *A Philosophical Enquiry into the Origin of Our Ideas of the Sublime and Beautiful* of 1756.
63. Scruton, *Beauty*, 157.
64. Ibid., 171.
65. Ibid., 178.
66. I used the following issue of the book: David Watkin, *Morality and Architecture. The Development of a Theme in Architectural History and Theory from the Gothic Revival to the Modern Movement* (Oxford: Clarendon Press, 1977). An extended version of the book has since appeared, published in 2001.
67. Sir Herbert Butterfield, *The Whig Interpretation of History* (1931), 41–2.
68. Augustus Welby Northmore Pugin, *Contrasts: Or, A Parallel Between the Noble Edifices of the Fourteenth and Fifteenth Centuries and Similar*

Buildings of the Present Day. Shewing the Present Decay of Taste. Accompanied by Appropriate Text (London: Charles Dolman, 1836), Nikulaus Pevsner, *Pioneers of the Modern Movement: from William Morris to Walter Gropius* (London: Faber and Faber, 1936).

69. Watkin, *Morality*, 1.
70. Ibid., 3.
71. Ibid., 4.
72. Ibid.
73. Ibid., 11.
74. Ibid., 12.
75. Roger Scruton, "The Architecture of Stalinism," *Cambridge Review* xcix, (16 Nov, 1976), 36–41.
76. Watkin, *Morality*, 14.
77. It is crucial for Scruton, that Watkin's own stance is one he has deliberately chosen, as a result of the impact on him of the Catholicism, characteristic of the Monsignor, Alfred Gilbey.
78. Watkin, *Morality*, 71.
79. Ibid., 72–3.
80. Ibid., 77.
81. Ibid., 81.
82. Susie Harries, *Nikolaus Pevsner: The Life* (London: Chatto and Windus, 2011).
83. Watkin even points out that in later editions of the book, totalitarian is replaced by the term "universal." See: Watkin, *Morality*, 96, footnote.
84. Stephen Games: *Pevsner—The Early Life: Germany and Art* (London: Continuum, 2010), Harries, *Nikolaus Pevsner*. For a more concise, yet detailed overview of the issue of Pevsner and the Nazi temptation, see Iain Boyd Whyte, "Nikolaus Pevsner: art history, nation, and exile," *RIHA Journal* 0075 (23 October 2013, URL: http://nbn-resolving.de/urn:nbn:de:101:1-20131113230, URL: https://journals.ub.uni-heidelberg.de/index.php/rihajournal/article/view/69832, accessed May, 2021.
85. Boyd Whyte, *Pevsner*, 3.
86. Games, *Pevsner*, 185–206.
87. Boyde Whyte, *Pevsner*, 5.
88. Watkin, *Morality*, 82.
89. Ibid., 97. Of course, this opposition between individual and collectivity does not leave much place to ordinary patriotism, either.

90. B. Miller Lane, *Architecture and Politics in Germany, 1918–1945* (Cambridge MA: Harvard University Press, 1968), 2–3.
91. Watkin, *Morality*, 103.
92. Pevsner, *Studies in Art*, vol. ii, 244.
93. Karl Popper, *The Poverty of Historicism* (London: Routledge, 1957), 10.
94. *The Philosophy of Karl Popper*, ed. P. A. Schilpp, 2 vols, (La Salle, Illinois: Open Court, 1974), vol ii. 925.
95. Jacob Burckhardt, *Die Renaissance in Italien* (Stuttgart, 1867), 165.
96. Roger Scruton, *The Aesthetics of Architecture* (Princeton: Princeton University Press, 1979), ix.
97. Ibid., x.
98. Ibid.
99. For Scruton, a well-designed public building can easily change its function, as the need of the community dictates.
100. Scruton, *Architecture*, 14.
101. See the entry "vernacular" in the *Online Etymology Dictionary*.
102. Literature is another of the art forms in which the local variant is crucial.
103. Scruton, *Architecture*, 17.
104. One should be aware of the fact that Roman virtue of prudence itself is not exactly the same, as the Greek notion of *phronésis*.
105. Scruton, *Architecture*, 30.
106. Ibid.
107. In some of his earlier works, Scruton seemed to be more Kantian, in disjoining the aesthetic entirely from the moral.
108. Scruton, *Architecture*, 36.
109. Ibid., 69.
110. Though dogs are said to be able to dream.
111. Scruton, *Architecture*, 101.
112. Ibid.
113. Geoffrey Scott, *The Architecture of Humanism* (Boston and New York: Houghton Mifflin Company, 1914), 232.
114. Scruton, *Architecture*, 113, referring, of course, to the enchanting speech by Socrates at the end of the Symposium.
115. Ibid., 133.
116. Ibid., 176.
117. Ibid., 192–3.

118. Nikolaus Pevsner, *An Outline of European Architecture* (London: Pelican Books, 1943, 7th edition, 1963), 255. The fact that Scruton uses Pevsner as a bibliographic source shows that he appreciated his professional knowledge as an art historian.

119. Scruton, *Architecture*, 196.

120. Ibid.

121. One should be cautious, of course, in the case of the work of art: attributing certain qualities to it should always depend on the clear sight of artistic intention recognised. Otherwise, we can easily fall victim of an impressionistic kind of subjectivism.

122. Ibid., 215–6.

123. For the rich vocabulary of the appropriate, Scruton draws on the work of Hans-Karl Lücke, *Index Verborum to Alberti's 'De Re Aedificatoria'* (München: Prestel, 1970 onwards).

124. Roger Scruton, "Alberti and the Art of the Appropriate," in Scruton, *The Classical Vernacular. Architectural Principles in an Age of Nihilism* (Manchester: Carcanet, 1994), 85–95.

125. Scruton, *Architecture*, 244, referring to Scruton, "Self-knowledge and Intention," *Proceedings of the Aristotelian Society*, 1977–1978, as well as a paper by D.C. Dennett.

126. Scruton, *Architecture*, 246–7. See John Grote's *Exploratio Philosophica, Rough Notes on Modern Intellectual Science*, Part I. (Cambridge, etc., 1865), 16: "at home in the universe".

127. Scruton, *Architecture*, 249.

128. Ibid., 253.

129. Ibid., 253.

130. Sir Denys Lasdun, "Architectural Aspects of the National Theatre," *Journal of the Royal Society of Arts* 125, no. 5256 (November, 1977), 780–92, quoted by Scruton, 255. Scruton does not deal with Lasdun's own plan of the National Theatre, which does not fulfil the above requirements.

131. Carroll William Westfall, "Tradition in the Vernacular and the Classical," *Traditional Building* (Aug. 1, 2019)

132. Scruton, *The Classical Vernacular*, xvii.

133. As mentioned earlier, Hegel's *The Philosophy of Right* is a major influence on Scruton's thought.

134. Scruton's distinction can be associated with the friend-enemy opposition of Carl Schmitt.

135. Scruton, *The Classical Vernacular*, 29.
136. Jacobs, *American Cities*.
137. Scruton, *The Classical Vernacular*, 32.
138. The term "tacit knowledge" derives from Michael Polányi's works, including *Personal Knowledge* (1958) and *The Tacit Dimension* (1966).
139. T. S. Eliot, *Notes towards the Definition of Culture* (London: Faber and Faber, 1948, 1962), 117.
140. Scruton, *The Classical Vernacular*, 37.
141. Ibid., 38.
142. Ibid., 39.
143. Ibid.
144. See Michael Wheeler, "Martin Heidegger," *The Stanford Encyclopedia of Philosophy* (Fall 2020 Edition), Edward N. Zalta (ed.), URL = https://plato.stanford.edu/archives/fall2020/entries/heidegger/.
145. Scruton, *The Classical Vernacular*, 106.
146. Ibid., 107.
147. Ibid.
148. Ibid., 107–8.
149. Ibid., 109.
150. Ibid., 86.
151. Lücke, *Index*.
152. Scruton, *The Classical Vernacular*, 89.
153. Ibid.
154. Ibid.
155. Ibid., 90., referring to Alberti, *The Architecture of Leon Battista Alberti in Ten Books*, Bk. VI, chap. 2.
156. Scruton does not give the source of the quote. It is *Alberti 1485: IX.v*, opposite fol. y, quoted by Cohen, M A 2014 Introduction: *Two Kinds of Proportion. Architectural Histories*, 2(1): 21, pp. 1–25., 19., n37.
157. See Franco Volpi, "In Whose Name?: Heidegger and 'Practical Philosophy'," *European Journal of Political Theory* 6, no. 1, (2007): 31–51.
158. Scruton, *The Classical Vernacular*, 93. He is criticising Leoni's translation, as far as the rendering of the philosophical parts is concerned. The original edition is: Leon Battista Alberti: *The Architecture of Leon Battista Alberti in Ten Books, of Painting in Three Books, and of Statuary in One Book*. Translated into Italian by Cosimo Bartoli. And Now First Into English, and Divided Into Three Volumes by James Leoni,

Venetian Architect; To Which Are Added Several Designs of His Own, For Buildings Both Public and Private, published 1726.

159. Martin McLaughlin argues that beyond Cicero, Alberti refers to Xenophon as his source of inspiration. McLaughlin, "Leon Battista Alberti and the Redirection of Renaissance Humanism," *Proceedings of the British Academy* 167, 2009 Lectures.

160. Scruton, *The Classical Vernacular*, 94.

161. It is, therefore, somewhat confusing that later he quotes Barbaro's reference to metaphysics, as if it was the same argument. What is called metaphysics in the post-scholastic literature is the opposite of practical knowledge, and is instead what Aristotle called theoria.

162. Roger Scruton, "A Plea for Beauty: A Manifesto for a New Urbanism," *American Enterprise Institute for Public Policy Research* (AEI), no. 1 (March 2012).

163. Siddhartha Sen, "New Urbanism," in *Encyclopedia of the City*, ed. Roger W. Caves (London and New York: Routledge, 2005), 332–3.

164. *The Charter of the New Urbanism*, https://www.cnu.org/who-we-are/charter-new-urbanism.

165. Friedrich Hayek, *The Constitution of Liberty*. The Definitive edition (Chicago: University of Chicago Press, 1960, 2011), 466.

166. A Jucker, "The Eighteenth Century: The Age of Politeness," In *Politeness in the History of English: From the Middle Ages to the Present Day* (Cambridge: Cambridge University Press, 2020), 117–34.

167. Once again, I am grateful to Robert Grant, who called my attention to this point.

168. Edward Banfield, "The Logic of Metropolitan Growth," ch. 2 in *The Unheavenly City Revisited* (Boston: Little, Brown and Company, 1974).

169. Scruton, *A Plea for Beauty*, 7.

170. I am suggested that similarly stringent requirements apply in the English Cotswolds, and the result is good.

171. Scruton, *A Plea for Beauty*, 8.

172. Press Release: James Brokenshire, building better and beautiful will deliver more homes, published November 3, 2018., available at: https://www.gov.uk/government/news/james-brokenshire-building-better-and-beautiful-will-deliver-more-homes.

173. Press release: Commissioners appointed to new home design body, published February 13, 2019, available at: https://www.gov.uk/government/news/commissioners-appointed-to-new-home-design-body.

Wilkie was later replaced by Adrian Penfold, a planning expert and government adviser.

174. The journalist, George Eaton, subsequently published an Instagram picture of himself, drinking champagne, with the caption: "The feeling when you get right-wing racist and homophobe Roger Scruton sacked."

175. See his summary of the events, *Press Statement from Sir Roger Scruton* in response to the apology from The New Statesman 8 Jul 2019, available at: https://www.roger-scruton.com/articles/617-press-statement-from-sir-roger-scruton-in-response-to-the-apology-from-the-new-statesman-8-jul-2019.

176. Creating Space for Beauty. The Interim Report of the Building Better, Building Beautiful Commission, https://assets.publishing.service.gov.uk/government/uploads/system/uploads/attachment_data/file/929630/BBBBC_Commission_Interim_Report.pdf. The Interim report has been signed by Interim Chair Boys Smith, and members Mayhew and Parsons.

177. Creating Space for Beauty, 8–9.

178. Ibid., 10.

179. Ibid., 69.

180. Available at: https://assets.publishing.service.gov.uk/government/uploads/system/uploads/attachment_data/file/861832/Living_with_beauty_BBBBC_report.pdf.

181. One should also note that the report has a very attractive design, which sends the same message as the meaning of the text: that how things look, their external form, shape and style matters.

182. Roger Scruton, *Beauty* (Oxford: Oxford University Press, 2009), 31. Later, it was published with the title: *Beauty: A Very Short Introduction* (2011).

183. See the entry "Steward" in the *Online Etymology Dictionary*.

184. Edmund Burke, *Reflections on the French Revolution* (The Harvard Classics. 1909–1914), paragraph 162. Available at: https://www.bartleby.com/24/3/7.html.

185. This opera was finished before he published his first volume on the aesthetics of music.

186. Scruton and Dooley, *Conversations with Roger Scruton*, 200.

187. Roger Scruton, *The Ring of Truth. The Wisdom of Wagner's Ring of the Nibelung*.

188. Famously, though, Hitler greatly admired Lehár's operettas, too.

189. To balance those misrepresentations of his life, Scruton advises the reader to turn to the description of Wagner's life by John Deathridge in John Deathridge and Carl Dahlhaus, *The New Grove Wagner* (London: Macmillan, 1984).

190. See especially Girard's *La violence et la sacré* (1972).

191. "The Sorrows and Grandeur of Richard Wagner," in Thomas Mann, *Pro and Contra Wagner*, trans. Allan Blunden (London, Faber and Faber, 1985), 100.

192. Importantly, Scruton's religiosity did not include a firm belief in after-life, either.

193. Robert Grant suggests to me that "there are this-worldly thoughts very like this in Oakeshott's Notebooks", though he also adds "I don't think Roger had read them".

194. This quote is once again a comment of Robert Grant, for which I am really grateful.

195. Scruton, *Sexual Desire*.

196. Rémi Brague, *La Loi de Dieu* (Paris, 2004).

197. Wagner discusses Antigone in *Prose Works*, vol. 2. Opera and drama (Lincoln, Nebraska: University of Nebraska Press, 1994), 265–71.

198. Richard Wagner, *My Life*, trans. Andrew Gray, ed. Mary Whitall (Cambridge: Cambridge University Press, 1983), 388.

199. Preface to the Bloomsbury Revelations edition, in Roger Scruton, *Understanding Music. Philosophy and interpretation* (London, etc.: Bloomsbury Academic, 2009, 2016), ix-x., x.

200. Plato, *Republic*, 4.424c.

201. Josef Pieper, *Leisure, the Basis of Culture*, intr. Roger Scruton, trans. Gerald Malsbary (South Bend, In: St. Augustine's Press, 1998), 36–7. To be sure, workaholics sometimes forget even to live "rightly".

202. Pieper, *Leisure,* 13–15.

203. Martin Heidegger, *Being and Time*, trans. Joan Stambaugh (Albany: State University of New York Press, 1996), par. 35, 169.

204. Roger Scruton, "Introduction," in Pieper, *Leisure*, 13–15, 14.

205. Ibid., 14.

206. Ibid.

207. Ibid., 15.

208. Importantly, Kant's idea already appears in the Scottish Enlightenment, in particular in Smith's notion of the impartial spectator.

209. Daniel J. Kapust, "Cicero on decorum and the morality of rhetoric," *European Journal of Political Theory* 10, no. 1 (2011): 92–112.

210. Daniel J. Kapust and Michelle A. Schwarze, "The Rhetoric of Sincerity: Cicero and Smith on Propriety and Political Context," *American Political Science Review* 110, no. 1 (February 2016): 100–11.

211. Notice the notion of imagined community, coming from the work of Benedict Anderson on the birth of nationalism.

212. This can be compared with Peter Jones, *Hume's Sentiments, Their Ciceronian and French Context* (Edinburgh: Edinburgh University Press, 1982).

213. See Ferenc Hörcher, *The Political Philosophy of the European City* (Lanham: Rowman and Littlefield), 2021.

214. This works only so long, one should add, as life itself, or the actual is not unbearable.

215. Scruton is aware of the relevance attributed by Iris Murdoch to the notion of attention in her philosophy.

5

From the Philosophy of Art to Metaphysics (Vita Contemplativa)

For much of his professional career, Scruton's philosophy had two focuses: on the one hand, he was interested in political philosophy and on the other hand in aesthetics. While he is best known around the world for his pronounced conservative political philosophy, his main personal scholarly interest was in the theory of art. In his overall history of Modern Aesthetics, Paul Guyer could confidently claim that: "After Wollheim, the most significant British aesthetician has been Roger Scruton."[1] Scruton published a short introduction to general Aesthetics, titled *Beauty*, and two detailed analyses of the aesthetics of specific branches of art, *The Aesthetics of Architecture* and *The Aesthetics of Music*.[2] In his early career he published two other works on general aesthetics, *Art and Imagination: A Study in the Philosophy of Mind* in 1974, and *The Aesthetic Understanding: Essays in the Philosophy of Art and Culture* in 1983. He also published Platonic dialogues; works of art in which art was a major theme. Scruton is also known as a practising artist: he composed operas which were publicly performed and wrote novels and poetry which were published.

In the final decade of his life, Scruton made an important step forward in his philosophy, opening up a new vista. He published two slim volumes which directly addressed the issue of metaphysics, and indirectly,

F. Hörcher, *Art and Politics in Roger Scruton's Conservative Philosophy*, Palgrave Studies in Classical Liberalism, https://doi.org/10.1007/978-3-031-13591-0_5

that of religion. The first of these two books *The Face of God*, was first published in 2012, while the second, *The Soul of the World*, was published not long afterwards, in 2014. In this chapter, I would like to make two main points about these important works. One is that his philosophy of art and theory of politics became richer and deeper by entering the realm of metaphysics. Arguably, these late works are the products of a philosopher at the peak of his professional abilities, proving his prowess in venturing right up to the highest peaks of nature—and God. The other point I would like to make is that these works are still less known than some of his others and they are somewhat underrated. I would like to show that they are worked-out yet concise philosophical edifices, worthy both of further reflection on them and to be read for sheer enjoyment. They represent Scruton, the philosopher, at his best, self-critical of being able to reach the highest realms of the divine, but at least daring to strive to reach that point. These two late volumes will also serve as the final destination in our panoramic overview of Scruton's views of politics and art, in accordance with the ancient Platonic-and-Aristotelian scheme of dividing life into an active and a contemplative part. Although I will deal with the two books separately, it is important to stress that they were written close to each other, and therefore they are connected to each other in a number of ways.

Scruton held the Kantian view that we can never reach God through philosophy. We will not make an attempt here to decide of Scruton's own religiosity. If he did not want to, or found himself unable to reveal his own final and explicit position concerning a belief in the existence of God, an interpretation of his philosophy should not "force" him to do so. In fact, we shall not directly focus on Scruton's religiosity, because this is a book about his philosophy of art and philosophy of politics. Religion is only relevant for us, therefore, as it comes up in his thought on art and politics.[3] The present venture will be careful not to cross the threshold of metaphysics, therefore. Although in a number of places we will address Scruton's references to metaphysics, we shall look at them from a perspective which focuses on art and politics, which excludes a philosophical explication of religion and God.

Metaphysics I. The Face of God

Once again, let us start out from how the book was conceived by its author. According to its Preface, the philosophical material of *The Face of God* was first delivered as the Gifford Lectures in the University of Saint Andrews. Apparently, it was John Haldane, the analytical Thomist, residing at the Philosophy Department of the University, who invited him and who himself took a deep interest in its topic. This book can be read as Scruton's contribution to a dialogue with Haldane, a religious thinker and a formal papal adviser of the Vatican. It is also important to note that Scruton was ten years older than Haldane, and thus the senior partner in this exchange of ideas. Yet obviously, his partner's views have their reflection in Scruton's own thoughts.

Painting the Fall of Man

I tend to attribute a more than usual significance to the two paintings which were used for the cover of these two books. *The Face of God* presents Adam and Eve, naked, apparently in the Garden of Eden, from Pere Mates' painting: *Adam and Eve in the Garden of Eden.* The Spanish Renaissance painter presented the pair at the moment when God, who appears at the top of the painting, expels them from the Garden, as a punishment for what came to be called the original sin. Unlike the rendering of the same scene in Masaccio's painting, which was produced a century earlier, and which also appears in the text of the book, the Spanish painter presents the two of them with an apparently tranquil state of mind, their bodily language and their facial expressions calm and serene, apparently accepting the judgement of God with obedience and gratefulness. Although the action presented on the panel focuses on the pair and God, the painter is keen to show further aspects of the Garden, including both the natural scenery and the wildlife in it. Even a part of the rising sun is visible in the painting. Both the animals' behaviour as well as the weather suggests that this is a moment of peace and harmony.

This calmness is due to the fact that this scene occurred at a moment before the fall of man. The first humans, Adam and Eve, are naked. They still live in apparent harmony with God and Nature. This is expressed by the face of Eve, turned upwards, her eyes directed towards God in the sky, depicted on a cloud dressed as a king, with a crown on his head, surrounded by the escort of his angels. Moreover, Eve's hands are clasped, as if she was in fact praying. Adam, too, looks up, spreading his hands, and his left hand is also raised up as if he was in the midst of an argument, or pointing to something. In fact, they are aware of the weight of their deed. Their face reflects their repentance. God himself is not friendly any more, holding up the fingers of his right hand, expressing a kind of warning. He must be making a pronouncement in a moment, and the first couple is ready to hear this divine message with awe, but also accepting God's will.

The painter chooses a moment apparently before the fatal decision was taken. The connection between the three, the human couple, God and nature is still strong, but there are clouds in the sky, and the onlooker cannot help recalling the story of the Bible of their expulsion from this peaceful coexistence with nature under the rule of God. The first humans still feel at home in the Garden, even if their faces look scared, and they are somewhat apart from the animals. Their attention is directed at God instead of towards the animal world, and their pose is also free and easy, their muscles not showing much tension. They naturally accept their subordinate position compared to God. They are also fully attentive to God.

The moment presented by the painter here antedates and anticipates the moment chosen by Masaccio, entitled *Expulsion from Paradise*. This other fresco, as Scruton explains in the book, is in the Brancacci chapel in Florence, within the Santa Maria Carmine in Florence. In the latter painting, the deed had been committed, and God's angel is expelling them from the Garden with a sword in his hand. The couple are in total despair, Adam burying his head in his palms, Eve, covering the genitals of her body, as if suddenly realising her nakedness. The two of them step out of a city gate, presumably that of the Garden of Eden. This is one of the crucial moments of the narrative of the Book of Genesis, explaining original sin committed by the fallen nature of the human being, and its consequences.

The fact that Scruton's book-cover presents the earlier moment, that of the peaceful coexistence of the creatures of God in the Garden of Eden, can be seen as an effort to refer back to the doomed moment of harmony.

The painter is interested in the relationship between Man and God, which is, as we have just noted, a relationship of subordination. The pair is ready to accept the judgement. The Renaissance master painted the human body with great care, yet the human condition is still determined by an intimate connection with the creator.

The Gifford Lectures and Natural Theology

Lord Gifford, the eponym of the lectures, defined the aim of the public lectures to "promote and diffuse the study of natural theology in the widest sense of the term – in other words, the knowledge of God."[4] Scruton was invited to deliver his own contribution to that famous lecture series by John Haldane who had himself published an article, in which he tried to explain the significance of the lecture series.[5] Scruton notes that Lord Gifford held the firm belief that "our relation to God is the most important relation we have," and Scruton contrasts this nineteenth-century view with our disbelief and scepticism.[6] Lord Gifford expected the lecturers to approach natural theology as a science, in other words without relying on revelation. Yet how could one take the exercise of natural theology granted in an age when people do not believe even in the existence of God? Scruton is ready to apply the strict meaning of natural theology to his own endeavour; his philosophical method takes for granted all the methodological self-constraints of scientific inquiry. According to the standard understanding of it, natural theology "aims to adhere to the same standards of rational investigation as other philosophical and scientific enterprises, and is subject to the same methods of evaluation and critique."[7]

Alluding to the composition of Pere Mates' painting on the front cover, Scruton argues that those who operate within the atheistic culture of our age, are in fact trying to escape from "the eye of judgement."[8] It is as if Adam and Eve no longer wanted to maintain eye contact with God any more. As if the painter painted the picture without the upper part of the composition, cutting out of it the divine sphere, where God and the angels dwell. As if people wanted to wipe out the face of God. Scruton provides a phenomenological description of the three faces he claims the

Spanish painter presents in this picture: the face of the person, the face of the earth and the face of God. Certainly, "face" is a more complex concept here than in a simple description of human anatomy. Yet before we can embark on the journey which the philosopher invites us on, to encounter the face of the human being, of nature and of God respectively, we have to summarise the findings of Scruton's intellectual pilgrimage to date.

Community and Communion

Let us take as our starting point Scruton's reference to the methodological problem of the philosopher who embarks on a project like this. If he plans to provide a description of the faces represented in the painting, he has to be able to say something about the perspective from which the composition allows us to look at its subject.

Natural theology would require a perspective from which the whole of the world can be seen—a universal aspect, which is nothing less than "the 'transcendental' perspective that God alone sees."[9] Given the methodological constraints of science, Scruton needs to confine his own perspective. He admits that his enquiry is in fact driven by an interest in the moral basis of the existence of human beings. However, he hopes that his modest approach to the question can indeed be covered by philosophy. His confined, yet still general question is as follows: "why, to what end, and for what reason, is there a world that contains creatures like us?"[10]

If this is a reasonable question, in other words if this question is answerable by philosophy, then it might lead us to the idea of God. For if there is an end and a reason for the world we inhabit, someone must have given it that reason and end. And to give end and reason to a world like ours, requires the sort of power which human imagination, or simply our language, attributes to God. Yet this being, endowed with divine powers, is by definition not available to our senses. His perspective on the world is a different one from ours—we do not enter the same stage at the same time with God.

Referring once again to the painting, Scruton recalls the typical way in which we try to contact God—through prayer. In prayer, we address someone, who is not present in person—which makes it a rather specific kind of communication. Yet it is also something more than an irrational effort to talk to someone who is not there. Prayer is a rite, part of the cult that we call religion. Human beings participate in rituals of religion as part of their participation in the life and practice of a particular community, the community of believers. In our efforts to speak to God, who is by definition not available to us, we are not left alone, but joined by others around us. Scruton's reference point here is Durkheim: it was the French anthropologist who described in an objective manner the ideal sense and practical life of a religious community. Durkheim highlighted that people naturally come together to celebrate God, whom they cannot confront directly and individually. Yet, his description of the culture of religious communities does not make the problem of humans in search of their God the less difficult to solve. We all need to answer our questions about the purpose or reason of our world and our lives in it.

The next question concerns how our search for meaning can be reconciled with religion being a cooperative exercise. Scruton refers to the Christian notion of communion at this point. As he sees it, communion is a communal act, in other words a religious exercise we do together with others. It is also something else: it is "the real presence of God among us."[11] In other words, it enables us to experience Him, without giving up His godly nature. There is a transcendental dimension in the act of communion. It is a form of communication comparable to prayer. In both cases, we naturally address God, who by his very nature cannot be present, and therefore we need to invoke him. This leads Scruton to make the bold claim that: "It is through the communion that we come face to face with God."[12] In other words, in the communion we succeed in making the view from nowhere (science's perspective as well as the perspective of God) and the view from somewhere—the subjective human point of view—overlap.

In what follows Scruton explores the semantics of what he calls three "critical" words—the meaning of "I," "you" and "Why?", in order to prepare his discussion of the face of the person, the face of the world and the face of God, respectively.

The starting point is the question of the distinguishing mark of human experience, as an experience of the external world. The second chapter bears the title "The View from Somewhere," in contrast to the first chapter's title, "The View from Nowhere." This distinction, which Scruton takes from Thomas Nagel, serves to show that science itself has no clue as to the above-mentioned distinguishing mark of the human.[13] This is because the human experience is based on the experience of oneself (of the "I"), in communicative interaction with the other (with "you"). In a more or less Kantian manner, Scruton argues that the human being is a moral being, and her morality is based on the capacity to maintain an "inter-personal" relationship. "Personhood is a relational condition."[14]

Interpersonal Dialogue

The precondition of the I-You relationship is an awareness of the "I" of myself, which is itself based on my experience of the others who relate to one. Scruton certainly had Martin Buber and his book *Ich und Du* (1923) in mind when exploring this relational nature of one's awareness of oneself in the mirror of others' experience. Levinas, who based his concept of morality on the notion of the face of the other, as the source of the individual's self-awareness, is not referred to in this context, but he must also have been in the back of Scruton's mind, and indeed he appears in later parts of the book. What Scruton calls the "interpersonal dialogue" is based on the idea of the mutual interchangeability of the position of "I" and "you." "I" cannot help recognising "your" personhood, if I am aware of myself, as it helps me to imagine your own awareness of "yourself." Such recognition also works the other way round. As soon as I am able to recognise your personhood—in other words your ability to make sense of yourself, I must therefore also suppose that you are able to make sense of my own personhood as well. In other words, I can suppose that you are aware not only of yourself, but also, in a similar way, of my own awareness of myself. In this way the two of us mirror each other, which initiates a dialogue to be generated between the two of us. My ability to imagine your own perspective of yourself, as well as your ability to recognise my own self, is the bedrock of what Kant calls the "transcendental freedom" of the human being. If I am aware of both myself and you, I am aware of a realm created by the two of us, in interaction, in other words, in the social realm.

Kant's idea of transcendental freedom brings Scruton's description of the human condition to Hegel's notion of mutual recognition, in the famous dialectic of the master-slave relationship. As such, references to "the recognition of the other as another like me" lead by logical necessity to the idea that the two of us share a common world, the social realm, established by our voluntary interaction. If I am aware of myself, it follows that I am responsible for my actions. And, as soon as I am aware of you, my responsibility expands to my responsibility for you as well. I am held accountable for my actions concerning the other, in other words, I have to be able to explain why I did what I did to the other person.

Due to our freedom of choice, human actions cannot be explained simply by causes; one also has to give the reasons for one's actions. The requirement to explain our reasons for our actions forges a strong link between the concepts of "I" and "you": this link is the notion of "why?". When you ask me why I did what I did, you do it because you are aware that I am aware of myself, which makes my actions free actions, in the sense that my action is the result of my own will or intention. One cannot explain human action without comprehending its intentionality: that it is the action of a being who is aware of herself, and who has freely chosen the deed in question. A human being cannot help attributing intentionality to human action—this is a necessary consequence of their self-awareness, and of their parallel awareness of the self of the other. It is this inbuilt, implied intentionality of human action which creates the realm of moral responsibility: I cannot help thinking of myself as a person to be judged by others. Even in the moment of deliberating what to do, I am aware that I will have to be able to account for my deed to others. It will be an action to which intentions will be attributed by others. In other words, human beings cannot expect to inhabit a world of total freedom, which would mean a freedom from the judgement of others. Scruton explains this essential social nature of the human being with the help of a theatrical metaphor: the community—which comprises all the others, who are aware of themselves, and who recognise my personhood, attributing intentionality to my deeds—"stands as though on a balcony above our projects, expecting us to play our part," and judging our performance.[15] This account of the rationale of human responsibility prepares the ground for his account of a divine perspective.

Aesthetic and Moral Judgement

The above metaphor of the theatre is crucial, because it portrays the common perception of an art critic's point of view and the point of view of a moral or political critic: both of them make use of their ability to judge, with the help of which they can make judgements about the performance they saw. In what follows we compare artistic and political judgement, to discover the differences between the two activities, but also to show a similar mechanism in work in the intellectual part of these activities. Just as the critic judges the artistic perfection of a performance, so too the moral or political critic judges the moral or political perfection of the moral or political actor's performance. In both cases, judgement is made possible by the attribution of intentionality to the performance. In other words, in both cases the judge is able to imagine what it feels like to be the person she judges. My self-awareness makes it possible for me to imagine what it feels like for you to be aware of yourself. When I judge your action, I imagine your perspective during your deliberative process, in order to see what alternatives faced you at that moment. This introspective analysis of your situation is the condition which allows me to judge your case, and this is the basis of the "face-to-face encounters" which establish the human community. For me, your face is not only an object of the external world, but it is also a viewpoint, from which the world opens up from a certain perspective. When I "read" your face, what I am doing is imagining what it feels like to see the world from that particular point of view, then and there. My reaction to your facial expression will be a response to that point of view. Our interaction is based on our common ability to share our world with the other, in other words on the ability to join a dialogue in a common dramatic performance.

The Latin term "persona" meant both character and the mask, which was used by the actors to enable them to play their roles better, in a more pronounced way, by hiding their own private personality. Scruton also contemplates the connection of person to persona, and considers the role of the mask in the ancient theatre. Looking back at the history of Western theatre, he mentions the mask of Dionysius, the God of the theatrical performance. He also describes Roman theatre, which leads him to the courts of Roman law. He takes from Roman law the concept of the "right-and-duty bearing" person. Roman law, he reminds us, attributed to the subject of judgement the appropriate legal status. Scruton also writes about the Venetian mask, and the historical changes of its role, from simple concealment to framing. By the eighteenth century, he stresses, it served not to separate people, but to secure a certain intimacy and autonomy for the one who wears it, "within jealously guarded limits."[16]

When Scruton speaks about the face of a person, he has in mind all these different layers of the term. As he interprets it, the face is the interface between "I" and "you," which makes their intentionality to some extent readable. The face initiates dialogue; it is the medium of interaction. The intention of an individual is readable on her face. Without making sense of the why of the action, without deciphering the intentional dimension of it, human action will remain silent and meaningless.

Scruton keeps emphasising the duality of our nature—that the human being is part of the animal world, and far above it, distinguished by the ability to act, to realise intentions. This emphasis on the duality of human nature is not, however, meant to explain away the philosophical difficulties of the concept of personal identity. What is it that connects my intentional act in my childhood and my intentional act half a century later as an adult? If my deeds are simply the outcomes of physical, physiological, chemical and biological preconditions, how, and in what sense can I be claimed to be free? There is no "I" without the "non-I": this is the sense of Hegel's analysis of recognition, of that curious mirror-effect between "I" and the other, which is crucial for self-esteem. Social life, which Scruton describes as "a negotiated life among strangers" is not possible without a very detailed map of moral concepts, including "justice, desert and punishment,"[17] all of which are made possible by the dynamic and long-term interactions between "I" and the other, between one generation and another, between strangers.

When Scruton describes the process of mutual recognition between the "I" and the other, he is drawing on a number of philosophical sources, from Aristotle's account of the *zoon politikon*, to the concept of sympathy employed by eighteenth-century Scottish authors, like Hume and Smith, and also to the inheritors of the Hegelian German philosophical tradition. Of the latter, he mentions Max Scheler and Robert Spaemann by name. He is also aware of the relevance in this context of French thinkers like Levinas and Ricœur, but he does not seem to be satisfied with their opaque language. It is obvious, however, that in his discussion of the metaphysical problem of the self, he keeps returning to Kant, and frames the problem in Kantian terms, "discussing the place of freedom in the world of causality."[18] Scruton is ready to admit that he has no clear-cut answer to the metaphysical dilemma of human personality. Instead, he returns to the concept of the face, as a symbol both of human intentionality and of the enigma of the human condition.

At this point, Scruton restarts his investigation of the riddle of the face, in three consecutive chapters, leading from the face of the human being, through the face of nature, to the face of God, which human beings cannot see in this world, according to the Torah.

The Human Face

In the first of these consecutive chapters, he approaches the specific operation of the human face through portrait painting, in other words through a genre of painting that depicts the human face as an entity which can convey meaning. Communication has two directions: one leads from the sitter to the viewer, the other one directly from the painter to the viewer. Of course, these two phases are not independent from each other: one cannot attribute an intention to the painter, without making sense of the sitter's face. The case is even more complicated with the self-portrait: there the sitter's face is both the object and the subject of meaning-attribution. Yet even here, there is a need for someone else, the onlooker, who deciphers the meaning by looking at the surface of the canvas, with or without the background-knowledge of the face of the painter.[19]

A number of difficulties are involved in painting self-portraits. One important difficulty is that the painter knows the sitter internally, and cannot forget about that knowledge, while he has to paint the face based on the facial attributes, the external signs, as if he were viewing an object of the external world. A further difficulty is connected to the viewer's assumptions: if we know that the painter and the sitter are the same, the painted face will serve rather as a mask to cover, rather than simply a helpful guide to allow us to uncover the essence of that human being, from his facial expressions.

Scruton illustrates his point with two portraits by Rembrandt. Presumably, Rembrandt was selected as the paradigm case of the painter who succeeds in avoiding the trap of idealisation even in his self-portraits. Intellectual honesty and self-knowledge are characteristic of Rembrandt's art. Obviously, he does not want to look better. What we see in his late self-portraits is the face of a disillusioned old man—and who would wish to look like a disillusioned old man? Scruton interprets the self-portrait of the Dutch master as presenting himself in the process of experiencing mortality. The philosopher himself was not much younger, when writing this—so his analysis of the self-portraits by the Dutch painter has something to say about Scruton's own mortality. The equivalents of the self-portraits are the autobiographical reminiscences, *Gentle Regrets*, and the autobiographical dialogue with Mark Dooley, entitled *Conversations with Roger Scruton*.

One more word about Rembrandt. Although the viewer tends to hear the furtive steps of death creeping up behind the sitter, the painting has a consoling power as well. It is not self-pity that moves the brush of the painter, to leave those thick daubs of paint on the canvas. It is more like an effort to understand the human condition, an acceptance of what happens to all of us, a wisdom which comes with age, experience and with reflection on what had happened to or had been committed by him in his life. Perhaps the simplest way to sum up Scruton's point is that the self-portraits suggest that Rembrandt had a close familiarity with death. By the end of his life, he had basically lost all those whom he had loved: parents, wife, lover and children, including his most beloved son, Titus. All of those events had the function befriend his own personal death. Yet one will never meet one's own death face to face. The only thing the sharp-eyed and unerring painter can do as an observer is to collect the signs, the external marks of death left on his own face. His portraits excel in that: they present the self in the final state of his lifelong progress, "embraced by its own mortality, and present like death on the unknowable edge of things."[20] Rembrandt's innovation is to paint not only what he looked like in his life, but also "the death that is growing in the folds"—presumably of his own face.[21]

To paint one's death without much self-pity is a task that requires great fortitude. Rembrandt, the painter proved to be stronger than Rembrandt, the man. If someone can be so unsparing with himself, then he can take one further step, and present a portrait of his mother, when she has grown so old that she has actually become ugly. This is the theme of the painting known as Rembrandt's Mother. The face has lost its form, thus divesting the person of all her sexual appeal. Yet in spite of the fact that one cannot find the remnants of female beauty on that face, it still has a warmth which is hard to explain. The eyes are tired, and cannot see much of the world around. The lips cannot close fully, and therefore do not hide well enough what lies beyond them in the cave of the mouth. However, if the viewer leans close enough to the canvas or the screen, she can recognise that she actually has a smile on her face. A smile that is not only intimate, but also loving, and not only loving, but also forgiving. The face expresses a self which has passed beyond all the suffering a human life can bring to the soul, but which still does preserve that most elementary link which anchors her to this life: her love of her son. Scruton does not mention the fact that this painting was probably finished not by Rembrandt himself, but by someone from his studio.[22] This is perhaps because it was painted soon after an etching by the artist himself of his mother, from 1628, assuring us that the painting itself, which is of the genre called a tronie, or a character study, rather than a portrait, does indeed follow closely the original intention of the artist. Art historians have established that Rembrandt's mother served as the model for other artists as well. Nevertheless, the smile on her face is still seen by them as being addressed to her son.

When describing the painting as "one of the greatest smiles in all painting," Scruton emphasises the interaction between painter and model, son and mother.[23] The canvas presents a face which expresses the soul in full engagement with her son, smiling at him (and only him)—the only one who can represent that smile on the canvas. As Scruton phrases it, the smile is "bestowed on Rembrandt by his aged mother, and by Rembrandt on her."[24] This is a magic circularity, that links the two of them in an interaction which the viewer can never join, but with which all of us can sympathise with as viewers, and which makes the experience of viewing the painting heart-warming. The lips do not actually act out the smile, yet they are suggestive of it. It is the way the eyes are presented that achieves the desired effect. As Scruton puts it, they are "bright with maternal affection."[25] A letter by Rembrandt reveals that what he wanted to achieve by his art was to express "the greatest and most natural movement," translated from the Dutch expression "de meeste en de natuurlijkste beweegelijkheid."[26] This striving to create a natural way of representation is indeed confirmed in the painting, even if it was not painted by his own hand. All the finely observed and represented details work together to produce the same overall effect. Following the intentions of the original drawing, it presents the mother's smile, according to Scruton, as "shining with the whole self in a moment of self-giving."[27] That expressivity of the face is made possible by the fact that the face is "a point of intersection of soul and body, person and animal,"[28] "the threshold at which the other appears."[29]

As a result of his dualist account of human nature, Scruton's human being resembles the figure of prudence: it is a figure with two faces. The animal face and that of the person—both belong to us, and both represent us. Scruton's explanation of erotic love describes the embodied subject, in other words the person as it animates the body. The solution of the "problem" of blind desire, which moves the human being when in love, is "not to overcome it, but to ensure that it retains its personal character."[30] The way to secure the personal dimension in one's sexual interaction with the other is to ensure "the redemption of the erotic," which is crucial for the survival of social order.[31] This is why sexual union is usually conceptualised by religions as a "rite of passage," a milestone in the pilgrim's progress. C.S. Lewis compares the special relationship of erotic love to friendship, claiming that "friends are side by side, while lovers are face to face."[32] On the one side of erotic love looms the abyss of the pornographic sexual act, when the person is absent or excluded from the body copulating, while on the other side stands the love of God, which is usually expressed in terms of the erotic love, in Plato, in the Song of Songs of the Old Testament, or in later Christian mystical art and writings. This fact reminds Scruton that, by having described the face as participating in an inter-personal relationship, he has made the first step towards God and the sacred.

The Face of Nature

Yet the fact is that this-worldly love will not reveal God face-to-face. It is therefore crucial to have places around us, which can serve as hiding places for God in this world. Sacred places are created or built to bring us as close to God as possible in this life—and they can be found in artistically built cities just as much as in nature.

One such example of a sacred place is the place of burial, requiring the rites that accompany the act of burial. Interestingly, the architecture and spatial arrangement of cemeteries are evidence that humans have a reverence towards the landscape, even in the most developed contemporary urban settings: some of the best-known scenes of cemeteries of Western culture can be found on friendly hills.[33]

Talking about sacred places, Scruton stresses that to have such a place we need to act out certain things, in a ritual manner, including suffering, sacrifice, revelation or prayer. These acts need to be marked by certain visual-architectural signs, like a stone, an altar or a shrine. It is also important that sacred places are witnessed by the whole community—even if they serve as a personal memento for you of your most intimate, personal love-relationship; when such a place is turned into a holy site, it becomes public.

Scruton's chapter on the face of the Earth starts out from a description of the Promised Land "as an inheritance, to be cared for and passed on."[34] His language connects geography and sanctity. This is why we call the land of a community both a gift and a resource.[35] Landscape is viewed with a sacred awe, an attitude expressing the utmost reverence towards the environment by the human being. Scruton refers in this context to Simon Schama.[36] Schama's opus magnum connects the visual effects of the landscape to the memories of human beings. His examples of the combination of these two acts, the visual perception and the mental operation of recollection, include the Old Testament, the Polish national epic poem *Pan Tadeusz* or Proust's *Combray*, a town both fictional and remembered, created and remembered by the novelist. All of these examples of commemorating the locality to which one belongs portray the protective relationship of the community to its locality as a sacred duty. The paradigm case is the Israelites' relationship to the Promised Land and to their Holy City, which was strictly determined by their religion.

Scruton uses all these examples to argue that environmental consciousness is not new, and that there is in fact "a religious memory at the heart of it."[37] He also refers to the ancient custom according to which if one wants to establish a new settlement, the first duty is to consecrate the land, and to build a temple at its centre, because "God's dwelling… is the model for all other dwellings."[38] The architecture of ancient Greco-Roman temples determined the vocabulary of classical architecture. Its elementary building blocks, such as its steps, the colonnade built from columns, the architrave and the tympanum, all return in the structure of the ordinary buildings of classical architecture, too. This architecture preserves its sacred origins. Furthermore, the relationship of the parts of a building to each other and to the final whole is again well defined, based on ideas borrowed from religion, like the idea of *concinnitas*, which was a crucial term for the Renaissance theorist, Alberti. As a result of this tradition-based language of architecture, buildings and even collections of buildings are all meaningful for the viewer, including the citizens of a particular location and their guests.

This is especially true of the façades of buildings, which have the same function as the face has in the human figure, mediating the message by an interface which connects the inside and the outside. Even more generally, the ancients drew a parallel between the building of the temple and that of the human body. Both the built temple and the temple of the body served as a dwelling place of God. This parallel determined the architectural character of ancient buildings and ancient cities: their proportions were based on the scale of the human body. In particular, the column was seen as an abstraction of the human body, having a foot, torso and head, all of which are parts of the human body. Similarly, the ancients sometimes used realistically modelled human figures as the columns of their buildings, this way giving a soul as well to the building.

According to Scruton, the vernacular style of Western cities preserved this ancient tradition of viewing the building as a meaningful and organic unit, which takes the structure of the human body as its model. Buildings in this tradition can serve as homes for us because of their human character. "Our towns are home to the people who live in them in part because their buildings perpetuate the experience of the face."[39] In making sense of the human settlement with the help of a philosophy of human nature, Scruton is inspired by Heidegger's famous short piece on the building as dwelling.[40] He uses the poetic language his forerunner used: "The way of settlement" tries to "fit our lives into an existing and already consecrated pattern… to honour the spirit of the place," while affecting "the way of disruption," as "the iconoclast seeks to replace old gods with new, to disenchant the landscape and to mark the place with signs of his defiance."[41]

Similarly, when discussing nature conservation, ecology and environmentalism, Scruton proposes returning to the idea of the sacred land, in order to bring dead words to life. When looking at the landscape, both natural and humanly built, two conditions have to be taken into account. First, one has to realise that consecrating a piece of land requires that we relearn how to converse with it—one has to be able to find the right interaction with it, which is in accordance with its properties. Secondly, in order to do so, we also have to be able to decipher the meaning a landscape conveys specifically to us.

Scruton compares the townscapes of Los Angeles and Venice to illustrate his point. If you look at a randomly selected photograph of Los Angeles, it will present a scene that is confused, or as Scruton rather acerbically puts it, "a pile of man-made junk," while a random detail taken from Venice will be not only simple and well ordered, but also calm and relaxed. This difference in our perception of the two cityscapes is due to the fact that in one of them it is easy to attribute meaning to architectural details, while in the other it is not, partly due to the presence of oversized hoardings. In other words, in one cityscape the city has a recognisable face while in the other one, this face is covered up, or simply does not exist. This example powerfully illustrates Scruton's point: the built environment needs to be able to address us, and it can only do so, if that specific environment has a recognisable face. The philosopher goes so far as to claim that there is no aesthetic experience without a face-to-face encounter between the viewer and the aesthetic object.[42] From this it follows that if the face is eliminated, the aesthetic experience also disappears, and possibly an act of desecration takes place.[43]

Scruton gives two examples of such desecration of the built environment: one is graffiti, consisting of "acts of aggression against the public realm" and the other is the service provided at fast-food restaurants, which replaces having a common meal, something that Scruton considers crucial for feeling at home. It also "desecrates townscapes and landscapes with childish logos." Moreover, it generates "a trail of packaging and waste across the surface of the world."[44]

Aesthetic judgement, for Scruton, is not only about aesthetic enjoyment but also concerns "what is right and wrong, what fits and harmonises, what looks and sounds appropriate."[45] In this sense, it is also connected, in fact, to practical moral judgement.

Aesthetic judgement connects to our feeling at home in the world through these moral judgements. This is where the German Romantic concept of *Heimkehr*, homecoming, becomes relevant. One feels at home among the members of one's community, among relatives and friends. Such a feeling of being at home is raised by the known and the familiar—and without beauty, we lose that sense of belonging. In this sense, "beauty is the face of the community."[46] In the modern age the sacred retreats and disappears. According to Scruton, it is beauty, which is supposed to take over its role. This is a further confirmation of the aesthetic quality's function of ensuring that we do not feel lost in the world. Scruton explains even the great landscape painting achievements of European art in terms of the ability to show that nature has a face which it can turn towards us, creating an "I-to-I" encounter, a true dialogue between us.

As he views it, the debate between the brutal desecration of the townscape by modernism and the balancing, counterweighting efforts of New Urbanism concerns our ability to make sense of our surroundings and to preserve the friendly, homely nature of our places of habitation. The modernist attack on the façade deprives buildings of their faces. It turns the street into meaningless space, taking away its power to invite and foster members of the community. As soon as this defacing happens, our environment becomes meaningless and desecrated, because it has lost its ability to communicate, to have meaning. If our environment loses its character of beauty, it cannot fulfil its basic function, which is to lead us to the recognition that we are not alone in this world, that our being here is a "gift, and receiving it is a task." This is just as true of our relationship to the environment as it is of our relationship to God. The face of the earth guides us to the face of God.

The Face of God

In the last chapter of the book, Scruton arrives to the main topic of the book. There, he starts out from the assumption that the form of existence human beings have is characterised by a sense of loneliness. This loneliness is something that is a result of human nature. There is an unavoidable gap between the subject who is endowed with awareness and her world, which the subject is aware of, including a gap between the "I" and the other. Scruton regards this gap that causes loneliness as a "supernatural defect," which amounts to admitting that we shall never be able to find God in the world. This view of the human condition, characterised by an unavoidable loneliness, is close to the thinking of such writers as Kierkegaard, Levinas and Berdyaev, all of whom were heavily influenced by Hegel. *Entäußerung* meant for them a kind of alienation which the self needs to achieve a distance from itself, in order to be able to catch sight of itself. This is described by Hegel in the dialectic of the self and the other. The conclusion of that dialectic is that the self needs to project himself into another, to turn into an object, in order to become aware of itself. Such *Selbstbestimmung*, the condition of a full awareness of the self, is always and inherently accompanied by the realisation that the self views itself as something that is necessarily separated from itself, as something that is out there, taking the form of an external object.

The split that dissects me into two halves—one of which is the one who is aware, the other one which I am aware of—distracts the original unity of the self. It can only be healed, if I find a viewpoint from where the two halves grow together and become congruent—and that is God's perspective. Scruton recalls here the Jewish and Christian narrative of the expulsion from Paradise, but he also refers to divine grace, or in other words, to God's redemption. As Hegel saw it, it is art and religion which can help us in our loneliness by healing the wound of the schism within the self. For Scruton, the main examples of this healing power of art include the poetry of Hölderlin and that of T.S. Eliot. It is religion, however, which directly addresses this quest of returning us to our original unity with ourselves. Religion unites me with my other, who is looking at me from the outside, and who is therefore able to judge me. The promise of religion is that it will lead me back to a unity with my other, to the original community of object and subject. "For the religious being… redemption is an emancipation from the things of this world, and an identification with a transcendental 'I AM'."[47]

To achieve an external view of ourselves, humans build up the institutional framework of society, including laws and morals, which views us in an unbiased, neutral way, as their objects. This is still only an externalisation of the internal dichotomy of the self, however. It does not accomplish what is promised by religion: if we are able to admit our guilt, we will be forgiven, and embraced by God in the community of the faithful. To tell us why we still miss that moment, we have to analyse the relationship between the two components of this event. Scruton views the genuine community which characterises religion as a preparation for our unification with God, and a revelation of God.

The individual needs society in order to have a clear view of herself. Without that external view, gained by her loss of the original unity of her self, she would be unable to judge herself. Kantianism claims an autonomy for the self—when we are in full command of our mental capacities, we are able to perform within ourselves the interaction between the "I" and the "You." In so doing we assume the responsibility for judging our own acts, as they appear from the perspective of the other, the "impartial spectator." In fact, the Kantian-Rawlsian argument is that, since as persons we are able to process this interaction within our own self, which is called our conscience, the community should recognise our freedom to do so, and to accept the moral rights of the person.[48]

Scruton argues, however, that this noble picture of the human person does not give full credit to the human phenomenon. For the individual cannot be identified by a fully controlled rationality. As Scruton emphasises, in accordance with the Christian religious tradition, "guilt, shame and remorse are necessary features of the human being,"[49] because the human agent can be "polluted, desecrated, defiled."[50] This is why Scruton refers at this point to the obligations of piety, beyond the enlightened notion of the unalienable rights of the person, which are derived from the ability of the individual to take responsibility for the acts performed. Beyond the latter, an enduring community also requires individuals to honour obligations of piety.

The ancient Latin term *pietas* covered both a reference to domestic obligations and community, and a reference to religion. Scruton defines piety as the semantic opposite of the notion of freedom, which is guaranteed by personal choice. "Piety is posture of submission and obedience towards authorities that you have never chosen."[51] The example Scruton uses is that of filial obligations: a family relationship which, it is assumed, determines one's action even if it is not freely chosen by the individual. To enable the individual to accept her position, the ancient notion of piety connects this sort of communal obligation with ideas of sacredness and sacrifice. We accept our position, as determined by certain relationships, if we see its sacred nature, or if it is required from us as a sacrifice. Entering into such human bonds is typically regarded as an exceptional moment in an individual's life, and therefore it is regarded as God-given or sacred. Entering into such a relationship is, in most traditional societies a religiously governed "rite of passage."[52] These rites include birth, initiation, sex and marriage and finally, fatal illness and death. All are milestones of human life, the starting points of which are specifically celebrated to distinguish them from the ordinary process of life. They are witnessed by the whole society, including the dead and the unborn, but also by the gods worshipped by the particular society. Such religious celebrations or festivities are moments outside of the normal routine of historical time. They belong to the gods and are hence part of the potentially eternal life of the community. The unlimited nature of the temporal is supplemented by the perception of the unlimited also in spatial terms: according to Scruton, the festivity lets the individual feel the perspective of the unlimited, a "bottomless chasm," on the edge of which the plot of our life has its turning points.

Scruton mentions two such experiences of the unlimited. One is a full sexual union in which the partners are involved with their whole personalities, with an emotional attachment of love. In giving ourselves fully to another we experience the other's total attachment to us. The other one is the experience of the dead body, which contradicts our usual experience of the cohabitation of body and soul. The dead body is regarded as sacred—because of the exit it reveals from the normal process of life.

In traditional cultures, sacredness serves as the defence-mechanism of the gods, while desecration is a violation of the order of the gods. To honour the sacred is to accept the taboo, things which cannot be questioned. The sacred is perceived by human communities through acts of ritual and acts of purification. In such ceremonial acts, "we are in some way standing at the horizon of our world, in direct but ineffable contact with that which does not belong to it."[53] The ritual gives a face to the event, in the case of both sexual union and death. Desecration, on the other hand, demolishes our sense of the world, depriving it of its meaning. Our civilisation is afraid of the sacred, and this is the reason behind its cult or culture of desecration. As a result of our scientific worldview, and our secular perception of reality, we have lost our ability to perceive that in fact there is a God beyond the mortal realm of our world, or at least something sacred. A society which honours the sacred does not give full licence to the liberty of the individual choice, and therefore it does not confirm individuality, the centre of the modern account of human life. Our world, exclusively centred around the individual, is a world in which God is defaced.

Is it still possible, then, to make sense of the traditional society and its god(s)? To answer this question, Scruton refers to Rudolf Otto's famous effort to define the sacred.[54] If the sacred is the interface with the transcendental, with that which is beyond our mortal world, then it is by definition undefinable. Interestingly, this is exactly, how we feel in those moments in which we think, feel or sense the sacred: it takes us beyond the realm of causal connections, which is the territory of scientific enquiry.

The same is also true of human subjectivity. We have no satisfactory account of what exactly it means to be a self, a complex web of experiences. If our inner self is undefinable, it obviously leads us into a logical nonsense, if we search for God as the cause of our subjectivity. A cause cannot lead us out of the world of causes, which is the world we know through science and through the empirical experiences of human beings. Theologians try to replace the notion of cause with that of reason: they say they seek the reason for our being or for our world. This search requires having a view from nowhere, from where the whole of our world—the world as we know it—is visible. The fact that we can imagine and we try even to describe this ideal view of the whole empirical world from a God's eye perspective comprises an argument that it might be possible. Science, however, is not able to provide this view for us, because its realm is the causal. In other words, this view includes, in a way, God himself. Which is to say that the view includes the physical as well as what is labelled traditionally as the metaphysical. Another way of expressing this is to call it the transcendental.

At this point, having mentioned William James' argument in *The Varieties of Religious Experience*, Scruton returns to Aquinas, and the medieval notion of transcendentals. He reminds his reader that for St Thomas, whatever is real has the following features: it has truth, unity and goodness. In other words, whatever partakes of being, has these as its *a priori* categories. Correspondingly, Scruton argues, medieval Christian thought introduced the notion of values into the world of contingencies. Whatever exists contingently is a carrier of value, or meaning. If so, however, we cannot help but *attribute* that value and meaning to existing phenomena.

This train of thought about the a priori quality of value brings us to the conclusion that we cannot help viewing whatever appears in the contingent realm as the gift of someone or something. Scruton connects the idea of being-as-a-gift to the notion of grace (*gratia*). He claims that all the major world religions see our world as having been given (to us). "The idea that the world is sustained by gift is second nature to religious people."[55] In this sense agape, the Christian notion of love is also connected to this idea of a gift. Agape is received by us, humans, from God, as a gift, and God expects us to distribute it among our neighbours. Here Scruton's reference is C.S. Lewis, and his book *The Four Loves*, where we can read of the term gift-love, which is the love of God towards humanity. This is identified with the Greek notion of agape, which Scruton describes as "following the path of gift and sacrifice."[56] The British philosopher is referring here to the Christian teaching of agape, when he claims that the human being is able to transform his life of contingency, which is by definition prone to lead to suffering, into one of sacrifice and gift. Hence, the human being experiences a "spiritual transformation," and can partake in redemption, which is itself, in fact, the gift of God. Scruton identifies such gift-giving acts with the notion of self-sacrifice, and he claims that this capacity is characteristic of humans only. It presupposes an "I-to-I" encounter, and it is a sign of freedom on the part of the gift-giver. Therefore "to make sacrifices for others' sake, including that of the community, is to walk with God."[57]

It must be admitted that Scruton's train of thought here leads us to risky paths on the verge of a precipice, above the depths of nothing.

When experiencing the contingent realm as a gift of God, for which the human being is grateful, the believer experiences something transcendental, something beyond the realm of the contingent. Moreover, the individual believer's experience is shared with other believers, who have the same experience, and who celebrate it in communion with the community.[58] Religious rituals centre around occasions of communal thanksgiving for the gift of life, as in the rites of passage. When we celebrate birth, initiation into adulthood or marriage, or when we nurse someone who is terminally ill or for other reasons unable to take care of herself, or mourn the death of someone, we witness human life as a gift. Sacrificial religions express this nature of gift-giving and the receiving of our life as a gift in the form of the sacrifice. What we, Christians offer on the altar ritually is also a gift to God, in memory of the gift he gave us by his own self-sacrifice, liberating us from our guilt, and thus bringing us redemption from the suffering which is part of earthly life. By the ability to give a gift, by the chance to self-sacrifice we can all serve as windows, through which humans can glimpse the light beyond.

The way we can experience the presence of God is the way we can experience the other through her face. This is explained in the Christian teaching of the incarnation of God. The meaning of the coming of Christ among us is that it provides us an example of suffering, which can show us the potential of our own lives, to transform it into a gift to others. Scruton freely admits that he is borrowing here from the illuminating ideas of Max Scheler.[59] His description is on the verge of what is possible in philosophy, and it still does not solve the riddle. The concept of incarnation is not easier to make sense of than the concept we sought to explain by it. But perhaps that is the limit of human understanding.

Wagner and Redemption Through Suffering

Admitting the shortcomings of his words, Scruton once again turns back to Wagner and his *Ring* at the end of his lectures on *The Face of God*. He suggests that Wagner, who was a non-believer and an agnostic, and a follower of Feuerbach, was able to make progress towards solving this metaphysical riddle. The question he starts out from in the *Ring* concerns Wotan, "king of the gods and lord of the world."[60] How can he succeed in becoming the object of love? Although he succeeds in creating the human world, paying the high cost of defying the moral law, he still lacks something that the humans have.[61] This is the combination of freedom and love. Humans have "freedom to defy laws, fate, death itself, for the sake of another – the freedom to make a gift of oneself."[62] This sacrifice is only possible if it is accompanied by personal suffering, which makes it really valuable.

Scruton illustrates Wagner's point by recalling the dialogue between Siegmund and Brünhilde. The former, a human being, offers his suffering as a gift, and as a result of it, the latter, a goddess, is turned into someone who learns "to account for herself," encountering Siegmund eye to eye, or indeed "I to I," "and so falls into the human world of love and suffering."[63] By losing her divine attribute of eternal life, she receives a real face, one which is "ready for love and destined for sacrifice."[64] Her fate is to lose her loved one, as the price she has to pay for the experience of being loved.

Scruton's argument here is that Wagner's symbolic story offers an artistic explanation of the riddle of incarnation. Brünhilde's example is an example of incarnation: it is, quite simply, the ability "to accept suffering for the sake of love."[65] The message is a paradox: in order to prove his divine nature, even a God needs to be able to give up divine power. It is through incarnation, that is, accepting a human fate, that a God becomes able to love and by offering such a sacrifice, a God, too, can become an object of love. The price a God pays for this experience is even greater than that paid by human beings. What a God loses is not only a mortal life, but immortality itself. On the other hand, what is gained by this act of self-sacrifice, mutual love, is also more than what a human being can achieve by her own will: it is not less, than redemption.

Humans and divine entities are united in the price they have to pay for love: they need to become able to freely offer themselves as a gift for an other. It is at the moment of sacrifice that the beauty of their real face becomes visible. In case of a God, through the act of self-sacrifice the God learns to love, how it feels to be loved, and in this encounter the divine face becomes visible as a real presence. The moment of revelation is a face-to-face encounter, when a God turns into a free and loving human being.

Scruton is aware of the theological difficulties of this account, in particular as far as a "cogent theology of creation" is concerned, which could account for all of these.[66] However, the strength of the narrative is the possibility of a face-to-face encounter with God, even by a mortal being, made possible by the dual act of incarnation, in the form of divine self-sacrifice, occurring in this world of fallen human beings.

It is exactly this chance of meeting God face to face that has been lost in our disenchanted culture, claims Scruton, and this loss is the loss of a chance to give meaning to human life. Here he turns back to what he calls "the Socratic idiom," claiming that without a chance of that encounter, our life is "not a life for a human being."[67] Even at that moment of loss, he finds hope, however: at least the disquiet we feel about this lost opportunity "has a religious meaning."[68]

Metaphysics II. The Soul of the World

Let us now turn to the pair of *The Face of God*, the other metaphysical work by Scruton, *The Soul of the World*.[69] Most of its material comes from the lectures which he originally delivered as the Stanton Lectures of the Divinity Faculty of the University of Cambridge in 2011. My aim here will be to show the connections between metaphysics and both politics and aesthetics in the late thought of Scruton. He summarises the book's programme as follows: "My intention has been to draw on philosophical discussions of mind, art, music, politics, and law in order to define what is at stake in the current disputes over the nature and ground of religious belief."[70] There are at least two things to say about this description. First of all, one should note the remarkable contiguity between art and music on the one side, and politics and law on the other. It tells a lot about Scruton's philosophical interests that he finds these activities so closely linked. What aesthetics and moral and political thought shared was a reliance on human judgement. He, in fact, compared aesthetic judgement required in appreciating art and music to political judgements and the judgements of the judge in the court. The second point to stress is that he characterises the aim of the book as "making room, in some measure, for the religious worldview," even if he does not venture to defend theoretically, as a philosopher of religion, a particular religion's theological teaching or religious practice.[71] Yet he is ready to call his venture a "theological elaboration."[72]

Scruton always had a refined sense of the religious phenomenon—for instance in his recurring references to Girard. As we saw, he was engaged in a constant struggle with that thinker's ideas about victimhood and the birth of religion. However, except for the twin books of *The Face of God* and *The Soul of the World*, he never explicitly searched for the religious consequences of his views on the practical realm of human activity. Characteristically, his account of the religious underpinnings of human behaviour in this book has a personal layer, in other words it concerns the religious life of the individual, but it also addresses the dimension of the communal, in other words, the experience of the I in the midst of others with whom the I has close relations, all of them sharing the same horizon of meaning. In a certain sense, the two books, read together, represent the summa of Scruton's philosophical analysis of human life, both as a solitary and as a common experience. His effort to give a metaphysical account of the human condition in a condensed form makes the two books all the more difficult to decipher.

Poussin's Landscape

I would like to approach this book with the help of the painting that is used on its cover. Although one may argue that writers do not necessarily take direct responsibility for the covers of their books, I suspect that

Scruton very deliberately chose this painting here. It is a detail of a painting by the seventeenth-century French painter, Nicolas Poussin. Its title is *Landscape with a Calm* (1650–1651)—offering an ideal landscape, appropriate to a book entitled the *Soul of the World*. It is as if the landscape presented here was—at least symbolically—a representation of the world, offering a view of the metaphysical duality of nature. While neither Poussin nor the painting appears in Scruton's text, in another of his works he claimed that: "there is more meaning in a Beethoven quartet or a Poussin landscape than in the entire corpus of literature devoted to the truth-conditions of 'Snow is white'."[73] This claim, of course, is a rather explicit criticism of the hermetic tendencies of analytical philosophy, and it serves as an explanation of Scruton's lifelong concern with aesthetics and art criticism.

Let us have a closer look at this painting, trying to make sense of its message as a window on Scruton's intentions with his book. Poussin is regarded as one of the first landscape painters in European art—according to the standard narrative of art history, he was one of the first painters who represented landscapes in his paintings for their own sake. Importantly, the painter still keeps narrative elements in his compositions of natural beauty: he does not seem to be satisfied merely with representing natural (and humanly built) forms without a story of events happening among these sets, like a play unfolding on a stage. Sometimes those narratives are easy to decipher, from the paraphernalia represented in the picture itself. In certain cases, however, neither the story, nor the meaning of the story is easy to identify, leaving the significance of the picture somewhat opaque and unintelligible, most probably intentionally. Nevertheless, the viewer cannot help associating the events depicted with the visual features of the scene.

This is the case with the painting which has been selected for the cover of Scruton's book. A whole spectrum of visual codes is present in *Landscape with a Calm*. The main element of the composition is a lake, surrounded by trees. The lake organises the composition, as all the other things depicted have to be arranged around it, while the things placed behind it are all reflected in the mirror of the untroubled surface of the water of the pond. In the foreground, a goatherd stands with his dog and surrounded by his herd, looking upon the scene as we do. In the middle ground, behind the pond, in a central position, we see the contours, walls and tower of an ensemble of buildings, in fact, of an "Italianate villa," with some of its inhabitants also appearing.[74] Between the villa and the lake, which reflects the contours of the buildings, are more herders, this time with cattle. In the distant background we see the rocky cliffs of a mountain, with the smoke of a bonfire also visible from that direction. To the left of the scene we find further buildings, this time less colossal than the villa. In front of them two men are on horseback: one of them is spurring his steed to a gallop, while the other is calmly letting his horse drink or eat.

The scenery is calm and quiet, except for the two motives of the galloping horseman and the smoke in the background. These two signs serve as warnings, or more precisely, the tension between these two movements and the rest of the scene provokes the viewer to think about the exact nature of the events she is witnessing, and the possible meanings behind those events, which seem to be in contrast with the serenity of the scene.

A further point to be taken into consideration when we interpret this artistic representation is the fact that the painting has a pair, with the title *Landscape with a Storm.*[75] We read about the connection between the two in an early commentary by Félibien, who refers to "two landscapes, one representing a storm and the other a calm and serene scene."[76] Most probably, Poussin painted both of these works at about the same time, in 1651. They might be seen as the representation of contrasting weather conditions: a calm, sunny day opposed to a stormy one.[77] However, if we are inclined to look at the landscape as a stage where meaningful action takes place, its narrative seems to be burdened with a symbolic message. Weather conditions like storms or sunshine often refer to spiritual conditions, like emotional turmoil and the flow of spirits in the traditions of both visual narration and rhetoric. This is one reason why the viewer is entitled to suspect that there must be more to the painting than simply a depiction of natural scenery. While one painting presents the world in an almost unmoving order, even a homely place, nature in the other one turns into a hyper-dynamic agent, ready to destroy any human beings who happen to be in its way. While the stormy picture captures the singular moment of lightning, the other one presents an almost frozen stillness. Rosenberg's catalogue identifies a "riotous nature" in one painting, and an "eternal nature" in the other one.[78]

There is a further clue in the picture. Given the fact that shepherds are represented in it in a natural setting, and the general mood of the painting is quiet and ordered, the viewer can easily come to the conclusion that this is an Arcadian, bucolic or pastoral scene.[79] These adjectives recall an ancient Greco-Roman literary genre, established by Virgil, a narrative, presenting in an idealised form the way of life and thinking of stylised shepherds in a context of a rural scenery, and following conventional manners. This literary convention has its roots in the poetry of Virgil, an ancient Roman poet. This is why the viewer is not surprised that Poussin sets his bucolic scene in a landscape of Romagna, the area around Rome. The genre of the pastoral was popular in both poetry and theatrical performances—even in music—in Poussin's lifetime. There is an emphasis on peace and the order of nature in this genre, which might be connected to Poussin's own artistic intentions. The theatrical element of the genre is also obvious in this composition. Bellori recalls the painter's walks on the Pincio, "from where a most beautiful view of Rome opens out, with its handsome hills, which together with the buildings evoke a theatrical stage setting."[80]

It is also important to note that the poetic element often returns in the interpretation of Poussin's painting, and not only in connection with Virgil's theory and practice of poetry. Poetry is traditionally understood as a depiction of an imagined, ideal world. To be sure, the apparent harmony and undisturbed peace presented in the picture is—it might be supposed—momentary, since the two symbols of a running horse, and the smoke on the hillside, taken together with the clouds looming over the hill imply the risk of a story event to come. Hazlitt refers to a "perfect human bliss" in connection with another of Poussin's landscapes, "which is, however, on the point of being soon disturbed."[81] The poetic and bucolic mood is made the more pronounced by the threat of its loss.

For Scruton, perhaps this bucolic atmosphere might be relevant as a paraphrase of the human condition. The painting presents a world, where humans can feel at home. The villa might be a location of retreat for someone escaping from the upheavals of political life. The Roman villa had this function, as is well known from the lives of Roman statesmen like Cicero and writers such as Virgil and Horace, not to mention the exiled Ovid. The same habit of retreating from political conflict zones was reinvented by Petrarch, as well as the exiled Dante, and followed by a line of humanists who wanted to leave the world of politics. Scruton himself created such a place of retreat when he withdrew to a farm in rural Wiltshire, which he named Scrutopia. Arcadia, in this sense, is the world of contemplation, distant from the turmoil of public life. Claire Pace refers to Justus Lipsius who in the Italian translation of his book *De Constantia* (1584) "praises gardens as offering refreshment and 'calm to the spirit' and 'a sure refuge from irritations and disturbances', citing 'philosophers and sages' who took refuge in gardens."[82] This retreat from urban life could mean the loss of all the advantages of friendship and other forms of human sociability. Yet country life has a more Epicurean understanding of it, as well, when the enjoyments of the garden were seen as the dominant value, for example in Horace's poetry.[83] Recall also Cato the Elder, in Cicero's *De Senectute*, which praises also the villa, as the site of friendship.[84]

In both cases, the distance of a peaceful nature from the town recalls the contrast between private life and public life, and with it, the difference between action and contemplation. Poussin's visual contrast between the two can also be associated with Montaigne's "long comparison of the solitary and the active life."[85] Another French author, Pierre Charron, referred to creative energies, imprisoned in cities, but liberated in country life, encouraging, in an indirect fashion, the "contemplation of the landscapes."[86]

Contemplation itself, as a mental activity, aims to identify and reflect upon the principles of living in accordance with nature. The homeliness of nature—its perfect composition—directs our attention to final caretaker of this order, as suggested in two paintings by Poussin, presenting the solitary Evangelists, Saint Matthew and Saint John. Poussin tends to connect the theme of the withdrawal to the countryside with the contemplation of the "divine Creator."[87] In fact, church leaders also encouraged such reflections on God's omnipotence through the contemplation of nature, as exemplified by a poem of Pope Urban VIII praising the "eternal beauty" of his own scenery at Castelgandolfo.[88] Poussin himself, in his late landscapes, seems to have come close to this understanding of natural beauty. In his late landscapes, like this one, the painter reflected on both "contemporary scientific interpretations of the natural world as well as antique philosophy," "contemplating the cyclical processes that rule the universe."[89] In this sense, the painting serves very well to prepare the reader for Scruton's efforts in this late book to answer some of the most profound metaphysical questions of the human condition.

The Religious Urge

The Soul of the World was written approximately at the same time as *The Face of God*. They may be seen as parallel efforts to approach some of the most fundamental questions of human life.

The Soul of the World addresses the question how to make sense of the religious drive of human beings. Both the starting and the finishing chapter are about the human being's earnest quest for a transcendental God. This fact makes the book a narrative of human quest. It is not a straightforward story leading the reader from uncertainties to certainties, however. On the contrary: while the first chapter bears the title "Believing in God," the last one deals with "Seeking God." This is because Scruton, as a trained analytical philosopher, always found it extremely difficult to talk about what he called the religious experience in conceptually well-founded language, and as a Kantian, he had serious problems with the whole Western tradition of the philosophy of religion.

Nevertheless, he makes every effort to find and develop a language and vocabulary suitable to address the human being's experience of something transcendental. He seems to take seriously the Enlightened philosophy of Kant and Hume. He accepts their disillusioning point: "the two ways to the transcendental – the cosmological and the psychological – are both effectively blocked."[90] Yet this is not the end, but the beginning of his story. For he also takes at least two other thinkers quite seriously. These are Durkheim and Girard, who convincingly proved to him that the religious experience is crucial in human societies. Both of them have something to say about the human potential to sacrifice, and in particular to self-sacrifice, which seems to be directly connected to the religious experience. In other words, he returns here to the problems of sacrifice and the sacred. It is true of both that they "stand at the horizon of our world, looking out to that which is not of this world." Or to be more precise "they seem to be both *in* our world, and also *out* of it."[91]

Obviously, such a claim is contradictory, according to elementary logic, and therefore disproved by it. And yet there is an urge in us, and Scruton keeps returning to this phrase in this chapter, which pushes or draws us in that direction. The story that Scruton tentatively reconstructs with the help of Girard (with Freud in the background) and Durkheim is the story of making sense of human violence. According to this story, violence or conflict is a part of human society. To contain this violence and "resolve the conflict," "the experience of the sacred is born."[92] Societies taken over by conflict have to find a scapegoat, who can assume the burden of being the target of violence. "By uniting against the scapegoat, people are released from their rivalries and reconciled. Through his death the victim purges society of its violence."[93] The victim of ritual violence is thus imbued with a sanctity, which distinguishes him from anything and anybody else in society, the "victim is thus both sacrificed and sacred."[94]

While for Girard the important thing is communal violence against a victimised individual and its function, for Durkheim the important thing about sacrifice is the relationship between the particularities of individual life and communal continuity. He presents the desire to belong as the main motivating force behind sacrifice, which explains why it becomes a meaningful choice for the victim himself. This is a crucial point once again for Scruton's understanding of Durkheim: that it is the Christian religion's moral claim that it can turn sacrifice into self-sacrifice, through the example of the consciously chosen self-sacrifice of Christ.[95] Durkheim stresses membership as the core idea of self-sacrifice: one can regain one's membership of a community, or belonging, by the act of self-sacrifice. Significantly, at this point Scruton also cites Jan Patocka, the contemporary Czech philosopher of phenomenology, who presents a similar case for the victims of totalitarian regimes, arguing for the meaning of their sacrifice for their community. This is, of course, in most of the cases, not a voluntarily chosen destiny, but the sacrifice has the same function, as in Gerard's and Durkheim's paradigms. Patocka himself fell victim to the Communist regime, thus authenticating his own theory by his own personal example. Scruton found Patocka's teaching and his personal example crucial. The Czech philosopher was a disciple of both Husserl and

Heidegger, but he became an original thinker, who worked out a personal version of phenomenology, applied to social and political philosophy. This contemplative thinker, at a certain historical moment joined Charter '77, an opposition movement against the oppressive measures of the Communist regime. Patocka had well-founded conscientious scruples about the totalitarian impulse, and died as a result of the violent police interrogations he had to endure for participating in the movement. By referring to him in this context, Scruton broadens the focus of his analysis, claiming that the religious urge has a communal, and sometimes even a political context.[96] By the end of the first chapter of his book, Scruton comes to the conclusion that the transcendental urge prevails in humans, even in those without religion, and that it can help us to reach the limits of our horizon, no matter whether we look at it from the "cosmological," the "psychological," the "cultural anthropological" or the "political" perspective.

Human Nature

The next four chapters of *The Soul of the World* are about human nature, the topic of his later book *On Human Nature*. In his philosophical anthropology, Scruton basically remained a Kantian, emphasising the cognitive dualism which defines the human being. In what follows I shall concentrate first on this term, which is crucial, if we wish to understand his notion of the human being, including the idea of the person and intentionality. This will be followed by a discussion of Scruton's proposition of "overreaching intentionality." This leads us to his quasi-religious notion of the covenant, finally arriving at his understanding of the relevance of the face-to-face relationship between two persons.

Defending his argument for cognitive dualism, the philosopher first of all distinguishes it from ontological dualism. This second form of dualism he attributes to Descartes, and rejects, while cognitive dualism, as he understands the term, is a Kantian notion, and he embraces it.[97] He identifies it with a certain tradition of analytical philosophy, including such authors as Wilfried Sellars, John McDowell and Robert Brandom, and such classical Continental authors as Spinoza and Kant, the two thinkers on whom Scruton published short monographs, as well as Husserl, the father of phenomenology.[98] This is how he defined cognitive dualism: "the world can be understood in two incommensurable ways, the way of science, and the way of interpersonal understanding."[99] Scruton's point is that cognitive dualism is an epistemological position, which denies a simple scientism. According to this view, we should not understand the scientific approach as in some sense better, more precise and more developed than ordinary human thinking, the kind of thinking we rely on in our human relationships. Neither should we claim a primacy for the ordinary in human thought, as opposed to a scientific understanding, however. Instead, we should accept cognitive dualism, the view that one should not prefer one way of understanding as opposed to the other. Just as Wittgenstein's duck-rabbit example serves to show that humans are able to see the same thing in two different ways, we should be aware of the fact, that we can approach the phenomena of the world in two distinct ways. The great advantage of human thought is that we can alternate these two perspectives as the moment requires.

As he understands it, science is the most appropriate approach to the world for answering the question "what exists?" However, Scruton adds, there is another approach, the practice of *Verstehen*, the internal view of human beings, of themselves and their interactions with the world of external objects left out of their view. This is an "emergent" world, which exists only due to the *cogito* of the human being. This is not a world defined by the law of causation, as the world of nature is, but one defined by a system of reasons. A reason is a sort of mental operation, applied in the world of interpersonal relationships, by which we attribute meaning to actions and events in the human world.

It is in this second realm, namely the realm of the social that two further important notions arise in Scruton's account of the basic tenets of phenomenology: "first-person phenomenology" and "intentionality." We need to understand what he means by them before we can move on. In order to explain them, we have to rely on his idea of the person.

To understand the relevance attributed by Scruton to the notion of the person, we have to briefly return to his discussion of belief in God. There he emphasised the notion of real presence (*shekhinah*), which is a particular manner in which believers experience the transcendental God in this world, directly.[100] He calls such a direct encounter at the moment of religious illumination a "personal encounter," and he enumerates Saint Teresa of Avila, Margery Kempe, Saint John of the Cross, Rumi and Pascal as witnesses of it within Christian spiritual literature.[101] The point he wants to make is that whoever actually "meets" God in this life has an experience of a "personal" God. In other words, the meeting is made possible by the fact that God has a presence, a form of participation in the human realm, which allows the human being to be in touch with this being. The relevance attributed to the real presence of God is an indirect proof of the relevance of the notion of the person in Scruton's philosophy.

To substantiate his interpretation of the term "person," Scruton starts out from the Latin notion of *persona*, meaning a theatrical mask, and its reference to the character performed by the actor. He also recalls the Roman law concept of the person, denoting the rights and duties attributed to a human being as a legal entity.[102] He then turns to medieval Christian philosophy, recalling Boethius' account of the person as "an individual substance of a rational nature" (29). He also mentions Aquinas in passing, before arriving at Locke's early modern, "scientific" efforts to make sense of personal identity. For Scruton, though, the major thinkers to rely on for a proper understanding of the term are Kant and Hegel. As he sees it, for Kant, too, the rational capacity defines the person, which allows the rise of "self-consciousness and the use of 'I'" (29). It is this ability of self-identification, the grasp of one's self as a "transcendental unit of apperception" that allows us to grasp the human being as a transcendentally free being. The human being is distinguished from the non-human parts of the world, by the fact that the movements or states of being of humans are not determined causally. They have the ability to see themselves and to reflect on their selves as a decision-making agency, who can choose between alternatives, in a holistically determined world of objects and states of affairs. Self-reflection also allows to see the individual in a context of a network of interpersonal relations with others. Beyond Kant, Scruton also refers to Hegel, citing once again his famous dialectic of the master-slave relationship. This is important for him as a "poetic description" or analysis of the process, which leads to self-identification and the idea of a free being, who requires recognition from others, and to the claim that this being cannot be used as a tool, that such a being is an end

in itself. Although the Hegelian dialectic leads through temporary submission and obedience, the thought process ends up dealing with a relationship between two human beings characterised by mutual recognition
of each other's equal human dignity, a notion which is not frequently
used by Scruton. Neither does he refer too often to the Catholic teaching
of the person, a body of thought explicated in Papal encyclicals since the
Rerum Novarum in 1891. Not belonging to the Catholic tradition, neither John Paul II nor Benedict XVI appeared in Scruton's account of the
person, a relevant lacuna, in the case of an author who is interested in
religious conservatism.

Instead of the Catholic tradition, Scruton relies on Hegel in his explanation of the relevance of self-consciousness and mutual recognition in
his chapter on the person. This is crucial for him, too, because it explains
the existence of an interpersonal realm, explained by Scruton as "a life
negotiated with others," (30) defined by an "I-to-I" relationship. Through
reconstructing the line of argument of Hegel's master-slave relationship,
he confirms the ability of the human being to realise that the other closely
resembles the "I," in other words to recognise that there is a chance to
share ideas with the other, and through that to think and feel together. In
so doing, Scruton establishes the existence of a realm which operates as
an autonomous dimension of human life, distinguishable from the world
of determination and causal laws.

Besides the concept of the person as a sociable being, the idea of intentionality also plays a crucial role in Scruton's idea of "cognitive dualism."
It is remarkable that when he discusses intentionality, he does not fall
back on the classics of phenomenology, or refer to recent developments
in phenomenological theory. Instead, he refers to "hardcore" analytical
philosophers like Dennett and Searle and Anscombe—proving that he
was educated in that tradition, and that his real discussion partners, the
ones that he wants to convince, are participants in the analytical discourse.

Scruton connects his understanding of intentionality to his account of
the person.

Human cognition has a target: it is always about something, which
means that it is relational. The human mind has the capacity to deal with
certain things, in other words, in this sense "to contain" certain things.
When I think, I think of something, which appears in my mind, because

my mind is able to represent it. Scruton accepts here the most common understanding of intentionality: "intentionality is the power of minds and mental states to be about, to represent, or to stand for, things, properties and states of affairs."[103] However, intentionality also has a stronger meaning, for him. If we are able to think of something, we can assume that when we enter into an interaction with it, we do so because we formed an intention to do so beforehand. This can be illustrated by the example of a piece of chocolate. If there is a piece of chocolate in front of me, lying on the table, I can perceive and recognise it, and as a result of that procedure I will be able to conceptualise its presence there: I will be aware of the chocolate lying in front of me. As soon as I have become aware of it I can make a decision to taste that piece of chocolate. If that is so, when I taste the chocolate, a correct description of what is happening to me and to the chocolate will have to include a reference to my intention to taste that chocolate. The mental representation of the chocolate which led to the decision to taste it, along with my tasting of it, belong to one continuous line of events, one in which one event leads to another one, and one event explains the other. It is because I know about the chocolate in front of me that I make a decision about my tasting it (or not), and it is because of my intention to taste it that I actually taste it.

Scruton's concept of intentionality goes even beyond that. He also stresses the fact that there is a "first-person awareness" connected to human intentionality. His point is that when I explain why I ate the chocolate, I can give an account of it without much thinking. I am in the privileged position of being able to give that account because it was me who had the perception of the chocolate lying there, and who made the decision to taste it, and who actually tasted it. Given my privileged position which I have for the explanation of the event, I am ready to accept the fact that I am accountable for what happened with the chocolate. This accountability is partly the result of my acknowledging that I indeed have a "first-person awareness" of the events. A further condition of accountability is that others also find it natural that I have a privileged access to all those phases of the line of events, and therefore that I have to be able to give reasons for why those events happened. They know this due to the fact that they can imagine themselves how they would have behaved in such a case where a piece of chocolate was in front of them.

In other words, when I or you give an account of what happened with the chocolate, there is a mutual awareness of my "first-person awareness," and therefore both of us can give a full description of what exactly happened to the chocolate with the help of my agency.

Further on, in our explanation of what happened, we will take into account further matters. We will take into account social institutions and systems of norms, like laws, customs and etiquette. These institutions and norms are internalised in the sense that adult persons acquire a first-person awareness of them. Anyone explaining what happened to me and the chocolate would presume that I am aware of the expectations concerning my behaviour, given those circumstances. They also presume that those circumstances can serve to limit my choices about whether to taste that chocolate or not. But they also know that I might decide to do what is outside of the realm of the socially accepted, in other words I might just as well disregard the expectations of others concerning my behaviour in that situation. Intentionality in this sense is not a private issue: following Searle, Scruton talks about social or collective intentionality, meaning by it "the shared sense that we are collectively under certain obligations."[104] This social intentionality is based on the "I-you" encounter, Scruton claims, referring to Hegel's master-slave relationship, Buber's notion of the "I-Thou" dialogue and to contemporary analytical philosophers such as Stephen Darwall and P.F. Strawson. It is through this philosophical analysis that Scruton arrives at an explanation of moral concepts like "right, duty, justice, virtue, purity, which inform our interpersonal exchanges."[105] Moreover, this line of argument allows him to explain the birth of a special realm of social reality, as a second level of understanding interpersonal relations, in other words the fact that "ours is a world of institutions, laws, and covenants."[106] To describe this social realm, Scruton needs to account for the rise of the perspective of the first-person plural.

From I to We

One of the acts which is specific to humans is that of making a promise. The history of Western philosophy finds this topic tantalising: from Aristotle to Scanlon a number of thinkers have struggled to make sense of the motive for keeping promises.[107] For Scruton, the crucial issue is the way that the act of promising creates social ties. He starts out from a classic essay by Searle.[108] A single promise seems to be restricted to the "I-you" relationship: I promise you something, which creates a lasting moral realm between the two of us. Scruton calls this an "institutional fact – a fact about the realm of human relations."[109] Institutions are not private matters, however—they are by definition public, maintained by the community we create and that we are both members of. This is why the keeping or breaking of promises can become legal matters. However, an interesting shift takes place from an individual's promise to a social acknowledgement of promise: Scruton uses the example of the legislature which passes a law. He understands the act of legislation as a mutual promise by all members of the community to assume the obligation of keeping to the norms of the law. This establishes a new institution which makes sure that individual behaviour follows a common pattern. The legislature proceeds in the name of the community, and its procedurally well-defined declaration of a law creates the realm of obligation for all the members of the community. Following Searle, Scruton is prepared to regard the legislative act as a kind of speech act, which creates a social fact simply by announcing it. The public realm which exists among human beings is defined by such speech acts, "undertaking obligations, making promises, committing themselves, and in general taking responsibility for the future and for the well-being of others."[110] This is made possible by the fact that humans feel at home in "this realm of institutions and laws," more at home, in fact, than they do in a world without it, in a state of nature. Scruton views this realm as being identical to Husserl's famous category, the *Lebenswelt*.

This realm is partly made up of the speech acts mentioned, which create obligations. They have relevance in our lives because the community ensures their enforcement. The social norms of the community demand that such personal relationships be safeguarded. The community will have organs, agencies or institutionalised bodies which guarantee that certain speech acts can be enforced. The reason behind this concern with enforcement is that humans feel that it is just or fair to keep promises. As Scruton argues, all human societies, no matter how developed they are, try to enforce these speech acts. This fact proves that they partake in what he calls "ordinary practical reasoning," or that they recognise what is traditionally called natural law.[111]

Scruton addresses this issue with reference to both common law principles and the early modern language of contractual obligations, specifically mentioning Adam Smith's concept of the impartial spectator. He argues that for a community to operate smoothly, "I-you" relations need to fit into a horizon of common expectations, which should be identified as the norms "an impartial spectator would readily go along with."[112] Thus, both me and you have to be aware that our dealings with each other are under the scrutiny of this impartial spectator. In other words, the idea of the impartial spectator is a personification of what Scruton terms a "calculus of rights, responsibilities, and duties,"[113] which defines ordered human interactions.

The Transcendental Ties of a Covenant

Of particular interest to Scruton is the concept of a covenant. He defines it as a binding agreement, and sees it as originally referring, as in the Old Testament, to the relationship between God and his people.[114] This is a special kind of religious teaching, in which God makes a promise and contract with the people, as a human being would do with another one. Scruton carefully describes how promises and obligations can arise, as a result of the emergence of different forms of contract law, including both the Roman law and the English common law variants. As he sees it, all these developments are due to the natural sense of justice of human beings, which can be observed even in childhood, in the playground, where children, too, try to enforce fair play among themselves. This sense ensures respect for what the tradition calls natural law, a "treasure trove of ordinary practical reasoning."[115] As Scruton points out, the analytical philosopher, J.L. Austin described the concepts of common law reasoning as the "natural outgrowth" of the "I-thou" relationship of human beings. The same applies to Adam Smith's reconstruction of the historical rise of the principles of law and morality.[116] This, too, is based on the idea of an "impartial spectator," in other words, on the fact that "we are judged in all our dealings" by others.[117] From here, it is only one more step to concede that there are certain rights which should be seen as unalienable, because they belong to us, human beings, as an unquestionable part of our human nature.

While Scruton accepts the concept of human rights, he also points out its tendency to become inflated in modern Western societies. He points out that even Bentham had drawn attention to the danger of rights inflation, and therefore preferred what he calls "noncontractual obligations."[118] Conservatism should avoid falling into the trap of too much talk of rights. Although conservatives accept the idea that our sense of justice establishes certain truths as evident, and makes promises and rights meaningful, they are keen to emphasise that "many of the relations that are most important to us cannot be captured by the terms of a contract," including "affection and love."[119] These latter are relationships which can be characterised as "transcendent" or "eternal."

The first example Scruton gives of this form of human commitment is the marriage vow. It has an existential character, generating the tie of a "shared destiny."[120] The third observer of the marriage vow is God himself. Since the ritual of the marriage ceremony is held in public, the community will also observe it as the communal witness of the relationship of marriage. Marriage was, and still remains mostly a religious act in our culture, in which two people (traditionally, but by now in many countries not exclusively a man and a woman) commit themselves to connect their lives for the whole length of their lives. Beyond marriage, Scruton highlights and analyses two further concepts as examples of non-contractual commitments, namely piety and love. Like marriage, they involve a commitment which is way beyond what is useful and enjoyable, creating non-transferable engagements, and comprising offerings that cannot be withdrawn. These represent transcendental self-obligations, which are made eternal by the individual's religious faith or respect for tradition and institution. As soon as the Enlightenment started to push the issue of secularism, in the name of the individual's rationality, it created a brave new world, which Scruton admits is completely different, and which is, according to him, one "in which we humans are not truly at home."[121]

The World in Which We Feel at Home

The second part of the book undertakes to describe in philosophical terms the world in which we feel at home. He lists four aspects of such a world. First of all, we need others to share our fate with. The human person is born into interpersonal relationships. We are also born into a home in a human settlement, built by our parents or others. The fact that we feel safe in this place is recognised in the idea that we fell at home there. We are embedded there in a social net, called family, and a conventional set of activities, the shared life of the family. Beyond satisfying our animal appetites, there are further forms of activity, which turn the events of our life meaningful: we are engaged in the life of the mind as well, in culture. Science and fine art, architecture, literature and music are forms of activity which turn our lives into the object of our own understanding. Finally, to feel at home, we need religion, divine support, and the description of the home arrives here to death and transcendence, issues which largely lie beyond the scope of philosophical analysis.

Here, too, Scruton addresses the issue of the face, discussed in a more detailed fashion in his book *The Face of God*. The face connects I and you. Scruton calls it a boundary and a threshold, recalling Dante's expression about the mouth and eyes being the "balconies of the soul."[122] It is also "the place where the self and the flesh melt together."[123] We address each other through each other's face. Looking at the other's face reveals the real presence of the other. On the other hand, the face can also serve as a mask covering up the real self, in which case decoding the "message" of the face becomes a difficult task. To reveal more about this masking, it is necessary to understand the mechanism of the different functions of the face when it provides the real presence for the I.

Scruton's phenomenological account of the various actions of the face focuses here on the problem of voluntariness. This is because some of these actions need to be involuntary in order to be interpreted as "real" or "honest," and not "false" or "fake" gestures (take for example a smile), while others, in contrast, need to be voluntary to mean sincere involvement (this is the case with the kiss as well as with the look). A kiss is a kiss, as soon as the whole of the self becomes involved in it, changing one from a passive recipient into an active contributor to the exchange. Similarly, a look turns into something different when it is returned, when it becomes what Scruton calls a "reciprocated glance."[124] This happens when it turns from a one-directional address to a mirror-act, me looking at you and you looking at me, "me seeing you seeing me."[125]

There are other gestures of the face, which cannot be willed or intended. Yet even these, such as blushes and tears, are seen as expressions of the self, even if they are not intended as its signals. It is precisely the involuntary nature of these gestures which makes them relevant and meaningful for me, even if the message they convey is to leave the self alone. Interpersonal human communication is, in this sense, double-channelled. When we try to understand the other, we make an effort to read the other's signs, both on the level of the voluntary as on that of the involuntary.

Once again, when discussing the covering up or masking of the self, Scruton returns to the theme of responsibility. One of the key features of the self is its temporal continuity, as well as its awareness of that very temporality. Remembering the past and harbouring intentions for the future prove that the human being is an accountable agent, who needs to take charge of both intentions and actions. Scruton's moral-juridical approach to the self, that is, his approach based on the notion of responsibility, is informed by both the analytical tradition's discussions of individuality or the "I."

If I disguise my identity, it might be because I want to avoid this responsibility, the recognition of my self by others. It is worth recalling the theatrical use of masks as well as the interesting social function masks had in Venetian society. In Greek drama or in Japanese Noh theatres the mask is meaningful, and reveals or even strengthens the real presence— although not that of the actor, but, through the mask worn by the actor, that of the protagonist of the plot represented on the stage. In its use in the Venetian carnival, the mask functions to support interaction by abolishing social distance, and wiping away social prohibition. Echoing Bakhtin, Scruton refers to the "carnivalesque" moment, as a specific attitude to social reality. By wearing a mask, I rid myself of the obstacles entailed by others being acquainted with my face, and let myself open to a reassessment by others. In this carnivalesque moment, I am allowed to experience what is forbidden normally, thus allowing the self to become involved in new, momentary affairs with others without the usual price of accountability paid for it.

This is the point where we can refer to one of Scruton's most exciting topics, the nature of human sexual interaction. His point again concerns human responsibility. Scruton's bold thesis, apparently borrowed from Continental phenomenology, is that my own identity depends on my fundamental interpersonal relations. The love with which one turns to another in an intimate relationship has an "individualizing intentionality" which takes the loved and the one who loves more than simply a body, and also more than simply a thinking being. Instead, when you love me, the object of your attention is my whole being. It is through your attachment to me in my totality, and my own attachment to your totality, that our relationship "creates" me as an embodied subject. Once again, the issue is accountability. If I am the subject of your sexual desire, it means that you perceive me as more than simply a body from which sensual pleasure can be gained.

To ensure that sexuality is more than simply what is dictated by animal instincts, society surrounds sexuality with norms of prohibition, or taboos. The taboos of "shame, guilt" and of purity and pollution help to preserve the spiritual component of the interaction. Without them, the spirit would not be present in our relationship, and sexual arousal and its consummation would be nothing more than a physical and physiological intercourse.[126]

Taboos on sex are usually associated with the religious teachings of a community. Scruton specifically focuses on the genre of origin myths. He argues that myths of origin are forms of storytelling which enables a culture to tell the foundational claims about itself to its members. To explain this function, he refers partly to Wagner, and partly to the Bible. A comparison of Scruton's two examples reveals what modern art and religious teaching have in common: both of them can help us understand ourselves, both as individuals, enabling us to confront our own personal fate, in terms of our responsibility for others, and through that, for the fate of our community, too.

To substantiate this point, Scruton rephrases the Hegelian dialectic, interpreting it as a myth of origins. This is crucial for him, because it is this understanding which leads the individual through the birth of real self-consciousness to freedom. As he interprets it, it is through the birth of self-consciousness that the individual becomes aware of the distinction between herself and the external world. The external world is further divided into the realm of objects, and the realm of other people. It is in the process of making sense of both external factors and other people that we learn to tackle the world of objects as well as to deal with others, who possess the same sort of self-consciousness that we do, and who are just as interested in handling the world of objects as the self is. To make sense of these two realms requires a common language, and creates the *Lebenswelt*, the shared world of the self and others. The self, as much as the other, becomes aware of both the world of objects and the *Lebenswelt*, as well as herself as the point at the intersection between the world of objects and the *Lebenswelt*, from where the self is able to perceive or conceive of both realms.

The process of negotiation enables us to describe what freedom is for the individual. The self discovers both that she is a subject from the per-spective of others, and that there can be a conflict of interests between herself and others. Both the self and others wish to handle the world of objects, and the negotiating process between and among them decides who will do what. At the end of that process, the freedom of the indi-vidual is embodied in an action affecting the external world in accor-dance with the agreements with the others. Our agreements are based on our common considerations of our reasons for doing certain things. We can make those agreements only if our partners are taken also as subjects, who have free will, rationality and the moral concern which allows them as much as it allows us to match each other's reasons to actions. This mutual acceptance is called social recognition, which is the requirement of both self-consciousness and individual freedom, and which creates and preserves the social realm.

The individual's freedom is certainly limited in the social realm—not theoretically, but practically. The body has a location in space, and the human being as a living animal has a certain amount of time for her life. These spatial and temporal constraints—that I am here and now, and not there and then—are crucial for the individual. They determine her rela-tionship to her immediate environment and her own times. With respect to the sense of home, the first, spatial aspect seems to be obviously crucial, yet the second, temporal aspect is just as relevant. Human life is too short and human powers are too limited to allow each and every generation to create ex nihilo. To live in a comparatively comfortable manner, humans need to cultivate the place where they find themselves, and the work of their ancestors contributes to the success of that cultivation. The result of that cross-generational activity is the city, the human settlement, based on the cooperation between individuals within a generation, and also between generations. Cities have myths of origins in order to enable the individual to learn about the background of what he finds around her.

Scruton recalls three myths of origins, specifically of the origins of cities—that of Rome (based on Fustel), that of Jerusalem (based on the Torah) and that of the Christian City of God, based on Augustine, before returning to the myth of origins he himself wrote, entitled *Perictione in Colophon*, continuing his own Xanthippic Dialogues.[127] All three are about settling down, and creating a world which turns a friendly face towards those who dwell in it. All three are built around the temple, which serves as the home of the gods, making it possible to the God of the city to move in, and take care of the city. The temple is the archetypal, true form of architecture, which determines the architectural language of all the other buildings of the town, and its location defines the placement of the other buildings, and prescribes the lines of the streets and the places of squares.

The urban environment, which is called the city, is formed as an ensemble of the temple and other public and private buildings around it, arranged in organic ways along patterns of streets and squares. Both the external and the internal forms applied in the architecture of the buildings, and their arrangements are crucial—they determine whether a place will be homely. Homeliness is a result of the fact that humans have an interest in appearances, in the way things present themselves to their eyes and ears and touch—as they perceive them aesthetically. We find things aesthetically agreeable if they reveal their meaning to us, in other words when we find them morally valuable as well. In this regard, Scruton draws heavily on Kant and Hume. After all, it was Kant who famously and paradoxically claimed that although our interest in beautiful objects is without direct utility, "the beautiful is the symbol of the morally good."[128]

Scruton translates this into the idea that by giving aesthetic qualities to our cities, we make them places of what the German Romantics called *Heimkehr* (homecoming). By ensuring that our buildings and their environment have beautiful features, we turn the city into an environment attuned to our tastes, creating a world which turns its face towards us and which is in accordance with our way of life and mental (rational and spiritual) makeup. Both in architecture and in urban design, "beauty is the face of the community, and ugliness the attack on that face by the solipsist and the scavenger."[129] A solipsistic loss of the face of buildings is characteristic of modern buildings, which do not share the traditional idea of having a façade, and which do not want to fit into their architectural environment. When put together, modern buildings do not combine, they seem to be there by accident and not by intention.

Classical European architecture, on the other hand, was able to create an order within the city wall which resembled the order of nature. Meaningfulness is crucial for the human eye in a natural as well as in an artificial scene. Scruton's description of European landscape painting (as exemplified by Constable, Crome, Courbet and Corot) is an effort to show that in them nature turns its face to us, reveals itself, and thus allows us to feel at home in it. Through sensually experiencing beauty, we arrive at an insight into "a fundamental truth about being – that being is a gift."[130]

The Gift of Music

As we saw above, Scruton wants to show that "Der Mensch ist ein heimatliches Wesen."[131] His account of what he calls "the aesthetics of everyday life" is followed by a section on music. He freely admits that his argument is based on the ideas taken from classical German idealism and other Continental sources, including French phenomenology.

Interestingly, he also refers to the disciplinary conditions of the discussion about art and music. He praises the humanities as a valuable idiom, contrasting them methodologically with the sciences. Referring to Dilthey's famous distinction, he recognises that, so far, no attempt to systematically work out the methodology of the humanities has been entirely successful, including hermeneutics, phenomenology or structuralism.

Music is one of the most difficult forms of art to make sense of by a conceptual language. To explain it reasonably, it is not enough to be able to listen carefully to music: to have an ear for music is a necessary but not a sufficient condition. Taking a tiny fragment of Beethoven's *Third Piano Concerto* Scruton illustrates his point. As he sees it, when we listen to classical music, we engage in a dialogue with it: we have questions about the musical turns and moves, and the music itself seems to pose as well as to answer questions.[132] This is because we attribute intentionality or goal-directedness to music. When we make sense of that intentionality, in other words, when we discover its intention, or the goal towards which a musical move points, what we experience is a fullness, a completeness that is rare in our ordinary life otherwise. This perfection of form is achieved by the sheer logic of the musical theme: it is a logic built up by well-defined expectations, and in a successful case by the end of the musical theme those expectations will be fully satisfied. Scruton calls this closed logical system of connections between its parts "internal necessity" or a "sense of compulsion"—admitting that these expressions are not more than metaphors, helping us to describe the actual phenomenon in a vague and underdefined manner. All talk about music is stuck in a metaphorical way of expression—we not only talk, we actually hear in the melody or the line of harmonies of a musical piece spatial movement where there is neither space nor movement of musical sounds. What seems to happen in music is determined by our ability to relate sounds, rhythms and harmonies to each other, and by our ability to follow what is actually audible carefully but also in an imaginative manner. The music happens to remain in our memory, and reverberate in our senses—once again taken metaphorically. The sequences of sounds and harmonies and rhythms in a piece of music evoke in us their equivalents (one could even say, transforming Eliot's famous term, their *subjective* correlatives), which allows us to sense and feel things, in other words to identify meaningful elements in what is actually happening in the musical space. Just as we are able to recognise the mysteriously expressive smile of Mona Lisa in Leonardo's painting, without catching the particular gestures which cause that impression or to be inspired by the height and detailed decoration of the interior space of a Gothic cathedral, even if it is less transparent, than a classical architectural unit, so we are able to translate for ourselves the intentionality embedded into the pattern of a piece of music, or, to put it more accurately, we cannot help attributing meaning to it, even if we cannot provide the exact conceptual equivalents of particular details. Clearly, there are certain conditions to allow the listeners to follow musical narration. The first of those requirements is a sophisticated enough texture of music. The second pre-condition is a sort of musical culture which can equip the listener with an apparatus to listen to music and to recognise its nuances and refinements. Scruton draws our attention to the significance of silence in music. Unlike pop music, classical music makes use of silence in many different ways. Silence has a general meaning: it is "the prime material from which the work is composed." But it can have diverse specific functions in the actual structure of a piece of music, lending to it meaning, colour and even weight. One has to learn how to listen to music, in order to learn to appreciate the interludes between sounds. To achieve that sophistication of listening requires a rather specific relationship to music. Unlike in most other cases when humans hear music—such as at rituals, when working together, waging war or relaxing—in the concert hall music has a value of its own. Here, members of the audience come together for the sole purpose of listening to music in order to make sense of it and enjoy it. Scruton stresses the importance of the fact that much classical music is instrumental. It does not need words to convey its message. On the contrary: apparently it is the wordless form of music that allows human phantasy to appreciate those complex formal structures which build up a piece of classical music, and which make it both understandable and enjoyable. Although confined by the spectrum of sounds that human ears can decipher, in instrumental music the composer is not confined by the grammar and vocabulary of natural language as the writer of literature is. She (why are female composers so rare?) only has musical confines—such as tonality, the rhetoric of rhythm and the virtuosity of musical performers, when building from musical sounds and their interludes those frozen cathedrals. As if architects only had to take into account physical laws, like gravitation when planning their buildings, irrespective of their non-architectural aspects, for example, their every-day or ritual functions.

Scruton is surprisingly hesitant to accept a concept of music which claims that it has a natural evocative power, a power to raise emotions in us, which would allow members of the audience react to it in one proper way to decode its meaning. He admits that musical interpretation is dependent on the use of metaphors. Yet he rejects the claim that musical interpretation is nothing more than a rhetorical exercise, consisting of finding linguistic equivalents to the building blocks of music—as he sees it, this approach can only touch the surface of the phenomenon, as when we assert that there "is sad, joyful, bitter, hesitant, noble, passionate, and diffident music."[133]

To find the music of the concert hall really meaningful we need to understand it as being the result of an act of communication. Like the transmission of a long and detailed message, we allow the sequence of melodies, harmonies and rhythms to convey messages between composer, performer and listener, creating the *Lebenswelt* of classical music itself. When you understand music, what you do, together with being "carried along by the music," is to discover the "pattern of pure intention," "as a kind of pure aboutness."[134] Scruton proposes two ways to do this. First, we pay attention to the musical syntax. In a sophisticated musical work of art each little detail has a well-defined function in the order of the whole sequence, and what we do when understanding music is to understand the particular role played in the whole by the particular parts we encounter in succession during the performance. Secondly, we interpret by sympathy. To achieve this, one's attention is directed neutrally at the details of the musical piece. The listener is expected to move together with the movement of music, but also to reflect on her own reactions to it. Although this sympathetic interpretation follows music only "imaginatively," not "bodily," Scruton takes the analogy of dancing as an illustration of what happens in this case. Dancers allow the sequence of sounds in music to move their bodies, and their bodily movements make visible what we hear. When one follows what one hears, with movements of one's body, one reacts like the dancers, whose steps and moves follow the rhythm of the music, as well as the movements of their partners. The audible leaves a trace on the body, changing not only the body's tension, but also, when done properly, its spatial position. What we do when following the music by bodily movements is to allow our bodies to react to the music. And as embodied beings we swim with the stream of music, we become able to make sense of its intentionality without the actual use of conceptual language or logical operators.

Scruton also adds that if we are able to make sense of music, our reception of its artistic impact has moral consequences. Those features which we associate with what we hear will leave their trace in us, this way temporarily affecting our character as well. Scruton attributes to music, in line with Plato, an exceptional persuasive power: for a while, it can transform us, and we can become better human beings when listening to music.

Scruton also compares audible music to spatial art, like architecture or sculpture. In both cases, the result of the creative effort is not simply an object, but also a space around it, in which the work of art itself takes a central position, but in which we too can move, as the interpreters of the work of art. If you allow it, you find yourself in an ideal world together with someone who is talking to you through the meaningful sound effects, the "phrases and sentences" of music.[135] According to Scruton, "the great works of instrumental music" demand from the audience "a kind of surrender, a recognition of their authority."[136]

Scruton flatly rejects the claim of Peter Kivy, who argues that music cannot articulate complex messages. According to Scruton, we interpret music in the same way that we assess character in another human being or decipher nature. We are, so to speak, intentionally tuned—we search for meaning "in a face, a look, or a gesture"; and in the same way we can "hear it in a tone of voice," or "in music."[137]

Scruton looks at music as a special kind of "éducation sentimentale," an exercise in the moral realm. Scruton refers in this respect to the music of Schubert, for example to his *String Quartet in G Major*. This piece of music "is one of the truly great pieces of chamber music… consistent from start to finish, not a note denying that intense stare into the void from which the work begins."[138] Scruton finds Schubert struggling with the same metaphysical questions, that he himself is struggling in his own philosophy. The void mentioned here is the fear of death, around which Scruton's own philosophical anthropology is built. To grasp this depth of music, however, requires exceptional interpretative capacities. Scruton is obviously aware of the fact that although everybody can sensually experience the threatening metaphysical power of this music, "not everybody can show how a composer like Schubert can make music that lifts itself out of its own despair, by purely musical devices."[139]

Yet the philosopher bravely claims that Schubert's music is actually able to convey spiritual or moral messages, without ever letting music fall into empty pathetic sentimentality. In order to draw a distinction between music as a transformative moral experience and music as a form of delusion, Scruton writes about a sort of Romantic obsession with the self, constituting a kind of moral narcissism, a tell-tale sign of musical sentimentality. This pitfall has not been avoided by César Franck's *Piano Quintet*, the late Skryabin, and the sickly sweet "Agnus Dei" in Duruflé's *Requiem*. In these cases, the composer allows music to seduce the listener's emotional awareness. Schubert's music, however, does not serve simply as a mirror of the composer's own suffering. Instead, his music invites us to reflect on the human condition in a way which might help us turn away from our own self, towards the other. This way this music has an unintended, morally and socially benevolent side effect.

It clearly requires practice to achieve the skills which enable us to distinguish between all the different manifestations of the intentionality of music. We also need the right sort of moral approbation. The end result of all those exercises which turn someone into an erudite critic is the understanding of great works of art properly. The exercises of sharpening one's aesthetic judgement will not leave one's character untouched. The perfect expert has to go through a moral baptism of fire. As Rilke's famous poem suggests, real artistic experience can indeed change our lives.[140]

The paradox is that if works of art are honest as well as artistically strong and confident, they can help us live a better life even if they deprive us of our naive optimism and reveal the metaphysical loneliness of the modern Western individual. Scruton does not deny that to learn how to properly understand what is at stake in a great instrumental piece of music, we also have to make sacrifices, which is not true when we simply enjoy sentimental music, with its fake sentiments and shortcuts of emotional turmoil, leaving us at the end in a state of moral shallowness and emptiness. When we select what sort of music we want to listen to, we determine if we want to "live in openness to others, accounting for our actions and demanding an account from them, or alternatively close ourselves from others."[141] Our choice of music serves as a moral test of our character.

"Seeking God"

The final chapter of Scruton's demanding book could hardly be anything else but "Seeking God". Although the question of the role and function of religion in human life was already raised at the beginning of the book ("Believing in God"), as we saw, much of the main argument did not seem directly touch upon this final question. Yet Scruton's persistent interest in serious art and its different forms, including architecture—the art of settling—literature and the sort of music which serves as a moral test of one's character logically leads to the search for the presence of God in the fallen world of fragile human beings. He seems to argue here that all of these art forms help us realise how much humankind harbours a need for religion.[142]

His final question concerns the mystery of whether God himself is indeed there, whether our whole need for religion is only a winning strategy of humankind in the evolutionary competition of adaptiveness, a safety belt to ensure that the "I-you" relationship will remain within the confines of what might be called the moral safe ground. In this last chapter, he finally reaches the conclusion that, indeed, for the self-conscious creature that we are, an order of creation exists, as too does its counterpart, an order of destruction and annihilation. Scruton's claim that the "I" "exists on the edge of things," facing its own disappearance, nothingness, is inspired by Sartre, for whom he reserves a special kind of philosophical appreciation, in spite of their tremendous distance from each other in politics. The final form of philosophical disillusionment that is present in Sartre's work is the challenge Scruton aims to confront in his own philosophy in its strongest form. In this final account of the human condition, Scruton, therefore, turns his focus on Sartre's fearful description of our state of being, encapsulated in the famous and worn-out dictum: "nothingness lies coiled in the heart of being, like a worm."[143] He is keen to discover if that is a valid claim, no matter what the consequences may be.

He certainly agrees with the French existentialist that, as conscious beings, humans have to confront the idea that they will soon perish, whatever happens. Moreover, all their most cherished relationships—parental love, marriage, love of children and further offsprings, friendship—are sooner or later destroyed by time. This is the background, in the forefront of which humans live their lives. They are aware of the certainty of their own and their loved ones' death. While all their instincts urge them to defend themselves against this scenario of perishing, as humans, they are also ready to perform the most perfect acts of self-sacrifice, and in extreme situations they are able to offer their lives to defend their family, home country or religion. However, most of the time these acts of heroic sacrifice are made necessary by the brutality of the intentions of other human beings, who threaten to take away their fellow beings' lives, property or human dignity. While aggression and war are seen as part of our nature, tit for tat, the possibility of acts of self-sacrifice show a way to turn away from the aggressive side of our nature. That human beings are able to surpass the lower part of their soul leads us to the idea of God's grace.[144]

According to the Christian teaching, human beings were created by God in his image. This teaching of the origin of humankind has the specific consequence that Christians look upon themselves, fallen human beings, as ones who can do unnatural good to others, and hence to imitate God's grace. As our whole life is the gift of God, we, too, can find resources to offer gifts to other people. Sometimes the existence of others seems to threaten human life. Human life, always lived in a community, is vulnerable to the often brutal demands of the community. Communal life has taught human beings that to handle crisis situations, the community might require from its members sacrifices as gifts to others. To enable their members to commit such acts, human communities have rituals as well as common narratives, such as myths of origins. These stories prepare us to accept the possibility of a fate, which cannot be accepted as a result of rational calculation. Often, rational calculation can help to solve the ordinary riddles of human life. Yet sometimes rational calculation does not take us far enough. In traditional human societies, faith leads humans beyond their rational faculty, beyond what can be accounted for by logical operations. Even if we acquire it naturally, faith brings us beyond the natural world; this is the internal contradiction of Scruton's explanation of the covenant, made possible by the cognitive dualism which he claims is a defining feature of human consciousness. Yet, even there, there is no assurance and no evidence. Our rational reflection has to admit that we "cannot deduce from this God-directed attitude that God really exists."[145]

Scruton's daring move at this point of doubt is to look once again at the idea of the self, which he takes from Kant and Sartre, both of whom he takes rather seriously. As we experience transcendence at the moment when we look into the eyes of another person (because we find there something which cannot be explained by science), in the same way, we can experience our selfhood, the personified nature of God in our own act of self-sacrificing love. Just as in our most personal, intimate relationships, we are able to offer gifts and make acts of self-sacrifice, in the same way, Scruton argues, we can in fact experience the presence of God in this world.[146] To do so we have to give up searching for the God of the philosophers, and turn to those accounts of him which we find in the writings of the great mystics of our cultural tradition. Scruton quotes, for example, the "medieval work of apophatic mysticism, The Cloud of Unknowing": "By love he can be grasped and held, but by thought, neither grasped nor held."[147]

Scruton relies on the Christian believer's experience of God in the act of offering a gift of love to the other. At the end of it, the human being is able to recognise that his life, taken as a whole, is itself a gift, that the human being is also able to give gifts, to others just as much as to God, by loving them. That we love God does not serve as a proof of God's existence. Giving up the search for the God of philosophers and theologians, Scruton turns towards the personal God of the ordinary Christian believer, who is ready to offer the act of love. We are all capable of that: we are all able to love others. Here, the philosopher recalls Scheler's notion of *Gottwerdung*, "the becoming of God."[148]

Scruton tries to distinguish between religion and faith. While many people are able to live a life of faith without adhering to a religion, the latter is in fact essential to the devotee: it offers in its formalised rituals "windows onto the transcendental."[149] Christian belief is basically a communal experience. It requires an inter-generational community. Besides the ritual, Scruton also refers to the liturgies of religion, which we owe to our revered ancestors, and which create a kind of absolute identity between the form and content of worship—which is only comparable to art, "in which the present moment and the eternal meaning are brought together in another way."[150]

The relationship between religion and faith is the relationship between ritual and doctrine. It is in a way easier to follow the pattern of behaviour prescribed in your religion than to rationally accept the doctrines of your religion, as yours. While Scruton finds a "war between ritual and doctrine" in the Reformation, he claims to find a "dialectical relation between ritual and doctrine," in the Orthodox Jewish religion. In that faith, all the details of the rituals are determined, including those "concerning dress, diet, language, ceremonies, mealtimes, and the divisions of the day."[151] This formalism helps the believing Jew to experience the presence of God by actively making himself "part of the eternal story," by re-enacting the words of the Torah. In the formalised ritual, the believer can "recognise that the world is suspended between creation and destruction," at the moment when "faith and ritual coincide."[152]

The final point in Scruton's elaboration of "metaphysics" is his account of death and transcendence. In the last subchapter of his book—as well as of his philosophical saga as a whole—he confronts the final dilemma of all human beings, no matter if they are believers or not. This quandary is how to make sense of death, the final annihilation of our personal being. What needs to be understood, as he sees this vexing question, is the Christian teaching that Christ's sacrifice is redemption.[153] We need more than religion, we need faith to open ourselves to a notion of death, which leads us beyond "the space-time continuum that is the world of nature."[154] According to Scruton's unorthodox view, it is not in an afterlife (a notion which remains within the framework of time and space), but in the abyss of death that we can experience our creator. Yet this acceptance of death as a clue to revelation is only achievable through an act of love and sacrifice, in accordance with our belief. For it is through love and sacrifice that we enter another framework, that of the eternal order. It is through love and sacrifice that we learn to perceive death as meaningful: it is no less than redemption, "it unites us with the soul of the world."[155]

Scruton stops at this point, with this enigmatic expression, which he keeps as the title of the whole book. He does not explain it, because he admits that he cannot articulate his message any better. To the ordinary reader this seems to be a pantheistic solution to the riddle of belief in an afterlife. Pantheism can be understood as "the view that God is identical with the cosmos, the view that there exists nothing which is outside of God, or else negatively as the rejection of any view that considers God as distinct from the universe."[156] To understand Scruton's final point correctly, however, we need to understand two things. First, he wants us to accept that religious belief can lead us almost to the end of what we know as nature, from where, he claims, new vistas open up. This insight can be achieved by prayer, love and sacrifice. The soul of nature is identifiable as that which is beyond nature, that which science cannot address. Scruton's idea of cognitive dualism is important here: that the human being is both a rational and a non-rational entity.[157]

Secondly, with the help of the enigmatic concept of "the soul of the world," Scruton invites us to rely on art, and more exactly, on poetry, when trying to make sense of death. His last reference is to the metaphysical poet and teacher, Richard Crashaw. Crashaw was for a time a fellow of Peterhouse, Cambridge, Scruton's own Cambridge college. Crashaw was a poet of the seventeenth century who lived a life in which art and poetry were closely intertwined with religious belief. His religion was a form of High Church Anglicanism, which was accompanied by royalist sympathies, and which provoked Puritan hatred and persecution. It was perhaps not difficult for Scruton, the outcast, to identify himself with this fate. Crashaw had to flee to France, from where he travelled to Rome and converted to Catholicism. Although Scruton never took that step, as far as we know, this Anglican cleric and poet, who died finally as a Catholic, was indeed a suitable role model for Scruton.[158] Scruton includes a brief extract of a long poem by him in the final chapter of his book. He does not analyse its meaning, letting us come to our own interpretation of it. The fact that at this crucial moment Scruton relies not on the authority of the conceptual explanation of philosophy (although he also refers to the words of Simone Weil, a twentieth-century mystic), but on that of poetry is a proof of the relevance he attributes to poetry. In his effort to address the final dilemma of our life, the philosopher can only offer the words of a poet, to substantiate his point about the redemptive power of self-devoted love, which can reconcile us with death, promising to bring us into the presence of God.

> Come Love! Come Lord! and that long day
> For which I languish, come away.
> When this dry soul those eyes shall see,
> And drink the unseal'd source of thee.
> When Glory's sun faith's shades shall chase,
> And for thy veil give me thy Face.

Notes

1. Paul Guyer, *A History of Modern Aesthetics: The twentieth century* (Cambridge: Cambridge University Press, 2014).
2. He certainly had further books on both architecture and on music.
3. For Scruton, the philosopher of religion, see James Bryson, *The Religious Philosophy of Roger Scruton* (London: Bloomsbury, 2016)
4. *The Gifford Lectures. Over 100 years of Lectures on Natural Theology*, available at: https://www.giffordlectures.org/.
5. John Haldane, "Scotland's Gift: Philosophy, Theology, and the Gifford Lectures," *Theology Today* 63 (2007): 469–76.
6. Roger Scruton, *The Face of God* (London: Bloomsbury, 2012), 1.
7. Andrew Chignell and Derk Pereboom, "Natural Theology and Natural Religion," *The Stanford Encyclopedia of Philosophy* (Fall 2020 Edition), Edward N. Zalta (ed.), URL = https://plato.stanford.edu/archives/fall2020/entries/natural-theology/.
8. Scruton, *The Face of God*, 2.
9. Ibid., 4.
10. Ibid., 7.
11. Ibid., 20.
12. Ibid. Once again, one should not forget about the communal dimension of religious rites—that we praise God in those rites—together.
13. Thomas Nagel, *The View from Nowhere* (Oxford: Clarendon Press, 1986).
14. Scruton, *The Face of God*, 35.

15. Ibid., 38.
16. James H. Johnson, *Venice Incognito: Masks in the Serene Republic* (Berkeley: University of California Press, 2011), 128.
17. Scruton, *The Face of God*, 61.
18. Ibid., 66.
19. Certainly, self-portraits can have further aims, like in the case of Reynolds' *Self-Portrait with a Bust of Michelangelo*, which is meant to present the social status of the Royal Academy, of which the painter was then the current president. For this example, I am grateful to Robert Grant.
20. Scruton, *The Face of God*, 79.
21. Ibid. A further difficulty of deciphering meaning in case of Rembrandt's self-portraits is caused by the fact that he often casts himself in a role, and this way checks the process of interpretation.
22. For this information, see Lloyd DeWitt, "Rembrandt's Mother" (2017). In *The Leiden Collection Catalogue*, ed. Arthur K. Wheelock Jr. and Lara Yeager-Crasselt. 3rd ed. New York, 2020–. https://theleidencollection.com/artwork/rembrandts-mother/ (accessed August 04, 2021).
23. Scruton, *The Face of God*, 82.
24. Ibid.
25. Ibid.
26. Robert Hughes, "The God of Realism," *The New York Review of Books* 53, no. 6 (2006).
27. Scruton, *The Face of God*, 82.
28. Ibid., 83.
29. Ibid., 93.
30. Ibid., 102.
31. Ibid.
32. Ibid., 105.
33. In connection with this fact, Scruton refers to Ken Worpole, *Last Landscapes: The Architecture of Cemeteries in the West* (London: Reaction Books, 2003).
34. Scruton, *The Face of God*, 117.
35. Certainly, the myth of the origins of the land of a certain people does not necessarily address all the historical facts of the case. It does not necessarily mention who else claimed that particular land as theirs.
36. Simon Schama, *Landscape and Memory* (New York: Alfred Knopf, 1995).
37. Scruton, *The Face of God*, 119.

38. Ibid. Scruton is here indirectly referring to the influential work of *The Ancient City: A Study on the Religion, Laws, and Institutions of Greece and Rome* by Numa Denis Fustel de Coulanges (1864), which argued that the foundation of ancient Greek and Roman cities was religious.

39. Ibid., 122.

40. Martin Heidegger, "Building, Dwelling, Thinking," in Heidegger, *Poetry, Language, Thought*, trans. Albert Hofstadter (New York: Harper Colophon, 1971).

41. Scruton, *The Face of God*, 124.

42. For this point, see also Robert Grant, "Locating the sacred," in Bryson ed., *The Religious Philosophy of Roger Scruton* 57–66.

43. Scruton's theory does not address such contrary cases as Hegel's account of the pyramids, which certainly do not have faces, or Shelley's Ozymandias, about the actual loss of face in case of a statue, due to external circumstances of weather conditions or history. For these examples I am grateful to Robert Grant.

44. Scruton, *The Face of God*, 134.

45. Ibid., 134.

46. Ibid., 135.

47. Ibid., 156.

48. This argument only works if the claim that human nature necessitates the existence of a conscience is true.

49. Scruton, *The Face of God*, 156.

50. Ibid., 158.

51. Ibid.

52. Scruton attributes the anthropological term rite of passage to Van Gennep: Arnold Van Gennep, *Les rites de passage* (Paris: Émile Nourry, 1909).

53. Scruton, *The Face of God*, 163.

54. Rudolf Otto, *Das Heilige*, 1917, trans. as *The Idea of the Holy* (Oxford: Oxford University Press, 1923).

55. Scruton, *The Face of God*, 169.

56. Ibid., 170. Lewis, of course, distinguishes agape from gift-love.

57. Ibid., 170.

58. In this celebration with others the ritual itself has an evocative power.

59. Max Scheler, "The Meaning of Suffering," in Max Scheler, *On Feeling, Knowing and Valuing*, trans. Harold J. Bershady (Chicago: Chicago University Press, 1992).

60. Scruton, *The Face of God*, 174.
61. Paradoxically, he also has the function to uphold the moral law.
62. Ibid.
63. Ibid., 175.
64. Ibid.
65. Ibid., 176.
66. Ibid., 177.
67. Ibid., 178.
68. Ibid.
69. Roger Scruton, *The Soul of the World* (Princeton and Oxford: Princeton University Press, 2014).
70. Ibid., vii.
71. Ibid., vii.
72. Ibid.
73. Roger Scruton, The philosophical hedonist: Arthur C. Danto on art, *New Criterion*, 1990/9, available at: https://newcriterion.com/issues/1990/9/the-philosophical-hedonist-arthur-c-danto-on-art.
74. This expression is from Hoakley, *Favourite Paintings 3: Nicolas Poussin, Landscape with a Calm*, 1651, February 13, 2015., available at: https://eclecticlight.co/2015/02/13/favourite-paintings-3-nicolas-poussin-landscape-with-a-calm-1651/.
75. In what follows I will rely on the catalogue description and essays in: *Poussin and Nature, Arcadian Visions*. ed. Pierre Rosenberg and Keith Christiansen, Catalogue by Pierre Rosenberg, The Metropolitan Museum of Art, (New York: Yale University Press, New Haven and London, 2008).
76. André Félibien, *Entretiens sur les vies et sur les ouvrages des plus excellens peintres anciens et modernes*, 2nd ed. 2 vols. (Paris, 1685–1688).
77. The catalogue refers to "two reflections of nature, alternately shown in its limpid tranquillity and in the violent unleashing of its elements." Rosenberg, *Catalogue*, 127–371., 260.
78. Ibid., 261.
79. It was Claire Pace who claimed that "The pastoral figures in the Landscape with a Calm" were "described by Kitson as Poussin's nearest approach to pure pastoral, signs evoking the bucolic tradition." Claire Pace, "Peace and Tranquillity of Mind: The Theme of Retreat and Poussin's Landscapes," in Rosenberg, *Catalogue*, 73–89., 81.

80. Giovanni Pietro Bellori, *Le vite de' pittori, scultori ed architetti moderni*, ed. Evelina Borea, intr. Giovanni Previtali (Turin, 1672) 1976, 451.

81. William Hazlitt, *The Complete Works*, ed. P.P. Howe after the edition of A.R. Waller and Arnold Glover, 21 vols. (London, 1930–1934), vol. 12 (1934), 291–2.

82. Pace, 82, referring to Marco Buonocore et al. Camillo Massimo, collezionista di antichita: Fonti materiali (Rome, 1996), 108 (fol. 26v, no. 93); Italian trans. of Lipsius (1620), 1381–v. One should also consider the Chinese tradition of retreating into the garden.

83. Pace refers to James S. Ackerman, *The Villa: Form and Ideology of Country Houses* (Princeton, 1990), 110–11, and the Epicurean expressions used by Charles Estienne (Carolus Stephanus): *De l'agriculture et la maison rustique*. Trans. into French by Jean Liébault, Rouen, 1657: "douceur, plaisir et liberté".

84. I am grateful to Robert Grant for this reference.

85. Quoted by Pace, 84, from Montaigne: *Essais*, i. chap. 39, De la solitude.

86. Pace, 84.

87. Ibid.

88. Ibid., 85.

89. Ibid., 87.

90. Scruton, *The Soul of the World*, 24.

91. Ibid., 15. One should recall here the notion of Panentheism.

92. Ibid., 19.

93. Ibid.

94. Ibid.

95. One should note that to make sacrifice so crucial in the well-being of a community requires the assumption that aggression and violence are indeed primordial in human behaviour, which seems to contradict the assumption of a basic sociability of human nature.

96. Obviously, after Wittgenstein, we can exclude the possibility of private religion.

97. For an argument that his cognitive dualism remains trapped in an ontological dualism see Fiona Ellis, "Cognitive dualism, ontological dualism, and the question of God," *Philosophy* 94, no. 3 (2019): 409–24. doi:10.1017/S0031819119000184. For another critique of Scruton's handling of cognitive dualism, see Anthony O'Hear, "The great absence. Scruton's cognitive dualism," in his book *Transcendence, Creation and Incarnation* (London and New York: Routledge, 2020).

98. He published his work on Kant in 1982 and his book on Spinoza in 1987, respectively.

99. Scruton, *The Soul of the World*, 34.

100. Scruton, *The Face of God*, 53, and *The Soul of the World*, 9–12., 10.

101. Scruton, *The Soul of the World*, 13.

102. We should recognise the difficulty raised by the use of masks, of losing personal identity, integrity and responsibility.

103. Pierre Jacob, "Intentionality," *The Stanford Encyclopedia of Philosophy* (Winter 2019 Edition), Edward N. Zalta (ed.), URL = https://plato. stanford.edu/archives/win2019/entries/intentionality/.

104. Scruton, *The Soul of the World*, 46.

105. Ibid., 48.

106. Ibid., 46.

107. For an overview of the major problems of this discourse, and some of the most relevant views on them, see Allen Habib, "Promises," *The Stanford Encyclopedia of Philosophy* (Fall 2021 Edition), Edward N. Zalta (ed.), forthcoming URL = https://plato.stanford.edu/archives/ fall2021/entries/promises/.

108. John Searle, "How to Derive 'Ought' from 'Is'," *Philosophical Review* 73, no. I (1964): 43–58.

109. Scruton, *The Soul of the World*, 77.

110. Ibid., 77.

111. Interestingly, Scruton does not directly refer to the Christian and medieval roots of the discourse of natural law (although he calls it an ancient concept), but identifies it through the work of Hugo Grotius, a par excellence early modern writer.

112. Adam Smith, *Lectures on Jurisprudence* (Indianapolis: Liberty Press, 2001), 87.

113. Scruton, *The Soul of the World*, 81.

114. Ibid., 78.

115. Ibid., 80.

116. Smith, *Lectures*, 87.

117. Scruton, *The Soul of the World*, 81.

118. Ibid., 89.

119. Ibid., 90. See also Burke, in *An Appeal from the New to the Old Whigs* (London: J. Dodsley, 1791).

120. Ibid.

121. Scruton, *The Soul of the World*, 94–5.

122. The expression is from Dante's *Convivio*.

123. Scruton, *The Soul of the World*, 97.

124. Ibid., 100.

125. Ibid.

126. In this venture I do not touch upon Scruton's philosophy of sexuality. For those interested in that field, Scruton provided a full-length study of sexuality. See Scruton, *Sexual Desire*.

127. *Perictione in Colophon. Reflection on the Aesthetic Way of Life*, trans. Roger Scruton from the Arabic. (South Bend, Indiana: St. Augustine's Press, 2000).

128. See Immanuel Kant, §59 in *The Critique of Judgement* (1790)

129. Scruton, *The Soul of the World*, 138.

130. Ibid.

131. This is a quote taken from Karen Joisten, *Philosophie der Heimat: Heimat der Philosophie* (Berlin: Akademie Verlag, 2003).

132. A procedure recalling what Collingwood said about ordinary linguistic discourse, in his *Autobiography*.

133. Scruton, *The Soul of the World*, 159.

134. Ibid., 162.

135. Ibid., 167.

136. Ibid., 168.

137. Ibid., 169.

138. Ibid., 170.

139. Ibid., 172.

140. See Rainer Maria Rilke, *Archaïscher Torso Apollos*. The final summons of the work of art towards the viewer is: "You must change your life."

141. Scruton, *The Soul of the World*, 174.

142. Scruton, on other occasions, seems to imply, like Wagner, that in fact art is able to substitute the religious urge in us, in other words that art is able to heal our need of God.

143. Ibid., 177, quoting Jean-Paul Sartre, *Being and nothingness* (Cornwall: Routledge, 1943), 21.

144. This proposition seems to work only if we suppose a pre-existing religious sense in us, or at least a benevolent inclination towards the teachings of religion.

145. Scruton, *The Soul of the World*, 188.

146. Of course, in an obvious sense, it is easier for us to experience the presence of the loving other than that of the loving God.

147. Ibid., 189. Quotation from *The Cloud of Unknowing and Other Works*, ed. and trans. A. C. Spearing (Harmondsworth: Penguin, 2001.)

148. Scruton, *The Soul of the World*, 192.

149. Ibid., 193.

150. Ibid. See Coleridge's famous claim is that the narrative in the Scriptures "gives birth to a system of symbols, harmonious in themselves, and consubstantial with the truths, of which they are the conductors." Samuel Taylor Coleridge, "The Statesman's Manual," in *Lay Sermons*, ed. R. J. White, Vol. 6 of The Collected Works, gen. ed. Kathleen Coburn (Princeton: Princeton University Press, 1972), 28 ff. I am grateful to Robert Grant for this reference.

151. Scruton, *The Soul of the World*, 195.

152. Ibid., 196. Admittedly, this is a rather enigmatic expression.

153. In this respect, of course, Christianity differs from most world religions, and therefore, Scruton's whole idea works only within a Christian context.

154. Ibid., 198.

155. Ibid. This is once again a poetic, metaphorical expression, which makes it more difficult for the sceptical to track the truth of it.

156. William Mander, "Pantheism," *The Stanford Encyclopedia of Philosophy* (Spring 2020 Edition), Edward N. Zalta (ed.), URL = https://plato.stanford.edu/archives/spr2020/entries/pantheism/.

157. Some of his readers go as far as to claim that this (the supposed relationship of spirit and nature in the human being) is already an ontological dualism, à la Spinoza. The present reading is based on Scruton's own terminology, however, accepting that he only means here an epistemic dualism.

158. See Richard Crashaw, *Selected Poems, Secular and Sacred*, ed. Scruton's friend, Robin Holloway (London: Carcanet Press, 2013).

6

Conclusion. The Duality of Scruton's Philosophy of Politics and Art

This book has aimed to provide a comprehensive overview of the life and work of the late Sir Roger Scruton, probably the best known British conservative philosopher of the turn of the century, focusing on his characteristic parallel interest in the arts and politics. The framework of this introduction was built around the classical distinction between a life lived in action and one lived in reflection. Our claim made about action and reflection was that Scruton was unable or perhaps not prepared to make a definitive decision on this issue. In other words, he lived two lives in parallel: that of the professional philosopher, struggling with concepts, in order to clarify them, under the constraints of universal truth, and that of the public intellectual, ready to fight in order to exercise influence on the state of affairs, to get involved in public affairs, and to make his voice heard, in order to work for the common good.

As a philosopher, Scruton was brought up in the analytical tradition, at Cambridge. This tradition saw philosophy as a professional toolkit which can be used to solve universal philosophical riddles, as long as one is able to preserve a detachment from practical concerns, while keeping one's ideas close to what is called common sense. It was Ludwig Wittgenstein who had a major impact on British analytical philosophy, and in particular in Cambridge, in the decades before Scruton's arrival

© The Author(s), under exclusive license to Springer Nature Switzerland AG 2023
F. Hörcher, *Art and Politics in Roger Scruton's Conservative Philosophy*, Palgrave Studies
in Classical Liberalism, https://doi.org/10.1007/978-3-031-13591-0_6

there. Preparing the ground for what came to be called the linguistic turn, the late Wittgenstein insisted on the claim that philosophy is basically concerned with our words and their usage. Philosophy in this interpretation is an activity which aims to help others have clear ideas, and clear ideas come via the right form of life. Wittgenstein famously compared the way we use words to a toolkit, opened at the beginning of the philosophical investigation: "Think of the tools in a tool-box: there is a hammer, pliers, a saw, a screw-driver, a ruler, a glue-pot, glue, nails and screw… The functions of words are as diverse as the functions of these objects. (And in both cases there are similarities.)"[1] The philosopher has no other tools but the words of ordinary language, in order to say something of the chaotic mass of reality. It is through an analysis of the way we use our words that philosophers can say something philosophically meaningful about reality. And that use of the words depends on our way of life. It is ironic, that in spite of the close relationship which Wittgenstein claimed to exist between words and deeds, the professionalisation of philosophy at analytical philosophy departments throughout the Western world led to a focus on clarifying concepts and their logical interactions, instead of viewing philosophy as an opportunity which allows us a direct interaction with reality through our analysis of our ordinary language.[2]

While the young Scruton and the people around him in Cambridge had a keen interest in Wittgenstein ("The university I attended was Cambridge and the philosophy I studied was that bequeathed by Russell, Wittgenstein and Moore,"[3]) he seems to have been unsatisfied with what he must have seen as the sterility of analytical philosophy, understood as a simple process of analysing logical operations. Although he was tutored by Wittgenstein's famous student, Elizabeth Anscombe, the main influence on his philosophical thought came from lesser-known people like the lecturer on aesthetics, Michael Tanner, the philosopher and literary critic John Casey and the art historian David Watkin. Behind them, one should be aware of the influence of the charismatic literary critic, F.R. Leavis, and what Scruton himself called his own "artistic inspirations."[4]

In his book of autobiographical recollections, *Gentle Regrets*, Scruton refers to Leavis as the source of his own convictions about the relationship between life and literature: "it is not life that is the judge of literature, but the other way round."[5] Leavis' impact upon Scruton's thought was reflected in a moral seriousness as well as a keen interest in the imaginative impact of literature and the arts—as a professional philosopher. Like Leavis, Scruton, too, had a sense of duty and calling—a rare attribute of a mind brought up in the analytical tradition. Leavis' influence on the intellectual life of the age is still debated, but no doubt it served for Scruton as a challenge of the somewhat grey and less imaginative side of analytical philosophy.

It was due to his primary interest in culture, art and literature that Scruton's original focus was on aesthetics and the philosophy of art. Compared to that interest, which emerged in his grammar school years, when he kept listening to records of classical music for hours, his political vein was secondary. His passion for listening to music was due to childhood experiences: he discovered first Mozart, and characteristically *The Marriage of Figaro*, and then Wagner. This early experience of classical music as the pinnacle of European high culture was his own path towards self-knowledge. It was not an overnight development, but one which lasted in fact for decades; and—somewhat surprisingly—Scruton identified himself with the help of music, literature and later architecture, much more than he did with political philosophy.

Was his conservatism connected to his interest in Mozart and Wagner? It was only later that he realised that there is a link between the two: "In opera we do not find drama alone; we rediscover, through the orchestra, the ancient experience of the chorus, the voice of community in which all our emotions, all our hopes and fears, all our unacknowledged destinies, are pooled and redeemed."[6] It took him a long time to discover this common root of art and politics. And it took even longer for him to discover the common thread of high culture and religion. He approached the latter through the former: "Myths, stories, dramas, music, painting—all have lent themselves to the proof that life is worthwhile, that we are something more than animals, and that our suffering is not the meaningless thing that it might sometimes seem to be, but one state on the path to redemption."[7] This connection was revealed to him, in fact, by Wagner. However, the connection between art, architecture and religion had already been revealed to him in his youth by the art historian, David Watkin and his spiritual father, Alfred Gilbey, the Catholic priest and

Chaplain to the University of Cambridge.[8] Watkin, the art historian, took his classical ideal, with which he fervently criticised his own earlier supervisor, the great advocate of modern architecture, Nicolaus Pevsner, from the monsignor. Gilbey "taught that chaos lies all around us, and that our first duty is to impose upon it whatever order—spiritual, moral, aesthetic—it can bear. The alternative to order is not freedom, which is a form of order and its highest purpose, but disorder, randomness and decay."[9]

It is not surprising, therefore, that Scruton's own research into art and politics was also connected with his conviction that in both fields order has priority—a view which led him naturally to conservatism in politics—even though that connection is not necessary. Abstract art is often ordered, but still rather revolutionary. In music, which he practised not only as a performer of piano pieces, but also as a composer, of opera as well as of songs, Scruton himself was not quite as old-fashioned as he was in his taste in politics or in architecture. To be sure, conservatism in politics does not necessarily imply a conservatism in one's artistic taste—think about the case of T.S. Eliot's politics and his modernist poetry. Art is not simply an illustration of politics, and artistic taste does not necessarily imply political judgement and practical wisdom, even if the operation of political and aesthetic judgement has the same structure. Scruton never mixed his politics and his views of art. He never considered art as a form of political propaganda, he was too much aware of the damages caused by propaganda art in the twentieth century. He took both politics and art seriously, and investigated both fields with the moral awareness he acquired from the examples of Ruskin, Eliot and Leavis.

Vita Activa: The British Idea of the Rule of Law

While Scruton, the art critic and artist, was a product of his teenage years, the conservative developed in him later, and could not have formed without further experiences of political disorder, decline and chaos. Famously, Scruton's major experience of political convulsion was his encounter with the student rebellion in Paris, which he was an eye witness of, while staying in the French capital. He describes the mood and morale of the case with a reference to the stage performance of the situationist theatre, inspired by Antonin Artaud, the theorist of the "theatre of cruelty."[10] His recollections of the cataclysm of the student revolution—while he himself was reading the *Mémoires de Guerre* by de Gaulle—show how even then he approached politics by way of art and aesthetic perfection. What he discovered in de Gaulle's memoirs was the French tradition of the promulgation of the glory of the nation through its art, exemplified by de Gaulle, as he stood among the mourners at the state funeral for Paul Valéry, right at the very end of the World War: "According to the Gaullist vision, a nation is defined not by institutions or borders but by language, religion and high culture; in times of turmoil and conquest it is those spiritual things that must be protected and reaffirmed."[11] In Scruton's mind this Gaullist vison was the opposite of the destructive irresponsibility of the youthful revolutionaries. Scruton chose Valéry's own vision of the nation in *Le Cimetière marin*, "that haunting invocation of the dead that conveyed to me, much more profoundly than any politician's words or gestures, the true meaning of a national idea."[12] Opposed to Valéry's grand poetic vision stood Foucault and his teaching of the oppressive power of the institutions, as manifested by the curriculum of the Western universities in the post-1968 era. Instead of the mesmerising influence of Foucault, Scruton turned towards the teachings of the past. Its cultural heritage meant for him not only art and poetry, however, but also the common law of England, perhaps the best single example to counter the simplifying prejudice that old-fashioned institutions are necessarily against freedom.

Although he did not become a lawyer, one should not underestimate the role of English common law in Scruton's mindset. After all, it was he himself who claimed: "all my political thinking grows, in the end, from a love for English law, for the Inns of Court and for what the Inns have represented in our culture."[13] One should realise that in England, to study law, traditionally one attended the courses at the Inns of Court, instead of studying it at a modern public university. The relevance of this fact is partly that by entering these centres of practical knowledge the would-be lawyer enters the temple of living tradition—after all, this is the place where English lawyers have been trained for centuries. Here lawyers are able to form the new generation of their profession according to their own professional standards, far away from the rather different world of higher education. Scruton seems to have enjoyed his legal studies—he won the Struben and Profumo prizes during those years, a recognition of the intellectual energies he invested in his studies, while already teaching philosophy at Birkbeck College.

If we take into account Scruton's love of his legal studies, which ended with his being called to the bar in 1978, not resulting in actual legal practice only because he "couldn't afford to take pupillage—which then meant a year of unpaid apprenticeship,"[14] we can formulate the somewhat astonishing claim that his conservative philosophy was indeed informed by a practical bent, rooted in English common law. Scruton's overall views of the polity were in line with the tradition of the great common law jurists, from Bracton to Blackstone.[15]

English common law is indeed a peculiar institution. Its special character derives from the fact that it was an early product of the Anglo-Saxon tribes, established by 1150, and that it was able to preserve its original nature over the centuries. It preserved its primary aim, to settle quarrels peacefully. Being a form of customary law, local judgements were preserved and recycled by later generations of judges. The collection of court cases provided the precedents, which were more important parts of the law than the statutes created out of touch with the reality of the life of the ordinary people. English common law is "a paradigm of natural justice,"[16] with an "admirable simplicity," because it mainly consists of these precedents, which embody its legal principles in their *ratio decidendi*, in a flexible form, in order to ensure their applicability to new cases. When a new case was brought before the court, the judge had to search the body of case law, in order to see if there were earlier judgements of comparable earlier cases. Also, the way they looked at the new case was defined by the practice of their profession. That legal practice was based on the idea that the judge does not invent the law, but only discovers it. This idea came from the assumption "that there is a law governing each judiciable conflict, and that its right application will provide a remedy to the person who is wronged."[17] The fact that in English law the precedent had the priority implied that "English legal thinking remained concrete, close to human life and bound up with the realities of human conflict."[18] Scruton, the philosopher, made the bold claim that this feature of the common law makes it a "consecration" of the daily life of the "ordinary individual."[19]

A further interesting part of the English law was equity, a special branch of it. Equity emerged from the practice of the court of chancery, and aimed to offer legal redress for those who did not find a remedy for their complaints in the ordinary courts. Even its name, deriving from the Latin *equitas*, meaning fairness, suggests that it is a legal tool offering natural justice in cases where the *strictum jus* was not able to resolve the conflict. Equity also managed to preserve its specific nature and function over the centuries, to "soften the strictness and supply the deficiencies of the law."[20] An important legal device created by equitable jurisdiction was trust—a legal institution which was relevant to Scruton's own political philosophy. He quoted Maitland who claimed that "the development from century to century of the trust idea" was the single "greatest and most distinctive achievement" of English common law.[21] The concept of trust is also crucial for English politics, since it helps to understand that there is a form of ownership which creates duties, without any associated rights. It "provided a model for the relation between the English and their country ... we find writers and statesmen explaining patriotism in such terms."[22] Scruton was clear-sighted enough to discover this principle already in Burke, the acclaimed founder of modern conservatism, who stressed the idea of "stewardship" over the landscape.

A further claim made by Scruton about the practice of common law concerns the relevance of the jury system, which ensured that "the law remained responsive to the ordinary conscience," ensuring the "involvement of all citizens in the administration of justice," and securing that the "law stood above power and politics."[23] The law was perceived as the common good of all the subjects, and not simply a tool in the hands of the powerful.

All these and further insights led Scruton to the conclusion that the English were dutiful people, who were aware of the fact that there are no rights without duties, and that society is nothing more than a "duty-bound relation between strangers."[24]

Although Scruton did not practise as a lawyer, he became acquainted with the spirit of the law, and that helped him to navigate in search of fundamental ideas about the essence of the political community. A further consequence of his study of common law was that he preserved a practical turn of mind throughout his life, which came from this early acquaintance with the practical responsibility of the lawyer. His sense of justice was rooted in his conviction that humans are indeed sociable beings, and that they need the institutions which emerge from their interactions spontaneously, and which have an authority over the members of their society, which helps them find the right way of doing things.

Scruton's activism is important for us for two reasons. For a long time, he was a public intellectual, working as a journalist, not only writing commentaries, but also commissioning and then editing articles about politics and public life. It is true, that conservatism is associated with a sharp criticism of the activism of the Leftist public intellectual. Yet there is a practical bent in the spirit of conservatism, reminding its proponents that political affairs are finally about settling day-to-day problems in communal life. A selection of Scruton's journalism has been collected by now by Mark Dooley, representing only the top of the iceberg. The body of his political commentary is remarkable not only for its size and scale, but also for its range and depth.[25] From it the future historian will be able to see the development of the Left, from the student revolution of the 1960s through the rise of Green philosophy and the ideology of New Labour, up to the brave new world of cancel culture and what he called the "culture of repudiation."

Scruton's involvement in public affairs caused his career a lot of harm, while making his name well-known all over the Western world and well beyond. He was prepared to sacrifice his academic career on its altar. His character was solid, determined by an inclination to live and die by his ideals. The Left, which had an ever-growing majority in these years and decades, both in the media and in the academic world, wanted to make a ritual victim of him: everyone had to understand that one cannot express views like those of Scruton without existential consequences. At one point, he even decided to leave his home country to escape the hostile atmosphere against him. Yet by his time even in the US, university posts were guarded by a closed network of gate-keepers and opinion-leaders. Anyone who wished to take a different path was ostracised. He felt to be barred from gaining a tenured job in academia again, and even though his journalism won him followers, even his editorial work was rendered impossible as time went by.

His views were not really welcome on the political Right, either. This is because the Western Right was not in the position to afford the luxury of having a spokesperson like Scruton. Scruton was an uneasy partner for politicians: he was always ready to test them with the principles of their party line. Yet his main target remained the left—as in his book *Thinkers of the New Left* (1985), a collection of sharp and provocative essays criticising the hotshots of the Left, including such superstars as Sartre, Foucault or Derrida. He republished the book later, with an even more provocative title: *Fools, Frauds and Firebrands: Thinkers of the New Left* (2015). Although his criticism was sharp and pointed, he was also ready to recognise the merits of Leftist ideologists, including such icons as the writer-philosopher Sartre. If you looked at the intellectual icons of the day through Scruton's eyes, you could discover for yourself the confusions, contradictions and logical fallacies in their standpoint.

A further battlefield of his activism was in Central Europe. Although British intellectuals were rarely interested in affairs of faraway lands like Central Europe, Scruton took an early interest in the art, literature and culture of this region. He was an uncompromising critic of the Russian-type Communist totalitarian rule which dominated these countries, and which terrorised its populations. In 1979, on the advice of Kathy Wilkes, a Cambridge-based leftist philosopher and a friend, Scruton joined an initiative of Oxbridge academics which aimed to help dissident thinkers and their students behind the Iron Curtain. As documented in Barbara Day's survey of the movement, *Velvet Philosophers*, he was actively involved in underground activities such as courses held in private homes, samizdat publishing of books and journals, illegally smuggling in books and magazines and the like.[26] He spent so much time and injected so much energy into that project that he even became quite fluent in Czech. He fell in love with the culture and subculture of that country, and therefore he was actively involved in the establishment of the Jan Hus Educational Foundation, which helped to manage the underground courses and to maintain the intellectual contacts between Czechoslovakia and the West. Scruton's adventures were also retold in a novel he later wrote about these years.[27] As a result of his political adventures, his view of the world was broadened, allowing some intellectual inspirations to reach him from the periphery of Europe.

Vita Contemplativa: Philosophy of Art

This is what Scruton basically remained until the last day of his life: a philosopher, in search of the Platonic ideal of truth and beauty. Beyond the troubled waters of politics, the world of art remained for him, a world of escape, a promise of beauty and harmony. By moving to the farm with his family, Scruton was seeking to leave the world of politics, to enjoy a more reflective style of life, spent with philosophy and agricultural activity, as well as with passions like fox hunting. This voluntary change in his way of life, from politics to art, from conflict to harmony, from urban hyperactivity to reflection in the countryside was a result of his search for a more harmonious "spirit," of a return to his original interests, including music and literature. After all, his doctoral research was in aesthetics, the philosophy of art, and not in political philosophy. The latter only came with his disappointing experience of the contemporary political world.

Yet even in his philosophy he preserved a practical orientation. He was keen to use a comprehensible language. Readers found most of his work comprehensible, which encouraged him to publish more and more—by the end of his relatively short life, he created a mighty oeuvre.

He surpassed the work of a professional analytical philosopher in at least two senses. First, he became a practising artist himself. He was ready to cross the divide: from the observer of artistic performance, he turned into an artistic agent. And his inclination to create determined his way of thinking even as a critic. This is why even in the arts his activity had a practical bent. He was always aware of the carnal and sensual character of art, and his critical reflections very often capitalised on his first-hand knowledge of the practical skills of the profession. In other words, he was able to recognise and appreciate craftsmanship in art—the technical achievement or mastery of the artist. He regarded criticism itself an art form. He had a legendary memory, which very usefully complemented his sophisticated intelligence. His imagination was also often at work:

through that he was able to approach classical topics of the philosophy of art with a fresh eye.

Scruton's views on art have a special attribute. This is the bold claim that culture in general, and beauty in particular, matters. They matter both socially and individually: after all, art can change our lives, as Rilke famously claimed. Scruton was always keen to see the impact of art on our ordinary lives. The search for beauty, the primary aim of art, in his opinion, had a well-defined anthropological function. It was in one of the essays of the *Confessions of a Heretic*, that he claimed: "Our human need for beauty is not something that we could lack and still be fulfilled as people. It is a need arising from our moral nature."[28] As he interprets it, the experience of beauty "tells us that we are at home in the world, that the world is already ordered in our perceptions as a place fit for the lives of beings like us."[29] Scruton's examples of artists who are able to evoke this feeling included Corot, Cézanne and Van Gogh, all of them modern French painters, and all of them masters of an honest art.

To reflect on the impact of art on human life, it is not enough to examine art—one also has to say something about human life in general. Scruton's philosophical anthropology was informed by his keen and searching interest in German philosophy, and in particular in classical German idealism (mainly Kant and Hegel) and the phenomenological tradition (from Husserl to Scheler, Gehlen and beyond). Although this part of his work was never to grow to full perfection, Scruton's late work in metaphysics was closely connected to his interest in Continental philosophy. The main pillar of his philosophical anthropology, inspired by contemporary German philosophy, was the transcendental direction in the human being's search for meaning. He agreed with his German predecessors that the human being is not enough for herself, she wants to surpass her animal nature, and look at her world from an external, neutral point of view as well. It is this transcendental inclination which is responsible for the human being's experience of loneliness and alienation, but at the same time this is a rather creative impulse. One of its consequences is human religiousness: the search for a personal God and his presence in one's this-worldly life.

The Philosophy of Politics, Art—and Religion

Having established that Scruton's interest in art had a practical, existential bent, which awakened in him an interest in the ultimate meaning of human life, it is no surprise to find that the late Scruton became interested in the chain of thought which leads from artistic activity through a sense of the religious to politics. His line of argument was the following. Art records the human being's search for God. Religion is a communal experience. Yet politics should not turn into a religion. It is better for believer and political subjects as well, if religion and politics remain disjoined, a great achievement of Christianity itself. Community life is connected to a certain location. After all, politics is about settling, the effort of a human group to find a home in a hostile world. In his late work, Scruton often returned to the concept of *homecoming*, as the clue to finding consolation in our this-worldly life. To make sense of such homecoming, he once again had to confront art.

The philosophical concern with the connection between politics, religion and art, so characteristic of Scruton, led him to describe this search for home with the term *oikophilia*, love of the place where one lives, or a "concern with home." In its finest elaboration, Scruton's conservatism in essence constitutes a detailed phenomenological account of *oikophilia*, as elaborated in his book on ecology, *Green Philosophy* (2011). The human being needs a shelter against the harshness of weather conditions and other external calamities. Groups, too, want to find their own place on the planet. When they think they found it, they consecrate it. They claim this resting place is given to them by God, according to the teachings of the main world religions. The Torah tells the story of Israel's wanderings in search of the Promised Land. Likewise, in Christianity: Scruton quotes St Augustine, who claimed that "Our hearts are restless, until they rest in You."[30] Earlier, in the Old Testament, the story of the Prodigal Son depicted a very powerful vision of the human being's homecoming. In the same vein, the Bhagavad Gita confirms: "even as the mighty winds rest in the vastness of ethereal space, all beings have their rest in me."[31]

What is at issue in homecoming is a switch between two different trajectories of human forms of life on Earth. One is that of a being lost in his wanderings, alienated, without a place to belong to. The other one has succeeded in finding "our home here, coming to rest in harmony with others and with ourselves."[32] Interestingly, the postmodern individual experiences something like a loss of home: she does not have contact with others and with her local environment, she is a global wanderer. This is why to find one's home becomes an urgent topic for philosophy. *Oikophilia* requires embeddedness in one's local community, and the rootedness in a particular environment.

It is in this context that architecture becomes an important, indeed a sacred activity. We invite the God(s) to dwell with our community, when we build a dwelling-place for ourselves and our families. Scruton learnt from the passionate, evangelical Christian British architect, Quinlan Terry, that "the first step towards settling is to make a home for the god. That is because the god is the spirit of your community and the thing that protects you, the thing that reminds you that you are together and under a shared obedience."[33] The idea certainly comes from classical Roman history, as summarised in the *Ancient City* by Numa Denis Fustel de Coulanges (1864). In *The Soul of the World* Scruton carefully reconstructs Fustel de Coulanges' effort to show how settlement, the foundation of the ancient city was conceptually connected to religion and politics: "the historian Fustel de Coulanges tells the story of the ancient city, which he sees primarily as a religious foundation, one in which people assemble to protect their households, their ancestors, and their gods, and in which each family gains an enduring foothold."[34]

It was in favour of these mythological origins of the European city that Scruton rejects the social contract as the basis of his political philosophy, and preferred to present the community established by a religious covenant as the archetypical example of what he has in mind. "Our life as free beings is a life in community, and the community depends upon the order of the covenant."[35] In order for families to unite, to enable the idea of the city to emerge, "as a political association, and of the town as its physical embodiment," "new and more public gods emerged, with the function of uniting people from several families in shared forms of worship and a shared loyalty to the common soil."[36]

Scruton describes all these as part of an unintended, natural process, one which derives from human nature. Human sociability is inborn in each individual, but it takes time to fully develop, both in the individual's own life and in the life of the community. This is because the individual depends on her community, and the community in turn needs the self-sacrificing service of the individual.

Self-sacrifice for the common cause is a crucial notion for Scruton. He explains its role and function first with the help of René Girard, whose account of the public relevance of religion had an impact on Scruton's thought. Scruton takes over Girard's concept of the scapegoat mechanism. Girard claimed that rivalry and conflict are necessary driving forces of progress in human society. It is to resolve the overgrown tension inherent in rivalry that the scapegoat mechanism comes into play. The community chooses a single person who can be accused of generating the conflict, and who can become the target of all the hostile feelings within the group. This victimised individual will be ritually murdered, in order to allow the community to reunite, and thus placate all the agitated passions. After the reunification of the hostile fractions made possible by the ritual murder, the scapegoat is often invested with sacred qualities, recognising his or her role in the process of pacifying enmities and bringing peace to the community.

Built on this account of the scapegoat mechanism in human societies, based on the field observations of anthropologists, Scruton generalises a theory of the demand for individual sacrifice in human communities.[37] He criticises the liberal account of the relationship between the political community and the individual—which is basically a defence of individual rights and liberties against the oppressive tendencies of the community. As he interprets it, the first prerequisite for making sense of the operation of a human community is the insight that the individuals united in a particular group are potentially required to make sacrifices for the common cause. Far from being eliminable, making sacrifices is part of communal life, and in fact it renders the individual's life more meaningful and humane.

Strong anthropological bonds link the individual to the community, bonds which are not easily relaxed or loosened, and which are, in fact, necessary for creating the individual's sense of self. Scruton borrows this strong description of self-identity from French and German phenomenology, discounting simplistic liberal accounts of the autonomy of the individual, and of the founding act as a kind of social contract, deliberately entered into by fully self-centred and responsible individuals.

Scruton's narrative of the role of sacrifice in the support of community life returns in his accounts of Greek tragedy and Wagnerian music. While the first is less surprising, his philosophical endorsement of Wagnerian mythology is perhaps more startling. One has to understand that, like Nietzsche, Scruton assumes that art generally, and music in particular plays a crucial role in the spiritual life of the human being. He seems to adopt the view of a close connection between religious inclinations and the rise of communal art also from Nietzsche. The explanation of the relevance of art comes directly from this presupposition: when religion is pushed into the background in public life, as happened in modernist secularism, something has to take over its function, and art seems to be the natural substitute for that role.

Scruton does not seem to be fully satisfied with Joachim Ritter's compensation theory, which claims that the rise of the arts as a uniting and stabilising force in the community comes after and as a result of the loss of religion in public life. Yet he is prepared to make sense of art as it relates to the primary importance of communal attachments in the individual's life. His perspective on Wagner is based on his full recognition of the German's genius. Scruton's enthusiasm for Wagner is a result of his philosophical views of art and high culture as metaphysically charged condition of communal life. Scruton returned to Wagner at several points in his professional career, publishing individual volumes on *Tristan*, the *Ring* and *Parsifal*. Above, I focused on his account of the *Ring*. Scruton surprisingly connects Wagner's message with the teachings of Christianity, which is quite an achievement given Wagner's serious reservations about Christianity.[38] Although Scruton is critical of Wagner's personality, and explicitly condemns his anti-semitism, he seems to be convinced that the negotiation between the two, Wagner's art and the teachings of Christianity, is not only possible, but also fruitful. His account of the *Ring* proceeds, therefore, in that direction. In the crucial chapter on Love and Power, he straightforwardly presents love as the necessary cement of all well-functioning human political communities. While power seems to rule the world, it cannot sustain its effect long without an opposite force, love. But how can love exert its influence on a whole community? In

Scruton's detailed interpretation of Wagner, love is no less than one of those exceptional forces in human life, which are able to awaken in us an awareness of the transcendent. In other words, even if most of the time love is connected to the phenomenon of the erotic, it is also connected to the idea of the sacred. To explain what he means by these high-sounding terms, Scruton relates to the anthropological concept of "rites of passage." These are turning points in the individual's life, and occasions which serve to reconfirm the cohesion of the human community in public. Rites of passage are sacred moments, when we experience something special, when "timeless sentiments find their temporal presence, and are thereby made real."[39] An acceptance of the human condition, that is, the fact that we are mortal beings, is possible in these sacred moments, when we understand that, although we cannot escape the oppressive power of death, choosing self-sacrifice freely "on behalf of a mortal love" can work as a kind of redemption, teaching us how to accept death. Through the exceptional devotion expressed in the act of self-sacrifice one is able to give meaning to one's mortal life, a meaning which has a transcendental dimension. "The moment of free commitment, the moment when I am fully myself in an act of self-giving—this has no place in the temporal order as science conceives it. And yet it is the moment that justifies my life."[40] The relevance of the moment comes from the fact that in this act love and sacrifice are both present, and these two acts help the human being to surpass itself, and to realise its full potential. The moment of self-giving is also a moment of the sacred, which is, for Wagner, the occasion which invites the metaphysical to enter human life, and the gods to appear on the human being's experiential horizon.[41]

By returning to the meaningfulness of love in the individual's life, as the way to redemption, Scruton once again returns to the Christian theme of personhood, of the person created in the image of God. In his late work *The Soul of the World*, Scruton discusses love in the context of our sociability, distinguishing a vow from a contract, and piety from justice. The liberal account of human sociability is conceptualised as a free relationship, dependent on a contract between partners. This account disregards the simple fact that the deepest of our personal relationships are not of this nature. Contracts are based on the understanding that they stand as long as their terms stand, and "(w)hen the terms are fulfilled, the contract is at an end."[42] Unlike contracts, vows do not necessarily have precise terms, and they are open-ended agreements. "They have an existential character, in that they tie their parties together, in a shared destiny and what was once called a 'substantial unity'."[43] In a flow of almost poetic language, Scruton also adds that a "vow is a self-dedication, a gift of oneself."[44]

Scruton takes the example of the vow of marriage. While it is understandable why marriage is important for the community, in other words, from an external point of view, it is hard to imagine what makes marriage vows work internally, if we disregard the fact that it is not a contract but a vow. A vow has a "transcendent" dimension, and a wedding is nothing less than an invitation of God or the gods to witness to it. This lends the vow a "sacramental" quality.[45]

A second contrast between a vow and a contract is that justice requires that the partners to the contract offer each other what the other has a right to, or what she deserves. (Scruton is careful to distinguish these two relationships of contractual indebtedness.) While justice requires that we return what we receive, this is not the case with "obligations of piety."[46] Scruton takes the term piety from the language of religion, where it is the expression of one's belief in God, expressed in an indirect way in one's manner of behaviour. A pious reverence towards God is the first requirement of religion. Scruton transposes this attitude to strong interpersonal relationships generally, in case they have a transcendent dimension. To address the other by fulfilling obligations of piety, the individual acknowledges "that we are not the authors of our fate."[47]

Scruton refers to Hegel's well-known account of family ties, when he compares familial obligation, like that which we owe to our parents, which also belongs to the sphere of piety, and political obligations. In both cases, he argues, we have to be aware of the requirement of piety, "as a distinct source of the 'desire-independent reasons' that govern our duties."[48]

Scruton turns here not only to Hegel, but also to Aristotle. When discussing the nature of a vow, he cannot avoid returning once again to the notion of friendship outlined in the *Nicomachean Ethics*. Obviously, Aristotle's notion of friendship (*philia*) is distinguished from his understanding of *eros*. The bond of friendship which is of the highest rank, connecting friends on the assumption of the merit of friendship as an end in itself, is still *philia*. Scruton adds, however, a Christian dimension to this discussion, when he introduces the Christian term *agape*, or "neighbour love."[49] The distinguishing mark of both of these forms of attachment to another person is that they are highly personal, in other words "non-transferable" relationships. Although we owe it to everyone, we are attached by it only to one at a time. Agape is also the strongest form of attachment. Breaking up this relationship opens a rift within one's self. In other words, love is an integral part of the identity of the one who loves and it is, in fact, "the ground of his being."[50]

When Scruton points out that this dimension of commitment to the common cause is part of our political belonging, he is certainly claiming something more than what is present in the liberal account of contractual obligations, and the demands of law. As he presents it, our membership in a political community is primeval, in the sense that it requires a commitment which is beyond a reasonable calculation of what is in my interest. Political membership here is based on the human being's dependence on others, which is an anthropological universal. What is more, in his comparison of the political community and the religious covenant, Scruton presents the strong claim that a well-functioning human community needs to have a transcendental dimension, in the sense that there are moments of the sacred in communal life, moments when our deeds and choices openly invite divine approval. To show this connection between politics and religion, Scruton is always ready to refer to works of art, which are able to portray these moments in tangible form. His examples range from ancient tragedies to Shakespeare, the opera of Wagner or modern poetry, as embodied in the oeuvre of Rilke, Eliot or Larkin. This is because, while Scruton is ready to admit that we live in an enlightened age, he thinks that we still seek the personal presence of God. What is special about the discourses and practices of art is that they can help us make explicit the moments of the sacred, not simply as substitutes for religion, but in their own right. It is this communal experience, of the presence of the transcendent, as evoked by art, which we need in order to achieve what is most valuable in human life: to feel at home in the world.

Notes

1. Ludwig Wittgenstein, *Philosophical Investigations* (Hoboken: Blackwell, 1953) §11.
2. See Wittgenstein's claim: "Philosophy... leaves everything as it is." *Philosophical Investigations*, I. 24.
3. Scruton, *Gentle Regrets*, 25.
4. See the somewhat anecdotal reference to Anscombe, as well as to Tanner and Casey in *Conversations with Roger Scruton*, 25.
5. Scruton, *Gentle Regrets*, 5.
6. Ibid., 136.
7. Ibid., 138.
8. Robert Grant, in his comments on an earlier draft of this text, invited me to "imagine the cruel fun Jane Austen would have had at the expense of them both. And they would have deserved it."
9. Roger Scruton, *Professor David Watkin Eulogy*—24th September 2018, Kings Lynn Norfolk, available at: https://www.roger-scruton.com/articles/547-professor-david-watkin-eulogy-24th-september-2018-kings-lynn-norfolk. One should admit, however, that too much social order can, on the other hand, be detrimental to personal liberty.
10. Scruton, *Gentle Regrets*, 34.
11. Ibid., 35.
12. Both of the above quotations are from *Gentle Regrets*, 35.
13. Ibid., 197.
14. Ibid., 43.
15. To do so, we shall rely on his chapter on English common law in his book *England: An Elegy*.
16. Ibid., 113.
17. Ibid., 115.
18. Ibid., 116.
19. Ibid., 117.
20. Ibid.
21. Ibid., 118.
22. Ibid.
23. Ibid., 120.
24. Ibid., 128.
25. See *Against the Tide. The best of Roger Scruton's columns, commentaries and criticism*, ed. Mark Dooley (London: Bloomsbury, 2022).

26. Barbara Day, *The Velvet Philosophers* (London: The Claridge Press, 1999), 281–2. See also: Jessica Douglas-Home, *Once Upon Another Time: Ventures Behind the Iron Curtain* (Norwich: Michael Russell, 2000).
27. Scruton, *Notes from the Underground*, 2014.
28. Roger Scruton, *Confessions of a Heretic* (Kendal, Notting Hill Editions, 2021), 13–14.
29. Ibid., 14.
30. Scruton, *Green Philosophy*, 238. The quote is from the beginning of the first book of Augustine's Confessions, see Henry Chadwic's translation (Oxford: Oxford University Press, 1991), 3.
31. Scruton, *Green Philosophy*, 238.
32. Scruton, *Confessions of a Heretic*, 13–14.
33. Scruton and Dooley, *Conversations*, 91. Interestingly, here his example is Venice, of which he says: it is "a lasting work of the religious imagination, a vision of eternity rising like Venus from the sea." Ibid.
34. Scruton, *Soul of the World*, 119.
35. Ibid., 183. The religious sense of a covenant, of course, is different from the modern legal concept of the contract.
36. Ibid., 119.
37. Certainly, he means self-sacrifice, and not the sacrifice of others.
38. For the problematic relationship between Wagner and Christianity, see the account of Ieuan Ellis, "Wagner and Christianity," *Theology* 80, no. 676 (1977): 244–50.
39. Scruton, *The Ring of Truth*, 270.
40. Ibid., 271.
41. But not necessarily present in human communities—remember that the gods get lost in *The Ring*.
42. Scruton, *The Soul of the World*, 90.
43. Ibid., 90.
44. Ibid.
45. Ibid., 91.
46. Ibid., 92.
47. Ibid.
48. Ibid.
49. Ibid., 93.
50. Ibid.

Sir Roger Scruton's Own Works

"A Plea for Beauty: A Manifesto for a New Urbanism," *American Enterprise Institute for Public Policy Research* (AEI), no. 1 (March 2012).

A Political Philosophy: Arguments for Conservatism (London, etc.: Bloomsbury, 2006)

About the Salisbury Review, available at: https://www.salisburyreview.com/about/.

Against the Tide. The Best of Roger Scruton's Columns, Commentaries and Criticism, ed. Dooley, Mark (London: Bloomsbury, 2022).

"An Apology for Thinking," *The Spectator* (11 April 2019), available at: https://www.roger-scruton.com/articles/590-an-apology-for-thinking-11-april-19-the-spectator.

Art and Imagination. A Study in the Philosophy of Mind (South Bend, Indiana: St Augustine's Press, 1998 (1974)).

Beauty (2009a).

Beauty (Oxford: Oxford University Press, 2009b).

Confessions of a Heretic (Kendal, Notting Hill Editions, 2021).

Conservatism. An Invitation to the Great Tradition (New York: All Points Book, 2017).

Conservatism: An Invitation to the Great Tradition (New York: All Points Books, Horsell's Morsels Ltd, 2017).

Conversations with Roger Scruton (London, etc.: Bloomsbury, 2016) (with Dooley, Mark).

© The Author(s), under exclusive license to Springer Nature Switzerland AG 2023 **343**
F. Hörcher, *Art and Politics in Roger Scruton's Conservative Philosophy*, Palgrave Studies in Classical Liberalism, https://doi.org/10.1007/978-3-031-13591-0

Creating space for beauty. The Interim Report of the Building Better, Building Beautiful Commission, https://assets.publishing.service.gov.uk/government/uploads/system/uploads/attachment_data/file/929630/BBBBC_Commission_Interim_Report.pdf.

Culture Counts. Faith and Feeling in a World Besieged (New York, London: Encounter Books, 2007, 2018).

"David Watkin and the Classical Idea," in *The Persistence of the Classical* (Cambridge, 2008).

England: An Elegy (London: Chatto and Windus, 2000).

Gentle Regrets. Thoughts from a Life (London, Continuum: 2005).

Green Philosophy: How to Think Seriously About the Planet (London: Atlantic Books, 2012).

How to Be a Conservative (London, etc.: Bloomsbury Continuum, 2014, 2019).

Living with Beauty. Promoting Health, Well-Being and Sustainable Growth. The report of the Building Better Building Beautiful Commission, January, 2020. Available at: https://assets.publishing.service.gov.uk/government/uploads/system/uploads/attachment_data/file/861832/Living_with_beauty_BBBBC_report.pdf.

"Maurice Cowling's Achievement," *Open Democracy* (25 August, 2005), available at https://www.opendemocracy.net/en/2783/.

Modern Culture (London, New York: Continuum Books, 1998).

Notes from the Underground, a Novel (New York: Beaufort Books, 2014).

On Human Nature (Princeton and Oxford: Princeton University Press, 2017).

Perictione in Colophon. Reflection on the Aesthetic Way of Life, trans. Roger Scruton from the Arabic. (South Bend, Indiana: St. Augustine's Press, 2000).

Philosopher on Dover Beach (Southbend: St Augustine's Press, 1998).

Press Statement from Sir Roger Scruton in response to the apology from The New Statesman 8 Jul 2019, available at: https://www.roger-scruton.com/articles/617-press-statement-from-sir-roger-scruton-in-response-to-the-apology-from-the-new-statesman-8-jul-2019.

Professor David Watkin Eulogy—24th September 2018, Kings Lynn Norfolk, available at: https://www.roger-scruton.com/articles/547-professor-david-watkin-eulogy-24th-september-2018-kings-lynn-norfolk.

"Roger Scruton and Charles Taylor on the Sacred and the Secular," in *The Religious Philosophy of Roger Scruton*, ed. James Bryson (London, etc.: Bloomsbury Academic, 2016), 239–52.

"Self-knowledge and Intention," *Proceedings of the Aristotelian Society*, 1977–1978.

Sexual Desire. A Philosophical Investigation (London: Weidenfeld and Nicolson, 1986).

The Aesthetics of Architecture (Princeton: Princeton University Press, 1979).

"The Architecture of Stalinism," *Cambridge Review,* xcix, (16 Nov, 1976), 36–41.

The Classical Vernacular. Architectural Principles in an Age of Nihilism (Manchester: Carcanet, 1994).

The Face of God (London: Bloomsbury, 2012).

The Law of the Land—The Temple Church Sermon, 3 October, 2018, available at: https://www.roger-scruton.com/articles/548-the-law-of-the-land-the-temple-church-sermon-3-oct-18.

The Meaning of Conservatism (London: Macmillan, 1980, 2nd edition, 1984).

The Need for Nations (London: Civitas: Institute for the Study of Civil Society, 2004).

The Philosophical Hedonist: Arthur C. Danto on Art, *New Criterion,* 1990/1999, available at: https://newcriterion.com/issues/1990/9/the-philosophical-hedonist-arthur-c-danto-on-art.

The Politics of Culture and Other Essays (Manchester: Carcanet Press, 1981).

The Ring of Truth. The Wisdom of Wagner's Ring of the Nibelung (London: Penguin Books, 2017).

The Soul of the World, Princeton University Press, Princeton and Oxford, 2014.

The West and the Rest: Globalization and the Terrorist Threat (Wilmington DE: ISI Books, 2002).

Understanding Music. Philosophy and Interpretation (London, etc.: Bloomsbury Academic, 2009, 2016).

"Why I became a Conservative," *The New Criterion* 21, no. 6 (February 2003).

Secondary Literature

Ackerman, James S., *The Villa: Form and Ideology of Country Houses* (Princeton, 1990).

Alberti, Leon Battista, *The Architecture of Leon Battista Alberti in Ten Books*, (London: Edward Owen, 1755).

Alberti, Leon Battista, *The Architecture of Leon Battista Alberti in Ten Books, of Painting in Three Books, and of Statuary in One Book.* Translated into Italian by Cosimo Bartoli. And Now First Into English, and Divided Into Three Volumes by James Leoni, Venetian Architect; To Which Are Added Several Designs of His Own, For Buildings Both Public and Private, published 1726.

346   Sir Roger Scruton's Own Works

Alexander, Christopher, The Nature of Order (Berkeley: Center for Environmental Structure, 2002).

Arendt, Hannah, The Origins of Totalitarianism (originally published Berlin: Schocken Books, 1951).

Aristotle, Poetics, trans. S. H. Butcher, release date: November 3, 2008 [Ebook #1974], last updated January 22, 2013. http://www.gutenberg.org/files/1974/1974-h/1974-h.htm.

Attallah, Naim, *Singular Encounters* (London: Quartet Books, 1990), 129–31.

Augustine, of Hippo Saint; Confessions, trans. Henry Chadwick (Oxford, New York: Oxford University Press, 1991).

Baeumler, Alfred, *Das Irrationalitätsproblem in der Ästhetik und Logik des 18. Jahrhunderts bis zur Kritik der Urteilskraft* (Darmstadt: Wissenschaftliche Buchgesellschaft, 1967).

Balsdon, J. P. V. D., "Auctoritas, Dignitas, Otium," *The Classical Quarterly* 10, no. 2 (May, 1960): 43–50.

Banfield, Edward, "The Logic of Metropolitan Growth," ch. 2 in *The Unheavenly City Revisited* (Boston: Little, Brown and Company, 1974).

Beard, Mary, "A don's life. A tribute to David Watkin," *Times Literary Supplement*, https://www.the-tls.co.uk/articles/tribute-david-watkin/.

Belloc, Hilaire, *History of England* (London, 1915).

Bellori, Giovanni Pietro, *Le vite de' pittori, scultori ed architetti moderni*, ed. Borea, Evelina intr. Previtali, Giovanni (Turin, 1672, 1976).

Bentley, Michael, "Herbert Butterfield and Maurice Cawling," in The Philosophy, Politics and Religion of British Democracy. Maurice Cowling and Conservatism, ed. Robert Crowcroft, S.J.D. Geeen and Ricard Whiting (London, New York: Tauris Academic Studies, 2010), 85–107.

Bentley, Michael, "Maurice Cowling—Political historian and Conservative controversialist who craved the limelight," *Independent* (Saturday 06 July 2013), available at: https://www.independent.co.uk/news/obituaries/maurice-cowling-8691679.html.

Bloom, Allan, *Giants and Dwarfs: Essays 1960–1990* (New York: Simon & Schuster, 1990).

Böckenförde, Ernst-Wolfgang, *Staat, Gesellschaft, Freiheit* (Berlin: Suhrkamp, 1976).

Brague, Rémi, *La Loi de Dieu: histoire philosophique d'une alliance* (Paris: Gallimard, 2004).

Brenn, Eva, The Perfection of Jane Austen, *The Imaginative Conservative*, available: https://theimaginativeconservative.org/2018/07/perfection-of-jane-austen-eva-brann.html.

Bryson, James, *The Religious Philosophy of Roger Scruton* (London, etc.: Bloomsbury Academic, 2016).

Buonocore, Marco et al. Massimo, Camillo collezionista di antichita: Fonti materiali (Rome, 1996), 108 (fol. 26v, no. 93); Italian trans. of Lipsius (1620).

Burckhardt, Jacob, *Die Renaissance in Italien* (Stuttgart, 1867).

Burke, Edmund, *A Philosophical Enquiry into the Origin of Our Ideas of the Sublime and Beautiful* (1756).

Burke, Edmund, *An Appeal from the New to the Old Whigs* (1791).

Burke, Edmund, *Reflections on the Revolution in France* (1790), ed. with intr. and notes by J.G.A. Pocock (Indianapolis, Cambridge: Hackett Publishing Company, 1987).

Butterfield, Sir Herbert, *The Whig Interpretation of History* (1931).

Cannadine, David, *The Decline and Fall of the British Aristocracy* (New Haven, Yale University Press, 1990).

Čapek, Karel, *Letters from England* (1924).

Carlis, Silvia, "Poetry Is More Philosophical Than History: Aristotle on Mimesis and form," *The Review of Metaphysics* 64, no. 2 (December 2010): 303–36.

Casey, John, "Actions and Consequences," in *Morality and Moral Reasoning*, ed. John Casey (London: Methuen, 1971), 155–206.

Casey, John, "After Virtue," *The Philosophical Quarterly* 33, no. 132 (July 1983): 296–300.

Casey, John, "Emotion and Imagination," *The Philosophical Quarterly* 34, no. 134 (January, 1984a): 1–14.

Casey, John, "Human Virtue and Human Nature," in *The Limits of Human Nature*, ed. Jonathan Benthall (London: Allen Lane, 1973a).

Casey, John, "The Autonomy of Art," in *The Royal Institute of Philosophy Lectures vol. VI: Philosophy and the Arts*, ed. Godfrey Vesey (London: Macmillan, 1973b), 65–87.

Casey, John, "The Noble," in *The Royal Institute of Philosophy Lectures, vol. xvi: Philosophy and Literature*, ed. A. Phillips Griffiths (Cambridge: Cambridge University Press, 1984b), 135–53.

Casey, John, "Tradition and Authority," in *Conservative Essays*, ed. Maurice Cowling (London: Cassell, 1978), 82–100.

Chamberlain, Charles, "The Meaning of prohairesis in Aristotle's Ethics," *Transactions of the American Philological Association* (1974–2014) 114, (1984): 147–57.

Chignell, Andrew and Derk Pereboom, "Natural Theology and Natural Religion," *The Stanford Encyclopedia of Philosophy* (Fall 2020 Edition), Edward N. Zalta (ed.), URL = https://plato.stanford.edu/archives/fall2020/entries/natural-theology/.

Cicero, *Pro Sestio.*

Cohen, Matthew A., "Introduction: Two Kinds of Proportion." *Architectural Histories* 2, no. 1 (June 2014): 21, 1–25.

Coleridge, Samuel Taylor, "The Statesman's Manual," in *Lay Sermons*, ed. R. J. White, Vol. 6 of The Collected Works, general ed. Kathleen Coburn (Princeton: Princeton University Press, 1972), 28 ff.

Colley, Linda, *Britons: Forging the Nation, 1707–1837* (New Haven and London: Yale University Press, 1992).

Collingwood, R.G., *An Autobiography and other writings*, with essays on Collingwood's life and work, Edited by Boucher, David and Smith, Teresa (Oxford: Oxford University Press, 2013).

Corey, Elizabeth Campbell, *Michael Oakeshott on Religion, Aesthetics and Politics* (Columbia, MO: Inv. Of Missouri Press, 2006).

Covell, Charles, *The Redefinition of Conservatism. Politics and Doctrine* (London, New York: Palgrave Macmillan, 1986).

Crashaw, Richard, *Selected Poems, Secular and Sacred*, ed. Holloway, Robin (London: Carcanet Press, 2013).

Crawford, Donald W., "Review of Roger Scruton, Beauty [Book Review], *Notre Dame Philosophical Reviews* 12 (2009). Available at: https://ndpr.nd.edu/reviews/beauty/.

Cullen, Barry, "The Impersonal Objective: Leavis, the Literary Subject and Cambridge Thought," in: F. R. Leavis: Essays and Documents, ed. Ian MacKillop and Richard Storer (Sheffield, 1995).

Czigány, Lóránt, *A History of Hungarian Literature, From the Earliest Times to the mid-1970's*, available at: https://www.arcanum.hu/hu/online-kiadvanyok/MagyarIrodalom-magyar-irodalomtortenet-1/a-history-of-hungarian-literature-from-the-earliest-times-to-the-mid-1970s-lorant-czigany-47D8/chapter-xviii-the-writers-of-the-nyugat-i-4BEC/1-a-view-from-the-ivory-tower-mihaly-babits-4BED/.

Danto, Arthur, *The Abuse of Beauty* (Chicago and La Salle: Open Court, 2003).

Day, Barbara, *The Velvet Philosophers* (London: The Claridge Press, 1999).

Deathridge, John and Dahlhaus, Carl, *The New Grove Wagner* (London: Macmillan, 1984).

DeWitt, Lloyd "Rembrandt's Mother" (2017). In The Leiden Collection Catalogue, ed. Wheelock, Arthur K. Jr. and Yeager-Crasselt, Lara, 3rd ed. New York, 2020. https://theleidencollection.com/artwork/rembrandts-mother/ (accessed August 04, 2021).

Dilthey, Wilhelm, Introduction to the Human Sciences (Volume I), in SW.I, 47–242.

Dooley, Mark, Roger Scruton, *The Philosopher on Dover Beach* (London and New York: Bloomsbury, 2009).

Dooley, Mark, *The Roger Scruton Reader*, ed. Mark Dooley (London and New York: Bloomsbury, 2009 and 2011).

Douglas-Home, Jessica, *Once Upon Another Time: Ventures Behind the Iron Curtain* (Norwich, Michael Russell, 2000).

Eliot, T. S., "East Coker", *Four Quartets* (London: Faber and Faber, 1943a).

Eliot, T. S., "Little Gidding," *Four Quartets* (1943b).

Eliot, T. S., *Notes towards the Definition of Culture* (London: Faber and Faber, 1948, 1962).

Eliot, T. S., *On the Use of Poetry and the Use of Criticism* (London: Faber, 1933).

Eliot, T.S., *For Lancelot Andrewes* (1928).

Ellis, Ieuan, "Wagner and Christianity," *Theology* 80, no. 676 (1977): 244–50.

Estienne, Charles (Carolus Stephanus), *De l'agriculture et la maison rustique*. Trans. into French by Liébault, Rouen, Jean (1657).

Félibien, André, *Entretiens sur les vies et sur les ouvrages des plus excellens peintres anciens et modernes*, 2nd ed. 2 vols. (Paris, 1685–1688).

Fukuyama, Francis, *Trust: The Social Virtues and the Creation of Prosperity* (New York: Free Press, 1995).

Fustel de Coulanges, Numa Denis, *The Ancient City: A Study on the Religion, Laws, and Institutions of Greece and Rome* (1864).

Games, Stephen, *Pevsner—The Early Life: Germany and Art* (London: Continuum, 2010) Whyte, Iain Boyd, "Nikolaus Pevsner: art history, nation, and exile," *RIHA Journal* 0075 (23 October 2013) available: http://nbn-resolving.de/urn:nbn:de:101:1-20131113230, URL: https://journals.ub.uni-heidelberg.de/index.php/rihajournal/article/view/69832.

Garcia, Emmanuelle and Frederic Nef (eds.), *Métaphysique contemporaine* (Paris: Vrin, 2007).

Ginsborg, Hannah, "Kant's Aesthetics and Teleology," *The Stanford Encyclopedia of Philosophy* (Winter 2019 Edition), Edward N. Zalta (ed.), URL = https://plato.stanford.edu/archives/win2019/entries/kant-aesthetics/.

Girard, René, *La violence et la sacré* (Párizs: Grasset, 1972).

Grant, Robert, "Locating the sacred," in Bryson ed., *The Religious Philosophy of Roger Scruton*, London: Bloomsbury, 2016), 57–66.

Greenblatt, Stephen, *The Swerve: how the world became modern* (New York: W.W. Norton, 2011).

Gregory, Anthony, *The Power of Habeas Corpus in America* (Cambridge: Cambridge University Press, 2019).

Gross, Neil and Solon Simmons, eds., *Professors and Their Politics* (Baltimore: Johns Hopkins University Press, 2014).

Gross, Neil, *Why Are Professors Liberal and Why Do Conservatives Care?* (Cambridge MA: Harvard University Press, 2013).

Grote John, *Exploratio Philosophica, Rough Notes on Modern Intellectual Science*, Part I. (Cambridge, etc., 1865).

Guyer, Paul, "Beauty, Freedom, and Morality: Kant's Lectures on Anthropology and the Development of his Aesthetic Theory," in *Essays on Kant's Anthropology*, ed. Brian Jacobs and Patrick Kain (Cambridge: Cambridge University Press, 2003), 135–63.

Guyer, Paul, *A History of Modern Aesthetics: The Twentieth Century* (Cambridge: Cambridge University Press, 2014).

Guyer, Paul, *Kant and the Experience of Freedom* (Cambridge: Cambridge University Press, 1993).

Guyer, Paul, *Kant's System of Nature and Freedom: Selected Essays* (Oxford: Clarendon Press, 2005).

Habib, Allen, "Promises," *The Stanford Encyclopedia of Philosophy* (Fall 2021 Edition), Edward N. Zalta (ed.), forthcoming URL = https://plato.stanford.edu/archives/fall2021/entries/promises/.

Haldane, John, "Scotland's Gift: Philosophy, Theology, and the Gifford Lectures," *Theology Today* 63 (2007): 469–76.

Hamilton, Andy and Nick Zangwill eds., *Scruton's Aesthetics* (Basingstoke: Palgrave Macmillan, 2012).

Hankins, James, "Salutati, Plato and Socrates," *Coluccio Salutati e l'invenzione dell'Umanesimo, Atti del Convegno internazionale di studi*, Firenze 29–31 ottobre 2008, Rome: Edizioni di Storia e letteratura, 2010 [published in 2011], 283–93.

Harries, Susie, *Nikolaus Pevsner: The Life* (London: Chatto and Windus, 2011).

Hayek, F. A., "Postscript, Why I Am Not a Conservative," in Hayek, *The Constitution of Liberty*, The Definitive Edition, ed. Ronald Hamowy (Chicago: The University of Chicago Press, 1960, 2011a).

Hayek, Friedrich, *The Constitution of Liberty*. The Definitive edition (Chicago: University of Chicago Press, 1960, 2011b).

Hazlitt, William, *The Complete Works*, ed. P.P. Howe after the edition of A.R. Waller and Arnold Glover, 21 vols. (London, 1930–1934).

Hazony, Yoram, *The Virtue of Nationalism* (New York: Basic Books, 2018).

Hegel, G. F. W., *Elements of the Philosophy of Right* (1820).

Heidegger, Martin, "Building, Dwelling, Thinking," in Heidegger, *Poetry, Language, Thought*, trans. Hofstadter, Albert (New York: Harper Colophon, 1971).

Heidegger, Martin, *Being and Time*, trans. Joan Stambaugh (Albany: State University of New York Press, 1996).

Hills, Nicholas, "Oxford dons battle Czech secret police," *The Montreal Gazette* (4 June 1980).

Hoakley, *Favourite Paintings 3: Nicolas Poussin, Landscape with a Calm*, 1651, February 13, 2015, available at: https://eclecticlight.co/2015/02/13/favourite-paintings-3-nicolas-poussin-landscape-with-a-calm-1651/.

Hörcher, Ferenc "Prepolitical Values? Böckenförde, Habermas and Ratzinger and the use of the Humanities in Constitutional Interpretation" in Hörcher, *A bölcsészet-tudományok hasznáról/Of the Usefulness of the Humanities* (Budapest: L'Harmattan, 2014a), 87–101.

Hörcher, Ferenc, "A léptékhelyes város dicsérete. A herceg, az építész és a filozófus beszélgetése" (In Praise of the adequately Scaled City. The Dialogue of the Prince, the Architect and the Philosopher, *Magyar Építőművészet* 20, no. 114 (2020): 63–9.

Hörcher, Ferenc, "A Brief Enchantment: The Role of Conversation and Poetry in Human Life," in *The Meanings of Michael Oakeshott's Conservatism*, ed. Corey Abel (imprint-academic.com, Exeter, 2010), 238–54.

Hörcher, Ferenc, *Esztétikai gondolkodás a felvilágosodás korában. 1650–1800. - Az ízlésesztétika paradigmája* (Aesthetic Thought in the Age of Enlightenment. 1650–1800.—The Paradigm of the Aesthetics of Taste) (Budapest: Gondolat, 2013).

Hörcher, Ferenc, *The Political Philosophy of the European City* (Lanham: Rowman and Littlefield, 2021).

Hörcher, Ferenc, *Esztétikai gondolkodás a felvilágosodás korában (1650–1800)* (Budapest: Gondolat Kiadó, 2014b).

Houlgate, Stephen, "Hegel's Aesthetics," *The Stanford Encyclopedia of Philosophy* (Spring 2020 Edition), Edward N. Zalta (ed.), URL = https://plato.stanford.edu/archives/spr2020/entries/hegel-aesthetics/.

Hughes, Robert, "The God of Realism," *The New York Review of Books* 53, no. 6 (2006).

Hume, David, "Of the Standard of Taste," in *Essays, Moral, Political and Literary* (1777), 226–49.

Jacob, Jane, *The Death and Life of Great American Cities* (New York: Random House, 1961).

Jacob, Pierre, "Intentionality," *The Stanford Encyclopedia of Philosophy* (Winter 2019 Edition), Edward N. Zalta (ed.), URL = https://plato.stanford.edu/archives/win2019/entries/intentionality/.

James, Clive, *May Week Was In June: More Unreliable Memoirs* (London: Picador, 2009).

Johnson, James H., *Venice Incognito: Masks in the Serene Republic* (Berkeley: University of California Press, 2011).

Johnson, Samuel, *Preface to Shakespeare* (1755). The Project Gutenberg Ebook version, which has no page numbers: https://www.gutenberg.org/ebooks/5429.

Joisten, Karen, *Philosophie der Heimat: Heimat der Philosophie* (Berlin: Akademie Verlag, 2003).

Jones, Peter, *Hume's Sentiments, Their Ciceronian and French Context* (Edinburgh: Edinburgh University Press, 1982).

Jucker, Andreas, "The Eighteenth Century: The Age of Politeness," In *Politeness in the History of English: From the Middle Ages to the Present Day* (Cambridge: Cambridge University Press, 2020), 117–34.

Jung, Carl G. *The Archetypes and the Collective Unconscious*, tr. R. F. C. Hull (London, 1959).

Kant, Immanuel, *The Critique of Judgement* (1790).

Kapust, Daniel J. and Michelle A. Schwarze "The Rhetoric of Sincerity: Cicero and Smith on Propriety and Political Context," *American Political Science Review* 110, no. 1 (February 2016): 100–11.

Kapust, Daniel J., "Cicero on Decorum and the Morality of Rhetoric," *European Journal of Political Theory* 10, no. 1 (2011): 92–112.

Keay, Douglas, "Aids, education and the year 2000," *Woman's Own* (31 October 1987): 8–10, available at: https://www.margaretthatcher.org/document/106689.

Kundera, Milan, "The Tragedy of Central Europe," trans. from the French by Edmund White, 1 *New York Review of Books* 31, no. 7 (April 26, 1984).

Kunstler, James Howard, *The Geography of Nowhere: The Rise and Decline of America's Man-Made Landscape* (New York: Simon and Schuster, 1993).

Lane, B. Miller, *Architecture and Politics in Germany, 1918–1945* (Cambridge MA: Harvard University Press, 1968).

Lanier, Anderson R., "Friedrich Nietzsche," *The Stanford Encyclopedia of Philosophy* (Summer 2017 Edition), Edward N. Zalta (ed.), URL = https:// plato.stanford.edu/archives/sum2017/entries/nietzsche/.

Larkin, Philip, *Churchgoing* (1954, 1955).

Lasdun, Sir Denys, "Architectural Aspects of the National Theatre," *Journal of the Royal Society of Arts* 125, no. 5256 (November, 1977), 780–92.

Léon, Krier et al., *The Architecture of Community* (Washington, DC: Island Press, 2009).

Letwin, Oliver, "Defenders of a shared culture", *The Critic* (May 2020). Available: https://thecritic.co.uk/issues/may-2020/defenders-of-a-shared-culture/.

Lombardo, Paul A. "Vita Activa versus Vita Contemplativa in Petrarch and Salutati," *Italica* 59, no. 2 (Summer 1982): 83–92.

Lücke, Hans-Karl, *Index Verborum to Alberti's 'De Re Aedificatoria'* (München: Prestel, 1970 onwards).

MacIntyre, Alasdair, Three Rival Versions of Moral Enquiry. Encyclopaedia, Genealogy and Tradition (London: Duckworth, 1990).

Makkreel, Rudolf, "Wilhelm Dilthey," The Stanford Encyclopedia of Philosophy (Winter 2020 Edition), Edward N. Zalta (ed.), URL = https://plato.stanford. edu/archives/win2020/entries/dilthey/.

Mander, William, "Pantheism," *The Stanford Encyclopedia of Philosophy* (Spring 2020 Edition), Edward N. Zalta (ed.), URL = https://plato.stanford.edu/ archives/spr2020/entries/pantheism/.

Mann, Thomas, *Pro and Contra Wagner*, trans. Allan Blunden (London, Faber and Faber, 1985).

Mann, Thomas, *Reflections of an Unpolitical Man* (1918).

Mann, Thomas, *The Magic Mountain* (1924).

Masters, Roger D., "The Case of Aristotle's Missing Dialogues: Who Wrote the Sophist, the Statesman, and the Politics?" *Political Theory* 5, no. 1 (1977): 31–60.

McLaughlin, Martin, "Leon Battista Alberti and the Redirection of Renaissance Humanism," *Proceedings of the British Academy* 167, 2009 Lectures, 25–59.

Mill, J. S., *A System of Logic*, 10th edition (London, 1879).

Mill, John Stuart, *The Philosophy of John Stuart Mill: Ethical, Political and Religious*, ed. Marshall Cohen (New York: Modern Library, 1961).

Montaigne, *Essais* (1580).

Mumford, Lewis, *The City in History* (London: Martin Secker & Warburg Ltd., 1961).

Nagel, Thomas, *The View from Nowhere* (Oxford: Clarendon Press, 1986).

Nagy, Gregory, "Ancient Greek elegy" in Weisman, *The Oxford Handbook of the Elegy* (Oxford: Oxford University Press, 2010, 13–45.

Nardin, Terry, "Michael Oakeshott," The Stanford Encyclopedia of Philosophy (Spring 2020 Edition), Edward N. Zalta (ed.), URL = https://plato.stanford.edu/archives/spr2020/entries/oakeshott/.

Newman, J. H., "Knowledge and Religious Duty," in *The Idea of a University* (London, 1852).

Nietzsche, Friedrich, *The Will to Power*, trans. Walter Kaufmann and R. J. Hollingdale (New York: Vintage Books, 1967), 435.

Novalis, *Das allgemeine brouillon, Materialien zur Enzyklopädistik* (1798/1799).

Oakeshott, Michael, An Essay on the Relations of Philosophy, Poetry and Reality (1925).

Oakeshott, Michael, *Rationalism in Politics and Other Essays*, new and expanded edition, ed. Timothy Fuller (Indianapolis: Liberty Press, 1991).

Oakeshott, Michael, The Voice of Liberal Learning, ed. Timothy Fuller (New Haven: Yale University Press, 1989; reprinted Indianapolis: Liberty Fund, 2001).

Oakeshott, Michael: The Voice of Poetry in the Conversation of Mankind (1959).

Oakeshott, Michael, "On being conservative," in Oakeshott, *Rationalism in Politics and other Essays, New and Expanded Edition* (Indianapolis: Liberty Press, 1962/1991), 407–37.

Oakeshott, Michael, On History and Other Essays (Oxford: Basil Blackwell, 1983; reprinted with different pagination Indianapolis: Liberty Fund, 1999).

Orwell, George, *The Lion and the Unicorn: Socialism and the English Genius* (1941).

Otto, Rudolf, *Das Heilige*, 1917, trans. as *The Idea of the Holy* (Oxford: Oxford University Press, 1923).

Pace, Claire, "Peace and Tranquillity of Mind: The Theme of Retreat and Poussin's Landscapes," in Rosenberg, *Catalogue*, 73–89.

Parry, Jonathan, "Maurice Cowling: A Brief Life," in *The Philosophy, Politics and Religion of British Democracy: Maurice Cowling and Conservatism* (International Library of Political Studies), ed. Robert Crowcroft (London: I.B. Tauris, 2010), 13–24.

Pevsner, Nikolaus, *An Outline of European Architecture* (London: Pelican Books, 1943, 7th edition, 1963).

Pevsner, Nikulaus, *Pioneers of the Modern Movement: from William Morris to Walter Gropius* (London: Faber and Faber, 1936).

Pieper, Josef, *Leisure, the Basis of Culture*, trans. Alexander Dru, with an intr. T. S. Eliot (London: Faber and Faber, 1952).

Plato, *The Republic of Plato*, translated with notes and an interpretive essay by Allan Bloom (New York: Basic Books, 1968).

Pocock, J. G. A., "An Overview of The Decline and Fall of the Roman Empire," in *The Cambridge Companion to Edward Gibbon*, ed. Karen O'Brien and Brian Young (Cambridge: Cambridge University Press, 2018), 20–40.

Pocock, J. G. A., "Between Machiavelli and Hume: Gibbon as Civic Humanist and Philosophical Historian," *Daedalus* 105, no. 3 (1976): 153–69.

Polányi, Michael, *Personal Knowledge* (1958).

Polányi, Michael, *The Tacit Dimension* (1966).

Popper, Karl, *The Poverty of Historicism* (London: Routledge, 1957), 10.

Poussin and Nature, Arcadian Visions. ed. Rosenberg, Pierre and Christiansen, Keith, Catalogue by Rosenberg, Pierre, The Metropolitan Museum of Art, (New York: Yale University Press, New Haven and London, 2008).

Prado, C. G. ed., *A House Divided: Comparing Analytic and Continental Philosophy* (Amherst, NY: Prometheus/Humanity Books, 2003).

Press release: Commissioners appointed to new home design body, published February 13, 2019, available at: https://www.gov.uk/government/news/commissioners-appointed-to-new-home-design-body.

Press Release: James Brokenshire, Building better and beautiful will deliver more homes, published November 3, 2018., available at: https://www.gov.uk/government/news/james-brokenshire-building-better-and-beautiful-will-deliver-more-homes.

Pugin, Augustus Welby Northmore, *Contrasts: Or, A Parallel Between the Noble Edifices of the Fourteenth and Fifteenth Centuries and Similar Buildings of the Present Day. Shewing the Present Decay of Taste. Accompanied by Appropriate Text* (London: Charles Dolman, 1836).

Putnam, Robert, *Bowling Alone: The Collapse and Revival of American Community* (New York: Simon and Schuster, 2000).

Redding, Paul, "Georg Wilhelm Friedrich Hegel," *The Stanford Encyclopedia of Philosophy* (Winter 2020 Edition), Edward N. Zalta (ed.), URL = https://plato.stanford.edu/archives/win2020/entries/hegel/.

Roberts, Andrew, *Salisbury: Victorian Titan* (London: Faber & Faber, 2012).

Roochnik, David, "What is Theoria? Nicomachean Ethics Book 10.7–8," *Classical Philology* 104, no. 1 (January 2009): 69–82.

Salingaros, Nikos, *A Theory of Architecture* (Solingen: Umbau Verlag, 2006).

Sartre, Jean-Paul, *Being and Nothingness* (Cornwall: Routledge, 1943).

Schaff, Adam, *Alienation as a Social Phenomenon* (Oxford: Pergamon Press, 1980).

Schama, Simon, *Landscape and Memory* (New York: Alfred Knopf, 1995).

Scheler, Max, "The Meaning of Suffering," in Max Scheler, *On Feeling, Knowing and Valuing*, trans. Harold J. Bershady (Chicago: Chicago University Press, 1992).

Scott, Geoffrey, *The Architecture of Humanism* (Boston and New York: Houghton Mifflin Company, 1914).

Searle, John, "How to Derive 'Ought' from 'Is'," *Philosophical Review* 73, no. I (1964): 43–58.

Sen, Siddhartha, "New Urbanism," in *Encyclopedia of the City*, ed. Roger W. Caves (London and New York: Routledge, 2005), 332–3.

Shaftesbury, Third Earl of (Anthony Ashley Cooper), "An Inquiry Into Virtue and Merit," in *Characteristics of Men, Manners, Opinions, Times, 1699–1714*, vol. 2, ed. Douglas Den Uyl (Indianapolis, IN: Liberty Fund, 2001a), 1–100.

Shaftesbury, Third Earl of (Anthony Ashley Cooper), *Characteristics of Men, Manners, Opinions, Times, 1699–1714*, vol. 2, ed. Douglas Den Uyl (Indianapolis, IN: Liberty Fund, 2001b).

Simons, Peter, "Metaphysics in Analytic Philosophy," in The Oxford Handbook of The History of Analytic Philosophy, ed. Michael Beaney (Oxford: Oxford University Press, 2013).

Skinner, Quentin, *Machiavelli* (Oxford: Oxford University Press, 1985).

Smith, Adam, *Lectures on Jurisprudence* (Indianapolis: Liberty Press, 2001).

Smith, Adm, *The Theory of Moral Sentiments* (1759).

Soininen, Suvi, *From a 'Necessary Evil' to the Art of Contingency. Michael Oakeshott's Conception of Political Activity* (imprint-academic.com, Exeter, 2005).

Stearns, Wallace N., *Plotinus and the Ecstatic State*, The Open Court: Vol. 1920 : Iss. 6, Article 5., 356–61.

Taylor, Charles, "The Politics of Recognition," in *Multiculturalism: Examining the Politics of Recognition*, ed. Amy Gutmann (Princeton: Princeton University Press, 1994), 25–73.

Taylor, Henry Osborn, *The Mediaeval Mind, A History of the Development of Thought and Emotion in the Middle Ages*, in two Volumes, Vol. I. (St. Martin's Street, London: Macmillan and Co., Ltd., 1911).

The Charter of the New Urbanism (1996), available: https://www.cnu.org/who-we-are/charter-new-urbanism.

The Cloud of Unknowing and Other Works, ed. and trans. Spearing, A. C. (Harmondsworth: Penguin, 2001).

The Gifford Lectures. Over 100 years of Lectures on Natural Theology, available at: https://www.giffordlectures.org/.

The Oxford Handbook of the Elegy, ed. Weisman, Karen (Oxford: Oxford University Press, 2010).

The Philosophy of Karl Popper, ed. Schilpp, P.A., 2 vols, (La Salle, Illinois: Open Court, 1974).

Thomas, Sir Keith, *Man and the Natural World: Changing Attitudes in England, 1500–1800* (Harmondsworth: Allen Lane, 1983).

Tocqueville, Alexis de, *Democracy in America* (originally published in 1835 and 1840).

Unger, Miles J. *Machiavelli. A Biography* (New York, etc.: Simon and Schuster, 2011).

Van Gennep, Arnold, *Les rites de passage* (Paris: Émile Nourry, 1909).

Vinen, Richard review of The Philosophy, Politics and Religion of British Democracy: Maurice Cowling and Conservatism, (review no. 1130), https://reviews.history.ac.uk/review/1130.

Viroli, Maurizio, *For Love of Country: An Essay on Patriotism and Nationalism* (Oxford, Oxford University Press, 1995).

Volpi, Franco, "In Whose Name?: Heidegger and 'Practical Philosophy'," *European Journal of Political Theory* 6, no. 1, (2007): 31–51.

Wagner, Richard, *My Life*, trans. Andrew Gray, ed. Mary Whitall (Cambridge: Cambridge University Press, 1983).

Wagner, Richard, *Prose Works*, vol. 2. Opera and drama (Lincoln, Nebraska: University of Nebraska Press, 1994).

Watkin, David, *Morality and Architecture. The Development of a Theme in Architectural History and Theory from the Gothic Revival to the Modern Movement* (Oxford: Clarendon Press, 1977).

Watt, Ian, *Conrad: Nostromo* (Landmarks of World Literature) (Cambridge: Cambridge UP, 1988).

Westfall, Carroll William, "Tradition in the Vernacular and the Classical," *Traditional Building* (Aug. 1, 2019).

Wheeler, Michael, "Martin Heidegger," *The Stanford Encyclopedia of Philosophy* (Fall 2020 Edition), Edward N. Zalta (ed.), URL = https://plato.stanford.edu/archives/fall2020/entries/heidegger/.

Wilford, Paul T., "Das Geistige Tier: Roger Scruton's Recovery of Hegel," *Perspectives on Political Science* 50, no. 2 (2021): 119–37.

Wirszubski, Chaim, "Cicero's CUM Dignitate Otium: A Reconsideration," *The Journal of Roman Studies* 44, no. 1 (1954): 1–13.

Witte, John, *From Sacrament to Contract: Marriage, Religion and Law in the Western Tradition* (Louisville, KY: Westminster/John Knox Press, 1997).

Wittgenstein, Ludwig, *Philosophical Investigations* (Hoboken: Blackwell, 1953).

Wolloch, Nathaniel, "Cato the Younger in the Enlightenment," *Modern Philology* 106, no. 1 (August 2008): 60–82.

Worpole, Ken, *Last Landscapes: The Architecture of Cemeteries in the West* (London: Reaction Books, 2003).

Author Index[1]

A

Abel, Corey, 26n3
Abraham, 116
Ackerman, S., 318n83
Acton, Lord, 110
Adam, 257–259
Addison, Joseph, 144, 152
Adorno, Theodor, 19, 73, 216, 237, 238
Alberich, 220
Alberti, Leon Battista, 172, 182, 196–200, 250n159, 271
Alcibiades, 7
Alexander, Christopher, 133n173
Allen, Brooke, 52n52
Anaxagoras, 7
Anscombe, G. E. M., 150, 292
Antigone, 219, 224

Antisthenes, 231, 232
Aquinas, Saint Thomas, 38, 39, 63, 150, 278, 291
Arendt, Hannah, 18, 19
Aristotle, 2, 5, 12–14, 16, 17, 21–23, 25, 38, 40, 63, 66, 70, 83, 87, 89, 114, 140, 141, 156, 171, 172, 177, 190, 198, 199, 225, 230, 231, 233, 234, 250n161, 265, 294, 339
Arnold, Matthew, 38, 39, 84, 85, 96, 138, 145
Aron, Raymond, 164
Artaud, Antonin, 36, 327
Attallah, Naim, 51n32, 52n39
Austen, Jane, 43, 141, 243n15, 341n8
Austin, J.L., 296

---

[1] Note: Page numbers followed by 'n' refer to notes.

B

Babits, Mihály, 19
Baeumler, Alfred, 28n32
Bakhtin, Mikhail, 299
Bakunin, Mikhail, 227, 228
Balsdon, J. P. V. D., 29n41
Banfield, Edward, 250n168
Barbaro, Emolao, the
    Younger, 250n161
Bartoli, Cosimo, 249n158
Baudelaire, Charles, 101
Bauer, Peter, 96
Baumgarten, Alexander
    Gottlieb, 144
Beaney, Michael, 27n13
Beard, Mary, 43
Beethoven, Ludwig van, 283, 304
Bellori, Giovanni Pietro, 285
Bellow, Saul, 85
Benedict XVI, Joseph Ratzinger, 292
Bentham, Jeremy, 297
Bentley, Michael, 41, 51n33
Berdyaev, Nikolai, 274
Berlage, Hendrik PEtrus, 160
Bernini, Giovanni Lorenzo, 179
Betjeman, Sir John, 208
Bibó, István, 19
Bismarck, Otto von, 16
Blackstone, Sir William, 88, 89,
    243n24, 328
Blair, Tony, 49, 68, 105, 127n55
Bloom, Allan, 30n61, 95, 163
Bloom, Harold, 163
Böckenförde, Ernst-Wolfgang,
    123, 134n184
Boethius, 291
Borromini, Francesco, 181
Bourdieu, Pierre, 241

Boyd Whyte, Iain, 165
Boys Smith, Nicholas, 206
Bracton, Henry de, 328
Brague, Rémi, 223
Bramante, Donato, 181
Brandom, Robert, 289
Bretter, György, 59
Brokenshire, James, 205
Brown, Gordon, 69, 127n55
Brünhilde, 280
Bryson, James, 27n14
Buber, Martin, 262, 294
Buckley, William F. Jr., 96
Budd, Malcolm, 244n43
Bunyan, John, 102
Burckhardt, Jacob, 161, 163,
    164, 167
Burke, Edmund, 36, 37, 60,
    62, 68, 70, 74, 88–90, 95,
    113, 115, 116, 122, 123,
    130n100, 155, 190, 210,
    245n62, 329
Bush, George Jr., 69
Butcher, S. H., 27n23
Butterfield, Sir Herbert, 40,
    41, 60, 159

C

Cannadine, David, 99, 100
Čapek, Karel, 100
Carlis, Silvia, 28n26
Casey, John, 37–40, 55, 56, 60,
    169, 324
Cato the older, 147, 286
Cato the younger, 147
Caves, Roger W., 250n163
Cezanne, Paul, 333

Chadwic, Henry, 342n30
Chamberlain, Charles, 28n31
Charondas, 114
Charron, Pierre, 286
Chateaubriand, François-René de, 92
Chaucer, Geoffrey, 99, 100, 102
Chesterton, G. K., 105
Chignell, Andrew, 314n7
Christ, Jesus, 119, 218, 219, 226,
    279, 288, 312
Christiansen, Keith, 317n5
Cicero, 12, 14, 17, 147, 196,
    199, 200, 235, 250n159,
    285, 286
Cleopatra, 102
Cockerell, Charles Robert, 44, 178
Coleridge, Samuel Taylor, 93, 96,
    98, 321n150
Colley, Linda, 108
Collingwood, R. G., 4, 39, 170,
    173, 320n132
Conrad, Joseph, 100
Constable, John, 303
Corey, Elizabeth Campbell, 26n3
Coriolanus, 102
Corot, Jean-Baptiste Camille,
    303, 333
Coulanges, Numa Denis Fustel de,
    192–193, 316n38, 335
Courbet, Jean Désiré Gustave, 303
Covell, Stanley, 37, 39
Cowling, Maurice, 37, 39–43,
    51n33, 55–57, 60, 96
Cox, The Baroness, 58
Crashaw, Richard, 313
Crawford, Donald W., 244n41
Croce, Benedetto, 4, 38
Crome, John, 303

Crowcroft, Robert, 51n33
Cullen, Barry, 46
Czigány, Lóránt, 30n54

D

Dahlhaus, Carl, 252n189
Dante, Alighieri, 223, 286, 298
Danto, Arthur C., 85
Darwall, Stephen, 294
Day, Barbara, 331
De Gaulle, Charles, 35, 327
De Maistre, Joseph, 70, 92,
    123, 225
Deathridge, John, 252n189
Dennett, D.C., 292
Derrida, Jacques, 58, 331
Déry, Tibor, 19
Descartes, René, 289
DeWitt, Lloyd, 315n22
Dickens, Charles, 102
Dilthey, Wilhelm, 3, 4, 303
Diogenes Laertius, 33
Dion, of Syracuse, 16
Dionysos, 15
Diotima, 9–11
Disraeli, Benjamin, 93
Dolman, Charles, 246n68
Dooley, Mark, 34, 36, 46, 50n6, 68,
    267, 330
Dostoyevsky, Fyodr
    Mikhailovich, 227
Douglas-Home, Jessica, 58
Dru, Alexander, 129n75
Durkheim, Émile, 192, 261,
    287, 288
Duruflé, Maurice, 308
Dutilleux, Henri, 85

E

Eaton, George, 251n174
Elias, Norbert, 235
Elijah, 233
Eliot, T. S., 47, 73–76, 79, 84, 85,
    90, 93, 115, 116, 129n75,
    137, 138, 145, 156, 190, 191,
    214, 241, 245n44, 275, 304,
    326, 340
Ellis, Fiona, 318n97
Epicurus, 12
Epimenides, of Crete, 114
Estienne, Charles (Carolus
    Stephanus), 318n83
Eve, 257–259

F

Falstaff, John, 102
Félibien, André, 284
Ferguson, Adam, 236
Ferguson, Niall, 96
Feuerbach, Ludwig Andreas, 280
Filmer, Robert, 63, 64
Fitzgerald, Scott, 131n123
Foot, Philippa, 38
Foucault, Michel, 36, 241, 327, 331
Franck, César, 308
Fraser, Hugh, 37
Frazer, Sir James George, 88
Freia, 220, 221
Fukuyama, Francis, 126n26
Fuller, Timothy, 27n7, 27n8

G

Gadamer, Hans-Georg, 28n32
Games, Stephen, 165
Garcia, E., 27n13
Garton-Ash, Timothy, 58

Gascoyne-Cecil, Robert, the Third
    Marquess of Salisbury, 56
Gaunt, John of, 103
Gehlen, Arnold, 333
Gescinska, Alicja, vi, 128n56
Gibbon, Edward, 147, 148
Giedion, Sigfried, 161
Gierke, Otto von, 70, 216, 217
Gilbey, Alfred, 43, 246n77, 325, 326
Ginsborg, Hannah, 243n28
Girard, Gené, 72, 139, 218, 234,
    282, 287, 288, 336
Glasman, Baron, 77, 128n62
Glasman, Maurice, 77
Goethe, Johann Wolfgang von,
    101, 223
Gombrich, Ernst, 167
Goodhart, David, 209
Gramsci, Antonio, 241
Grant, Robert, 27n14, 28n25,
    30n51, 51n33, 125n15,
    126n29, 127n55, 128n62,
    244n43, 245n46, 315n19,
    316n43, 321n150, 341n8
Gray, John, 189
Green, S.J.D., 51n33
Greenblatt, Stephen, 29n47
Griffiths, A. Phillips, 51n29
Gropius, Walter, 160, 165
Gross, Neil, 128n64
Grote, John, 248n126
Grotius, Hugo, 319n111
Gruegmann, Robert, 203
Gutmann, A., 129n80
Guyer, Paul, 255

H

Habib, Allen, 319n107
Haldane, John, 257, 259

Hamilton, Andy, 52n49
Hamlet, 102
Hamowy, Ronald, 130n100
Hamvas, Béla, 19
Hankins, James, 29n48
Hardy, Thomas, 147
Hare, R. M., 38
Harries, Susie, 164, 165
Havel, Václav, 19, 59, 73
Hayek, Friedrich, 83, 90, 94, 95,
      130n100, 189, 190, 202
Hazlitt, Illiam, 285
Hazony, Yoram, 104, 105, 109
Heaney, Seamus, 85
Hegel, Georg Wilhelm Friedrich, 3,
      38, 39, 64, 70, 71, 82, 84,
      90–92, 95, 98, 113, 123,
      125n14, 125n16, 151, 155,
      169, 220, 224, 225, 245n44,
      263, 265, 274, 291, 292, 294,
      316n43, 333, 339
Heidegger, Martin, 18, 19, 115, 192,
      199, 232, 238, 272, 289
Herder, Johann Gottfried, 138, 142
Hesiod, 11, 114
Hills, Nicholas, 125n8
Hitler, Adolf, 41, 145, 165, 216
Hobbes, Thomas, 60, 88, 188
Hofstadter, Albert, 316n40
Hogarth, William, 102
Hölderlin, Friedrich, 115, 275
Hollingdale, R.J., 129n85
Holloway, Robin, 128n56
Homer, 11, 15, 116, 242
Honeyford, Ray, 56, 57, 80
Hooker, Richard, 88
Hopkins, Gerard Manley, 47
Horace, 285, 286
Hörcher, Ferenc, 28n32, 133n175,
      134n184, 253n213

Horkheimer, Max, 19, 73
Houlgate, Stephen, 245n62
Howard Kunstler, James, 120, 203
Huddleston, Andrew, 46
Hughes, Robert, 315n26
Hughes, Samuel, 128n56
Hull, R.F.C., 242n11
Hume, David, 18, 38, 40, 88, 89,
      117, 122, 145, 182, 235, 236,
      266, 287, 302
Huntington, Samuel, 97
Husserl, Edmund, 173, 288, 290,
      295, 333
Hutcheson, Francis, 144, 152

Ieuan, Ellis, 342n38
Iktinos, 15
Illyés, Gyula, 19
Isolde, 220

Jacob, Pierre, 203
Jacobs, Jane, 120, 189, 201, 203
James, Clive, 52n51
James VI, 63, 108
James, William, 278
Jefferson, Thomas, 88, 89
John Paul II, Karol József
      Wojtyła, 59, 292
Johnson, James H., 315n16
Johnson, Paul, 96
Johnson, Samuel, 28n25, 88
Joisten, Karen, 320n131
Jonas, Hans, 115
Jones, Peter, 253n212
Jucker, A., 250n166
Juliet, 102, 220

Julius Caesar, 102
Jung, Carl G., 140, 242n11

K

Kádár, János, 83
Kant, Immanuel, 4, 18, 33, 40, 85,
    90, 116, 117, 144, 150, 169,
    173, 182, 208, 222, 228, 235,
    239, 245n44, 252n208, 262,
    263, 266, 287, 289, 291, 302,
    311, 319n98, 333
Kapust, Daniel J.,
    253n209, 253n210
Kaufmann, Walter, 30n50, 129n85
Keay, Douglas, 128n68
Kedourie, Elie, 96
Kempe, Margery, 291
Kenny, Anthony, 58
Kierkegaard, Søren Aabye, 233, 274
Kirk, Russell, 96, 97
Kivy, Peter, 307
Koestler, Arthur, 18, 19, 73, 147
Kolakowska, Afnieszka, 58
Kolakowski, Leszek, 73
Kosselleck, Reinhart, 197
Kreon, 224
Krier, Léon, 121
Krotkin, Joel, 203
Kundera, Milan, 117
Kunstler, James Howard, 120,
    133n173, 203

L

Lane, Miller, 166
Leontes, king, 102
Langland, William, 102
Lanier, Anderson, R., 29n49, 30n50

Larkin, Philip, 137, 138, 340
Lasdun, Sir Denys, 184, 248n130
Le Corbusier, Charles-Edouard
    Jeanneret, 160, 172, 212
Lear, king, 102
Leavis, F. R., 26n4, 38, 39, 46–47,
    79, 93, 94, 96, 136, 138,
    239, 324–326
Lehár, Ferenc, 251n188
Lenin, Vladimir Ilyich, 145
Leonardo, Da Vinci, 304
Letwin, Oliver, 26n1
Lévinas, Emmanuel, 262, 266, 274
Lewis, C.S., 269, 278
Liébault, Jean, 318n83
Lipsius, Justus, 286
Locke, John, 18, 60, 63, 65, 81, 88,
    90, 220, 291
Lombardo, Paul A., 29n46
Longhena, Baldassare, 176
Loos, Adolf, 166
Lücke, Hans-Karl, 248n123
Lukács, George, 18, 241
Lukacs, John, 19, 130n88

M

Machiavelli, Niccolo, 17,
    18, 30n51
MacIntyre, Alasdair, 27n11,
    29n37, 40, 81
Maistre, Joseph de, 70, 92, 123
Maitland, F.W., 96, 329
Makkreel, Rudolf, 27n9
Malsbary, Gerald, 252n201
Mander, William, 321n156
Manent, Pierre, 97
Mann, Thomas, 147, 218, 229
Mannheim, Karl, 167

Mao, Zedong, 145
Márai, Sándor, 18
Marcuse, Herbert, 19
Marx, Karl, 90, 91, 220, 230
Masaccio, Tommaso di Ser
    Giovanni di Simone,
    257, 258
Mates, Pere, 257, 259
Matraszek, Marek, vi, 128n56
Matthews, David, 128n56
Mayhew, Gail, 206, 251n176
McDowell, John, 289
McLaughlin, Martin, 250n159
Meager, Ruby, 169
Medici family, 178
Michelangelo, Lodovico Buonarroti
    Simoni, 155, 167, 178
Mill, John Stuart, 18, 60, 104
Millar, John, 236
Milosz, Czeslaw, 73, 147, 164
Milton, John, 102
Minogue, Kenneth, 96
Molière, Jean-Baptiste
    Poquelin, 102
Montaigne, Michel Eyquem
    de, 14, 286
Montesquieu, Charles Louis de
    Secondat, Baron de La Brède
    et de, 88
Moore, G. E., 46, 324
Morris, William, 160, 165,
    166, 203
Möser, Justus, 70
Moses, 116, 193
Mozart, Wolfgang Amadeus,
    156, 325
Mumford, Lewis, 120, 201, 203
Murdoch, Iris, 253n215
Murray, Douglas, 69, 207

N
Nagel, Thomas, 262
Napoleon, Bonaparte, 89, 217
Nardin, Terry, 3, 4
Nef, Frederic, 27n13
Németh, László, 19
Newman, Cardinal, 100
Nietzsche, Friedrich, 15, 16, 30n49,
    38, 40, 72, 86, 150, 227,
    241, 337
Novalis, Georg Philipp Friedrich
    Freiherr von Hardenberg, 115
Nussbaum, Martha C., 81

O
Oakeshott, Michael, 1–7, 9, 26n3,
    27n11, 35, 38, 41, 60, 81, 83,
    90, 94–96, 123, 126n29, 190,
    192, 252n193
Obama, Barrack, 69
O'Connor, Flannery, 94
O'Hear, Anthony, vi, 2, 26n2,
    31n64, 244n43, 244n44
O'Keeffe, Dennis, 58
Orpheus, 15
Orwell, George, 18, 73, 95, 102,
    128n66, 129n74, 147
Otto, Rudolf, 227, 277
Ovid, 285

P
Pace, Claire, 286, 317n79
Palladio, Andrea, 174
Parry, Jonahtan, 51n31, 51n35
Parsons, Mary, 206
Pascal, Blaise, 233, 291
Patocka, Jan, 59, 288, 289

Peacham, Henry, 99
Péguy, Charles Pierre, 147
Penfold, Adrian, 251n173
Penn Warren, Robert, 94
Pereboom, Derk, 314n7
Pericles, 6, 16
Peruzzi, Baldassare Tommaso, 174
Petrarch, Francesco, 13, 14, 286
Pevsner, Nikolaus Bernhard Leon,
    Sir, 44, 159–167, 172, 179,
    248n118, 326
Pfitzner, Hans Erich, 156
Phidias, 5, 15
Philip II, 16
Pieper, Josef, 83, 129n75, 231–233
Plato, 2, 5–9, 16, 17, 21–23, 94,
    176, 223, 229, 231, 269, 307
Pocock, John G.A., 148
Polányi, Michael, 249n138
Pole, David, 169
Polybius, 17
Polyclitus, 5
Popper, Karl, 91, 164, 167
Portia, 102
Pound, Ezra, 47, 156
Poussin, Nicolas, 282–287
Powell, Enoch, 39
Proust, Valentin Louis Georges
    Eugène Marcel, 270
Pugin, Augustus Welby Northmore,
    160, 163, 171, 196
Putnam, Robert, 122, 124, 134n181

R

Rawls, John, 40, 60, 81
Redding, Paul, 125n14
Reeve, C. D. C., 7, 28n27

Rembrandt, Harmenszoon van Rijn,
    267–269, 315n21
Renan, Joseph Ernest, 130n88
Reynolds, Sir Joshua, 315n19
Richard II, king, 103
Richards, Ivor Armstrong, 39
Ricoeur, Paul, 266
Rilke, Reiner Maria, 85, 214, 308,
    333, 340
Rimbaud, Arthur, 85
Ritter, Joachim, 197, 337
Roberts, Andrew, 124n2
Romeo, 220
Roochnik, David, 29n39
Rosenberg, Pierre, 284
Roth, Joseph, 94
Rougemont, Denis de, 220
Rousseau, Jean-Jacques, 18, 33, 90,
    116, 147
Rowthorn, Robert, 104
Rumi, Jalāl al-Dīn Muḥammad, 291
Ruskin, John, 93, 96, 116, 171, 176,
    189, 203, 326
Russell, Bertrand, 46, 324
Russell, Michael, 342n26

S

Sachs, Hans, 221, 239
Saint Augustine, 13, 33, 48, 116,
    302, 334
Saint John of the Cross, 291
Saint Matthew, 286
Saint Teresa, of Avila, 179, 291
Salingaros, Nikos, 133n173
Salisbury, the Third Marques of, see
    Gascoyne-Cecil, Robert, the
    Third Marquess of Salisbury

Salutati, Coluccio, 13, 14
Sartre, Jean Paul, 18, 19, 173, 309,
    311, 331
Scanlon, Thomas Michael, 294
Schaff, Adam, 84
Schama, Simon, 122, 270
Scheler, Max, 115, 266, 279,
    311, 333
Schiller, Friedrich, 83, 84, 116, 144,
    154, 230, 237
Schilpp, P.A., 247n94
Schmitt, Carl, 18, 248n134
Schoenberg, Arnold, 156
Schopenhauer, Arthur,
    219, 222
Schubert, Franz, 307, 308
Schwarze, Michelle A.,
    253n210
Scott, Geoffrey, 176
Scruton, Sir Roger Vernon, v, 1, 2,
    24–26, 33, 55, 135,
    255, 323–340
Scruton, Sophie, v, 77
Searle, John, 292, 294, 295
Sellars, Wilfried, 289
Sen, Siddhartha, 201
Shaftesbury, Thrid Earl of,
    8, 28n33, 85, 144,
    150, 236
Shakespeare, William, 98, 101–104,
    155, 156, 220, 223, 225,
    242, 340
Shelley, Percy Bysshe, 316n43
Sidney, Sir Philip, 103
Siegfried, 218, 220, 225, 226
Sieglinde, 221
Siegmund, 221, 280
Simmons, S., 128n64

Simons, Peter, 27n13
Simpson, John, 85
Skinner, Quentin, 30n51
Skryabin, Alexander
    Nikolayevich, 308
Smith, Adam, 81, 88,
    89, 91, 95, 122,
    235, 236, 252n208,
    266, 296
Smyth, Charles, 40, 41
Socrates, 2, 9, 11, 29n48,
    231, 247n114
Soininen, Suvi, 26n3
Solzhenitsyn, Aleksandr Isayevich,
    18, 73, 147
Sophocles, 15, 222, 224
Spaemann, Robert, 266
Spearing, A.C., 321n147
Spengler, Oswald Arnold Gottfried,
    132n138, 142
Spinoza, Baruch (de), 34,
    244n44, 289,
    319n98, 321n157
Stalin, Ioseb Besarionis dze
    Jughashvili, 145
Stambaugh, Joan, 252n203
Stearns, Wallace N., 29n45
Stein, Edith, Saint, 115
Strauss, Leo, 87, 94, 95
Stravinsky, Igor Fyodorovich, 236
Strawson, P.F., 294

Tacitus, 17
Tamás, Gáspár Miklós, 59
Tanner, M.K., 150
Tate, Allen, 94

Taylor, Charles, 84, 125n16,
    129n79
Taylor, Henry Osborne, 13
Tchaikovsky, Pyotr Ilyich, 155
Terry, Quinlan, 85, 335
Thales, 7
Thatcher, Margaret, 79, 80,
    128n68
Theocritus, 114
Thomas, Keith, Sir, 122
Thucydides, 17
Tippett, Michael, 85
Titus, 267
Tocqueville, Alexis de, 18, 83, 92,
    122, 123, 134n181
Tomin, Julius, 58
Travolta, John, 241
Tristan, 220
Trump, Donald, 105
Tyndale, William, 102

U

Unger, Miles J., 30n52
Urban VIII, pope, 286

V

Valéry, Paul, 35, 327
Van Gogh, Vincent, 333
Vaughan-Wilkes, Kathleen, 100
Vinen, Richard, 52n37
Viollet-le-Duc, Eugène
    Emmanuel, 160
Virgil, 14, 285
Viroli, Maurizio, 104
Vitruvius, 172, 196, 200
Volpi, Franco, 249n157

W

Wagner, Otto, 166
Wagner, Richard, 15, 72, 74,
    213–242, 252n189, 280–281,
    300, 320n142, 325, 337, 338,
    340, 342n38
Watkin, David, 37, 43–45, 52n42,
    55, 158–169, 199, 245n66,
    246n77, 246n83, 324–326
Watt, Ian, 131n123
Weber, Max, 164
Weil, Simone, 313
Welty, Eudora, 94
Westfall, Carroll William, 185
Wheeler, Michael, 249n144
Wheelock, Arthur K. Jr., 315n22
White, Edmund, 125n7
White, R. J., 321n150
Whiting, Ricard, 51n33
Wiggins, David, 128n56, 244n43
Wilford, Paul T., 125n16
Wilkes, Kathy, 58, 331
Wilkie, Kim, 206, 207
Williams-Ellis, Clough, 204
Winckelmann, Johann Joachim, 160
Wirszubski, Chaim, 29n41
Witte, John, 126n32
Wittgenstein, Ludwig, 23, 38, 46,
    150, 169, 171, 245n44, 290,
    323, 324
Wölfflin, Heinrich, 161, 163
Wollheim, Richard Arthur, 255
Wolloch, Nataniel, 244n36
Wordsworth, William, 116
Worpole, Kent, 315n33
Wotan, 220–226, 280
Wright, Frank Lloyd, 160
Wycliffe, John, 102

X

Xenophon, 250n159

Y

Yeager-Crasselt, Lara, 315n22
Yorick, 102

Z

Zalta, Edward N., 26n5, 27n9,
    29n49, 125n14, 243n28,
    245n62, 249n144, 314n7,
    319n103, 319n107, 321n156
Zangwill, Nick, 52n49
Zweig, Stefan, 82, 94

Subject Index[1]

A

Absolute, 4, 9, 18, 123, 227, 312
Abstract-utopian, 61
Accommodation, 48, 205
Accountability, 80, 106, 110, 111, 293, 300
Adapt to, 118, 187
Administrative state, 71
Aesthete, v, 37, 186
Aestheticism, 2
Aesthetics, 11, 28n32, 36, 38–40, 44–46, 97, 119, 136, 151, 153, 157–212, 215, 255, 281–283, 324, 325, 332
   appreciation, 116–118, 170, 181, 198, 200
   education, 124, 146, 150, 198
   effect, 23, 122
   of everyday life, 171, 303
   experience, 38, 150, 156, 157, 173, 177, 272, 273
   order, 121
   quality, 9, 23, 151, 170, 187, 205, 273
   response, 177
   standard, 194
The Aesthetics of Architecture, 168–185, 209, 255
The Aesthetics of Music, 213, 229, 232, 255
Aesthetic Understanding, 185, 255
Affordability, 211
Africa, 111
Agape, 278, 340
Age of Reason, 89
Alienation, 84, 91, 142, 230, 237, 274, 333
Allegiance, 20, 62, 63, 105

---

[1] Note: Page numbers followed by 'n' refer to notes.

American Enterprise
Institute, 68, 201
Analytical, 4, 22–24, 33, 37, 46, 58,
60, 137, 150, 257, 287, 292,
294, 296, 299, 323, 325, 332
philosophy, 23, 33, 46, 136, 283,
289, 323–325
Ancien regime, 36, 89, 216
Ancient, 2, 5, 7, 9, 12–14, 16, 17,
45, 84, 88, 101, 114, 120,
147–149, 154, 172, 177, 180,
182, 184, 185, 188, 189, 195,
196, 199, 200, 222, 229, 231,
233, 234, 245n44, 256, 265,
271, 276, 285, 316n38,
319n111, 325, 335, 340
Anglican, 43, 86, 213, 313
Anglican Church, 86, 148
Anthropology, 25, 99, 149, 171,
186, 231, 289, 307, 333
Anthropomorphic, 179
Anti-Christian, 80
Anti-Communism, 95
Anti-intellectual, 79
Anti-modernist, 87
Anti-semitism, 216
Anxiety of influence, 159, 163
Application, 24, 157, 168, 178, 328
Apprehension, 156, 175, 177, 235
Appropriate, 5, 34, 100, 172, 177,
182, 194, 197–199, 204, 208,
235, 240, 265, 273, 283, 290
Appropriation, 156, 173
Aptus, 182, 197
Arbitrary power, 49, 62, 89
Arcadia, 286
Arcana imperii, 104
Architectural criticism, 180

Architecture, 14, 16, 25, 37, 44, 45,
92, 121, 136, 138, 148, 151,
152, 157–213, 236, 242, 270,
271, 298, 302, 303, 307, 309,
325, 326, 335
Architrave, 194, 271
Arendtian, 73
Aristocracy, 75, 92, 235, 236
Aristotelian, 5, 8, 30–31n62, 69, 81,
83, 114, 117, 120, 140, 171,
190, 199, 209, 225, 234
Art, 1–26, 33–49, 73, 75, 76, 79,
82–86, 89, 92, 93, 95, 97,
102–104, 114–117, 119,
129n85, 135–242, 244n43,
255–314, 323–340
Art and Crafts, 160
Art and Imagination, 150, 173, 255
Art critic, v, 93, 116, 179, 264, 326
Art history, 37, 158, 159, 163,
192, 283
Artist, 21, 74, 119, 154–156, 178,
196, 200, 238, 255, 268, 332
Art of conversation, 83
Art theory, 159, 168
Athenian theatre, 141

Bhagavad Gita, 116, 334
Bible, 97, 242, 258, 300
Bildung, 83
Bildungsbürgertum, 235
Bill of Rights, 5, 111
Biography, 34, 164
Birkbeck College, 328
Blairism, 77
Bloomsbury, 34, 121

Blue labour, 77
Body, 2, 10, 11, 29n38, 46, 151,
    178, 201, 205, 212, 241, 258,
    259, 269, 271, 272, 277, 292,
    300, 301, 306, 328, 330
Bologna, 198
Bon gout, 236
Boston University, 57
Boundary, 193, 298
Brancacci chapel, 258
Brexit, 74, 87, 105, 109
British conservatism, 1, 35, 60, 87,
    92, 95, 97
Brussels, 80
Budapest, vi, vii, 59, 134n184
Building Better, Building Beautiful
    Commission, 121, 200–212
Built environment, 118, 122, 124, 136,
    186, 204, 208–210, 272, 273
Bürgerliche Gesellschaft, 91, 188

Cambridge, 20, 23, 30n56, 35, 37,
    41–43, 46, 55, 60, 79, 96,
    136, 149, 150, 158, 159, 281,
    313, 323, 324, 326
Cancel culture, 79, 87, 207, 330
Canon, 47, 84, 145, 208
Capitalism, 82, 87, 148, 237
The Captive Mind, 73
Carnivalesque, 299
Cartesian, 88
Castelgandolfo, 286
Catharsis, 141, 155, 156, 234
Cathedral, 195, 196, 305
Catholic, 37, 43, 83, 162, 163, 292,
    313, 325

Catholicism, 41, 45, 163,
    246n77, 313
Causal law, 292
Central Europe, 35, 58–59, 73, 80,
    83, 100, 125n7, 135, 331
Central planning, 203
Chaos, 45, 85, 165, 326
Character, v, 8, 65, 98–102, 110,
    146, 152–154, 156, 158, 163,
    179, 180, 182, 184, 216, 217,
    221, 228, 229, 232, 240,
    243n24, 264, 268, 269,
    271–273, 291, 297, 307–309,
    328, 330, 332, 339
Charisma, 46, 103
Charter '77, 58, 289
Chastity, 221
Chatto and WIndus, 68
Chelsea, 121
Chivalry, 99, 100
Christian, 12, 13, 25, 63, 72, 75, 80,
    92, 101, 119, 139, 164, 195,
    218, 223, 261, 269, 274, 275,
    278, 279, 288, 291, 310–312,
    319n111, 321n153, 338, 340
Christianity, 42, 75, 132n141, 143,
    219, 226, 321n153, 334,
    337, 342n38
Christ, Jesus, 119, 218, 219, 226,
    279, 288, 312
Church, 75, 83, 88, 122, 132n141,
    137, 138, 163, 176, 181, 189,
    195, 196, 209, 213, 214,
    237, 286
Citizen, 15, 21, 64, 65, 69, 106,
    109, 112, 120, 123, 125n15,
    134n184, 141, 145, 147, 194,
    271, 329

City, 11, 12, 14, 16, 17, 48, 117,
    118, 120, 121, 124, 153, 158,
    168, 187, 189–191, 194–196,
    202–205, 216, 229, 235–237,
    242, 258, 270–272, 286, 302,
    303, 316n38, 335
    of God, 302
Civic virtue, 189, 225
Civil association, 83, 84, 91, 123,
    124, 126n29
Civilised behaviour, 199
Civility, 45, 78, 83, 88, 151, 188,
    189, 195
Civil law, 71
Civil society, 64, 83, 84, 91, 113,
    122–124, 125n15, 134n181,
    188, 211, 217, 224
Classical, 4, 7, 33, 44, 74, 76, 89,
    94, 121, 155, 158, 167, 172,
    174, 178, 182, 185, 191, 192,
    195, 199, 213, 215, 220, 228,
    229, 236, 239, 271, 289,
    303–306, 323, 325, 326,
    333, 335
    liberalism, 91
    vernacular, 186
Cognitive, 145, 152, 174, 177
    dualism, 289, 290, 292, 311,
    313, 318n97
Cold War, 94
Collective intentionality, 294
Collective spirit, 165
Collectivism, 91, 166
Collectivistic society, 162
Colonnade, 44, 174, 193, 194, 271
Combray, 270
Comedy, 21
Commercial society, 89, 148, 236

Commodus, 182, 197
Common good, 14, 66, 101, 120,
    139, 146, 194, 323, 329
Common law, 48, 49, 61, 77, 79,
    86, 95, 107, 108, 111, 112,
    210, 243n24, 296,
    327–330, 341n15
Common sense, 60, 76, 151, 206,
    210, 235, 323
Communal belonging,
    107, 139–141
Communal rite, 139, 141
Communion, 260–262, 279
Communism, 59, 94, 111
Communist, 19, 24, 58–59, 73, 74,
    83, 288, 289, 331
Community consent, 206
Concentration camp, 227
Conception, 72, 99, 198, 199
Concordance, 198
Conditio sine qua non, 87
Conflict, 13, 17, 59, 68, 91, 101,
    107, 108, 132n141, 157, 188,
    218, 222, 224, 225, 237, 285,
    288, 301, 328, 329, 332, 336
Connoisseur/ship, 235, 236
Conquest, 113, 327
Conservation movement, 116,
    121, 124
Conservatism, 5, 34–36, 39–42, 47,
    55–124, 135, 149, 292, 297,
    325, 326, 329, 330, 334
Conservative ecology, 113
Conservative party, 35
Conservative thought, 2, 87, 96
Consoling power, 267
Constitution, 5, 35, 62, 88,
    94, 96, 103

Contemplation, 12–14, 187, 233, 234, 286
Contemplative activity (*theorein*), 12
Contemporary art, 47, 242
Continental philosophy, 20, 24, 333
Contract theory, 105
Contractual agreement, 188
Conversation, 3, 34, 36, 60, 83, 95, 129n79, 165, 192, 213, 230
Conversion, 35, 36, 45, 74, 93
Coordinating device, 118
Coordination problem, 152, 153
Cornaro Chapel, 179
Cornice, 178, 195
Corporate person, 103
Corporate personality, 91
Correspondence, 26, 31n64, 122, 178, 180, 198
Countryside, 12, 69, 77, 79, 98, 120, 137, 149, 204, 286, 332
Courtesy, 99, 100
Court philosopher, 79
Covenant, 289, 294, 296–297, 311, 335, 340, 342n35
Covid, 130n87
Craft knowledge (*technê*), 5–7
Creed, 35, 82, 107, 110
  community, 106, 107
Critical judgement, 180, 184
Critical Regionalism, 212
Criticism, 8, 13, 24, 38, 39, 46–47, 60, 67, 68, 74, 82, 88–90, 92, 93, 105, 111, 129n74, 147, 148, 158, 161–164, 180, 186, 187, 200, 201, 203, 212, 219, 239–242, 283, 330–332
Crown, 103, 108, 258

Cult, 14, 15, 72, 120, 139–142, 165, 193, 201, 233, 261, 277
Cultural anthropology, 171
Cultural conservatism, 39, 76, 86, 87, 92–94, 96, 97, 137
Cultural critic, 47, 93, 135, 136, 241
Cultural studies, 47, 138
Cultural tradition, 9, 143, 311
Culture, 8, 9, 11, 14–16, 18, 33, 37, 38, 40, 45, 47, 56, 59, 66, 72, 75, 76, 79, 83–87, 89, 90, 92, 93, 96–98, 101, 102, 116, 135–242, 259, 261, 270, 277, 281, 297, 298, 300, 305, 325, 327, 330, 331, 333
Culture war, 59, 71, 72, 97, 109
Culture warrior, 97
Cunning of reason, 91
Custom, 63, 64, 68, 84, 87, 88, 90, 107, 119, 120, 139, 143, 154, 163, 235, 236, 238, 271, 294
Customary law, 328
Czech, 58, 288, 331
Czechia, 125n7
Czechoslovakia, 58, 331

D

Dead, 35, 70, 75, 107, 115, 116, 137, 159, 235, 272, 276, 277, 327
Death, v, 109, 121, 138, 141, 209, 216, 218–221, 226, 240, 267, 268, 276, 277, 279, 280, 288, 298, 307, 310, 312–314, 338
  of God, 86
Decadence, 185
Decency, 100, 195

Decens, 182, 197

Decline, 43, 93, 94, 147, 148, 185, 186, 202, 223, 241, 242n5, 326

Decorative art, 170

Decorum, 43, 101, 154, 200, 235

Deliberate choice (*prohairesis*), 8, 78

Delusion, 308

Democracy, 75, 80, 91, 96, 106, 109, 211, 225, 229

Democratic deficit, 111

Democratic opposition, 59, 73

Density, 204, 232

Desecration, 78, 156, 157, 196, 273, 277

Design, 44, 73, 152, 155, 160, 175, 178, 187, 191, 195, 200–202, 205, 206, 208, 209, 251n181, 303

Detachment, 22, 323

Detail, 34, 42, 44, 118, 148, 154, 155, 158, 168, 172, 175, 180–184, 186, 197, 198, 203, 204, 209, 239, 269, 272, 283, 305, 306, 312

Dialectic, 84, 91, 123, 263, 274, 291, 292, 300

Dialogue, 11, 21–23, 31n62, 140, 255, 257, 262–265, 267, 273, 280, 294, 304

Dignitas, 99

Dignus, 197

Discrimination, 175, 177

Disposition, 35, 82, 199

Dissident, 45, 58, 83, 331

Divine, 9–11, 14, 25, 194, 219, 256, 258–260, 264, 274, 280, 281, 298, 340

Doctrine, 34, 35, 39, 42, 60–97, 163, 166, 186, 312

Dogmatics, 61

Door, 44, 144

Doric column, 181

Downtown, 203, 204

Drawing, 24, 84, 91, 145, 152, 154, 192, 210, 212, 229, 265, 269

Duty, 21, 24, 101, 128n68, 271, 291, 294, 296, 325, 326, 329, 339

Dwell, 192, 259, 302, 335

Dwelling, 45, 115, 120, 139, 192, 271, 272
    place, 86, 194, 271, 335

Eastern Europe, 58, 80, 122, 125n7

Ecology, 25, 70, 113, 135, 202, 272, 334

Economic history, 41

Ecstasy, 13, 156

Education sentimentale, 34, 78, 307

Egoistic, 64, 236

Ekphrasis, 179

Elegeia, 98

Elegy, 98

Elitist, 138

Embodied, 23, 40, 67, 162, 227, 269, 300, 301, 340
    being, 23, 307

Emotions, 21, 75, 141, 155, 173, 178, 179, 239, 306, 325

Emotivism, 38

Empathy, 115

Empire, 12, 16, 94, 97, 100, 105, 108, 109, 147, 148

Enchanted, 103, 104, 158
Enchantment, 103
Enclosure, 192, 193
English law, 36, 48, 49, 53n59,
    107, 327–329
Englishman, 100, 108, 111, 138
Enlightened, 88, 90, 232, 276,
    287, 340
Enlightenment, 16, 18, 28n32, 72,
    73, 85, 88, 90, 92, 147, 172,
    224, 235, 243n27, 297
Entäußerung, 274
Environmentalism, 82, 272
Ephesus, 189, 190
Epics, 14, 21, 270
Epicurean, 286, 318n83
Epistemology, 2, 25
Equilibrium, 70
Erklären (explanation), 3
Erlebnis, 241
Eros, 10, 232, 339
Eternal, 5, 45, 85, 103, 219, 276,
    280, 297, 312
Ethics, 40
Ethnic, 109, 110, 112
Eudaimonia, 12, 172
Europe, 16, 73, 74, 105, 107, 111,
    118, 120, 121, 147, 148, 203,
    229, 332
European city, 117, 118, 120,
    236, 335
European unification, 73, 74, 87
European Union (EU), 73, 74, 80,
    105, 109, 111
Everyday beauty, 151–153
Everyman, 102, 104
Evil aesthete, 145, 147
Expressive function, 180, 195

Expressive value, 178, 179
Expulsion from Paradise, 258

F

Façade, 44, 155, 174, 175, 179, 183,
    184, 186, 189, 191, 192, 195,
    271, 273, 303
Face, 179, 184, 189, 205, 258–262,
    264–274, 277, 279–281, 298,
    299, 302, 303, 307,
    314, 316n43
The Face of God, 4, 256–282,
    287, 298
Face-to-face, 261, 267, 269, 270,
    272, 281, 289
Faith, 92, 157, 225, 233, 297,
    310–312, 314
Family, 20, 44, 63–66, 69, 70,
    77–79, 83, 84, 91, 99, 102,
    106, 107, 113, 114, 119, 120,
    123, 125n15, 126n17,
    128n56, 129n68, 149, 157,
    188, 193, 195, 196, 199, 224,
    276, 298, 310, 332, 335, 339
Fascist, 18
Fear, 21, 74, 105, 155, 307, 325
Fellow traveller, 19
Financial Times, 68
Fine art, 16, 158, 298
First-person awareness, 293, 294
First-person perspective, 66
First-person phenomenology, 290
First-person plural, 67, 70, 87, 105,
    106, 231, 234, 240, 241, 294
Fittingness, 151–153, 172
Fitting together, 182
Flesh, 298

Flexibility, 108
Florence, 17, 155, 258
Florentine, 16, 17
Folly, 43, 56, 57
Fortitude, 268
France, 20, 35, 50n11, 97, 101, 313
Frankfurt school, 19
Freedom, 41, 57, 62, 77, 78, 86, 91,
    102, 118, 123, 128n61,
    134n184, 154, 167, 184, 202,
    203, 211, 218, 220, 222–224,
    263, 266, 275, 276, 279, 280,
    301, 326, 327
  of conscience, 110
  of expression, 86
Free market, 36, 56, 87
Free press, 110
Free speech, 57, 86
French Revolution, 36, 88–90, 111
Friendship, 5, 59, 81, 83, 84, 95,
    117, 209, 225, 230, 234, 269,
    286, 310, 339, 340

G

Galleries, 93, 171
Garden of Eden, 257, 258
Geisteswissenschaften, 3
Gemütlich, 191
Genealogy, 15, 108, 144, 164, 165
Genossenschaft, 70
Genteel, 99
Gentleman, 43, 69, 98–101, 104
Georgian, 179
German idealism, 94, 219, 222,
    303, 333
Germany, 16, 73, 101, 165,
    216, 217

Gesamtkunstwerk, 215
Gifford Lectures, 57, 257, 259–260
Gift-love, 278, 316n56
Global capitalism, 87
Globalisation, 86
Globalising movement, 171
God, 4, 12, 13, 15, 41, 49, 65,
    119, 139, 155, 166, 193, 194,
    196, 214, 218, 219, 223, 226,
    234, 241, 256–261, 265,
    269–272, 274–281, 286, 287,
    290, 291, 296, 297, 302,
    309–314, 314n12, 320n142,
    320n146, 333–335,
    338–340, 342n41
Gonville and Caius, 60
Good, 6, 8, 10–12, 14, 15, 25, 41,
    56, 59, 66, 70, 78, 103, 136,
    145, 146, 165, 191, 192, 204,
    205, 208, 210, 211, 214, 235,
    236, 250n170, 302, 310
  manners, 118, 188, 189, 192, 195
  place, 208
Gothic, 195, 196, 305
  cathedral, 195, 196, 305
Gothic Revival, 92
Göttingen, 164
Gottwerdung, 311
Grace, 119, 180, 199, 274, 310
Graceful, 100, 179
Grace (*gratia*), 278
Grassroots, 77
Great tradition, 2, 26n4, 47,
    86–97
Greek tragedy, 141, 145, 219, 337
Guilt, 96, 102, 127n39, 139,
    275, 279
Gymnasium, 15

H

Habeas corpus, 5, 79, 111, 128n61
Half-column, 178
Harmonious, 178, 182, 199, 241, 332
Harmony, 108, 119, 149, 151, 152,
    156, 170, 172, 178, 180, 181,
    183, 189, 194, 195, 198, 199,
    229, 238, 241, 257, 258, 285,
    304, 306, 332, 335
Hegelian, 38, 39, 63–67, 84, 91,
    105, 123, 125n14, 125n16,
    170, 183, 188, 245n62,
    292, 300
Heimat, 115
Heimkehr, 115, 273, 303
Hellenic, 139
Heritage, 72, 86, 327
Heroic, 21, 146, 310
    death, 102
High art, 86, 140, 171
High culture, 40, 59, 87, 93, 102,
    137, 138, 140–142, 145–147,
    149, 229, 237, 325, 327, 337
Historicism, 39, 165–167
History of architecture, 37, 44, 159
Holistic, 25, 26
Holy City, 271
Holy site, 270
Home, 36, 45, 65, 66, 68, 69, 77,
    79, 80, 86, 99, 103, 104,
    114–116, 119–121, 136, 149,
    152, 153, 183, 184, 188,
    191–195, 200, 205, 209–211,
    213, 217, 230, 242, 258, 272,
    273, 285, 295, 297–303, 310,
    330, 331, 333–335, 340
Homecoming, 273, 303, 334
Homeliness, 70, 286, 302

Homeostasis, 122
Homesickness, 115
Homo oeconomicus, 81
Hubris, 222, 223
Human being, 1, 8, 9, 13, 15, 20,
    25, 45, 64, 66, 67, 72, 73, 81,
    82, 84, 85, 87, 89, 114, 115,
    117, 119, 122, 143, 146, 151,
    152, 155, 170, 173, 179, 183,
    187, 189, 193, 197, 199, 200,
    204, 213, 219, 220, 222, 226,
    227, 232, 233, 258, 260–263,
    265–267, 269, 270, 274, 275,
    277–281, 284, 287, 289–292,
    295–297, 299, 301, 307,
    309–313, 321n157, 333, 334,
    337, 338, 340
Human condition, 20, 24, 35, 47,
    102, 114, 155, 157, 200, 225,
    226, 235, 236, 259, 263, 266,
    267, 274, 282, 285, 287, 308,
    309, 338
Human dignity, 292, 310
Humanities, vi, 20, 78, 82, 158,
    180, 235, 278, 303
Human nature, 25, 45, 47, 61, 82,
    103, 117, 139, 143, 146, 158,
    161, 172, 186, 187, 197, 200,
    215, 222, 229, 231, 241, 265,
    269, 272, 274, 289–294, 297,
    316n48, 318n95, 335
Human phenomenon, 21, 275
Human reason, 14
Human rights, 110–113, 297
Human scale, 196
Hungary, 19, 58, 59, 83, 125n7
Hunting, 181, 332
Husserlian, 114

Idea, v, vii, 2–5, 9, 13, 16, 18, 19,
    22, 23, 34, 36, 38, 40, 45, 56,
    59, 60, 62, 63, 70, 76, 80, 81,
    83–85, 87–91, 93–96, 106,
    107, 109, 111–114, 121, 123,
    130n100, 132n138, 137, 138,
    144, 152, 154, 160, 163–165,
    167–170, 173, 178, 182, 184,
    189, 192, 193, 195–197, 200,
    201, 203, 206, 208, 211, 215,
    217, 228, 229, 235, 239, 240,
    252n208, 257, 260, 262, 263,
    271, 272, 276, 278, 279, 282,
    288–292, 296–298, 303, 310,
    311, 313, 321n153, 323, 324,
    326–332, 335, 338
Idealism, 4, 7, 38, 94, 219, 222,
    303, 333
Ideal landscape, 283
Identity, 108, 109, 112, 191, 216,
    265, 291, 299, 300, 312,
    319n102, 340
Ideology, 18, 19, 44, 45, 56, 57, 69,
    77, 82, 83, 87, 91, 93, 110,
    159, 162, 164–167, 171, 186,
    200, 217, 242, 330
ILO, 111
Imagination, 38, 141, 145, 146,
    155–157, 161, 162, 173–175,
    228, 260, 332, 342n33
Imaginative, 89, 174, 175, 177,
    304, 325
    attention, 175, 176
    perception, 176
Imperialism, 113
Impartial spectator, 89, 252n208,
    275, 296

Implied order, 195, 196
Impression, v, 35, 43, 48, 80, 114,
    175, 177, 180, 182, 198,
    204, 304
Incarnation, 279–281
Individual freedom, 62, 63, 220,
    224, 229, 301
Industrialisation, 93
Inner Temple, 48
Inns of Court, 47, 49, 61, 86, 327
Institute for the Psychological
    Sciences in Arlington, 68
Institutional fact, 295
Institution(s), vi, 38–40, 47, 48,
    62–66, 69, 71, 73, 75, 77, 78,
    82, 84, 87, 88, 92, 107, 110,
    111, 170, 188, 190, 193, 201,
    202, 294, 295, 297, 327–330
Integer, 197
Intellectual conservatism,
    41, 43, 122
Intellectual conservative, 78, 79
Intellectualism, 177
Intellectual pleasure, 173
Intellectual(s), 12–14, 16–20, 35,
    37, 39–43, 46, 55, 56, 58–60,
    68, 69, 74, 78, 79, 95, 96,
    101, 136, 143, 145, 149–151,
    158, 160, 163, 164, 173,
    175–177, 180, 185, 190, 200,
    206, 208, 223, 230, 231, 234,
    235, 260, 264, 267, 323, 325,
    328, 330–332
Intention, 23, 62, 98, 109, 152, 155,
    160, 161, 168, 169, 175, 181,
    188, 217, 248n121, 263, 265,
    266, 268, 269, 281, 283, 285,
    293, 299, 303, 304, 310

Intentionality, 152, 263–266, 289, 290, 292–294, 304, 305, 307, 308
Intergenerational justice, 210
Interim report, 207, 208
Internationalism, 82
Interpersonal, 71, 89, 115, 119, 144, 221, 223, 230, 234, 290–292, 294, 298–300, 339
Intrinsic value, 116, 117, 230, 234
Invisible hand, 91, 238
Iraq, 111
Iron Curtain, 58, 80, 331
Irrational, 38, 116, 223, 261
Islamic, 72, 132n141
Islamism, 80
Istanbul, 120
Italy, 17, 18
I-to-I, 115, 117, 273, 279, 292

J
Jagiellonian Trust, 58
Jan Hus Educational Association, 58
Jan Hus Educational Foundation, 331
Jesuitism, 164
Jewish, 44, 94, 274, 312
    tradition, 77
Journalism, 55, 330, 331
Jubilate Deo, 214
Judaic, 139
Judeo-Christian, 80, 116, 193
Judgement, 8, 9, 28n32, 38, 40, 48, 84, 102, 115, 117, 118, 124, 136, 140, 141, 143–145, 148, 150–153, 162, 164, 168–173, 176, 177, 180, 184, 187, 199, 209, 235, 257, 259, 263–266, 273, 282, 308, 326, 328

Jurisdiction, 49, 107–109, 132n155, 329
Justice, 11, 48, 49, 62, 79, 98, 115, 188, 194, 224, 225, 265, 294, 296, 297, 328–330, 338, 339

K
Kantian, 2, 3, 25, 38, 117, 136, 151, 152, 169, 188, 222, 245n46, 247n107, 256, 262, 266, 287, 289
Kensington, 121
Kinship, 106
Kiss, 298
Kitsch, 85, 157
Kunstgeschichte, 172
Kunstwollen, 172

L
L'art pour l'art, 119
Labour, 8, 62, 65, 68, 77, 79, 113, 212, 236, 239
Lady, 98–100
Landscape, v, 122, 128n66, 202, 206, 207, 270, 272, 273, 282–287, 303, 329
Landscape with a Calm, 283
Landscape with a Storm, 284
Lantern, 176
Laurentian Library, 155, 167
Law, 7, 47–49, 61–63, 73, 78, 80, 82, 87, 90, 91, 95, 98, 110–112, 123, 143, 193, 194, 210, 218, 222–227, 229, 275, 280, 282, 290, 292, 294–296, 305, 317n61, 327–329, 340, 341n15

Lebanon, 80
Lebenslauf, 34
Lebenswelt, 50n5, 114, 295,
 301, 306
Left, 39, 57, 59, 71, 78, 96, 101,
 104, 155, 159, 211, 241, 258,
 261, 267, 284, 290, 330, 331
Left wing, 58, 77, 82, 95, 104,
 162, 166
Legal, 13, 48, 49, 61, 63, 64, 70, 77,
 83, 89, 91, 107, 108, 111,
 121, 128n61, 132n155, 194,
 203, 204, 220, 223, 224, 265,
 291, 295, 328, 329, 342n35
Legislators, 15, 114, 120
Leisure, 12, 13, 81, 83,
 143, 231–233
Liberal, 41, 56, 59, 62, 63, 65, 81,
 94, 96, 101, 109, 123,
 134n184, 149, 336, 338, 340
Liberal conservative, 59, 92
Liberalism, 41, 42, 61, 62, 65–67,
 82, 86, 87, 91, 96, 142
Liebesverbot, 221
Life-world (*Lebenswelt*), 50n5, 114,
 295, 301, 306
Linguistic turn, 21, 23, 324
Literature, 14, 16, 37, 39, 42, 46,
 47, 73–75, 79, 81, 82, 93, 94,
 98, 99, 101, 115, 118,
 132n152, 140, 142, 143, 157,
 165, 170, 213, 236, 241,
 247n102, 250n161, 283, 291,
 298, 305, 309, 324, 325,
 331, 332
Little platoons, 90, 113, 122–124
Local, 16, 57, 59, 67, 69, 76, 77, 82,
 83, 87, 99, 109, 122–124,
 135, 152–154, 171, 201, 206,
 208, 211–214, 216, 239,
 247n102, 328, 335
 attachment, 70, 81, 86, 87, 122
 community, 113, 118, 121, 124,
 207, 211, 335
 history, 202
 knowledge, 206
 surroundings, 171
Localist conservatism, 87
Locality, 107, 112, 153, 170, 171,
 208, 271
London, 94, 121, 169, 191
Loneliness, 274, 308, 333
Los Angeles, 272
Love, 6, 9–11, 13, 59, 64, 65, 79,
 102, 104, 105, 114, 116, 117,
 122–124, 126n17, 151, 155,
 156, 165, 166, 185, 188, 191,
 215, 217–228, 230, 232,
 268–270, 276, 278, 280, 281,
 297, 300, 310–314, 327, 328,
 331, 334, 337, 338, 340
 of home, 114, 120, 191
 of place, 135
Lower middle-class, 40, 79, 101
Loyalty, 39, 40, 65, 87, 102–110,
 112, 113, 117, 126n18, 335
LSE, 95, 96

M

Mannerism, 164
Manners, v, 4, 22, 35, 41, 48, 60,
 64, 70, 76, 89–91, 95,
 98–101, 104, 118, 119, 139,
 144, 147–149, 152–154, 157,
 171, 174–176, 188, 189, 191,
 192, 195, 223, 226, 261, 262,
 270, 285, 290, 302, 304, 339

Market, 36, 56, 64, 81, 87, 89, 90, 95, 121, 189, 190, 202, 203, 236, 237
  economy, 89
Marriage, 71, 72, 91, 102, 114, 276, 279, 297, 310, 339
Marxist, 18, 41, 44, 62, 96, 160, 167, 177, 237, 241
Mask, 45, 264, 265, 267, 291, 298, 299, 319n102
Mass society, 93, 238
Master-slave relationship, 84, 263, 291, 292, 294
Materialist, 83
Maternal affection, 269
Meaningful, v, 42, 76, 113, 139, 140, 181, 183, 184, 195, 198, 218, 221, 226, 227, 271, 284, 288, 297–299, 304, 306, 307, 312, 324, 336
Mediality, 23
Medici chapel, 178
Meistersinger, 238, 241
Melody, 173, 174, 179, 235, 239, 241, 304, 306
Memoir, 33, 34, 214, 217, 327
Metaphysical, 4, 9, 25, 78, 90, 107, 136, 155, 195, 266, 278, 280–283, 287, 307, 308, 313, 338
Metaphysics, 4, 25, 38, 107, 115, 118, 213–242, 250n161, 255–314, 333
Middle class, 40, 79, 101, 203, 205, 238
Migration, 109, 113
Mimetic desire, 139
Mitteleuropa, 125n7
Moderation, 221, 240

Modernism, 44, 159, 162, 164, 167, 168, 171, 186, 199, 204, 238, 273
Modernity, 19, 45, 47, 75, 76, 82, 85, 94, 122, 159, 196
Modes of experience, 1–7, 26n3
Monarch, 65, 67, 88
Monsignor, 43, 246n77, 326
Morality, 37–40, 42, 102, 144, 161, 184, 262, 296
Moral Sciences, 46
Moral sense, 8, 184
Moral theology, 42
Moral virtues, 81, 148, 190, 209
Moulding, 44, 178, 184, 195
MP, 37
Multiculturalism, 56, 82, 97
Municipal authorities, 202
Museum, 171
Music, 10, 14–16, 22, 25, 74, 79, 82, 92, 115, 136, 138, 140, 150, 157, 158, 170, 171, 173, 180, 213–242, 244n43, 251n185, 282, 285, 298, 303–309, 314n2, 325, 326, 332, 337
Musical phrase, 174
Mutual recognition, 263, 265, 292
Myth, 15, 72, 139, 140, 217, 219, 300, 302, 310, 315n35, 325

N

Narcissism, 308
Narrative, 9, 10, 14, 15, 17, 21, 22, 34, 44, 50n11, 79, 86, 88, 94–96, 100, 105, 139, 141, 146–148, 168, 215, 216, 218, 219, 223, 227, 228, 237, 258, 274, 281, 283–285, 287, 310, 321n150, 337

Nation, 59, 69, 70, 83, 97, 104–113,
138, 216, 327
National conservatism, 97, 105
Nationalism, 82, 87, 104–106, 112,
130n88, 217, 253n211
Nationalist, 87, 104, 105, 165
National loyalty, 104–109,
112, 113
National socialism, 165, 166
Natural justice, 48, 328, 329
Natural language, 23, 178,
179, 305
Natural law, 9, 39, 94, 296, 319n111
Natural right, 39, 94
Natural science, 20, 33, 113, 136,
140, 145, 158, 244n40
Natural theology, 259–260
Nazi, 19, 115, 164–166, 216,
227, 246n84
Negotium, 12, 81
Neoconservatism, 69
Neoliberal, 87
Neo-Marxist, 59
Neo-traditional, 201
Newspeak, 73
New Urbanism, 200–212, 273
New Urbanist Movement,
120, 133n173
Nicomachean Ethics (*NE*), 5, 171,
190, 233, 339
Nihilism, 185–200
1984, 40, 56, 58, 73, 95, 187
1968, 35–36, 59, 71, 159
Noh theatre, 299
Non-reflective, 175
Nostalgic, 93
Numerus, 197
Nuremberg, 238

Obedience, 102, 106, 123, 188, 257,
276, 292, 335
Obelisk, 176
Objective harmony
(concinnitas), 180
Objective order, 183, 225
Obligation, 187, 188, 224, 276,
294–296, 339, 340
Oikophilia, 70, 81, 97, 112–124,
135, 191, 334, 335
Oikophobia, 70, 113, 122
Oikos, 66, 114, 122
Old Testament, 193, 269, 270,
296, 334
Old universities, 86
"One nation" conservatism, 93
Ontological dualism, 289,
318n97, 321n157
Opacity, 22
Order, 7, 8, 11, 12, 16, 18, 19, 25,
34, 36, 44, 45, 49, 56, 61–64,
67, 68, 70, 75, 81, 85–88, 91,
94, 96, 101, 102, 104, 114,
117, 118, 121, 124, 126n29,
140, 141, 144–146, 150, 152,
153, 161, 163, 167, 168, 172,
173, 176, 178, 181, 184, 187,
191–196, 199, 200, 203, 205,
208, 211, 216, 223–226, 230,
234, 236, 240, 241, 261, 264,
272, 274, 275, 277, 280, 282,
284–286, 290, 298, 302, 303,
305, 306, 308, 309, 312, 323,
324, 326, 328, 335, 336,
338, 340
Organic community, 93
Original sin, 139, 219, 257, 258

Ornament, 21, 43, 44, 186
Otium, 12, 81
Oxford, 58, 169, 178
Ozymandias, 316n43

P

Padua, 198
Painting, 170, 257–260, 266–269,
    273, 282–287, 303, 304, 325
Palazzo Massimo alle Colonne, 174
Palladian, 178
Pan Tadeusz, 270
Pantheism, 313
Paradise, 258, 274
Parliament, 48, 86, 88, 111
Parsifal, 219, 221, 337
Parthenon, 154, 155
Passions, 24, 25, 148, 179, 221, 325,
    332, 336
Pastoral, 285, 317n79
Patriarchalism, 64
Patriot, 104, 105
Pattern-book, 195
Pediments, 178
Perception, 2, 22, 25, 71, 116, 136,
    173–176, 180, 183, 198, 211,
    264, 270, 272, 276, 277,
    293, 333
Pergae, 189, 190
Persona, 47, 137, 264, 291
Personal identity, 265, 291,
    319n102
Personal life, 33, 75
Perspectivity, 22
Persuasion, 135, 178
Peterhouse, 37–45, 55, 96, 159, 313
Phaedrus, 223

Phenomenological, 115, 173,
    174, 259, 292, 298,
    333, 334
  analysis, 114, 115
Phenomenology, 173, 189,
    288–290, 292, 300, 303,
    304, 336
Philia, 339, 340
Philistine philanthropist, 145, 147
Philosophes, 18
Philosophical anthropology, 25, 99,
    186, 289, 307, 333
Philosophy, v, 1–26, 33, 37–39, 42,
    46, 47, 50n5, 50n6, 57,
    59–97, 101, 115, 116, 136,
    138, 149, 158, 160, 168–170,
    182, 183, 196, 202, 213,
    215, 217, 223, 226, 228,
    229, 233, 236, 253n215,
    255, 256, 260, 272, 279,
    283, 286, 287, 289, 291,
    307, 309, 313,
    323–340
  of art, 1, 25, 33–49, 97, 255–314,
    325, 332–333
  of religion, 25, 218, 287
  of sexuality, 25, 320n126
The philosophy of culture, 25
Photograph, 22, 209, 272
Phronesis, 5, 6, 12, 14, 171, 190,
    199, 247n104
Phronimos, 8, 40
Physical environment, 194
Pietas, 5, 39, 276
Piety, 67, 70, 119, 188, 276, 297,
    338, 339
Pious, 30n51, 119, 339
Pity, 21, 155

Place, 9, 10, 16, 21, 46, 66, 85–87,
    92, 103, 107, 110, 114, 116,
    117, 121, 122, 124, 135, 139,
    142, 149, 152, 183, 184,
    191–194, 199, 202, 204,
    207–211, 218, 225–227, 256,
    266, 270–273, 284, 286, 295,
    298, 302, 303, 327,
    333–335, 338
Placemaker, 211
Plan, 121, 178, 190, 193, 199, 211
Planning code, 211
Platonism, 94
Platonist, 157
Play, 9, 21, 90, 102, 103, 108, 148,
    150, 151, 153, 154, 157, 164,
    167, 170, 177, 179, 188, 198,
    214, 218, 220, 223, 230, 231,
    237, 239, 242, 263, 264, 283,
    292, 296, 336, 337
Poet, 7, 9–11, 19, 36, 73–76, 85, 88,
    92, 93, 114, 116, 138, 208,
    214, 285, 313, 314
Poetic justice, 141
Poetics, 5, 6, 21, 234
Poetry, 3, 6, 7, 9–11, 14, 15, 21, 22,
    26n3, 27n8, 38, 47, 74–76,
    92, 93, 95, 103, 115, 177,
    180, 229, 232, 241, 255, 275,
    285, 286, 313, 326, 327, 340
Poetry (*poiesis*), 5, 9, 10
Poland, 58, 83, 125n7
Polis, 14, 44, 66, 190, 192, 195, 225
Politeia, 225
Politeness, 100, 115, 192, 202
Political agent, 4
Political correctness, 87, 95
Political critic, 264

Political philosophy, 1, 4, 24,
    39, 42, 55–124, 135, 164,
    228, 255, 289, 325, 329,
    332, 335
Political science, 42, 94
Politics, 1–26, 33–49, 55, 56, 58,
    61, 62, 68, 73, 74, 76–79, 81,
    82, 84, 86, 87, 90, 91, 95, 97,
    103, 104, 107, 123, 136, 148,
    149, 157–242, 256, 281, 282,
    286, 309, 323–340
Pollution, 49, 139, 234, 300
Polyphonic music, 229
Polyphony, 229
Popular culture, 102
Portrait, 34, 266–268
Poundbury, 121, 200–212
Power, 16, 18, 19, 21, 34, 48, 49,
    62–64, 66, 69, 73, 77, 79, 80,
    88, 92, 102–104, 110–113,
    120, 155, 156, 160, 164, 176,
    202, 215, 217–220, 222, 223,
    234, 241, 260, 267, 273, 275,
    280, 293, 302, 306, 307, 314,
    327, 329, 337, 338
Practical knowledge, 39, 106, 172,
    182, 190, 191, 250n161
Practical life, 12–14, 155, 261
Practical reason, 169
Practical understanding, 172
Practical wisdom (*phronesis*), 5
Prague, 58, 59
Precedent, 48, 49, 90, 121, 328
Precinct, 193
Prejudice, 62, 190, 210, 327
Primary impression, 180
Primary perception, 175
Prime minister, 56, 79

Primordial, 218, 318n95
Principium individuationis, 222
A priori, 18, 146, 278
Private, 23, 33, 43, 73, 118, 123,
        186, 188, 189, 193, 195, 196,
        211, 264, 286, 294, 295,
        302, 331
    property, 66, 67
Progress, 44, 82, 160, 188, 267, 269,
        280, 336
Progressivist, 44, 164
Proletarian, 101
Promised Land, 270, 271, 334
Proportion, 44, 154, 172, 181, 194,
        197, 199, 200, 271
Propriety, 154, 178, 200, 235
Proprius, 182, 197
Protestant, 148, 163, 164
Prudence, 10, 11, 171, 190,
        247n104, 269
Psychoanalysis, 177
Public, 12–16, 19, 24, 38, 42, 57,
        62, 68, 71, 84–87, 102–104,
        107, 111, 121, 123, 137, 139,
        140, 146, 147, 158, 166, 169,
        170, 174, 183, 184, 186–189,
        193–196, 200–202, 205,
        207–209, 211, 212, 231,
        247n99, 259, 270, 273, 286,
        295, 297, 302, 323, 327,
        330, 335–338
    intellectual, 19, 58, 149, 185,
        323, 330
    spirit, 78, 80
Puritan, 47, 313
Puritanism, 148
Purity, 294, 300
Pythagorean, 172

Q
Queen, 49

R
Racism, 57, 112, 216
Radicalism, 72, 148, 162, 166
Ratio decidendi, 48, 328
Rational choice, 106
Rational faculty, 144, 228, 310
Rawlsian, 275
Reactionary, 56, 70, 78, 92
Real presence (*shekhinah*),
        261, 281, 290, 291,
        298, 299
Realism, 17, 102, 183, 217
Realm, v, 3, 4, 11, 24–26, 39,
        66, 79, 81, 83, 85, 102–104,
        115, 125n15, 132n155,
        151, 152, 156–158, 169,
        172, 176, 183–188, 201,
        202, 218, 220, 223–225,
        239, 241, 256, 263, 273,
        277–279, 282, 290–292,
        294, 295, 301, 307
Recognition, 16, 64, 65, 84,
        91, 129n77, 189, 201,
        234, 238, 262, 263, 265,
        274, 291, 292, 299, 301,
        307, 328, 337
Recorded music, 22, 238
Redemption, 156, 218, 219, 226,
        228, 269, 274, 275, 279–281,
        312, 325, 338
Regained religion, 214
Regeneration, 210, 211
Regulatory-institutional, 62
Relativism, 9

Religion, 4, 25, 27n14, 37, 38, 41,
42, 72–76, 84–86, 92, 95, 98,
116, 136, 138, 139, 142, 144,
160, 161, 193, 213, 214, 218,
226, 233, 234, 238–240, 256,
261, 269, 271, 274–276, 278,
279, 282, 287–289, 298,
309–313, 318n96, 320n144,
321n153, 325, 327, 334–340
Religiosity, 76, 160, 252n192, 256
Religious conversion, 93
Religious devotion, 116, 119
Religious revival, 162
Renaissance, 16, 17, 134n181, 164,
172, 174, 180, 181, 185, 197,
235, 257, 259, 271
Representation, 21, 28n25, 269,
283, 284, 293
Representative democracy, 106, 109
Repudiation, 37, 75, 79, 330
Rerum Novarum, 292
Resilience, 122
Resolve the conflict, 288, 329
Respect, 4, 9, 27n11, 38, 40, 63, 65,
67, 71, 78, 80, 81, 84, 112,
115, 116, 124, 132n155, 145,
177, 186, 188, 189, 211, 215,
296, 297, 301, 307, 321n153
Responsibility, vii, 56, 66, 101, 102,
128n68, 141, 183, 184,
210–212, 221, 263, 264, 275,
276, 282, 295, 296, 299, 300,
319n102, 330
Revelation, 259, 270, 275, 281, 312
Rhetoric, 16, 17, 36, 109, 161, 166,
177, 212, 284, 305
Rhythm, 139, 174, 240,
241, 304–306

Right, 8, 37–45, 49, 66, 67, 71, 74,
75, 78, 79, 90, 91, 94, 103,
104, 110, 111, 113, 152, 153,
166, 167, 183, 197, 198, 202,
205, 210, 212, 222, 233, 241,
256, 258, 272, 273, 275, 276,
291, 294, 296, 297, 308, 324,
327–330, 336, 339, 340
judgement (*orthos logos*), 124, 140
Ring, 215, 218–220, 227, 280, 337
Rite of passage, 226, 269,
276, 316n52
Ritual, 45, 106, 119, 120, 139, 141,
193, 194, 218, 233, 234, 261,
270, 277, 279, 288, 297, 305,
310–312, 316n58, 330, 336
Romagna, 285
Romania, 59
Roman law, 112, 243n24, 265,
291, 296
Romanticism, 16, 18, 86, 116
Romantics, 80, 116, 130n85, 138,
155, 156, 237, 238, 308
Rome, 120, 143, 181, 195, 285,
302, 313
Rule of law, 62, 63, 70, 89, 91, 106,
108, 110, 112, 222, 223, 225,
229, 326–332
Rule-following, 38, 154
Ruler, 16, 17, 49, 63, 103, 126n18,
145, 224, 225, 324
Russian constructivism, 212

S

Sacrament, 71, 139, 233, 234
Sacred, 4, 27n14, 72, 85, 115–118,
136, 151, 152, 156, 192–194,

196, 218, 226–228, 241, 270,
    271, 273, 276, 277, 287, 288,
    335, 336, 338, 340
land, 272
Sacrifice, 56, 66, 80, 102, 119, 139,
    141, 193, 217–220, 227, 233,
    234, 270, 276, 278–281, 287,
    288, 308, 310, 312, 313,
    318n95, 330,
    336–338, 342n37
Salisbury Group, 55–57
Salisbury Review, 55–58, 80
Salvation, 218, 226
Samizdat, 59, 331
San Carlino, 181
Sanctum, 193
Santa Maria Carmine, 258
Santa Maria della Salute, 176
Scale, 90, 115, 125n15, 154, 192,
    194, 196, 204, 207, 222,
    271, 330
Scallop, 180, 181
Scapegoat, 288, 336
Science, 3, 6, 7, 20, 28n27, 28n32,
    33, 38, 41, 42, 46, 88, 94,
    113, 140, 144, 145, 158, 171,
    200, 231, 244n40, 259–262,
    277, 278, 290, 298, 303, 311,
    313, 338
Scientific knowledge, 5, 6
Scientific knowledge (*epistémé*), 5
Scottish Enlightenment, 148, 202,
    236, 252n208
Sculpture, 5, 14, 178, 179, 307
Secular age, 76, 138
Secularism, 92, 297, 337
Secular religion, 116
Selbstbestimmung, 222, 223, 274

Self, 85, 103, 141, 142, 156, 157,
    182, 198, 221, 222, 227, 228,
    233, 262, 263, 266–269, 274,
    275, 277, 291, 298–301, 308,
    311, 336, 340
Self-giving, 226, 269, 338
Selfhood, 40, 103, 311
Self-knowledge, 182, 183, 220, 222,
    232, 267, 325
Self-pity, 267, 268
Self-portrait, 266, 267,
    315n19, 315n21
Self-sacrifice, 217–219, 222, 223,
    226, 279, 281, 287, 288, 310,
    311, 336, 338, 342n37
Sensation, 173, 176
Sense of beauty, 8, 117–119, 122,
    136, 150, 169, 180, 198, 199
Sense of detail, 180
Sense of home, 66, 86, 302
Sense of place, 124, 170, 210
Sense of the beautiful, 184
Sentimental education, 141, 145
Settlement, 87, 113–115, 120–122,
    124, 184, 192, 194, 196,
    204–207, 211, 271, 272, 298,
    302, 335
Settling down, 302
Sexual desire, 71, 156, 220, 221, 300
Sexual interaction, 269, 300
Shame, 115, 275
Shrine, 139, 270
Side constraints, 204, 205
Siena, 120
Sign language, 177, 195
Silhouette, 176
Sittlichkeit, 40, 64, 67, 91
Slavery, 89, 94, 233

Slovakia, 125n7
Smile, 114, 268, 269, 298, 304
Sociability, 81, 88, 89, 91, 187, 230,
    286, 318n95, 335, 338
Social cohesion, 71, 81, 242
Social conservatism, 56
Social engineering, 24, 72, 172, 201
Social hierarchy, 93
Socialism, 61, 82, 91, 94
Social media, 86, 206
Social order, 39, 63, 82, 90, 121,
    226, 269, 341n9
Social science, 42, 78
Social virtue, 119
Society, 37, 49, 55, 56, 63–66, 69,
    71, 80–84, 87–91, 93,
    98–101, 106, 107, 113, 118,
    122–124, 125n15,
    128–129n68, 134n181,
    134n184, 140, 142, 144–146,
    148, 153, 186, 188–190, 192,
    210, 211, 217, 224, 225, 228,
    229, 231, 235–241, 275–277,
    287, 288, 295, 297, 299, 300,
    310, 329, 330, 336
Socratic, 281
Soft power, 16
Soul, 9–11, 13, 21, 72, 77, 151,
    156, 187, 195, 220, 223,
    234, 239, 245n48, 268,
    269, 271, 277, 298, 310,
    312, 313
The Soul of the World, 4, 256,
    281–314, 335, 338
Soviet system, 124
Space, 22, 43, 66, 116, 119, 124,
    160, 172, 174, 175, 178, 179,
    181, 183, 184, 187, 189, 191,

192, 194, 195, 202, 204, 273,
    301, 304, 305, 307, 312, 334
Speech act, 295
Spirit of community, 210
Spirituality, 43, 44
Spiritual values, 80
Spontaneous order, 64, 83, 95,
    189, 190
Sprawl, 201, 202, 204
Sprawling, 120
Square, 14, 153, 184, 189, 209, 302
Stability, 187
Stagira, 16
Stalinist, 162
Stanton Lectures, 57, 281
Stare decisis, 48
State and church, 88
State of nature, 224, 295
Statesman, 10, 11, 14, 36, 74
Statue, 14, 15, 176, 193, 316n43
Status quo, 108, 161, 206
Stewardship, 71, 209, 210, 329
Stockholm-syndrome, 165
Straussian, 69, 87
Street, 14, 46, 117, 118, 153, 183,
    184, 186, 189, 191, 192, 205,
    236, 273, 302
Student revolution, 35, 327, 330
Stylobate, 194
Subjectivism, 9, 29n36,
    182, 248n121
Sublime, 151, 152, 155, 169, 218
Suburb, 120, 121, 201, 203
Suffering, 218, 221, 225, 227, 228,
    268, 270, 278–281, 308, 325
Supreme Court, 71
Surrounding world (Umwelt), 114
Sustainability, 122, 203

Sustainable neighbourhood, 211
Sympathy, 19, 89, 100, 115, 138, 164, 165, 237, 265, 306, 313
Syracuse, 16
Syria, 111
Szlachta, 98

T

Taboo, 277, 300
Tacit knowledge, 169, 189
Tactile, 175
Tannhäuser, 223
Taste, 8, 9, 28n32, 36, 38, 75, 100, 118, 143–145, 150, 153, 161, 162, 166, 168, 175–177, 184, 187, 199, 211, 212, 228, 235, 238, 243n27, 293, 294, 303, 326
Tempietto, 181
Temple, 15, 154, 193–195, 271, 302, 327
Terrorism, 109
Thatcherism, 77, 79, 87
Theatre, 14, 16, 21, 36, 141, 171, 234, 237, 264, 265, 299, 327
Theology, 11, 25, 42, 65, 140, 165, 259–260, 281
Theoretical knowledge, 190
Theoretical wisdom (*sophia*), 5–7
Third person perspective, 67
Tobacco, 68
Tocquevillian, 83
Tonality, 238, 239, 305
Torah, 116, 266, 302, 312, 334
Tory, 41, 130n100
Totalitarian, 18, 19, 57, 73, 82, 83, 86, 91, 94, 95, 110, 145, 147, 164, 166, 167, 199, 200, 288, 289, 331
Town, 121, 202, 204, 205, 237, 238, 242, 270, 272, 286, 302, 335
Town and Country Planning Act, 124, 203
Tradition, 2, 4, 5, 9, 20, 23, 24, 33, 37, 39, 40, 43, 44, 47, 57, 58, 60, 61, 63, 68–70, 74–81, 85–87, 89–94, 96, 102, 106, 107, 112, 115–118, 122, 123, 128n61, 138, 142, 145, 156, 160, 161, 163, 171, 205, 206, 229, 236, 238, 239, 266, 271, 272, 275, 284, 287, 289, 292, 296, 297, 299, 311, 323, 325, 327, 328, 333
Tragic drama, 21
Transcend, 119, 174, 227
Transcendence, 25, 72, 298, 311, 312
Transcendental, 3, 4, 80, 81, 151, 152, 157, 182, 222, 226, 227, 260–263, 275, 277–279, 287, 289–291, 296–297, 311, 333, 338, 340
    freedom, 262, 263
Transfiguration, 141
Transformation, 35, 71, 82, 177, 187, 278
Transgenerational responsibility, 210
Transnational, 105, 110
Transylvania, 59
Trial and error, 117, 153, 190
Tribal, 106, 107, 109–111
Tristanism, 220
Trust, v, 62, 69, 70, 88, 90, 100, 105, 106, 124, 188, 202, 225, 231, 329

Truth, v, 6, 8, 9, 16, 22, 23, 25, 34,
42, 56, 78, 82, 86, 151, 160,
162, 164, 172, 192, 214, 223,
278, 283, 297, 303, 323, 332

U

UN, 111
Unborn, 70, 115, 116, 235, 276
Understanding (*nous*), 3, 5, 6, 8, 9,
12, 16, 20, 23, 34, 66, 82, 91,
92, 94, 105, 109, 114, 115,
117, 123, 144, 159, 169, 170,
172, 175, 176, 183, 186, 193,
198, 199, 218, 226, 227, 233,
234, 243n22, 259, 279, 286,
288–294, 298, 301, 306, 308,
338, 339
UNESCO, 111
United Kingdom, 56, 68, 108, 205
United States (US), 24, 68, 69, 71,
77, 83, 88, 94, 96, 135,
201–203, 330
Unity, 176, 178, 182, 183, 211, 274,
275, 278
University, vi, 39, 48, 56–59, 86,
164, 185, 205, 257, 281, 324,
326, 327, 330
University of Virginia, 89
Urban development, 121, 124, 148
Urban fabric, 122
Urbanism, 148, 158, 183, 200–212
Urban texture, 120, 122
Utopia, 74, 161, 162, 186

V

Values, 40, 41, 57, 62, 71, 77, 78,
80–83, 89, 93, 95, 101,
116–119, 122, 136, 145,
148–150, 162, 172, 178, 179,
184, 187, 199, 209, 222, 227,
230, 233, 234, 240, 278,
286, 305
Velvet Philosophers, 331
Venice, 176, 203, 272, 342n33
Vernacular, 152, 153, 157–212,
222, 271
Verstehen (understanding), 3, 290
Victorian, 116, 166
View from Nowhere, 261, 262, 278
View from Somewhere, 261, 262
Vignolesque, 178
Villa Cornaro, 174
Violence, 72, 100, 146, 192, 221,
225, 288
Virtue, 5, 8, 10, 12, 14, 39, 40, 81,
83, 98, 100, 105, 109, 110,
119, 143, 147–149, 171, 176,
188–190, 195, 209, 225,
240, 294
Visual arts, 158, 244n43
Visual faculty, 175
Vita activa, 13, 14, 18, 25, 55–124
Vita contemplativa, 13, 14, 25, 95,
255–314, 332–333
Voices, 2–4, 19, 40, 47, 49, 74, 95,
171, 229, 233, 239, 307,
323, 325
Voluntarist, 121, 145, 161

W

Weimar, 166
Weltanschauung, 34, 225
Westminster, 121
Whig, 41, 96, 159
historians, 159
WHO, 111
Wiltshire, 286

Window, 35, 44, 178, 189, 226, 279, 283, 311
Work, v, vi, 2–5, 15, 17, 19, 24, 26n3, 31n64, 34, 37, 38, 42, 44, 46–48, 58, 61, 70, 72, 73, 81–84, 86, 88–90, 92, 94, 95, 97, 100, 102, 113–116, 118, 120, 137, 139, 144, 145, 149–152, 154–157, 160, 164, 168–171, 173, 175, 179, 181, 184, 187, 196, 197, 199, 205–209, 212–217, 219–221, 223, 225, 230–233, 235, 239, 247n107, 248n121, 255, 256, 262, 264, 269, 281, 283, 284, 302, 303, 305–309, 311, 316n48, 319n111, 320n144, 321n153, 323, 331–334, 338–340, 342n33
    of art, 14, 47, 151, 152, 154–157, 181, 215, 235, 239, 248n121, 306, 307
Worship, 45, 106, 110, 193, 239, 312, 335

Y

Yale, 59

Z

Zeitgeist, 163, 166, 172
Zoning, 203
Zoon politikon, 25, 265